Microsoft
Outlook 2013 Plain & Simple

Jim Boyce

Published with the authorization of Microsoft Corporation by:
O'Reilly Media, Inc.
1005 Gravenstein Highway North
Sebastopol, California 95472

ISBN: 978-0-7356-6935-2

2 3 4 5 6 7 8 9 10 QG 8 7 6 5 4 3

Printed and bound in the United States of America.

Microsoft Press books are available through booksellers and distributors worldwide. If you need support related to this book, email Microsoft Press Book Support at mspinput@microsoft.com. Please tell us what you think of this book at *http://www.microsoft.com/learning/booksurvey.*

Acquisitions and Developmental Editor: Kenyon Brown
Production Editor: Kara Ebrahim
Technical Reviewer: Vincent Averello
Copyeditor: Richard Carey
Indexer: Angela Howard
Cover Design: Twist Creative • Seattle
Cover Composition: Zyg Group, LLC
Illustrator: S4 Carlisle Publishing Services

[2013-04-05]

For my wife Julie, who continues to put up with me

for reasons known only to her.

Contents

1

About this book

In this section:

- A quick overview
- A few assumptions
- Adapting task procedures for touchscreens
- A final word (or two)

If you want to get the most from your computer and your software with the least amount of time and effort—and who doesn't?—this book is for you. You'll find Microsoft Outlook 2013 Plain & Simple to be a straightforward, easy-to-read reference tool. With the premise that your computer should work for you, not you for it, this book's purpose is to help you get your work done quickly and efficiently so that you can get away from the computer and live your life.

A quick overview

Your computer probably came with Outlook preinstalled, but if you have to install it yourself, the Setup Wizard makes installation so simple that you won't need my help anyway. So, unlike many computer books, this one doesn't start with installation instructions and a list of system requirements.

You don't have to read the sections of this book in any particular order. You can jump in, get the information you need, and then close the book and keep it near your computer until the next time you need to know how to get something done. But, that doesn't mean the information is scattered wildly about. The book is organized so that the tasks you want to accomplish are arranged in two levels—you'll find the overall type of task you're looking for under a main section title, such as "Working with contact groups," "Setting up email accounts," "Communicating with contacts," and so on. Then, in each of those sections, smaller tasks are arranged in a loose progression from the simplest to the more complex.

Section 2, "What's new in Outlook 2013," provides an overview of the most common changes and notable new features in Outlook 2013 such as the interface changes and new social networking features. If you have been a user of Outlook 2010 or earlier, Section 2 gives you a good idea of what's new.

Section 3, "Getting Started," introduces you to Outlook functions; it explains how to start and exit the program, work with the Outlook program window, and use the standard set of folders in Outlook. You also learn how to set up email accounts, import data into Outlook from other programs, and work with items such as email messages, contacts, and appointments. Information about how to get help and troubleshoot problems rounds out the section.

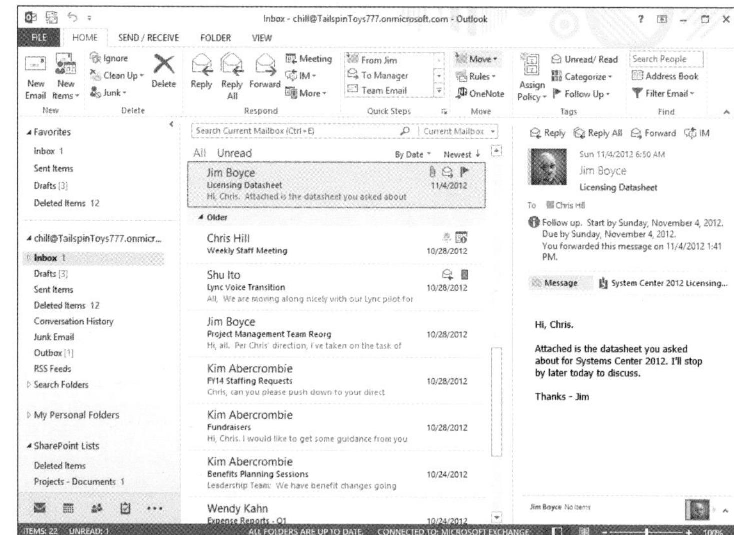

Sections 4, "Writing and sending email," and 5, "Receiving and reading email," explain how to work with email messages in Outlook, including addressing messages, using the Address Book, and working with contact groups. Section 4 teaches you how to change and format message text to add emphasis or highlight information. You also learn how to incorporate designs and color schemes to give messages the look of stationery. Section 4 finishes with a look at how to send files with messages, review messages you've already sent, and keep messages in the Drafts folder until you're ready to send them. Section 5 covers several topics about receiving and reading email and helps you manage, filter, and follow up on messages.

Keeping track of your contacts' addresses, phone numbers, and other information is one of the main uses for Outlook, and Section 6, "Working with the People Hub," acquaints you with this feature, which in previous versions of Outlook was referred to as the Contacts folder. You learn how to add social networking accounts such as Facebook and LinkedIn to Outlook. You also learn how to add new contacts, view and change contacts, and find a particular person. The section also explains how to organize contacts, schedule meetings for a contact, and communicate with people through the Contacts folder. The section finishes with a look at how to share contacts with others, keep track of phone calls, and associate contacts with items such as tasks.

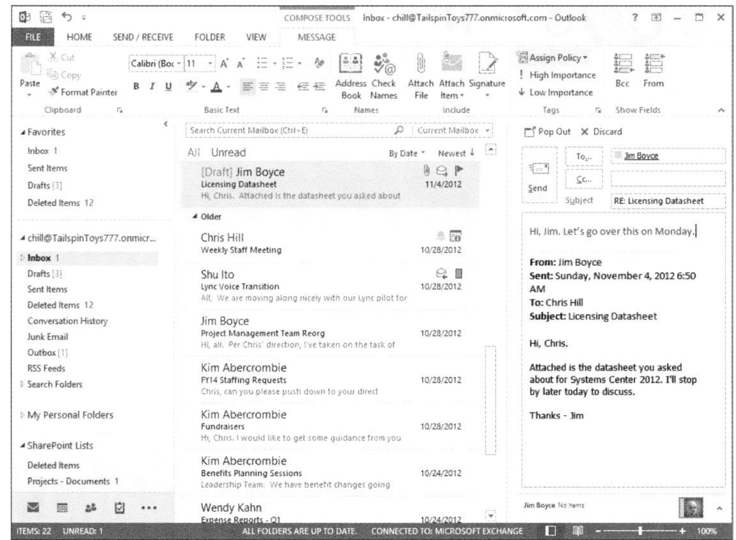

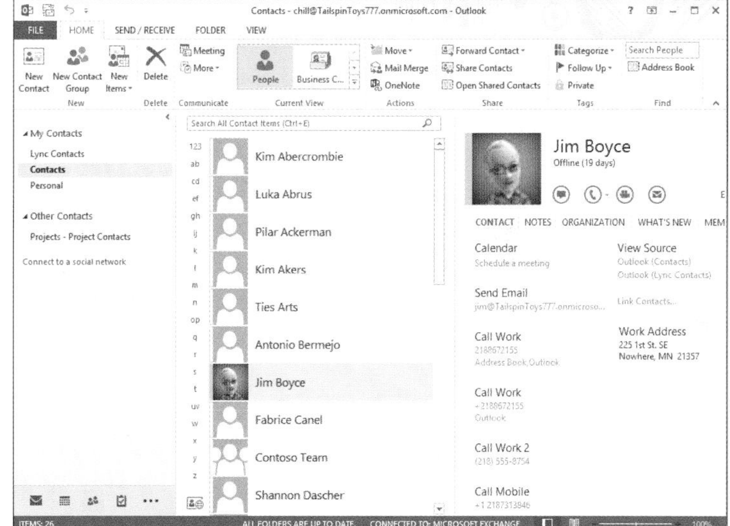

Section 7, "Managing a calendar," covers the Calendar folder and how to view your schedule, add appointments and meetings, associate files or other items with schedule items, and work with reminders. You also learn how to share your calendar, print calendars, and use the To-Do Bar to keep track of your tasks without leaving the Calendar folder.

Section 8, "Working with tasks," expands on Section 7's coverage of tasks and explains how to use the Tasks folder. You can assign tasks to yourself or to others, associate contacts and other items with tasks, and mark tasks as complete.

Section 9, "Using alerts and mobile features," covers the mobile features of Outlook 2013, such as setting up alerts to your mobile device for calendar events, messages, and voice mail.

Section 10, "Using Outlook with SharePoint," explains how to integrate Microsoft SharePoint sites with Outlook, which enables you to view shared calendars, contacts, document libraries, and other SharePoint items in Outlook. You can also work with those SharePoint items right from Outlook without ever opening the SharePoint site. Section 10 also looks at the presence features in Outlook that help you see when others are online.

Section 11, "Using Lync with Outlook," explores the integration between Outlook and Microsoft Lync. Here you learn how to join a Lync meeting from Outlook, create new Lync (online) meetings, and set online meeting options. The section also explores other that ways you can communicate with colleagues through Outlook and Lync, including instant messaging and voice calls.

Section 12, "Managing items and folders," helps you start to organize the data you keep in Outlook. Here you learn to create categories and organize Outlook items with categories, create and manage folders, delete items, and automatically move items out of your regular Outlook storage file and into an archive file. Archiving keeps your Outlook data file lean while still letting you hang on to important messages.

Section 13, "Managing your Outlook files," helps you work with and manage the files in which Outlook stores your data. You learn to create new data files, import and export items in Outlook, and back up and restore your Outlook data file.

Outlook offers a wealth of options that you can use to change the way the program looks and works, and Section 14, "Customizing Outlook," shows you how to set options for each of the Outlook folders and item types. The section also explains how to customize the Outlook folder pane, ribbon, and Quick Access Toolbar.

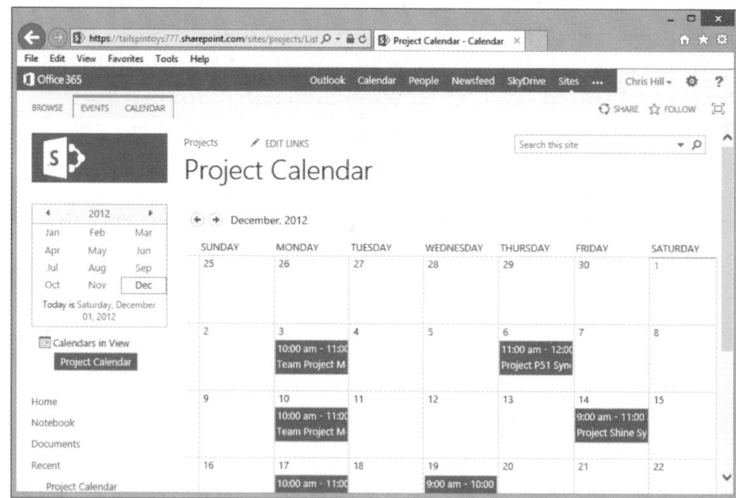

A few assumptions

I had to make a few educated guesses about you—my audience—when I started writing this book. Perhaps your computer is solely for personal use—email, surfing the Internet, playing games, and so on. Possibly your work makes it possible for you to telecommute. Or, maybe you run a small home-based business. Taking all these possibilities into account, I assumed that you either use a stand-alone home computer or have two or more computers connected so that you can share files, a printer, and so on. I also assumed that you have an Internet connection.

Another assumption is that—initially, anyway—you use Outlook just as it came, meaning that you use the standard views and standard menus rather than custom ones, and that you use your little friend, the mouse, in the traditional way: that is, you point and click to select an item and then double-click to open it. If you prefer using the mouse as if you are working on a webpage—pointing to an item to select it and then opening it with a single click—you can easily do so. To switch between single-click and double-click, open the Folder Options applet from the Control Panel. Use the Click Items As Follows controls to choose the method you prefer. However, because my working style is somewhat traditional, and because Outlook is set up to work in the traditional style, that's the style followed in the procedures and graphics throughout this book.

Adapting task procedures for touchscreens

In this book, I provide instructions based on traditional keyboard and mouse input methods. If you're using Outlook on a touch-enabled device, you might be giving commands by tapping with your finger or with a stylus. If so, substitute a tapping action any time I instruct you to click a user interface element. Also note that when I tell you to enter information in Outlook, you can do so by typing on a keyboard, tapping in the entry field under discussion to display and use the onscreen keyboard, or even speaking aloud, depending on how your computer is set up and your personal preferences.

A final word (or two)

I had three goals in writing this book:

1. Whatever you want to do, I want the book to help you get it done.
2. I want the book to help you discover how to do things that you didn't know you wanted to do.
3. And, finally, if I achieve the first two goals, I'm well on the way to the third: I want this book to help you enjoy using Outlook.

I hope you find *Microsoft Outlook 2013 Plain & Simple* a great learning tool. Of course, the best way to learn is by doing—so jump right in!

What's new in Outlook 2013?

2

Microsoft Outlook 2013 not only has a new look, but also has some great new features. These changes combine to make Outlook more visually appealing and easier to use. For example, reply emails no longer open up by default in a new window; instead, you can edit them right in the Reading pane. Other changes are more significant, such as the integration of social networking accounts like Facebook and LinkedIn, which brings all of your contacts together in one place.

We can't cover every new feature in this section, but we do cover some of the more popular features, along with the ones that will have the most impact. So, let's dig in!

In this section:

- Using message list commands
- Working in the Reading pane
- Using Calendar preview
- Working in the People Hub
- Using the Weather bar
- Working with cached Exchange mode

Using message list commands

Outlook 2013 adds features to make it easier to work in a single Outlook view without switching windows. One of these new features is the addition of a small selection of email commands that you can use right in the message list to mark messages as read or unread, flag messages, and delete them.

Work with message list commands

1 At the bottom of the Folder pane, click the Mail icon to open the Inbox.

2 Hover the pointer on the left edge of a message.

(continued on next page)

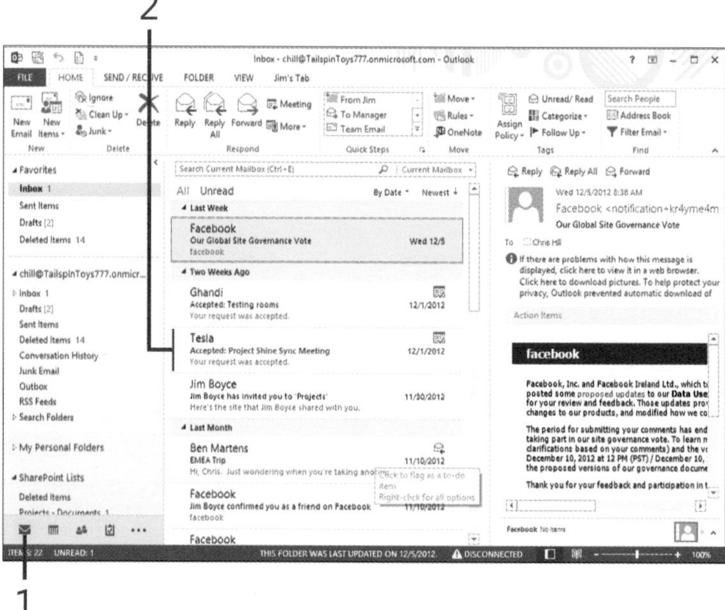

> **TIP** Some features in Outlook 2010 have been removed or deprecated. For example, the Journal features are no longer available. The Notes folder is still available, but most of the options for working with Notes have been removed.

Work with message list commands *(continued)*

3 Click to mark the message as read (or unread).

4 Click to flag the message for follow up.

5 Click to delete the message.

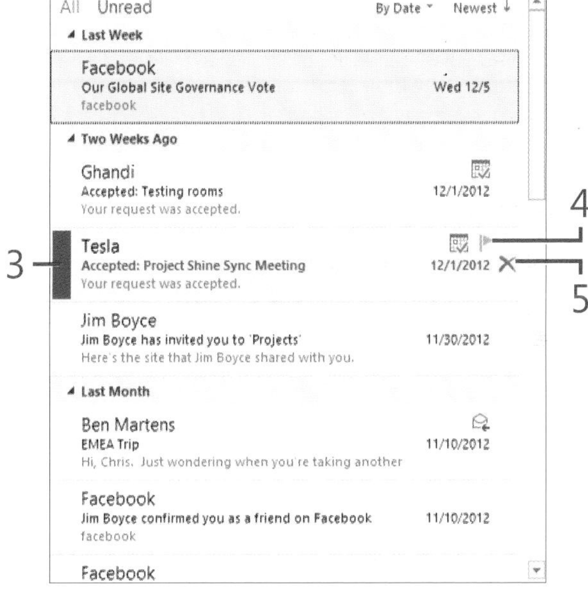

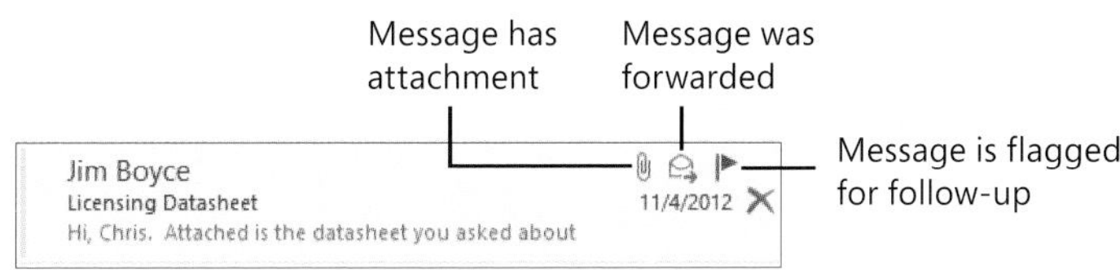

TIP Icons at the upper-right corner of the message provide status for the message, such as indicating that you have replied to or forwarded a message, that the message has an attachment, that a meeting invitation has been accepted or declined, or that the message is flagged for follow-up.

Working in the Reading pane

In previous versions of Outlook, you previewed messages in the reading pane but edited them in a separate window. In Outlook 2013, you can edit messages for replies and forwards directly in the reading pane. If you prefer not to edit in the reading pane (for example, you want to move the message window to a different monitor and continue to preview messages on another), you can pop out the message and edit in its own window.

Edit email in the reading pane

1 At the bottom of the Folder pane, click the Mail icon to open the Inbox.

2 Click a message to select it.

3 In the reading pane, click Reply.

(continued on next page)

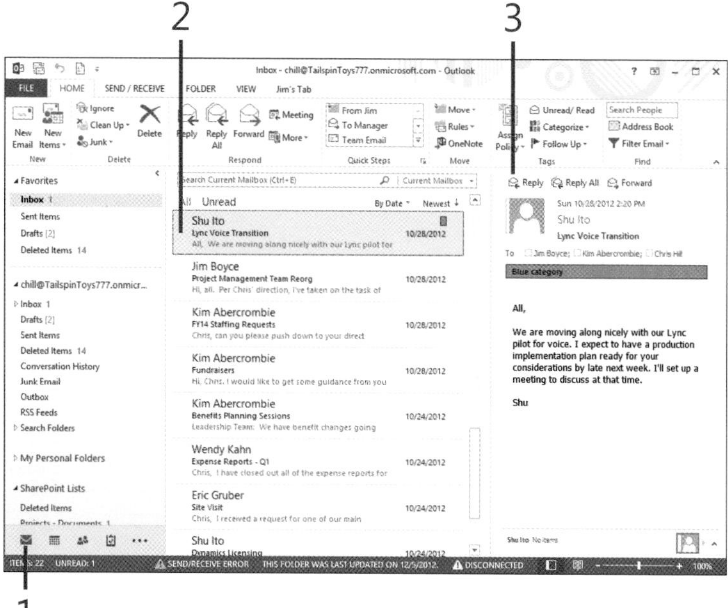

> **TIP** You can reply, reply all, or forward a message by using the buttons in the Reading pane. Also, if you start editing a message in the Reading pane and then decide you want to discard the edits, just click the Discard button.

Edit email in the reading pane *(continued)*

4 Type your reply.

5 Click Send.

6 Alternatively, to open the message in its own window, click Pop Out.

7 Finish editing the message and click Send.

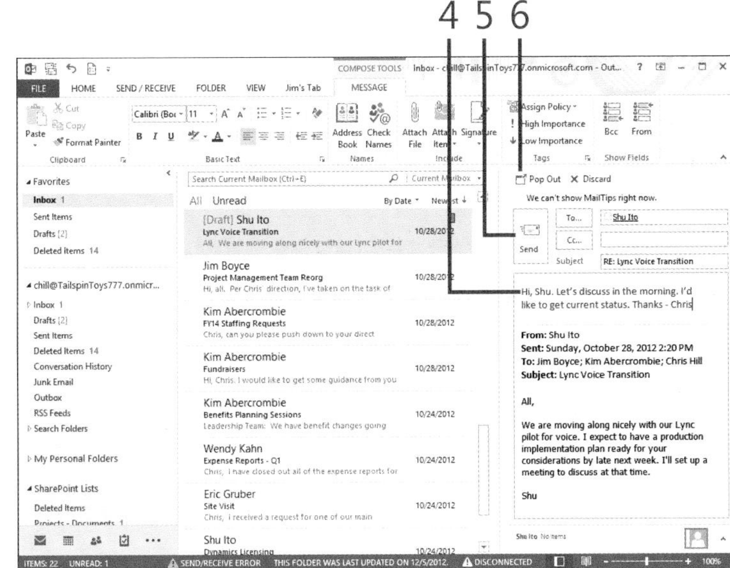

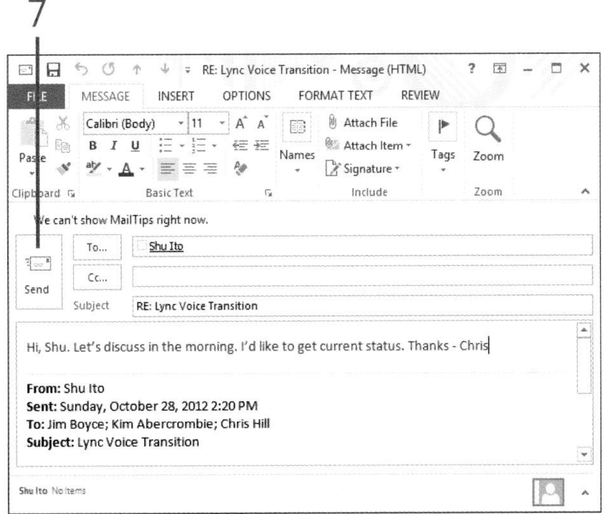

Using Calendar preview

If you have multiple monitors, you might keep your Calendar open on one monitor and your Inbox open on another. This way, you can see your Calendar without switching away from your mail. Outlook 2013 users now have a new way to preview their calendars right in their mailboxes. This handy new feature makes it possible to preview your calendar without ever leaving your mailbox.

Preview Calendar items in the Inbox

1 Click the Mail link to open the Inbox.

2 Hover the pointer on the Calendar link.

3 Click a date to view a day other than the current day.

4 Preview the calendar items for the selected day.

5 Double-click an item to open it for viewing or editing.

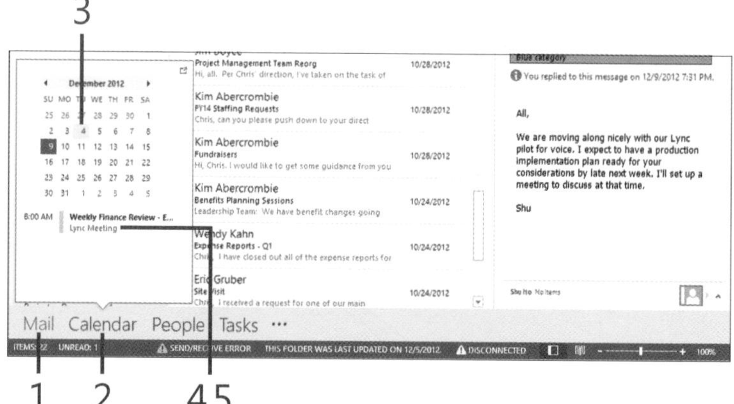

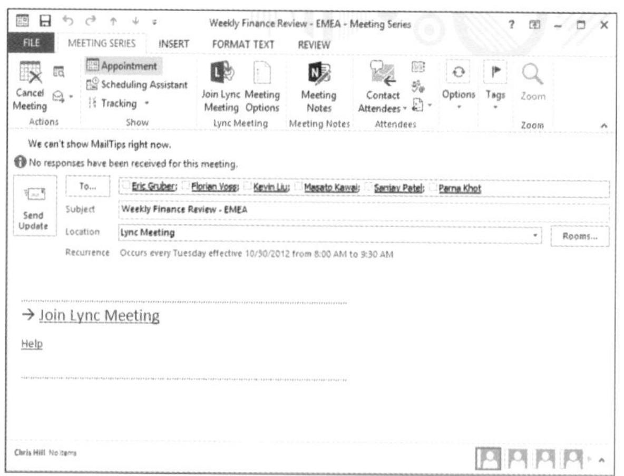

TIP By default, the Calendar preview in the Inbox shows calendar items from the current day. Use the arrows on either side of the month in the preview to choose a different month.

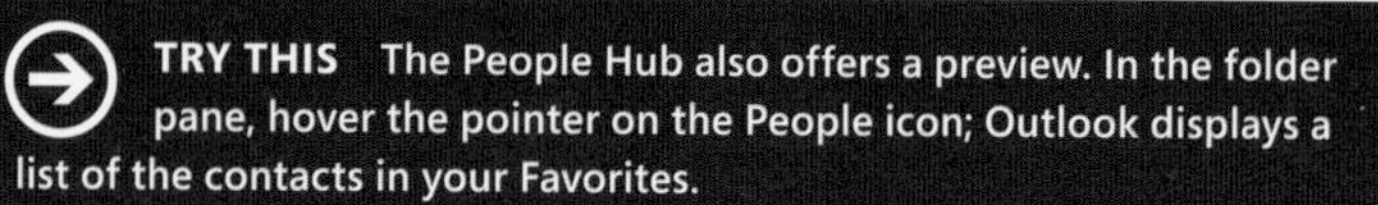

TRY THIS The People Hub also offers a preview. In the folder pane, hover the pointer on the People icon; Outlook displays a list of the contacts in your Favorites.

Working in the People Hub

The People Hub combines the new capability in Outlook 2013 to integrate social networking accounts, with a new People view that presents most of a contact's information in an easily consumed view. As you might expect, the new People view provides features to help you easily work with a selected contact. Thanks to Microsoft Lync integration, you can not only view contact information and start an email to a contact from the People Hub, but you can also start an instant message, voice call, or video call.

View contacts in the People pane

1. At the bottom of the Folder pane, click the People icon to open the People Hub.
2. In the People pane, select a contact.
3. View the contact information in the Contact card.
4. In the Folder pane, click the Connect To A Social Network link.

(continued on next page)

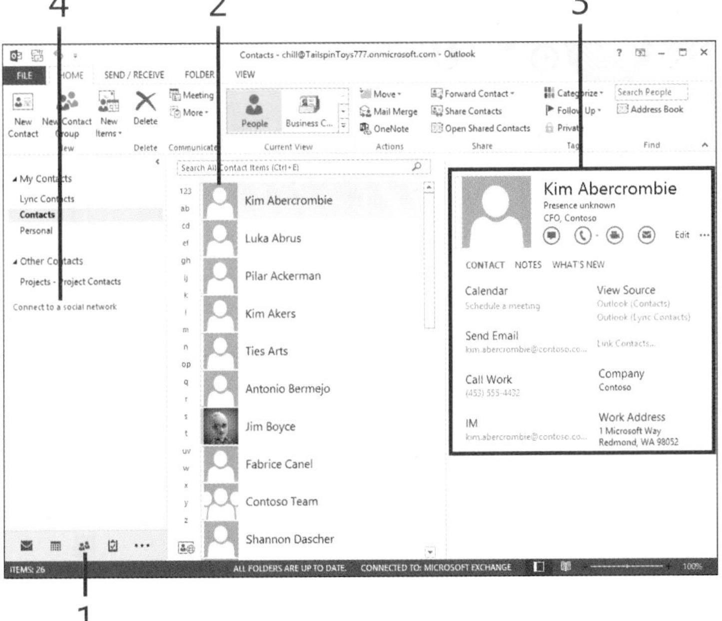

View contacts in the People pane *(continued)*

5 Select a social networking service and then click Connect to log on to that service and connect it to Outlook.

6 Click Finish.

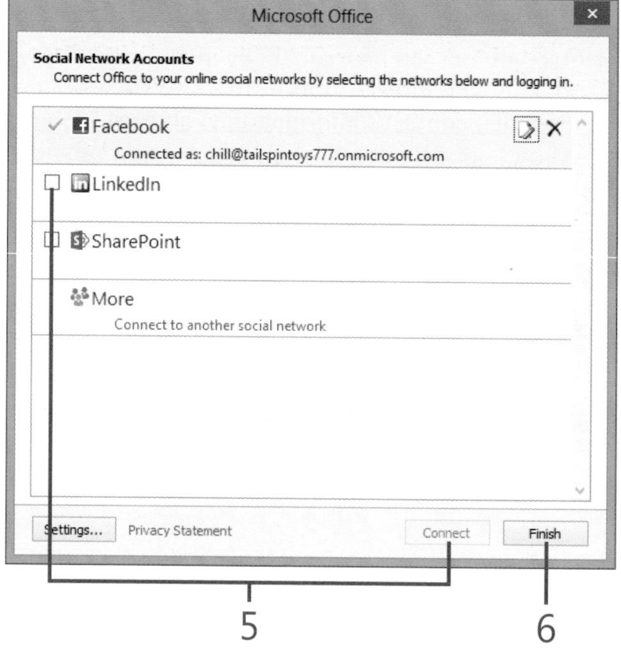

TIP Using the Facebook and LinkedIn connectors, you can connect your Facebook and LinkedIn accounts to Outlook and access contacts. With the SharePoint connector, you can incorporate SharePoint contacts.

Using the Weather bar

A new addition to the Calendar is the Weather bar, which shows a brief summary of the weather in selected locations. You can add locations by name or Postal Code. You can choose the location from a menu.

Add a location to the Weather bar

1 Open the Calendar.

2 View the sky condition and temperature for the selected default location.

3 Click the location name, click Add Location, and then type a location name or Postal Code and press Enter.

4 Hover the pointer on the displayed weather to view more details.

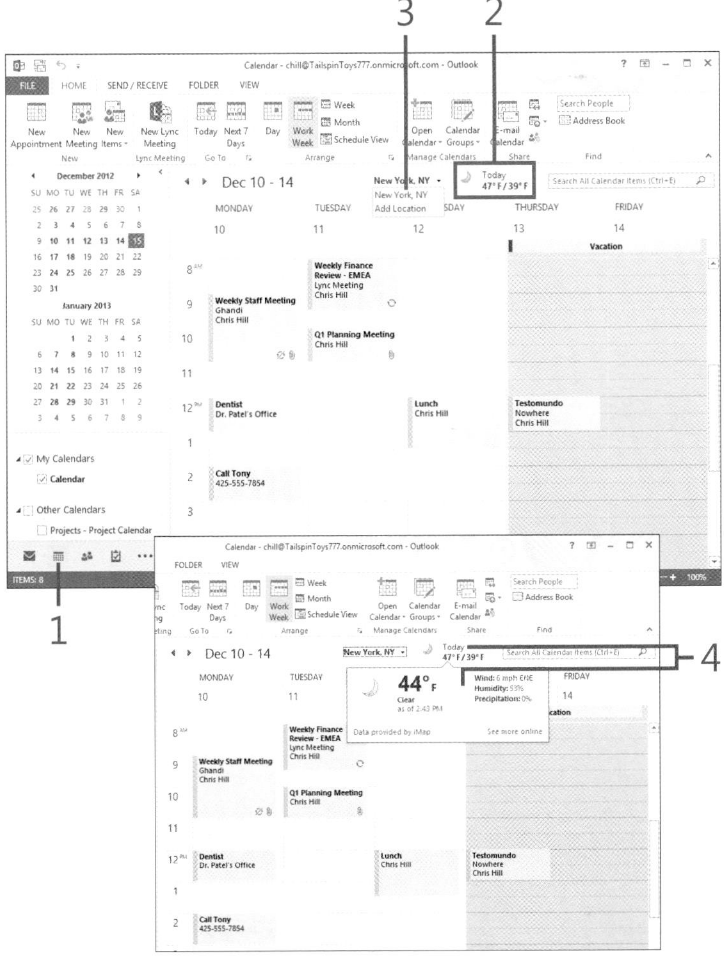

TRY THIS Enter a Postal Code or a location name to add a weather location to Outlook.

TIP The option to turn on or off display of weather in the Calendar is located on the Calendar page of the Outlook Options dialog box.

Working with cached Exchange mode

A new feature in Outlook 2013 when used in conjunction with Microsoft Exchange is the capability to specify how many months of content to keep cached locally. For example, if you are working from a tablet, you might want to limit Outlook to caching only a month's worth of data to conserve device storage space. You configure the amount of data Outlook will cache through the account settings for the Exchange account.

Configure offline cache

1 On the ribbon, click the File tab to display the Backstage view, click the Account Settings button, and then choose Account Settings.

(continued on next page)

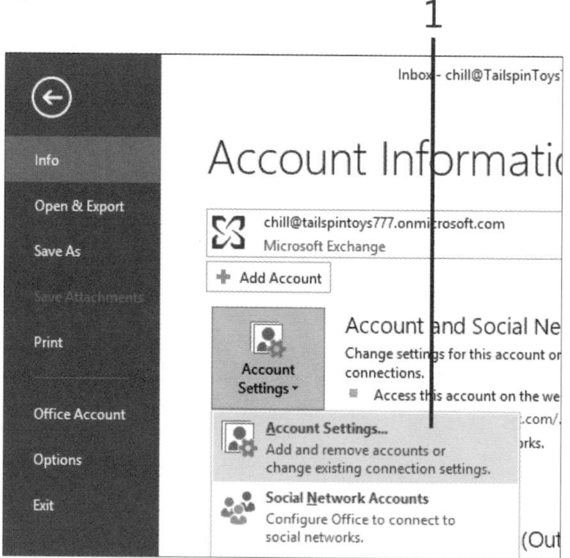

TIP You can configure the cache for a minimum of one month or a maximum of all. The latter causes Outlook to cache all data from your Exchange Server account.

Configure offline cache *(continued)*

2 In the Account Settings dialog box, click the Exchange Server account.

3 Click Change.

4 In the Change Account dialog box, drag the slider left or right to change the amount of data to cache.

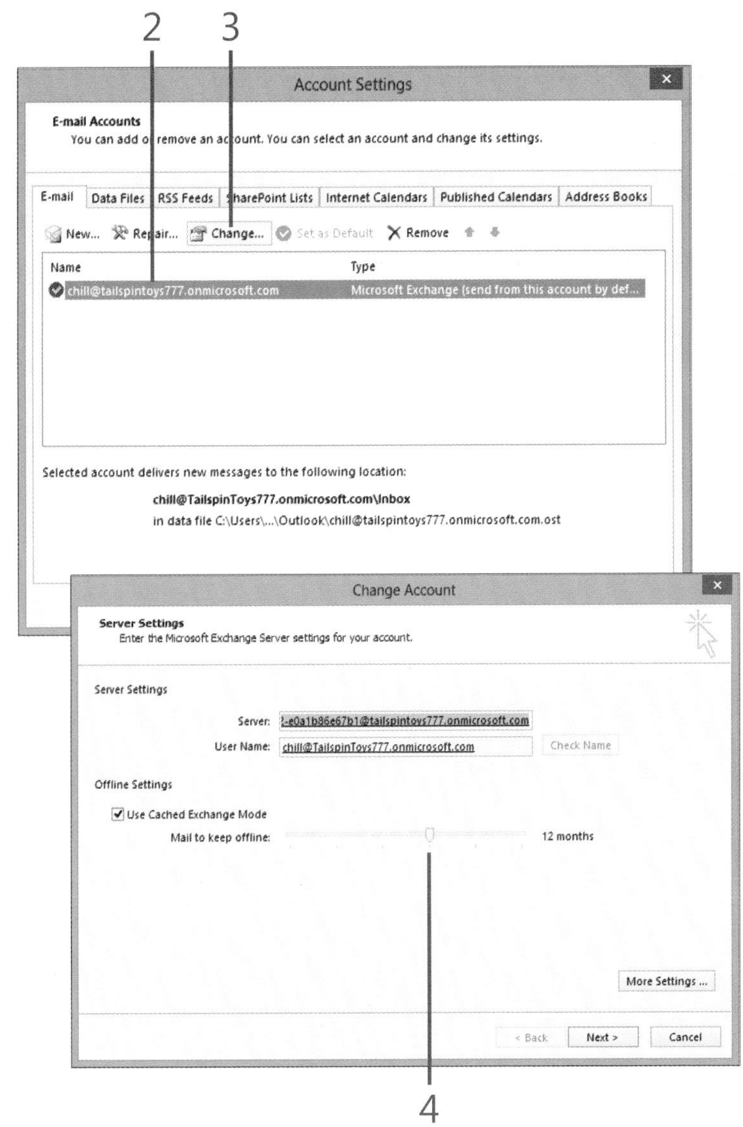

Getting started

3

In this section:

- Outlook 2013 at a glance
- Starting and exiting Outlook
- Exploring Outlook folders
- Working with Outlook items
- Setting up email accounts
- Viewing items and folders
- Getting help in Outlook 2013

Microsoft Outlook 2013 can help you manage almost every aspect of your day. With Outlook, you have tools to manage your email, contacts, calendar, and tasks. Using these tools, you can even keep track of your phone calls, time spent on documents, and other tasks and events. With new social networking features like Facebook and LinkedIn account integration included in Outlook 2013, you can bring much of your online experience—at least when it comes to communicating with family, friends, and colleagues—together in one place.

Even with all of its many features, Outlook is easy to use. It provides simple forms for creating and viewing messages, meetings, tasks, and other items. You can choose among several options for viewing your information in Outlook, and you can customize the existing views and create new ones. With this book in hand, you can be up to speed with Outlook in just a few hours.

This section of the book offers a quick overview of Outlook and how to start using it. You learn how to work with Outlook folders and items (such as messages, meetings, and contacts), add email accounts, and get help when you need more information about a particular feature or task.

Outlook 2013 at a glance

At first, the Outlook app window can seem overwhelming to new users because it contains so much information. However, after you understand how Outlook organizes and presents that information, you will have no trouble moving from folder to folder to view and arrange your information. The main program window organizes all of your Outlook folders for easy access, and individual windows help you to work with the different types of Outlook items.

Overview of the Outlook program window

Outlook provides several folders and ways to view the contents of those folders. The default view is the Inbox view, which shows email messages that you have received.

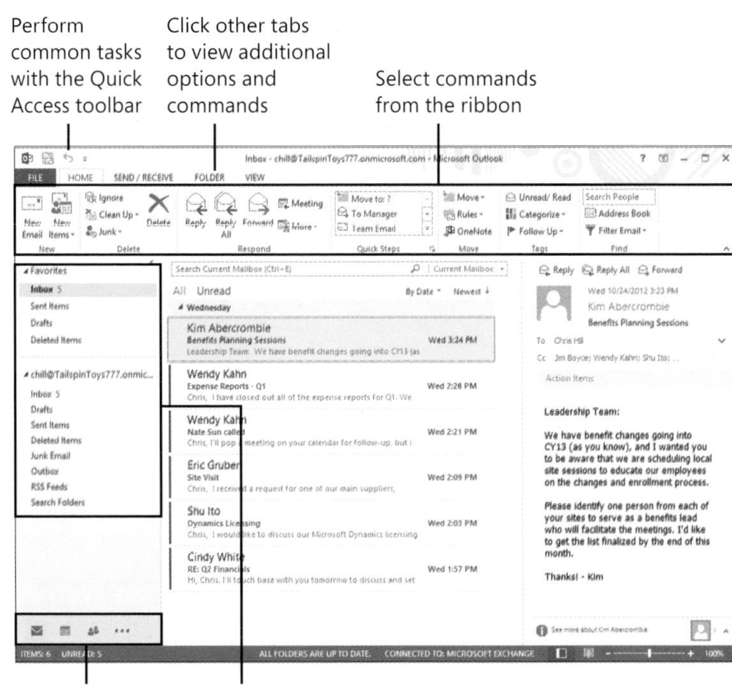

TIP If you need more space to display your schedule or other data, you can collapse the Folder pane or hide it altogether. Click the collapsed Folder pane or click the ellipsis button (...) at the bottom of the Folder pane to open a different Outlook folder.

SEE ALSO The Inbox is the default view in Outlook, but you can choose a different view as your default. See "Set the startup view" on page 33 for details.

Overview of an Outlook item window

Each Outlook folder uses a different type of form to let you view, create, and work with items. Simply double-click an item to open its form, or click the small arrow beside the New Items command on the Home tab on the ribbon and choose the type of item that you want to create.

1 Click the New Email button to create a new item of the default type for the current folder.

2 Click the New Items button to select the type of item that you want to create.

3 Double-click an item to open the item for viewing and editing.

4 View the opened item.

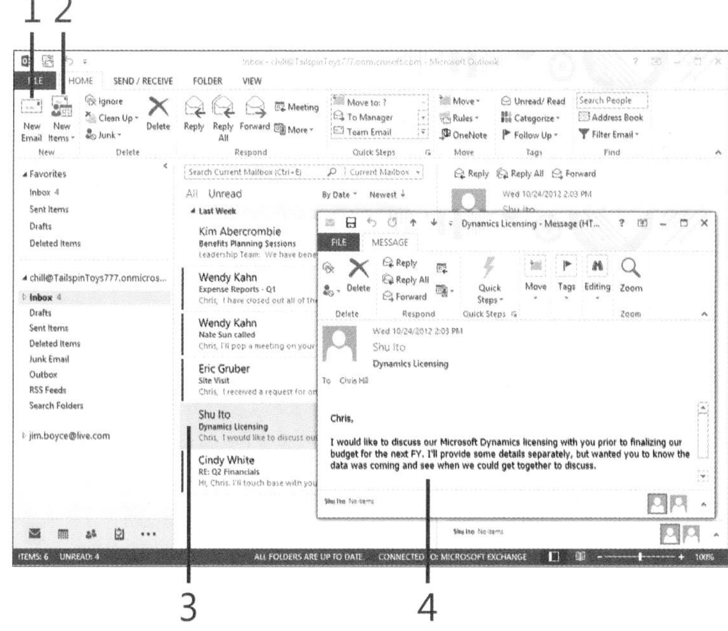

SEE ALSO For information about customizing the way folder icons appear in the Folder pane, see "Customizing the Folder pane" on page 253.

Starting and exiting Outlook

Before you can work with your Outlook items, you need to open Outlook. The app functions in much the same way as other traditional desktop Windows programs when it comes to starting, using, or exiting the program.

Start Outlook

1 On the Windows 8 Start screen, click the Outlook 2013 app tile.

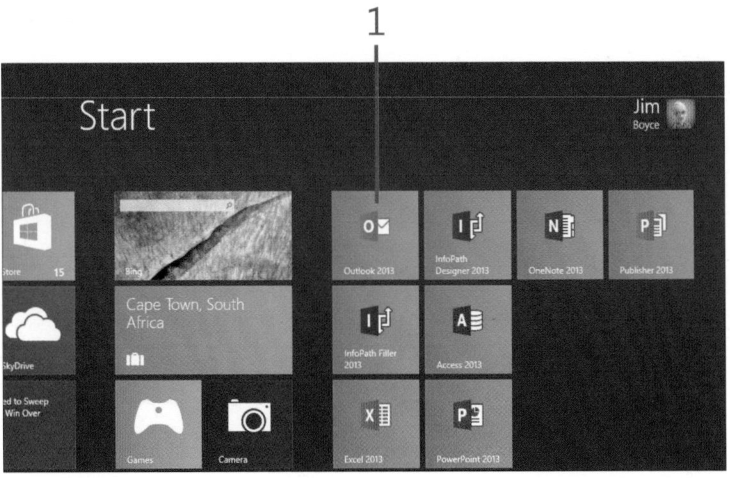

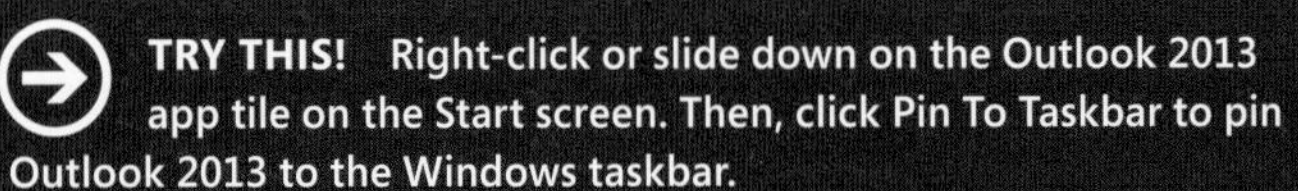

TRY THIS! Right-click or slide down on the Outlook 2013 app tile on the Start screen. Then, click Pin To Taskbar to pin Outlook 2013 to the Windows taskbar.

Exit Outlook

1 On the ribbon, click the File tab to display the Backstage view and then click the Exit tab.

2 As an alternative to step 1, click the Close button.

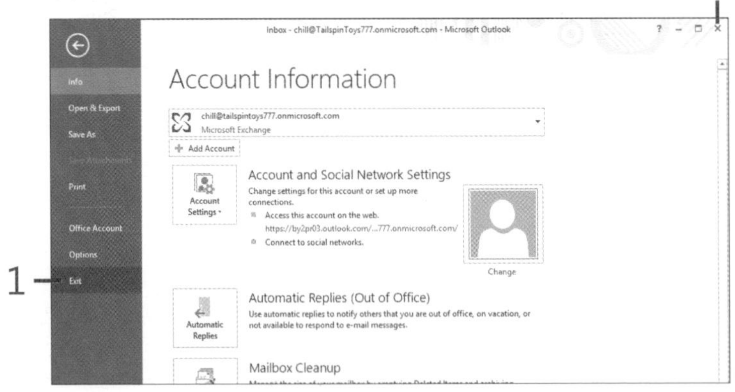

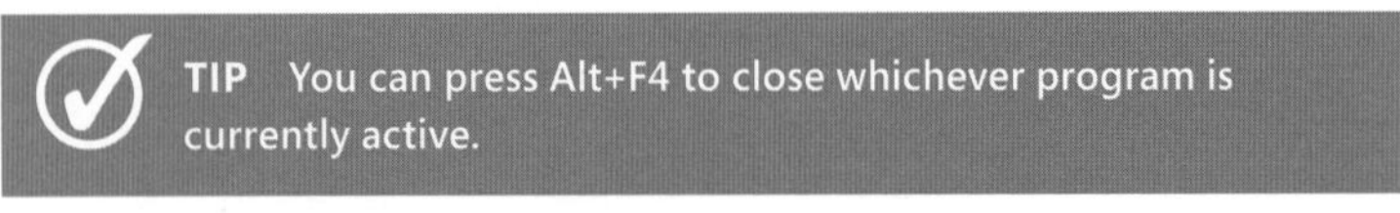

TIP You can press Alt+F4 to close whichever program is currently active.

Exploring Outlook folders

Outlook includes several folders that contain different types of data. The Inbox receives incoming messages, and outgoing messages depart through the Outbox. The Drafts folder holds messages that you're working on, and the Sent Items folder keeps a copy of each message you send. You can use the People Hub to store contact information and the Calendar folder to store your schedule. The Navigation pane and the folder list give you quick access to your folders.

Using the folder pane

1. Click Mail to open the Inbox folder.
2. Click the root of your default email account to open the Outlook Today view.
3. Click other icons to open items not shown in the Folder pane.

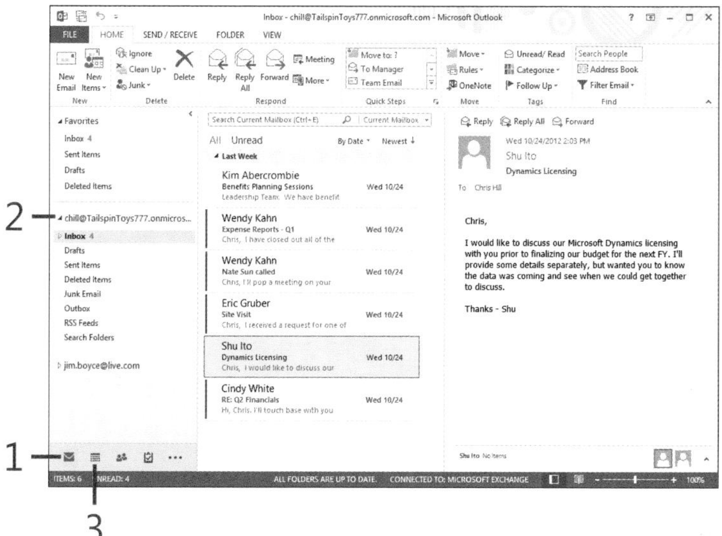

TIP If you work with Outlook much of the day or every time you work on your computer, pin Outlook 2013 and your other most frequently used Office apps to the taskbar.

TIP You can use more than one set of personal folders at a time, and Outlook shows them all in the folder list. For example, if you have a Windows Live account as well as an Exchange account, you see both sets of folders in the Folder pane.

Use the folder list

1 Click the ellipsis button.
2 Click Folders.
3 Click a white triangle to expand a folder's listing.
4 Click a black triangle to collapse a folder's listing.
5 Click a folder to open it in Outlook.
6 Click a different icon to display that folder's contents.

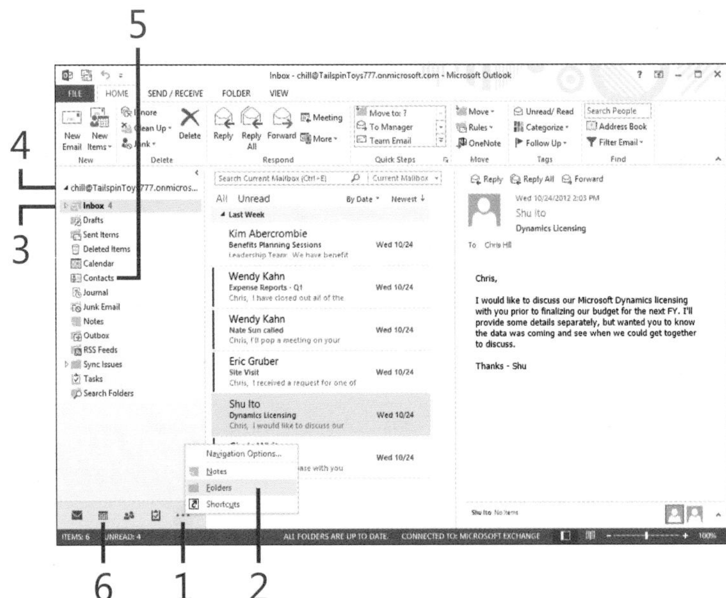

> **TIP** Unlike previous versions of Outlook, Outlook 2013 displays menu choices in text. This change makes the program interface well-suited to Windows 8. However, you might want to switch back to icons to save space.

> **SEE ALSO** For information about setting up email accounts for Windows Live and other email services, see "Setting up email accounts" on page 27.

Working with Outlook items

Outlook helps you to store information and send messages in a variety of ways. You can use messages, contacts, journal entries, tasks, appointments, meetings, and notes, each of which constitutes a type of Outlook item. Outlook stores each type in a particular folder and presents the information in a way that makes the most sense for that type of data. In many situations, you can retrieve the information you need simply by opening the folder without actually opening the item.

Review items in a folder

1 In the Folder pane, click the folder whose contents you want to view.

2 Use the scroll bar to view additional items.

3 View the item in the Reading pane.

4 In the People Hub, click the letter that corresponds to the first initial of other names that you want to view.

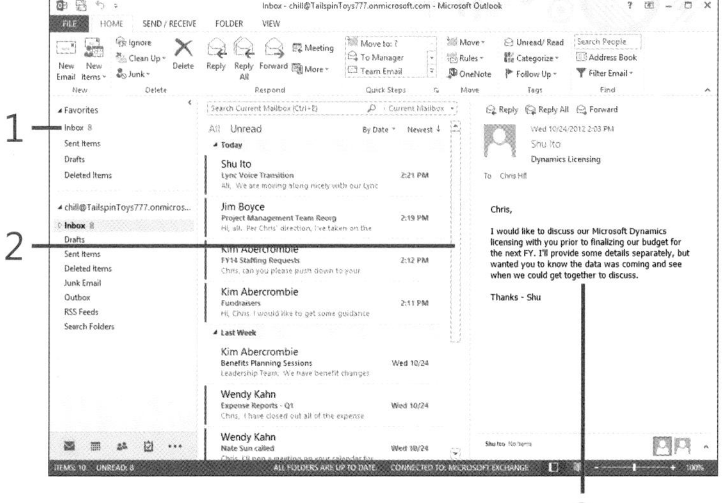

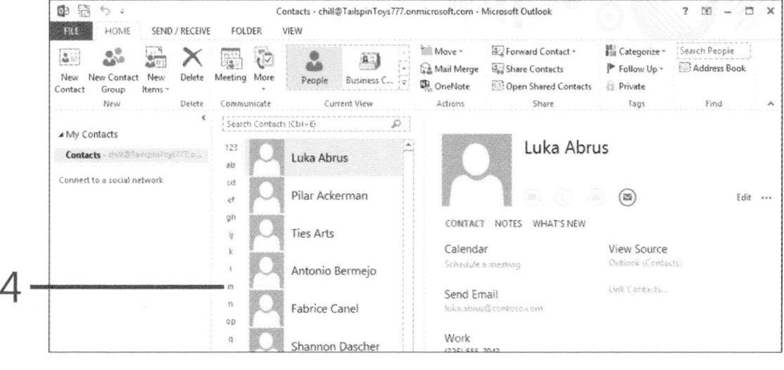

TIP The Reading pane appears below or to the right of the Contents pane and displays the contents of an item when you click it. To find the Reading pane, choose Reading Pane on the View tab.

TIP Outlook provides a Message Preview option for list views such as the default Inbox and Tasks folder views. When Message Preview is turned on, Outlook displays the first few lines of the item below the item's header. To turn Message Preview on or off, choose Message Preview on the View tab.

Open an item

1 In the Folder pane, click the folder that contains the item you want to open.

2 Locate the item in the Contents pane and double-click it.

3 View the item in its current form or make changes as necessary.

4 For a meeting, click Send Update to save the changes and send an updated invitation. For other types of items, click the Save & Close button to save your changes to the item and close the form.

5 As an alternative to step 4, click Close to close the form without making changes.

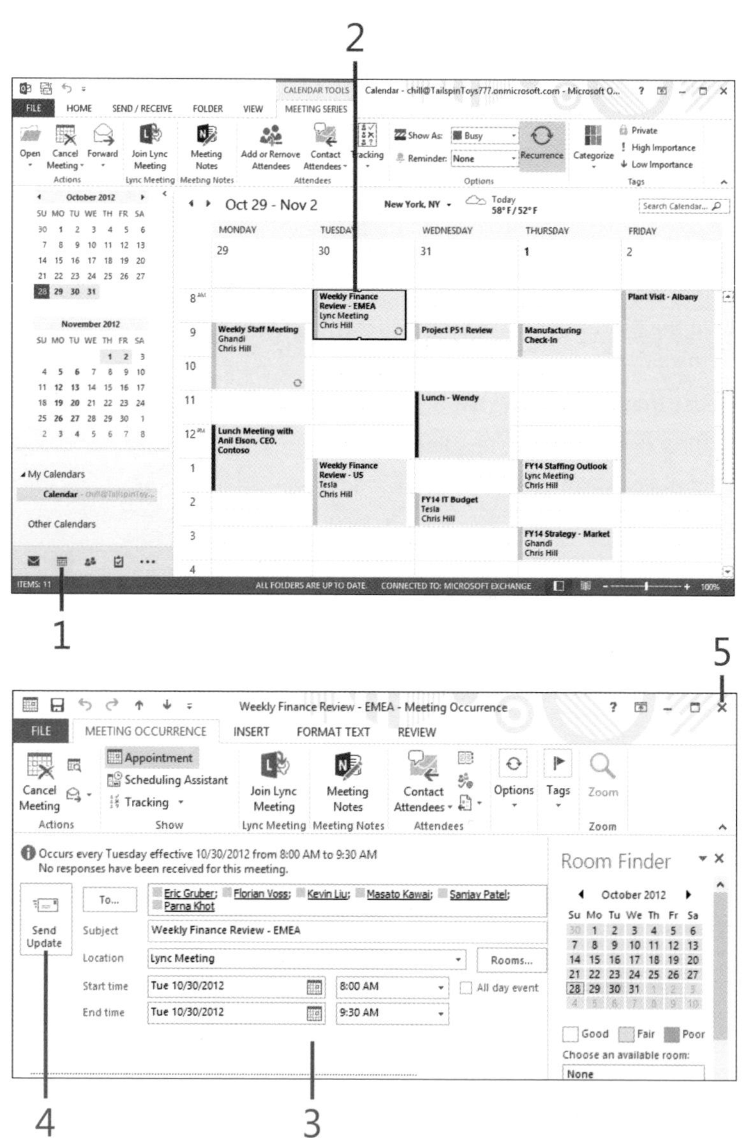

Setting up email accounts

You can use Outlook to send and receive messages for several different types of email accounts. Outlook supports Microsoft Exchange Server; POP3 services, such as a typical account from an Internet service provider (ISP); IMAP services; and Exchange ActiveSync compatible accounts such as Outlook.com accounts. You can easily add a new account, either automatically by using AutoDiscover or by manually entering the settings for the account. However, unlike previous versions of Outlook, you can't import email accounts from other programs into Outlook 2013. Instead, you must add them in the same way that you add a new email account.

Add an email account by using AutoDiscover

1 On the ribbon, click the File tab to display the Backstage view and then click Add Account.

(continued on next page)

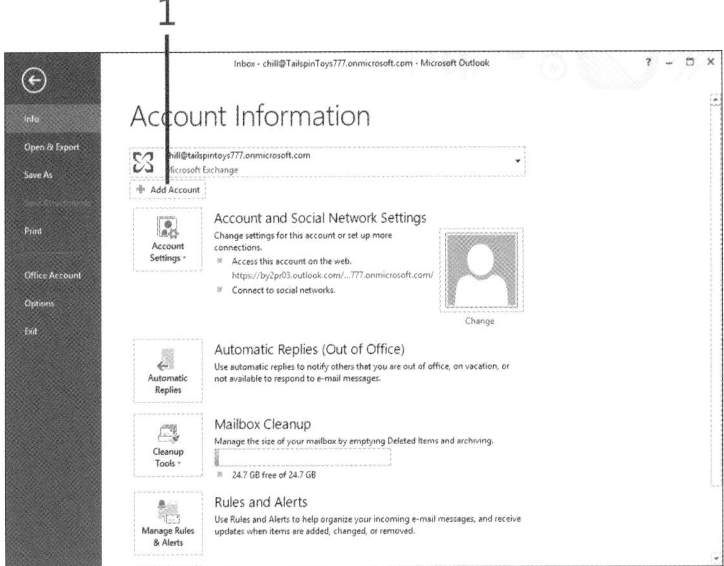

Add an email account by using AutoDiscover *(continued)*

2 Type your first and last name.

3 Type the email address for your email account.

4 Type your email account password.

5 Type your email account password again.

6 Click Next.

7 Click Finish.

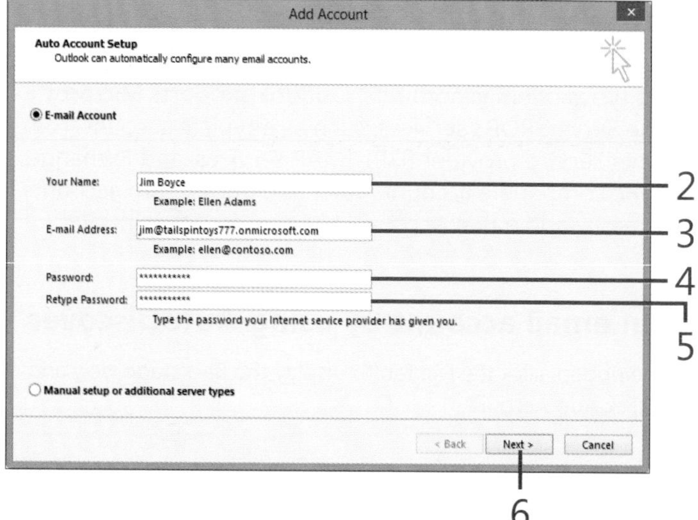

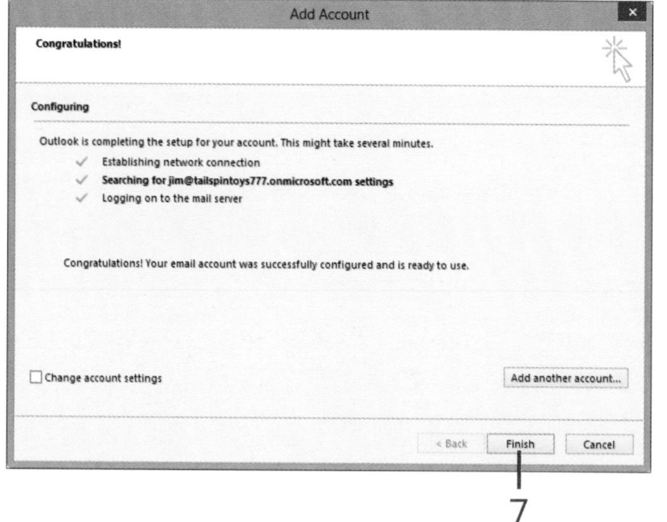

Add a POP or IMAP email account manually

1. On the ribbon, click the File tab to display the Backstage view and then click Add Account.
2. Click Manual Setup Or Additional Server Types.
3. Click Next.

(continued on next page)

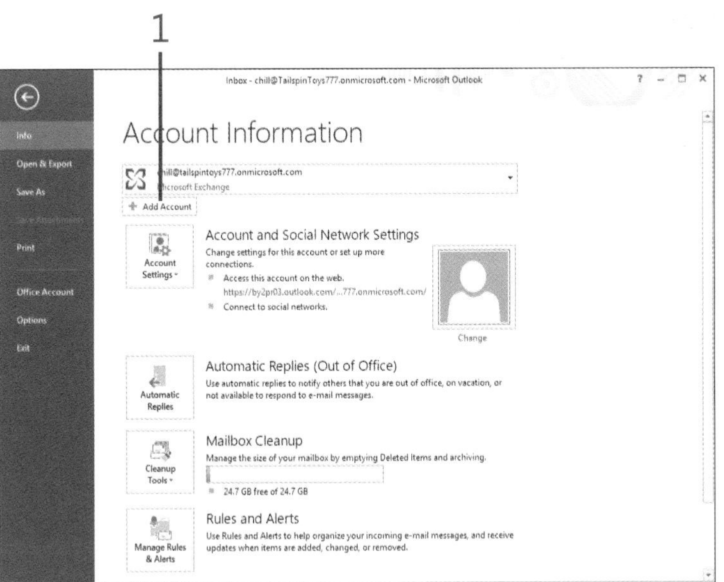

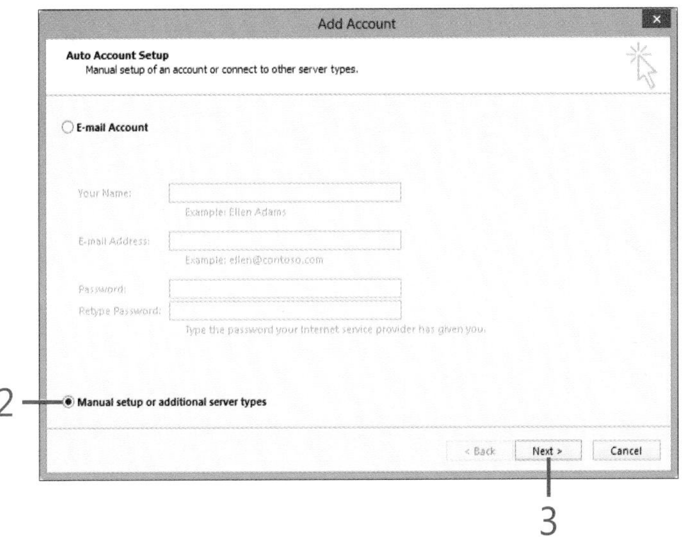

TIP You can manage Outlook email accounts, personal folders, address books, RSS feeds, SharePoint lists, and directory services through the Mail icon in Windows Control Panel.

TRY THIS! Outlook can often add email accounts automatically. In the Add New Account dialog box, fill in your name, email address, and password, and then click Next. Outlook attempts to identify the mail server based on your email address and performs some tests to verify that it can send and receive using the specified server. If Outlook can't determine the right settings, it prompts you to enter them manually.

Add a POP or IMAP email account manually *(continued)*

4 Select POP Or IMAP.

5 Click Next.

6 Type your name and email address.

7 Choose the account type.

8 Type the incoming and outgoing mail server names provided by your ISP or email administrators.

9 Type your user name and password for the server account you're testing.

10 Click Test Account Settings to have Outlook test your settings, and then close the test window when the test is completed successfully. Click Next, and then click Finish to return to the Account Settings window.

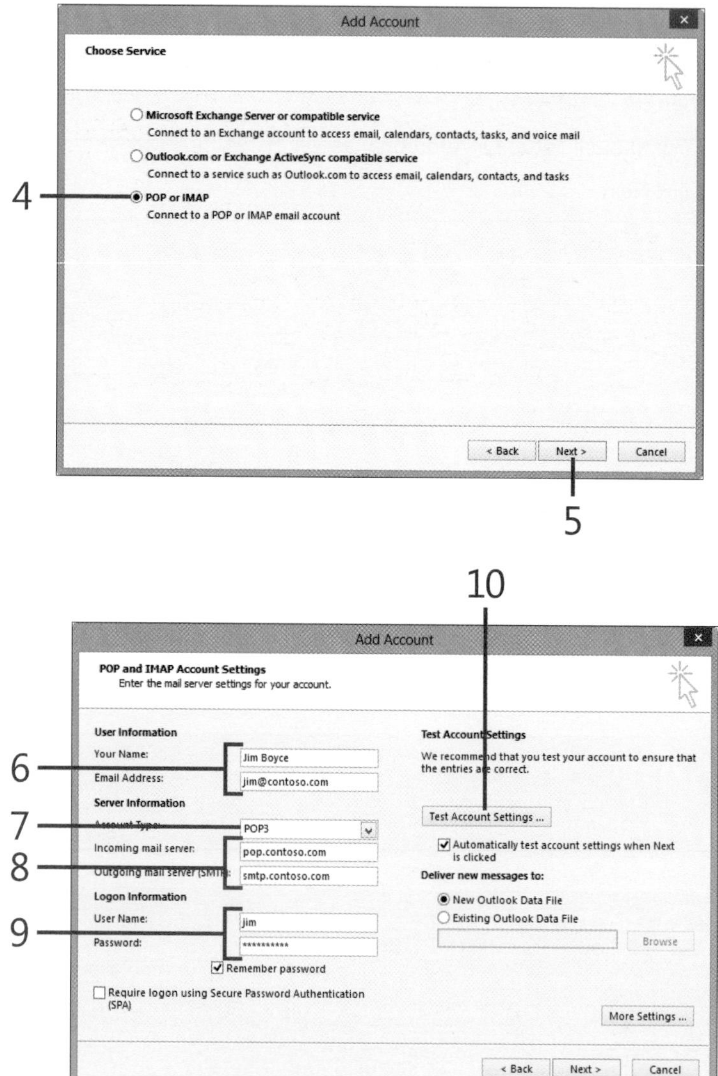

SEE ALSO For information about keeping messages from different accounts separated from one another, see "Working with the Rules Wizard" on page 81.

Viewing items and folders

Outlook offers several different views, depending on the folder you open. You can use the default views to work with the data in the folder or change the view to tailor it to your needs. The Outlook Today view gives you a single place to view your pending appointments, tasks, and messages, giving you a summary of your workday or workweek. You can also use the View tab to switch easily among the available views for a particular Outlook folder.

Use the Outlook Today view

1. In Outlook, in the Folder pane, click the email address for the account with which you want to work.
2. To open an appointment, in the Calendar list, click the appointment.
3. Select the check box beside a task to mark it as complete.
4. Click a task to open the task.
5. Click the Inbox or other folder to open the folder and work with your messages.

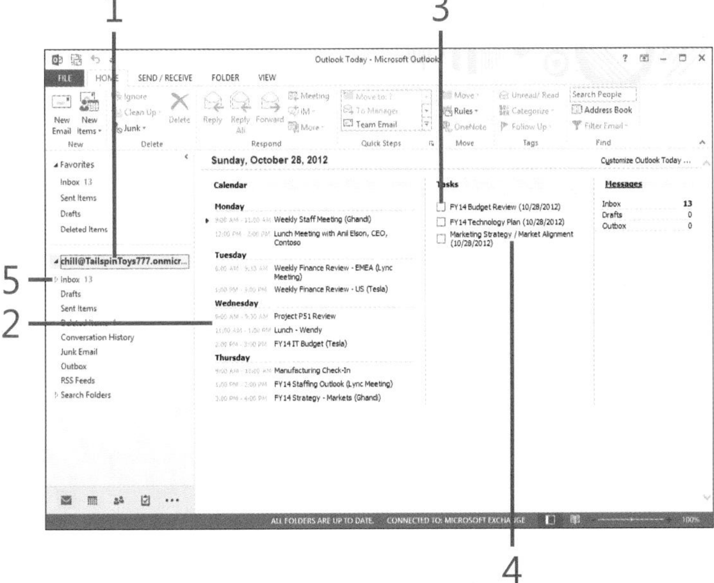

Use the Change View menu

1 In Outlook, select the folder that you want to view.

2 On the ribbon, click the View tab.

3 Click the Change View button.

4 In the gallery that opens, choose a view.

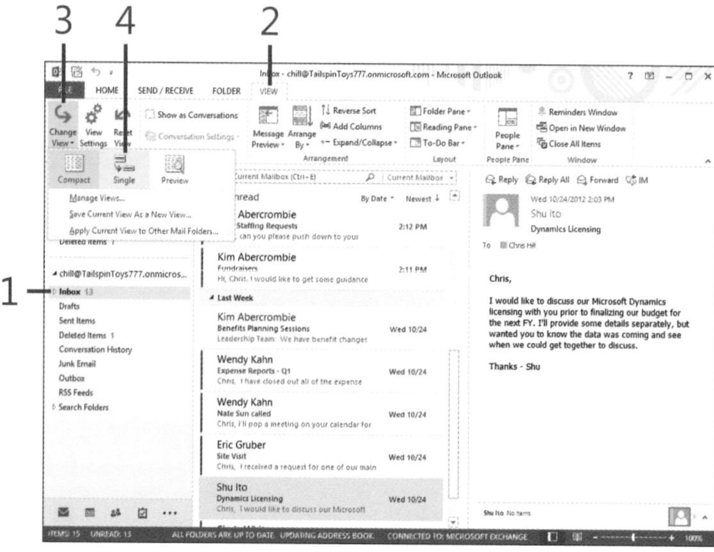

TRY THIS! Open the People Hub and click New Contact in the ribbon to create a new contact. Fill in the fields on the Contact page and click Save & Close to save the contact. With the People Hub open, click the View tab, click Change View, and then select Card. Outlook displays more information in the Contacts folder. Click Change View and then select Phone to change to a view that is handy for quickly locating phone numbers.

Set the startup view

1. In Outlook, click the File tab to display the Backstage view and then click the Options tab.
2. Click Advanced to show the Advanced page in the Outlook Options dialog box.
3. Click Browse, and choose the folder that you want Outlook to display when you first start the program.
4. Click OK to close the Options dialog box.

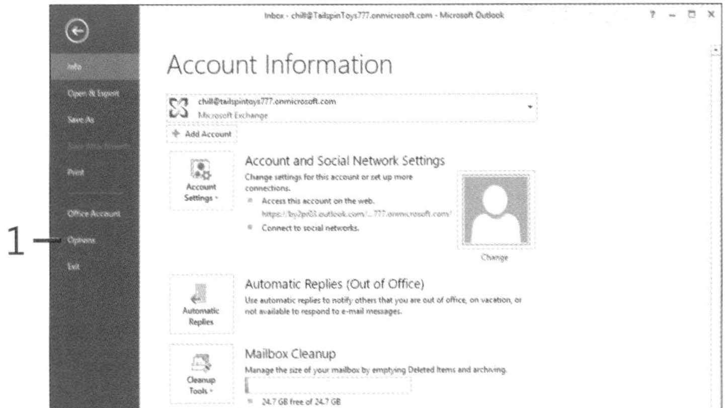

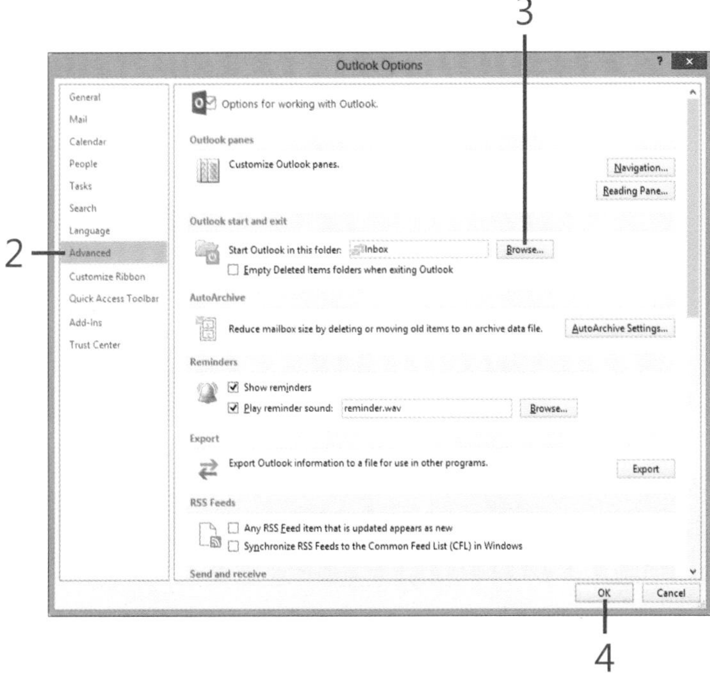

Getting help in Outlook 2013

Every new program has a learning curve. Getting up to speed with Outlook can take some time because of the number of features it offers. Even after you become comfortable using Outlook every day, you're likely to need some help with features you've never used before or those you seldom use. Outlook provides extensive Help documentation, and you can access this information in a couple of ways.

Use Outlook Help content

1 Click the Question Mark button above the ribbon.
2 In the Outlook Help window, click in the text box and type a word or phrase.
3 Click to search for the specified topic. Alternatively, use either of the following steps.
4 Click a topic heading to view the associated topic.
5 Click to choose between online and offline Help content.

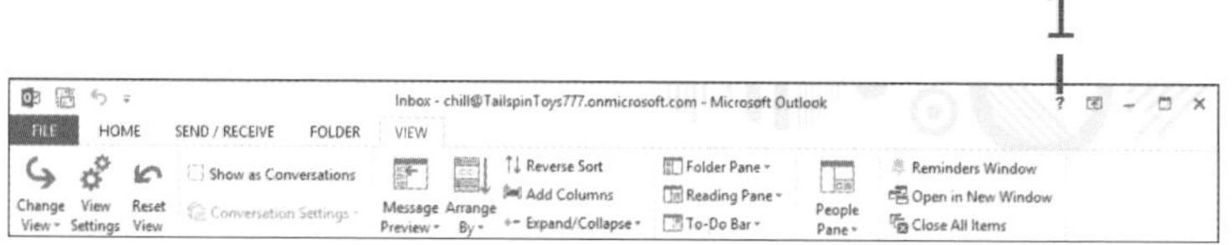

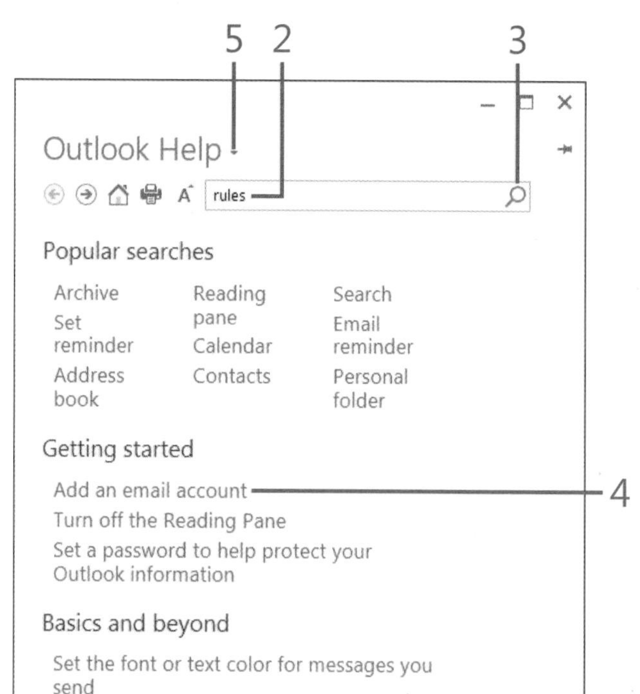

TIP Offline Help consists of Help content installed by the Setup program and stored on your computer. Online Help is content available on the Internet at the Microsoft website. Offline Help is great when you don't want or can't connect to the Internet. Online Help is generally more extensive.

Writing and sending email

4

In this section:

- Writing an email message
- Working with the Address Book
- Working with contact groups
- Changing message text
- Formatting message text
- Using signatures
- Working with HTML stationery
- Sending a file by email
- Sending messages manually
- Reviewing sent messages and drafts

Microsoft Outlook 2013 handles many daily tasks for you, such as keeping your calendar, collecting notes, and saving your contacts. But the main feature of Outlook is its electronic mail (email). Outlook is often referred to as a universal inbox—it can send, receive, and store messages from a number of different email sources, such as Exchange Server, Outlook.com, Windows Live, and other Internet email accounts.

The email features in Outlook make it possible for you to create and send email messages to others. With the help of the People Hub and Address Book, you can quickly access a recipient's email address when you're ready to address your new email message. You can also use contact groups in Outlook to send one message to multiple users, format email message text to contain rich content (such as HTML format) and to use HTML stationery, and to append signatures at the bottom of all your outgoing messages.

In this section, you learn how to write and modify email messages, send messages, and review messages you've already sent. In addition, you learn how to use the Address Book to select recipient names, create and use contact groups, format your messages, use signatures, send attached files, and work with HTML stationery.

Writing an email message

When you write new messages in Outlook 2013, you use the Message window. This window has a line for recipients (called the To line), a line for "carbon copied" recipients (the Cc line), a Subject line, and an area for the text of the message. Every new message must have at least one recipient. If you want, you can leave the Cc and Subject lines blank, but it's a good idea to give your messages a subject.

Address an email message

1 On the Home tab, in the New group, click New Email to display a new Message window.

2 To open the Select Names dialog box, click To.

3 In the Select Names dialog box, click the Address Book drop-down arrow.

4 Click the name of the address book you want to use, such as Contacts.

The addresses in the selected address book appear in the box.

5 Click the name of the person to whom you want to send the new message.

6 Click To, Cc, or Bcc; Outlook copies the name to the specified message recipients list.

7 Repeat steps 5 and 6 until the message recipients list includes all the recipients to whom you want to send the message.

8 Click OK.

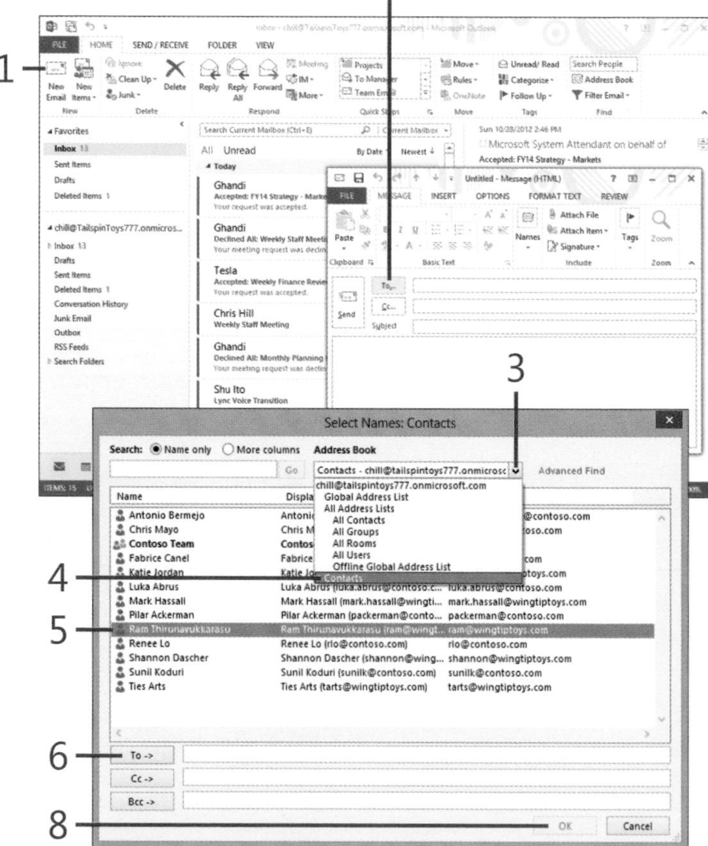

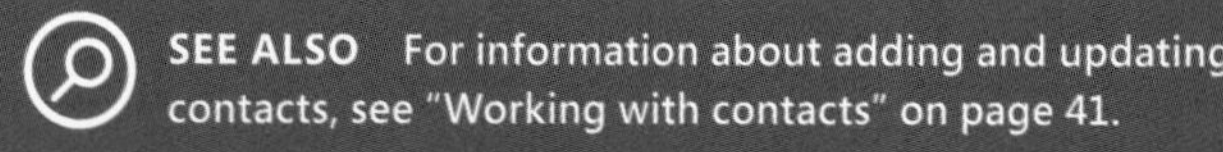

SEE ALSO For information about adding and updating contacts, see "Working with contacts" on page 41.

Type your message subject and text

1 In the new Message window, in the Subject field, type a subject for the new message.

2 Press the Tab key, or click in the message body area.

3 Type your message.

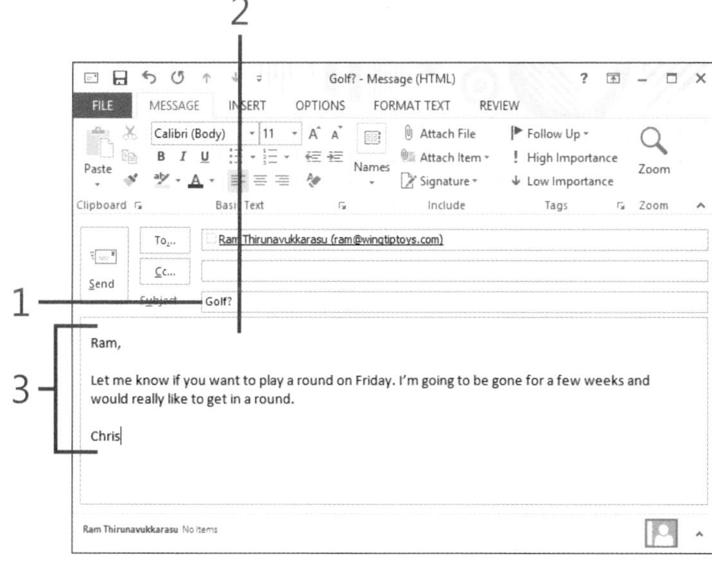

TIP As you write your message, you do not have to press Enter at the end of each line. Keep typing, and Outlook wraps the text to the next line. To create a new paragraph, press Enter. If you want each paragraph to be separated by two blank lines, press Enter twice at the end of each paragraph. This makes your messages easier to read than single-spaced messages.

CAUTION You can apply special formatting to your message (see "Formatting message text" on page 47), but you might not want to. If you send mail to people who use a different email program, they might not see the formatting that you intended. When in doubt, it's usually a good policy to keep your messages simple so that nothing gets lost in the translation.

Working with the Address Book

You can use the Outlook 2013 Address Book to search for and select names, email addresses, and contact groups. When you type a recipient name in the To field of the Message window, Outlook searches the Address Book for a match. The Address Book gives you access to any address books that you have set up (see the Tip about address books on page 40), as well as information from the Contacts folder, Microsoft Exchange Server Global Address List (if you have an Exchange Server mailbox), Internet directory services, and address books added by other services such as LinkedIn. Depending on the way you have Outlook set up, you can have information from only one of these sources or you can have contact information from multiple types.

Open the Address Book

1 On the Home tab, in the Find group, click Address Book.

2 In the Address Book drop-down list, click the selection arrow.

3 Click the address book from which you want to view addresses.

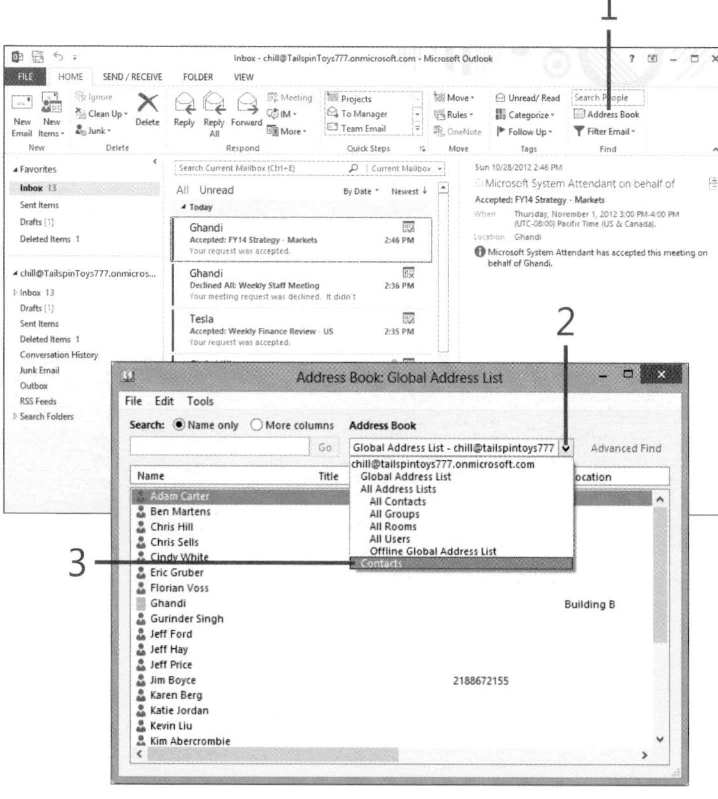

SEE ALSO For more information about working with your contact information, see "Working with contacts" on page 41.

TIP You can set up several different address books to store your email recipients' contact information. For example, you might have a company-wide address book that stores addresses and contact information for all internal employees. A second address book can be set up for external contacts, such as vendors, suppliers, and customers. A third address book could store personal contact information.

Find a name in the Address Book

1 In the Address Book dialog box, click in the Search text box.

2 Type the name of the contact that you want to find.

3 The first contact that matches the name you typed in the Search text box is highlighted in the list of names.

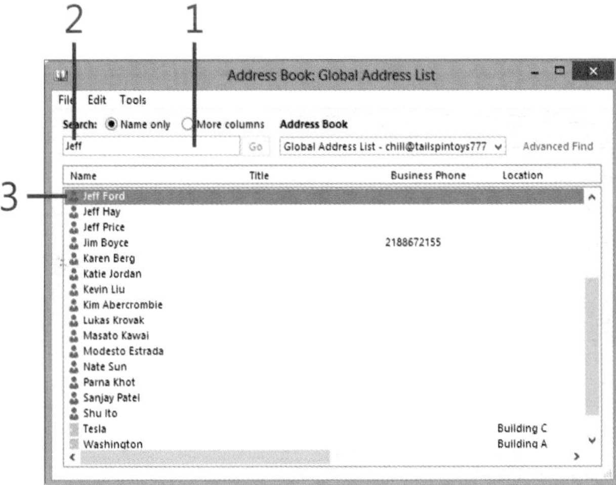

TRY THIS! Assume that you want to find a contact whose name is Dave. You're not sure whether you listed him as "Dave" or "David" in your Contacts folder. To find him, in your Address Book choose Find from the Tools menu, type **dav**, and then press Enter. Outlook displays all names containing "dav", such as "Dave," "Davey," "David," and so on.

TIP If you want to redisplay your entire address book after a search, select an address book from the Address Book drop-down list and click Name Only. Notice that Outlook now lists search results as a selection in case you want to return to your latest search results.

Send an email to a name in the Address Book

1. In the Address Book dialog box, click a contact to whom you want to send an email message.
2. On the File menu, click New Message.
3. Type a subject.
4. Type your message text in the message body area.

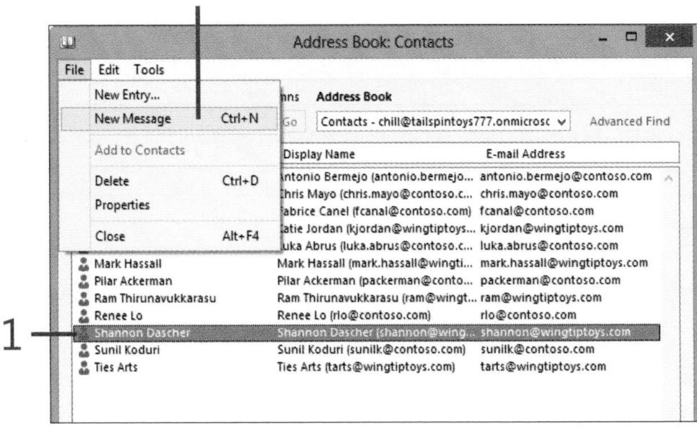

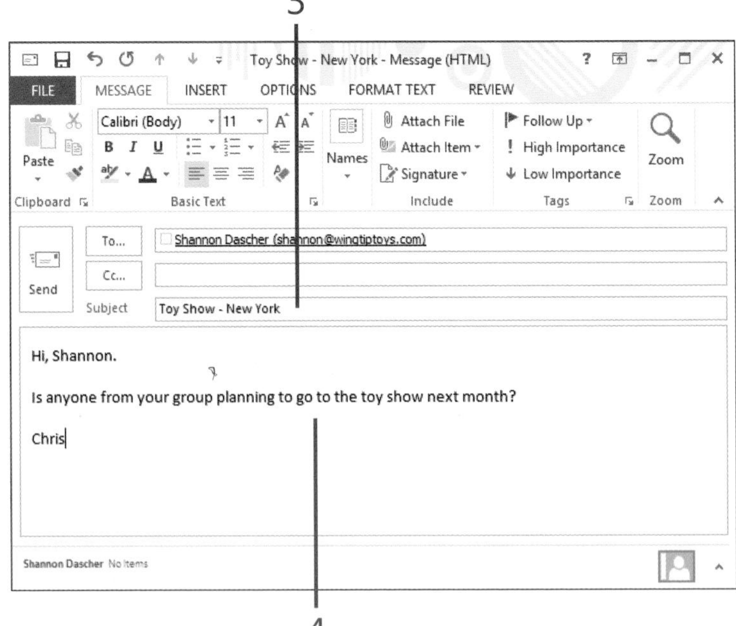

TIP When you finish with the Address Book, close it by choosing Close from the File menu.

TIP If your installation of Outlook is not set up for other address books, such as an Exchange Server Global Address List, the only address book that you can select from the drop-down list is the Outlook Contacts folder, which appears as "Contacts" under your email account. Note that the Outlook Address Book collects together all address books, but is not an address book itself in the sense that it stores addresses. Instead, it shows addresses from multiple address books.

Working with contact groups

A contact group is a group of contacts that are related in some way. For example, you could create a contact group that includes contacts working on the same project. Then, when you need to send messages to the entire project team, simply select the contact group for that project; Outlook 2013 sends the message to all the contacts in the group. Contact groups are stored in the Contacts folder (People Hub) by default. Contact groups are also referred to as distribution lists.

Create a contact group

1 On the Home tab, in the new group, click the New Items button.

2 Click More Items and then, on the submenu that appears, click Contact Group.

3 Click in the Name field and type a name for the new contact group.

4 On the ribbon, click Add Members and then, in the drop-down list that appears, choose From Address Book to open the Select Members dialog box.

(continued on next page)

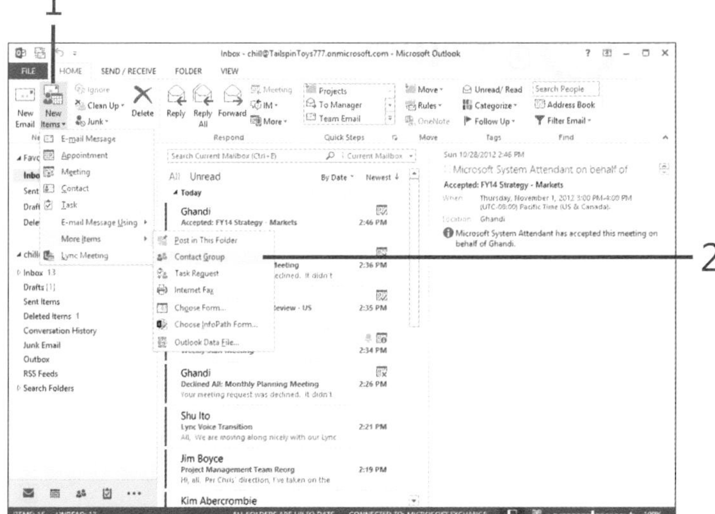

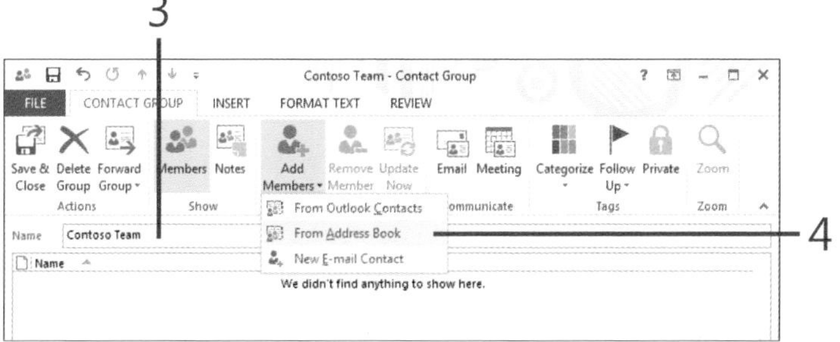

TIP You can share a contact group with other users. To do so, open a new message and click Attach Item, and choose Outlook Item from the Include group on the Message tab of the ribbon. In the Look In list, select the folder, such as Contacts, that includes your distribution list. In the Items list, select the distribution list you want to send. Click OK to attach the list to your new message.

Create a contact group *(continued)*

5 From the Address Book drop-down list, select the address book that contains the names you want to add to the distribution list.

6 Choose one or more names from the list that appears in the Name field.

7 Click Members to copy the name to the address list text box.

8 Click OK when your list is complete.

9 On the ribbon, click Save & Close.

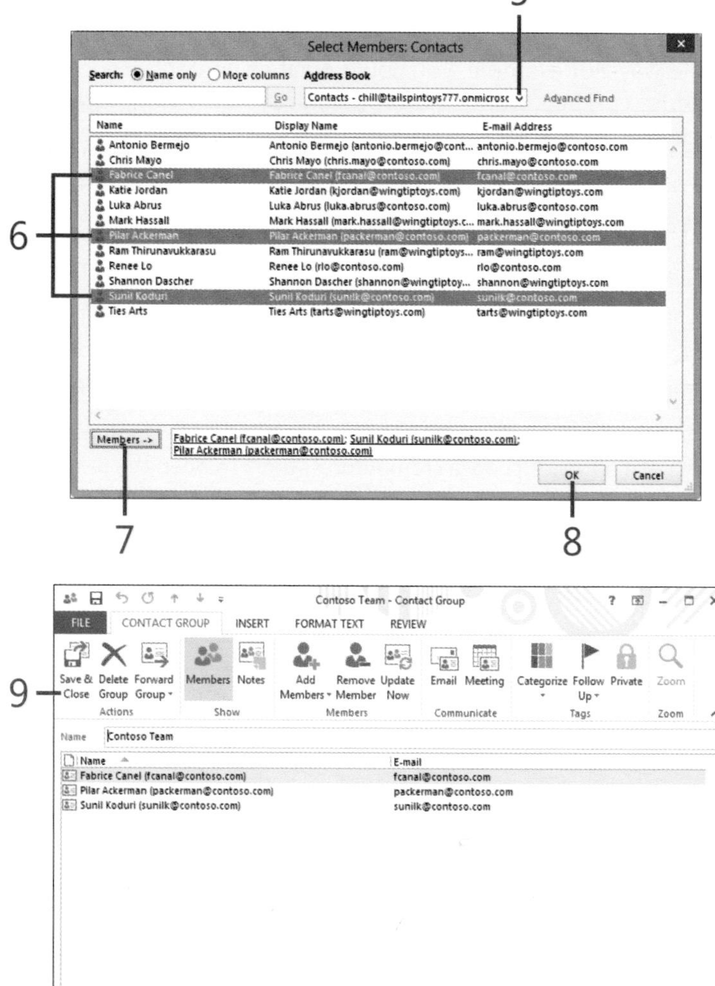

> **TIP** You can add existing contacts to a contact group, and you can also add other addresses for recipients who are not among your existing contacts.

Use a contact group

1 On the Home tab, in the New group, click New Email to start a new email message.

2 Click To.

3 From the Name list, click the contact group that you want to use to address your email message.

4 Click To.

5 Click OK.

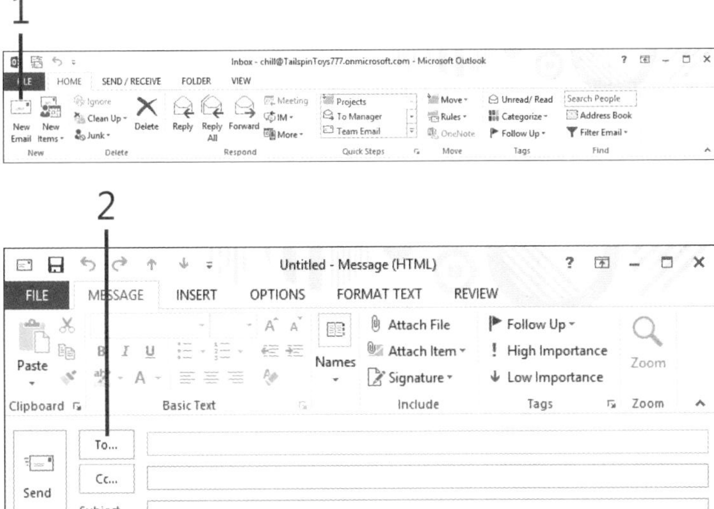

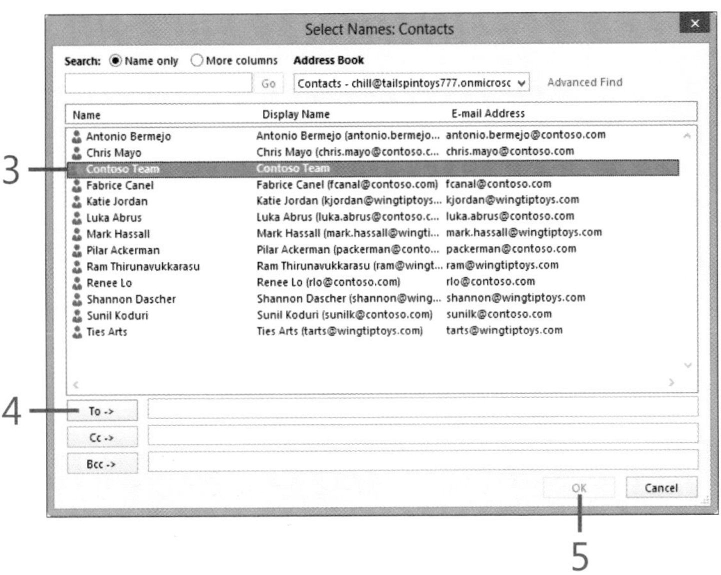

> **CAUTION** When you use a contact group, everyone on the list receives the same message. If you want to send a message to only a select few on the list, such as a confidential message that only specific recipients should read, create a new contact group for these recipients or select the recipients individually in the Select Names dialog box.

Changing message text

After you create a message in Outlook 2013 and before you send it, you should proofread it for errors or omissions. If you discover a typographical or other error, you can edit it in the same way you would a word-processing document. You can use familiar commands like Copy and Paste or operations like dragging to edit your text.

Edit your message

1 Create a new mail message with recipients, a subject, and message text.

2 To change the recipient, click To.

3 In the Select Names dialog box, click a name in the Name list and click To, which adds it to the Message Recipients list.

(continued on next page)

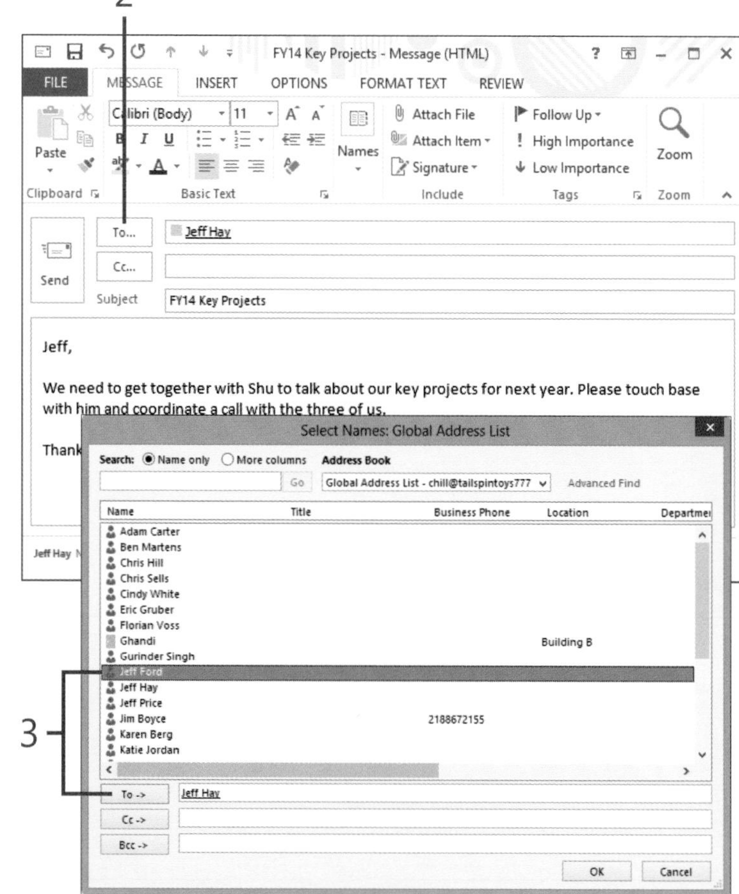

> **SEE ALSO** If you need to modify a contact's information, such as the email address or name, you can do so in the Contacts folder. See "Use the contact form" on page 98.

Edit your message *(continued)*

4 Click a name in the To list and press Delete or Backspace to remove that person from the list.

5 Continue adding or deleting recipients until your recipient list includes all those to whom you want to send the message.

6 Click OK.

7 Click in the Subject line where you want to change text.

8 Click in the message body area where you want to change text.

9 Add or delete text as needed.

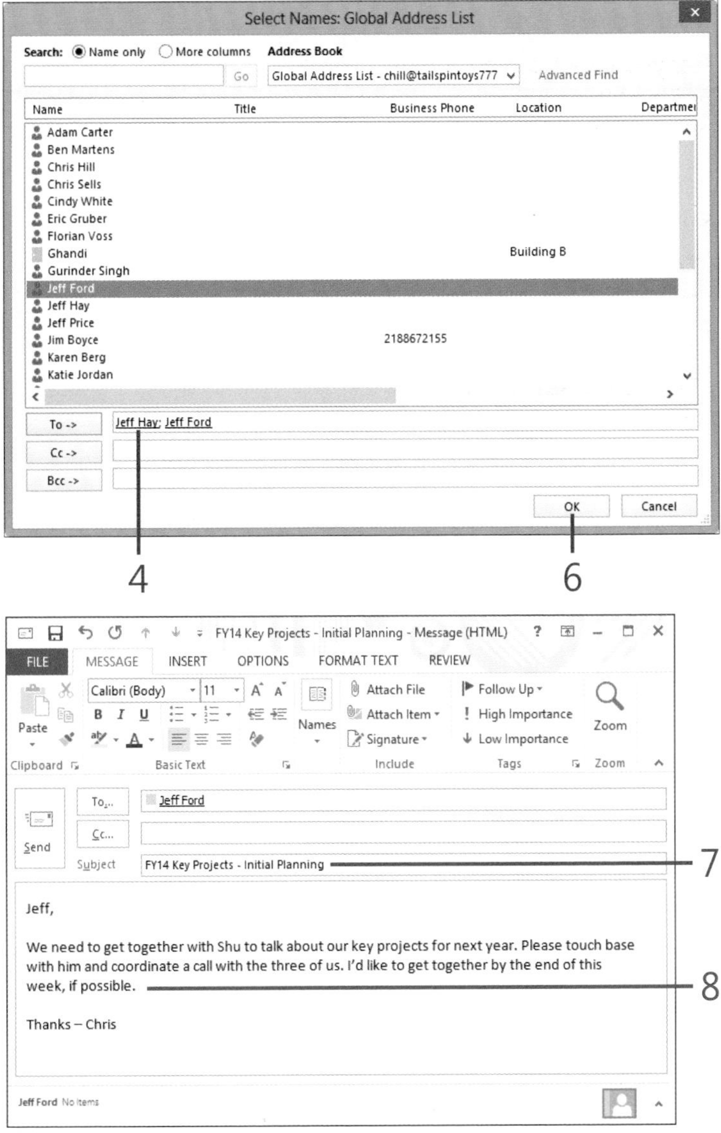

Move and copy message text

1. Display the message containing the text that you want to move or copy.
2. Select the text that you want to move or copy.
3. Drag the text to a new location. Or, to copy the text, hold down the Ctrl key as you drag.
4. At the new location, release the mouse button.

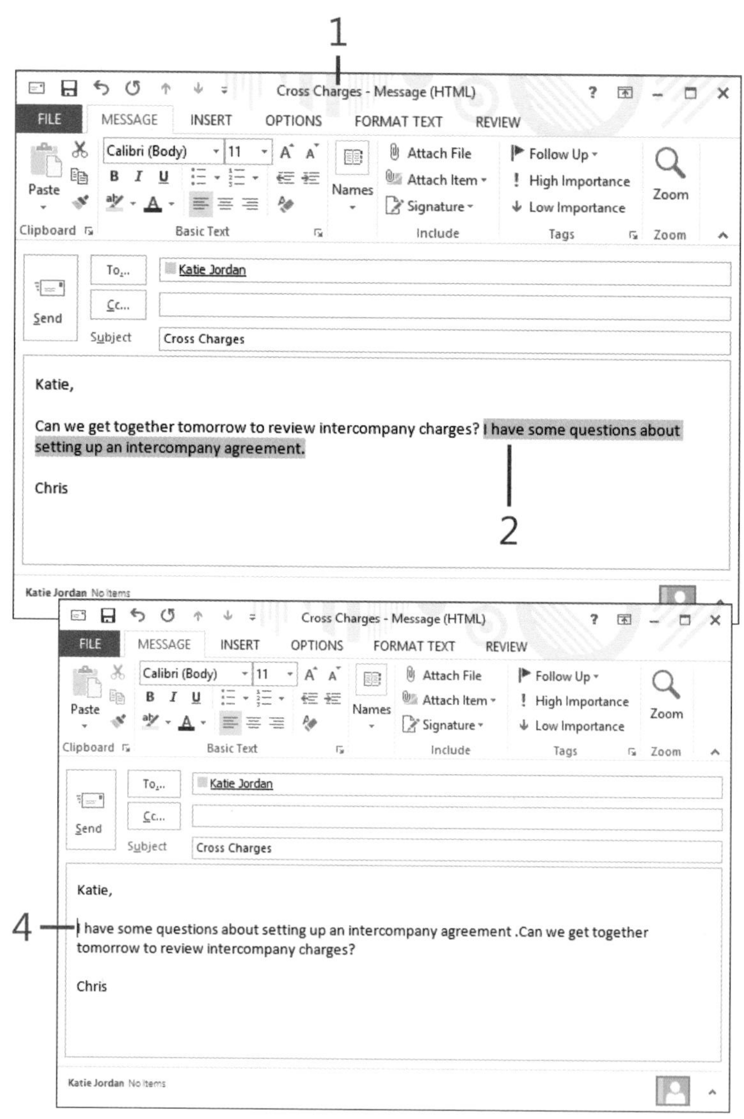

TIP Message text can be moved or copied within a message, from one message to another, and between Outlook and other applications. For example, if you have a selection of text that you want to use in several messages, you can select the text and press Ctrl+C to copy the text to the Clipboard. Then, click in the body of each new message and press Ctrl+V to paste the text into each message. You can also use the Copy and Paste buttons on the Message tab on the ribbon to copy and paste text.

TRY THIS! You can drag text from one message to another. Open both messages, and position them so that you can see both windows. Select the text you want to move, and drag it to the desired location in the other message window. Release the mouse button.

Formatting message text

In Outlook 2013, you can format text so that it looks more attractive to you and your recipients. For example, you can apply bold, italic, underline, colors, and other rich formatting to your messages. You also can add HTML formatting to your messages, including tables, hyperlinks, heading levels, and more.

Use a rich text or HTML message format

1 Create a new message, and add some text.

2 On the ribbon, click the Format Text tab.

3 In the Format group, Choose HTML or Rich Text.

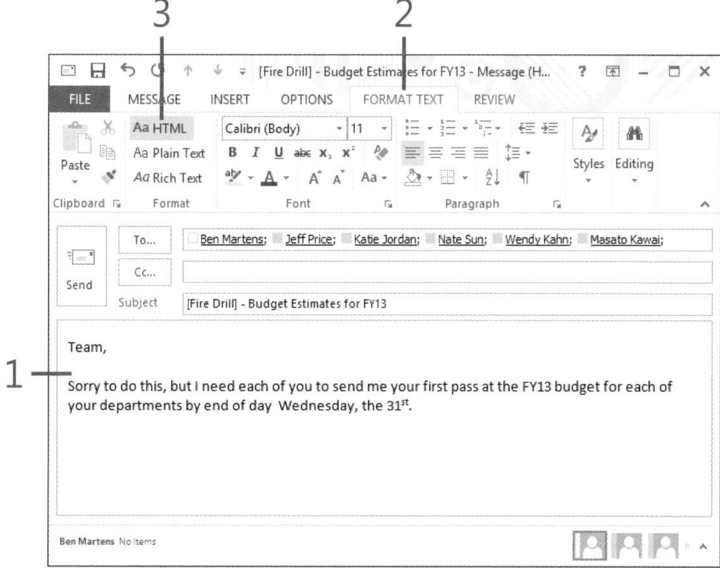

TIP You can see the presence status (online, offline, away, and so on) in the People pane at the bottom of the new message window.

CAUTION If you add a hyperlink to a message, your recipient needs access to that site or document. For example, if the document you specify in the hyperlink is on the Internet, your recipient must have Internet access. Likewise, if your link is to a document that you have stored locally on your hard drive, your recipient must have share privileges to that document.

Add formatting to a message

1 Select the text that you want to format.

2 On the ribbon, click the Format Text tab.

3 In the Font group, click Bold to apply a bold character style to the text.

4 Click Italic to italicize the text.

5 Click Underline to underline the text.

6 Click the Font drop-down arrow and then, in the list that appears, select a font name to change the text font.

(continued on next page)

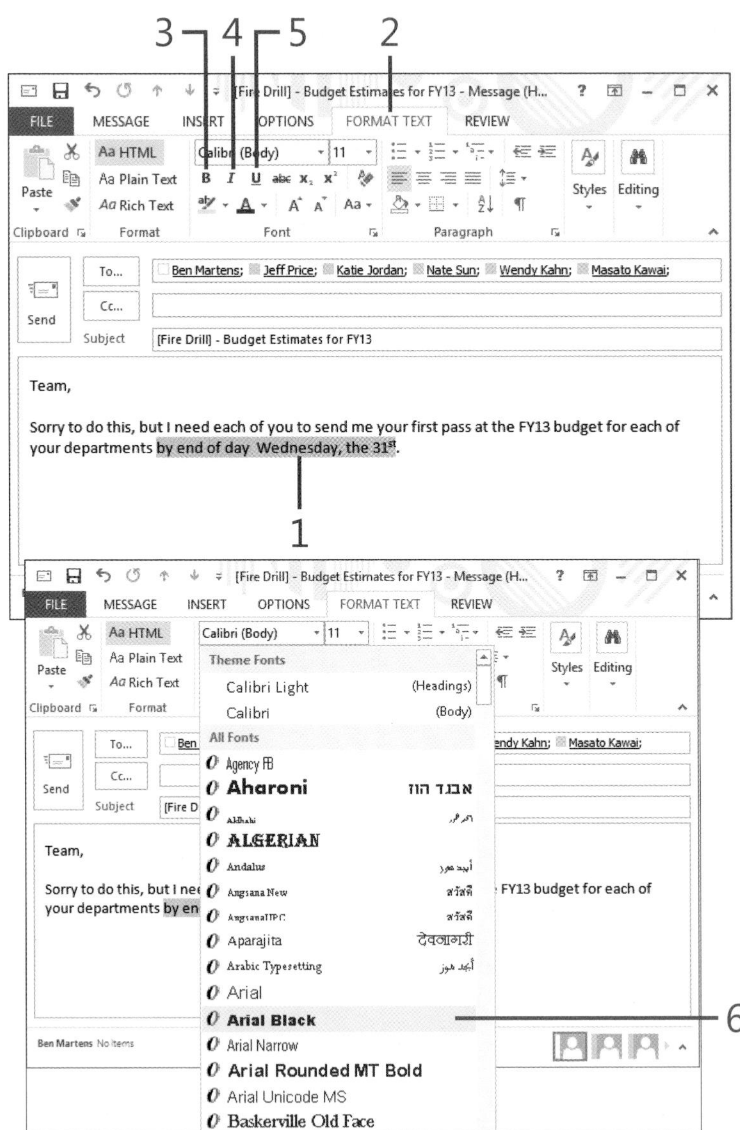

> **TIP** Some recipients might not be able to handle rich-formatted text. In these cases, the formatted text you see in your message window appears to your recipients as plain text or is converted to unrecognizable characters.

> **TIP** To add a hyperlink to an email message, type the hyperlink in your message; and Outlook converts it to a live link that your recipient can click. For example, you can add a hyperlink to the Microsoft website by typing *www.microsoft.com* in your message.

Add formatting to a message *(continued)*

7 Select a color from the Font Color drop-down list to change the text font color.

8 Select a value from the Font Size drop-down list to change the text font size.

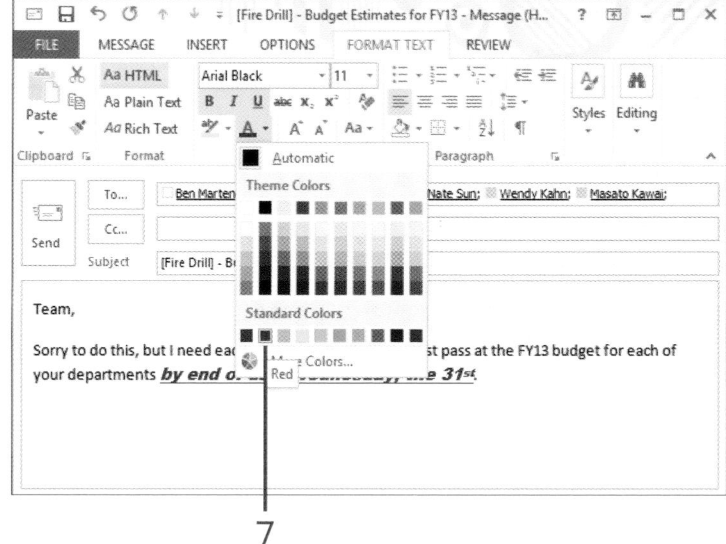

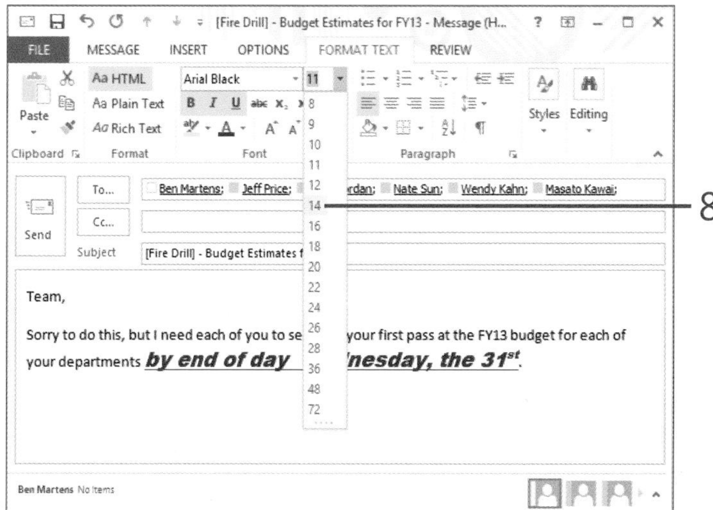

Using signatures

A signature is boilerplate text or an image that appears to any new messages you compose. The signature is positioned at the bottom of your messages. Many people include phone numbers and other information in their signatures.

Create a signature

1. On the ribbon, click the File tab to display the Backstage view and then click the Options tab.
2. In the Outlook Options dialog box, click Mail.
3. Click Signatures to open the Signatures And Stationery dialog box.

(continued on next page)

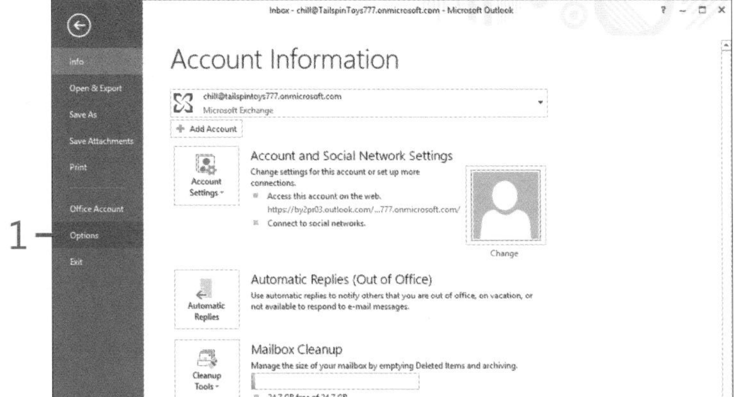

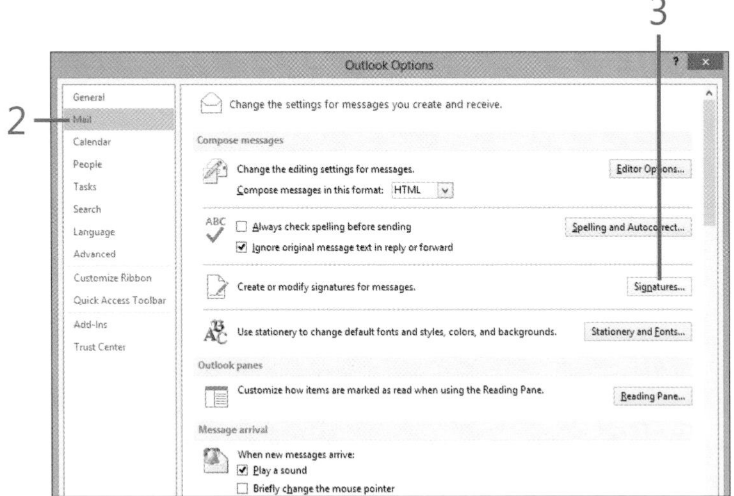

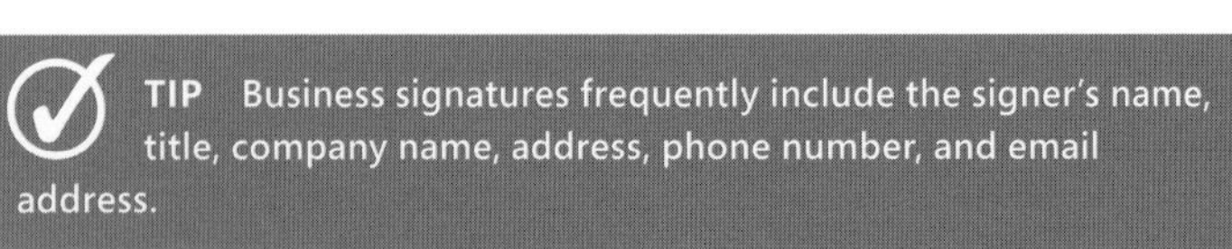

TIP Business signatures frequently include the signer's name, title, company name, address, phone number, and email address.

TIP You can create custom signatures for the type of email message you create. For example, you can create a friendly signature for messages intended for family or friends, and a more formal one for business recipients.

Create a signature *(continued)*

4 Click New to open the New Signature dialog box.

5 Type a name for the signature and click OK.

6 Choose a font and font size.

7 Select font format options.

8 In the Edit Signature field, type the text that you want to appear in your signature.

9 Optionally, add pictures or links to the signature.

10 Click OK to save your signature and close the Signatures And Stationery dialog box. Click OK again to close the Outlook Options dialog box.

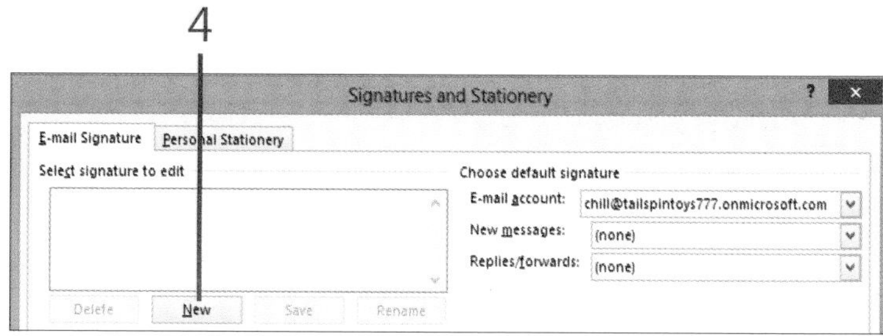

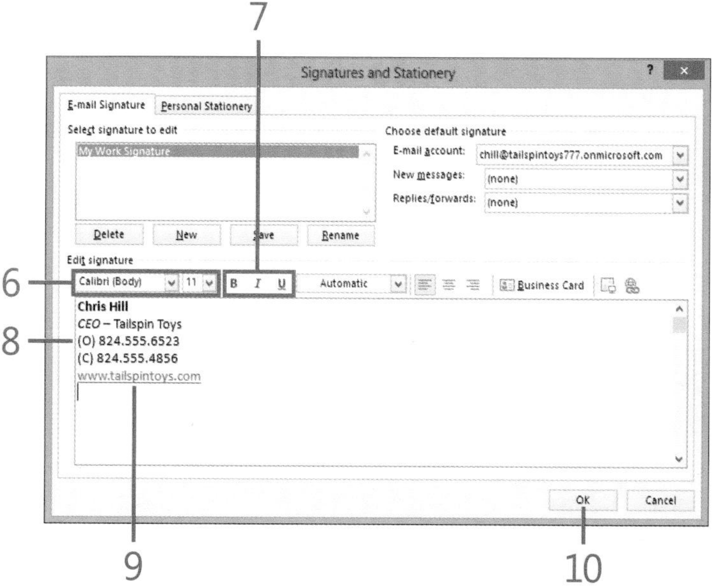

Associate a signature with an email account

1. On the ribbon, click the File tab to display the Backstage view, click the Options tab to open the Outlook Options dialog box, and then click Mail.
2. Click Signatures to open the Signatures And Stationery dialog box.
3. From the Email Account drop-down list, select the account to which you want to assign the signature.
4. In the New Messages drop-down list, select a signature.
5. Click OK to close the Signatures And Stationery dialog box. Click OK again to close the Outlook Options dialog box.

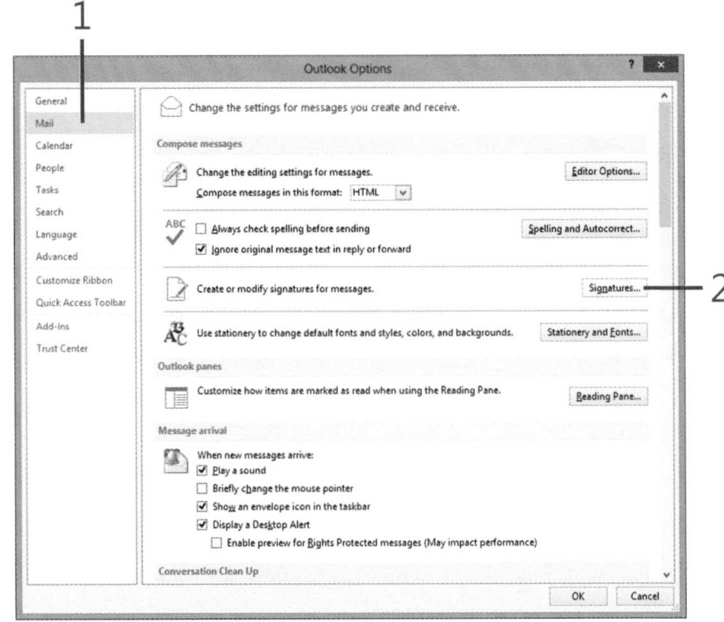

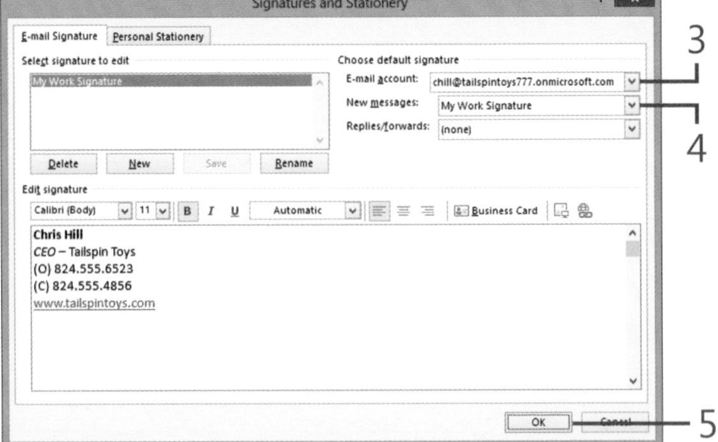

TIP If you want your signature to appear in messages you reply to or forward, select the appropriate signature from the Replies/Forwards drop-down list.

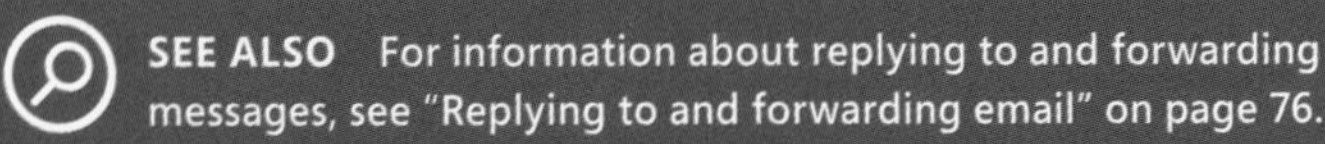
SEE ALSO For information about replying to and forwarding messages, see "Replying to and forwarding email" on page 76.

Choosing a signature for a message

1. Start a new email message.
2. If a signature is already included, select and delete it.
3. On the Message tab, in the Include group, click Signature.
4. In the drop-down list that appears, choose the signature that you want to use for the current message.
5. Add a recipient.
6. Type your message.
7. Click Send.

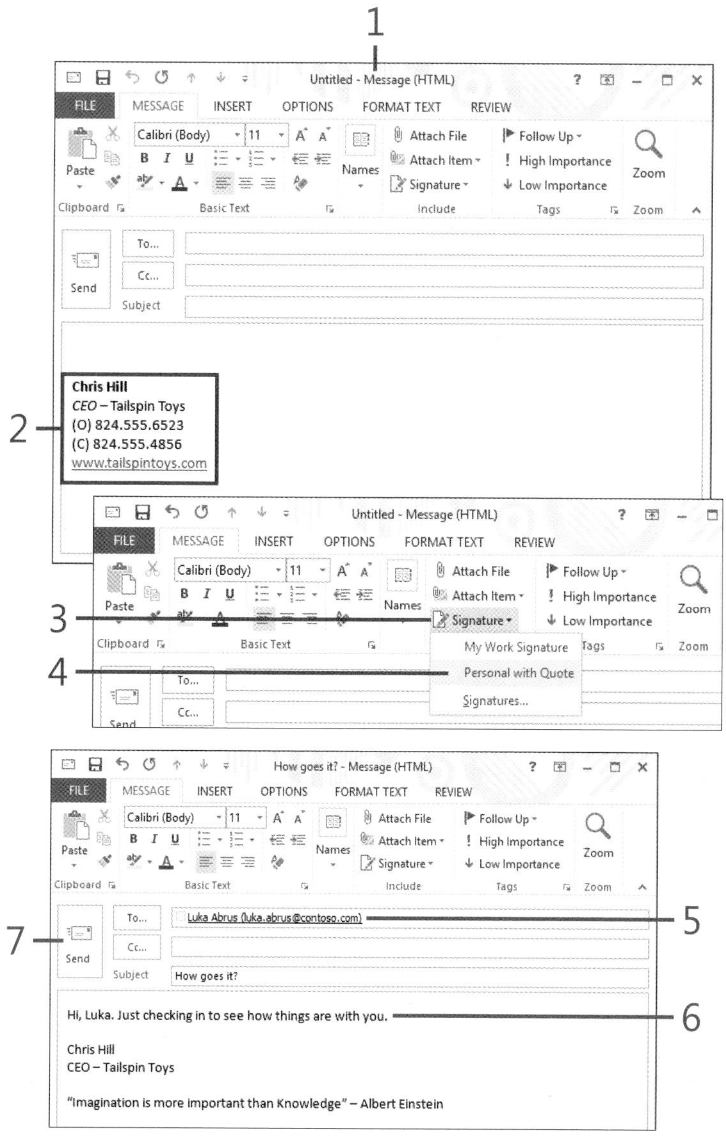

Working with HTML stationery

Outlook includes a set of predefined designs and color schemes that you can add to your rich text–formatted messages. These are known as HTML stationery. You can use or modify the stationery Outlook provides. When you create a message, you can specify which stationery you want to use, or you can set Outlook to use a default stationery pattern each time you create a new message. You can also specify the background image or color for an individual message.

Select stationery

1 On the Home tab, in the New group, click New Items and then, in the drop-down list that appears, point to E-mail Message Using.
2 On the submenu that appears, click More Stationery.
3 In the Theme Or Stationery dialog box, choose the stationery that you want for your new message.
4 Click OK.

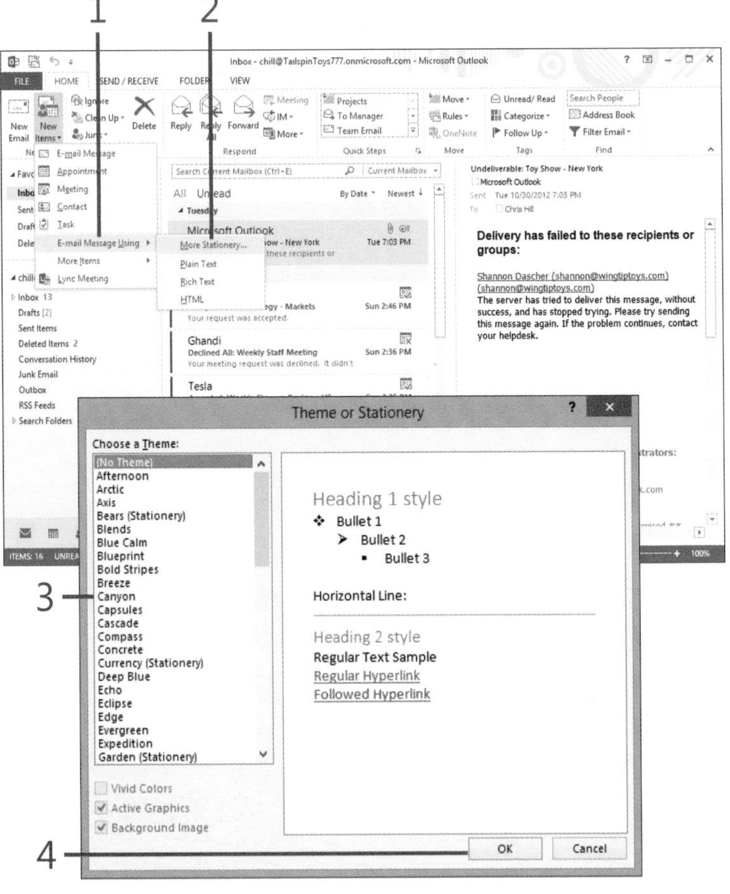

TIP You can also use Office themes for messages. To do so, on the ribbon, on the Options tab, click the Themes button. In the gallery that opens, you can select an existing theme, browse for themes, save the current them, or search the Microsoft Office Online website for more themes.

CAUTION To use HTML stationery, your message must be in HTML format. Your recipients' email programs must be able to read this type of formatting; otherwise, they won't be able to see the stationery or any other formatting on your page.

Edit stationery

1. On the ribbon, click the File tab to display the Backstage view, click the Options tab to open the Outlook Options dialog box, and then click Mail.
2. Click Stationery And Fonts to open the Signatures And Stationery dialog box.
3. Click Theme, choose the stationery you want to edit, and then click OK.
4. From the Font drop-down list, choose Always Use My Fonts.
5. Choose the font options that you want to modify.
6. Click OK to close the Signatures And Stationery dialog box. Click OK again to close the Outlook Options dialog box.

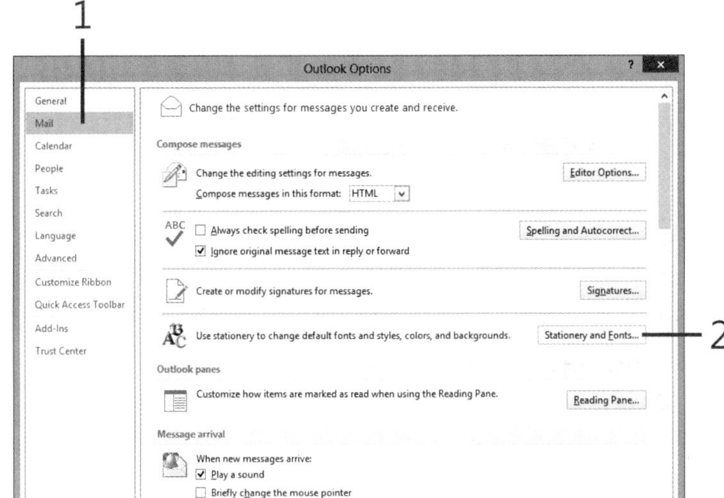

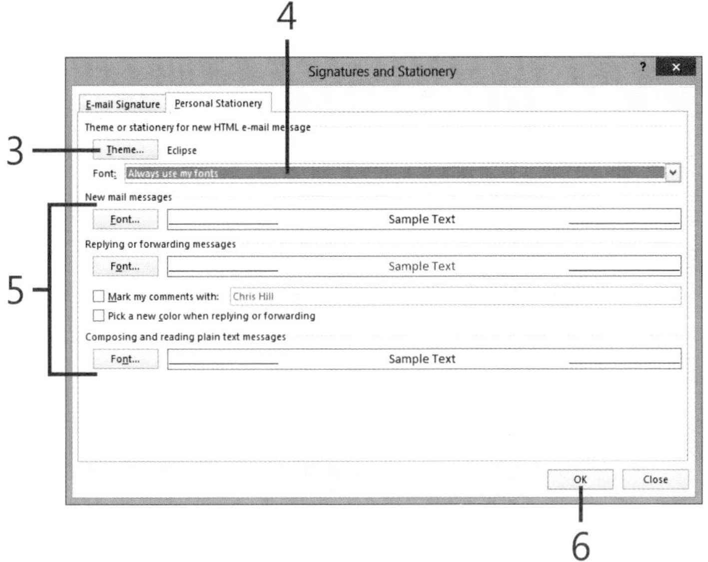

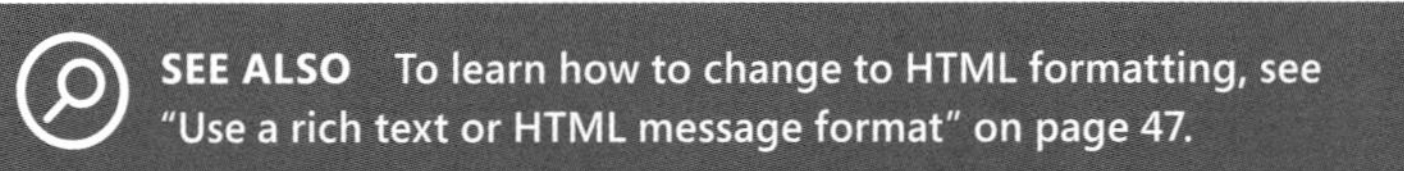

SEE ALSO To learn how to change to HTML formatting, see "Use a rich text or HTML message format" on page 47.

Sending a file by email

Sometimes, when you create an email message in Outlook 2013, you want to send along a file as well. Files sent with email are called message attachments. When you send the message, the file goes along with the message; the recipient can open it on his or her computer. You can also insert pictures into your email messages.

Insert a picture

1. To insert a picture in a message, you must choose either HTML or Rich Text format for the message. Open the message into which you want to insert a picture and then, on the Format Text tab, the Format group, choose HTML or Rich Text.
2. Click in the body of the message.
3. On the ribbon, click the Insert tab.
4. Click Picture to open the Insert Picture dialog box.

(continued on next page)

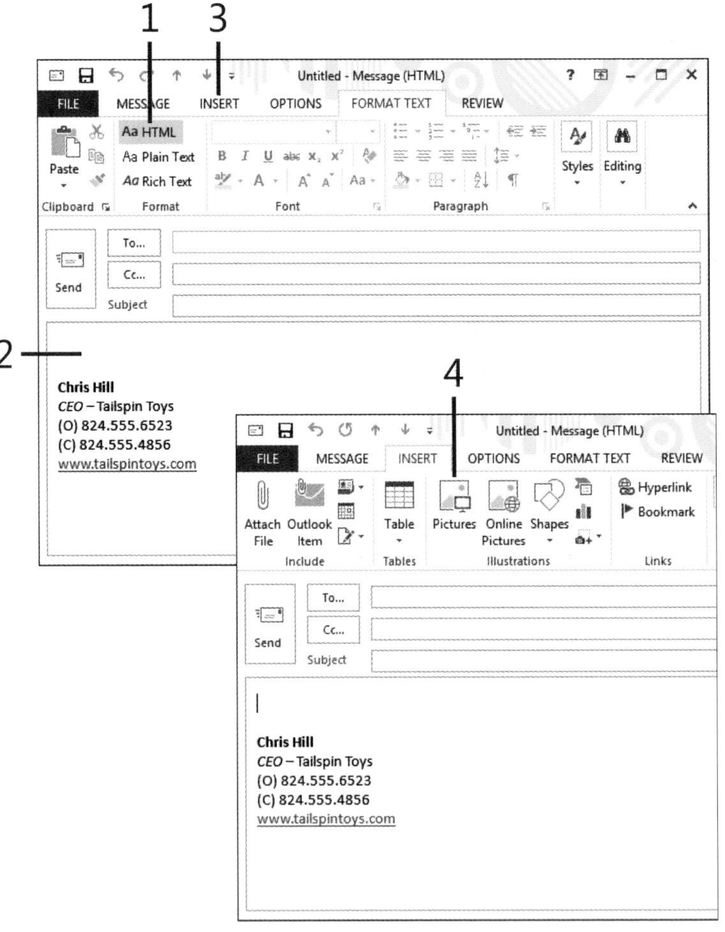

Insert a picture *(continued)*

5 Choose the picture that you want to insert.

6 Click Insert.

7 The picture is now part of the message.

(continued on next page)

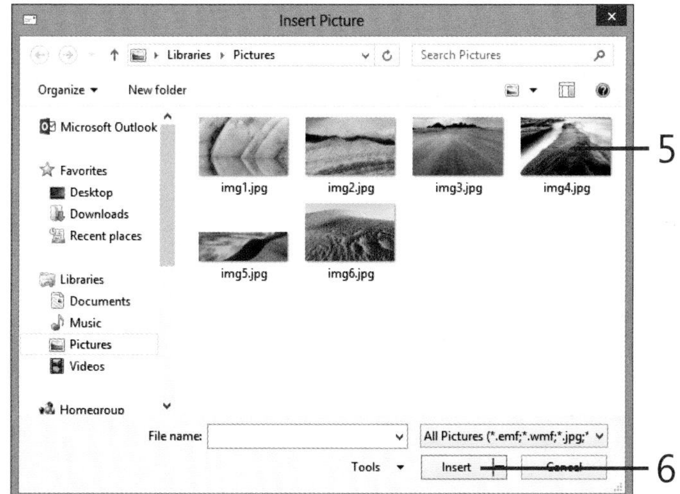

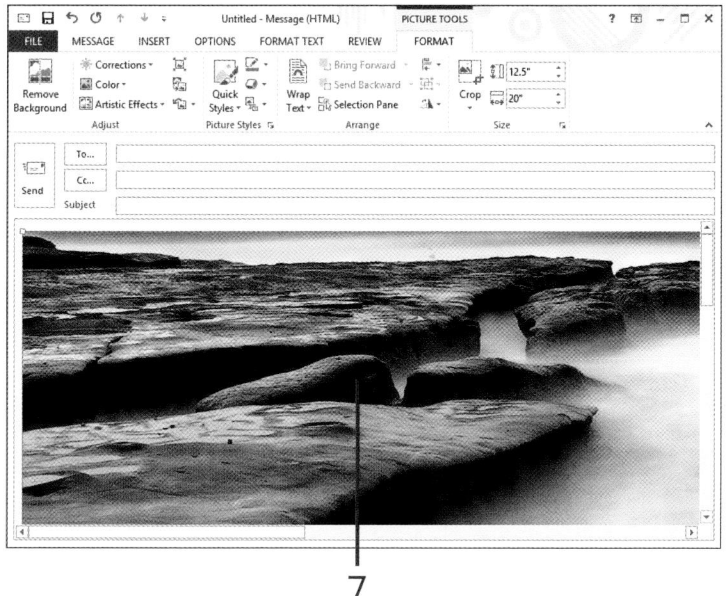

Insert a picture *(continued)*

8 Click the picture to select it.

9 On the ribbon, Click the Picture Tools|Format contextual tab.

10 Resize the picture as needed.

Attach a file

1 Open a new message. On the ribbon, click the Insert tab.

2 In the Include group, click Attach File.

(continued on next page)

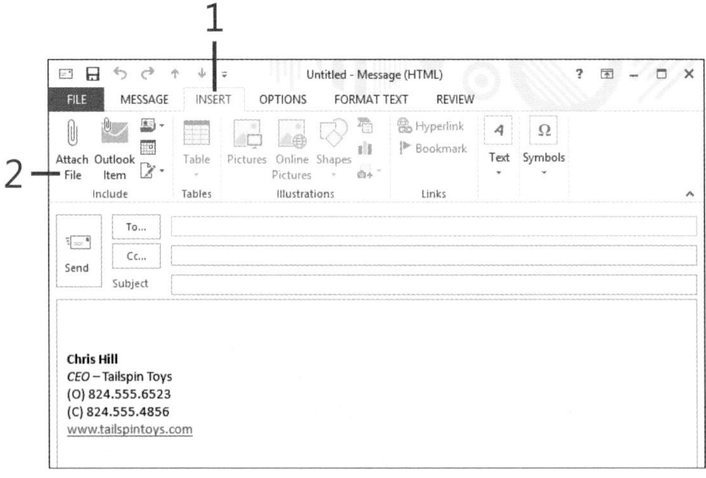

> **CAUTION** The recipient of an attached file must have an application on his or her computer that can open the attached file. If not, you might need to save the file in a format that your recipient is able to use, before sending the file.

Attach a file *(continued)*

3 In the Insert File dialog box, click the file that you want to attach.

4 Click Insert.

5 The file is inserted into the message.

6 Add a recipient.

7 Add a subject.

8 Add message text.

9 Click Send.

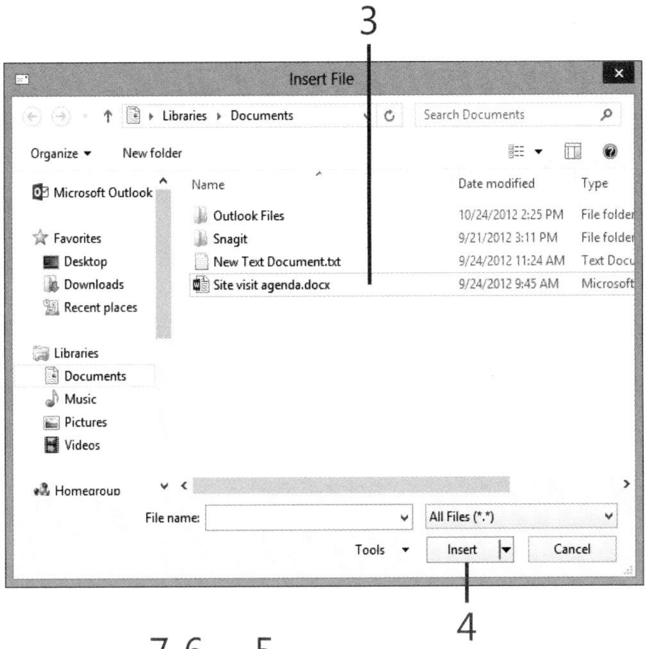

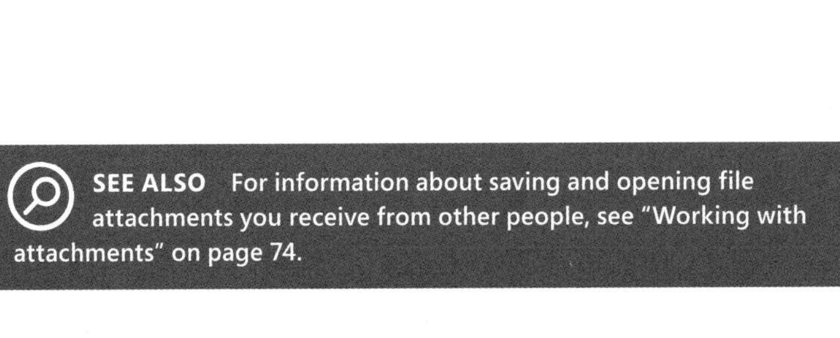

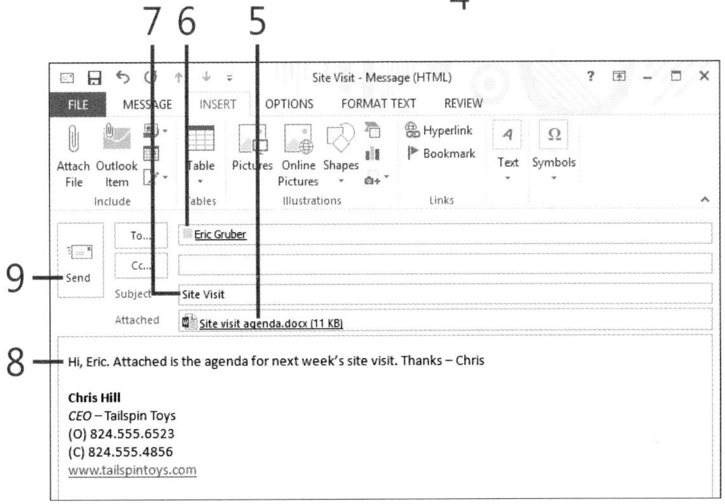

SEE ALSO For information about saving and opening file attachments you receive from other people, see "Working with attachments" on page 74.

Sending messages manually

When you send a message, it travels across the local area network or the Internet to the mailbox of the person you specify as the recipient. If you specify more than one recipient, Outlook 2013 sends a copy of the message to everyone you specify. By default, Outlook sends messages automatically as soon as they are placed in the Outbox. You also can configure Outlook to hold your messages in the Outbox until you're ready to send them. (Clicking Send places the message in the Outbox.)

Configure Outlook to not send messages automatically

1. On the ribbon, click the File tab to display the Backstage view, click the Options tab to open the Outlook Options dialog box, and then click Advanced.
2. Clear the Send Immediately When Connected check box.
3. Click OK to close the Options dialog box.

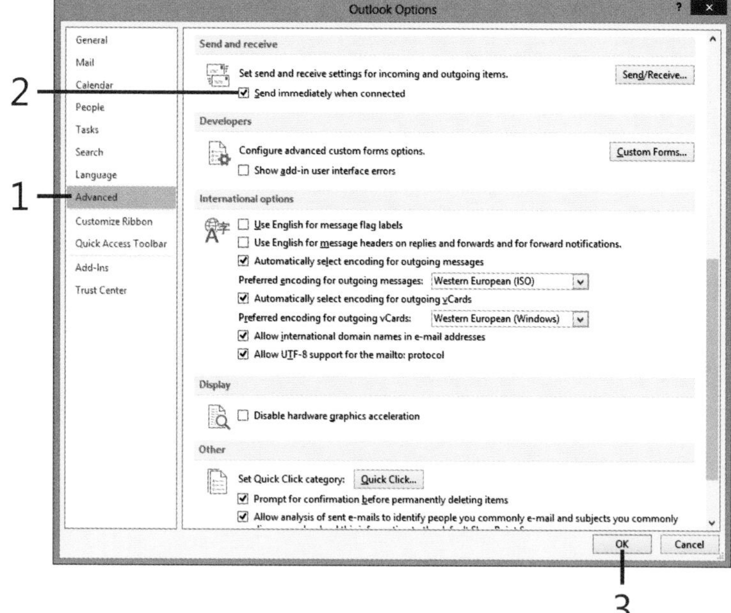

> **CAUTION** If Outlook is set up to send your messages as soon as you click the Send button, you can't change anything in your message before it's routed to your recipients. Even if your message is incomplete or contains confidential information, you can't recall the message (unless you're using Exchange Server).

Send and receive messages manually

1. Create a new message.
2. Click Send to send the message to the Outbox folder.
3. In the Folder pane, click Outbox.
4. Confirm that a message is waiting in the Outbox folder.
5. On the ribbon, click the Send/Receive tab.
6. Click the Send/Receive All Folders button.

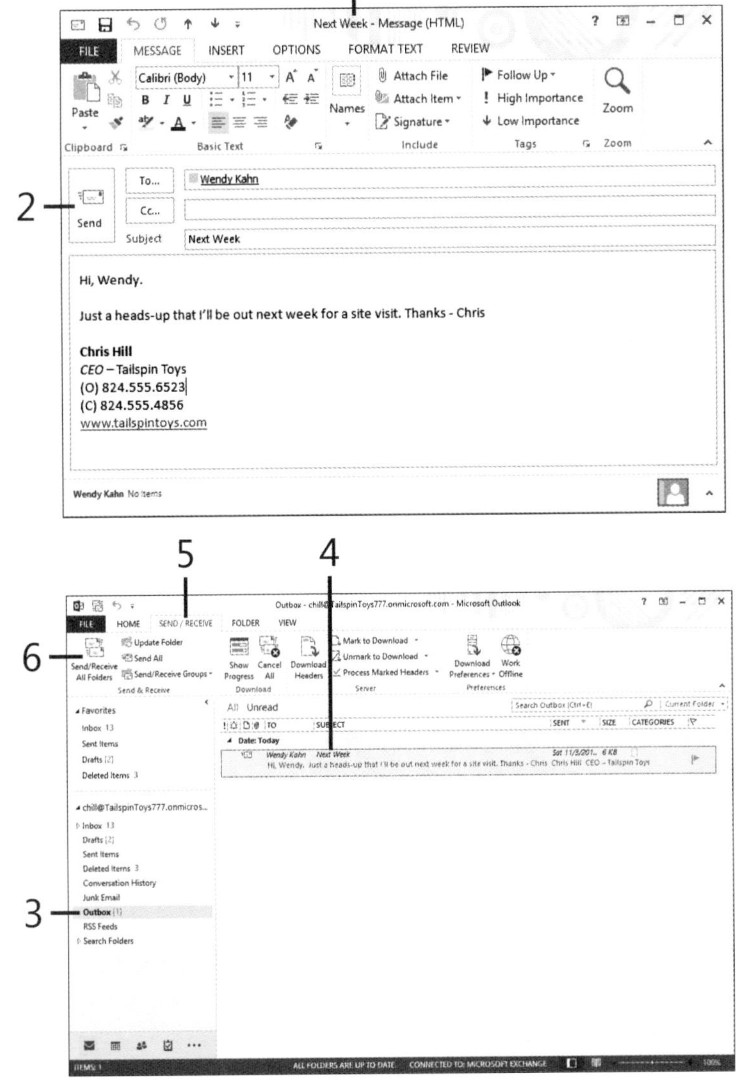

SEE ALSO For information about receiving email messages, see "Receiving and reading email" on pages 66 and 68.

Reviewing sent messages and drafts

When you send a message, Outlook 2013 stores a copy of it in the Sent Items folder. You can use this folder to keep track of all the messages you've sent to recipients. You can open this folder and review messages you've sent to other users. Outlook also includes a Drafts folder that stores new messages you're working on but are not ready to send.

Open the Sent Items folder

1 At the bottom of the Folder pane, click the Mail button.

2 In the Folder pane, click the Sent Items folder.

3 Review the contents of the Sent Items folder.

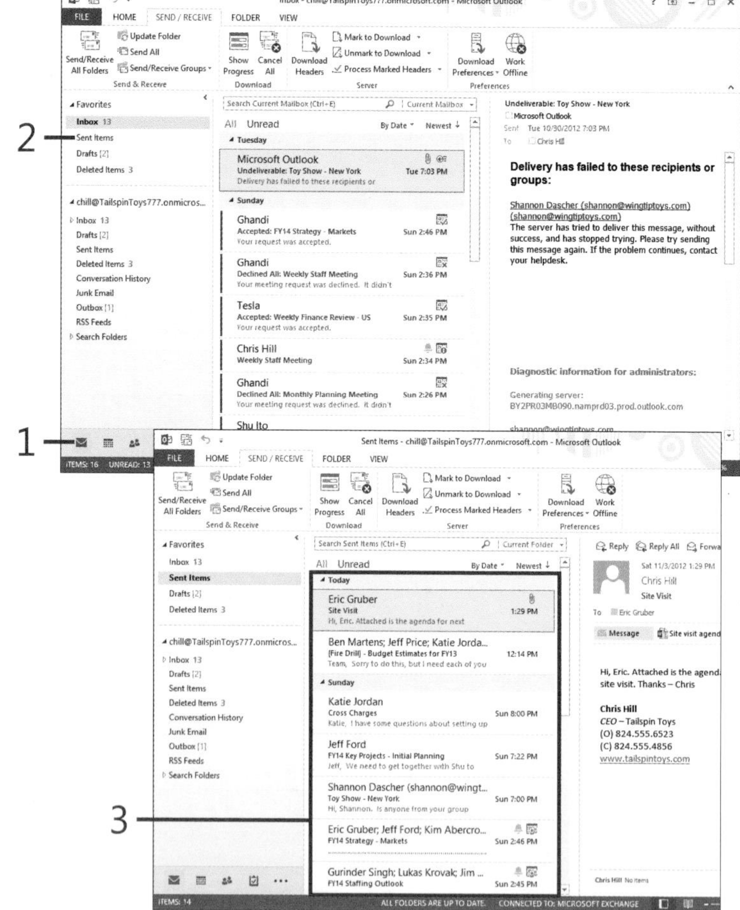

TRY THIS! Create and send a few messages to others. Then, open the Sent Items folder to see how the sent messages appear there.

Open a message from the Drafts folder

1. Create a new message with recipient, subject, and body text.
2. Click the File tab to display the Backstage view.
3. Choose the Save tab.
4. Click the Close tab.

(continued on next page)

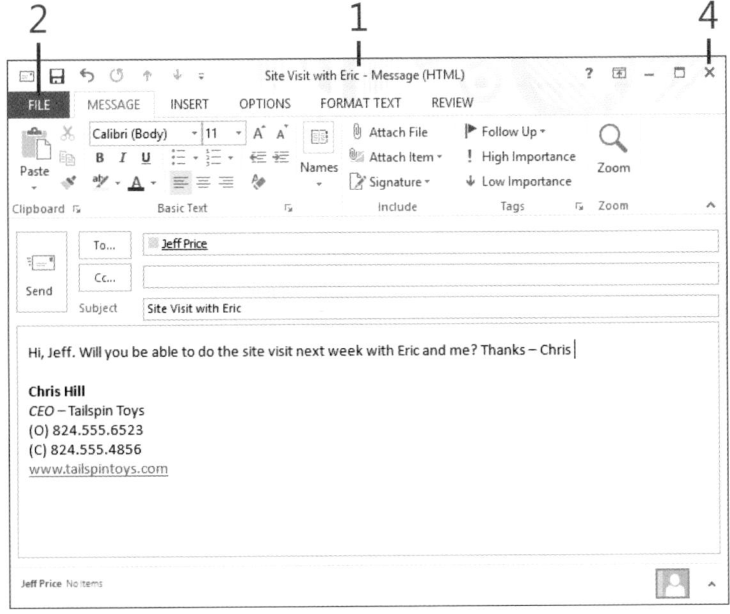

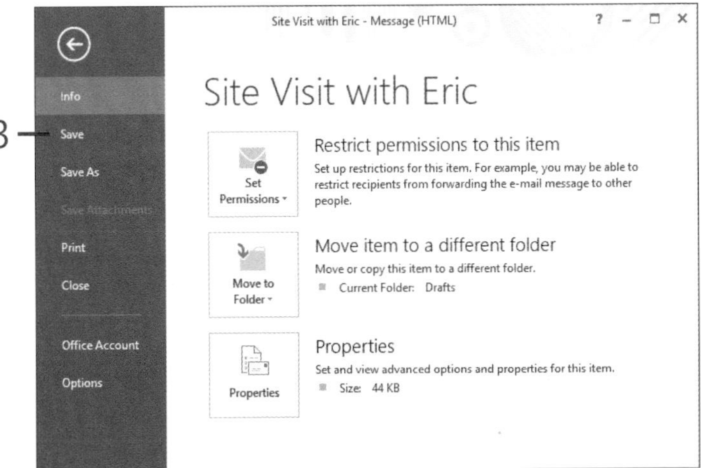

Open a message from the Drafts folder *(continued)*

5 In the Folder pane, click the Drafts folder.

6 Double-click the message that you want to open and then edit and send it.

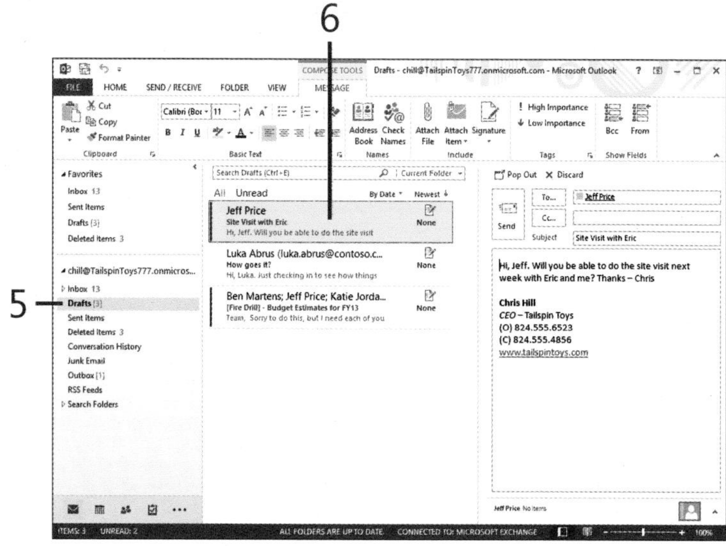

SEE ALSO You can move a message or group of messages from the Drafts folder to the Outbox folder without opening any first. To learn how to move items to different folders, see "Organizing with folders" on page 220.

Receiving and reading email

5

In this section:

- Receiving email
- Reading email
- Managing the Inbox folder
- Working with attachments
- Replying to and forwarding email
- Handling junk mail
- Working with the Rules Wizard
- Following up on a message

To receive email messages that have been sent to you, Microsoft Outlook 2013 connects to an email server on which messages are stored (such as servers located on a local area network or the Internet) and downloads the messages (or copies of them) to your Inbox folder. From there, you can read a message, reply, forward it to someone, flag it for later action, and open file attachments. In most cases, messages that you download are deleted from the server automatically after they're downloaded.

Outlook can also filter out junk email by placing in the Junk Email folder any mail that contains certain words or phrases or that arrives from certain addresses. You can adjust these filters to block mail from unwanted senders while still allowing through the mail that you want to read. You also can set up Outlook Rules, which help you to manage your messages by moving them to designated folders, flagging them, or otherwise processing messages in accordance with rules that you define.

This section shows you how to receive, read, reply to, follow up on, and forward messages in Outlook. You learn how to manage your Inbox by deleting, saving, and printing messages. Finally, you learn how to handle junk mail, set up rules that personalize your email experience, and work with email attachments.

Receiving email

Outlook 2013 makes it easy for you to receive your incoming messages. You can schedule Outlook to download your new messages, or you can manually download new messages when you want.

Configure Outlook to retrieve email automatically

1. On the Send/Receive tab, in the Send & Receive group, click Send/Receive Groups and then, in the drop-down list that appears, click Define Send/Receive Groups.
2. In the Send/Receive Groups dialog box, select the Schedule An Automatic Send/Receive Every *n* Minutes option.
3. Type the number of minutes between each download.
4. Click Close.

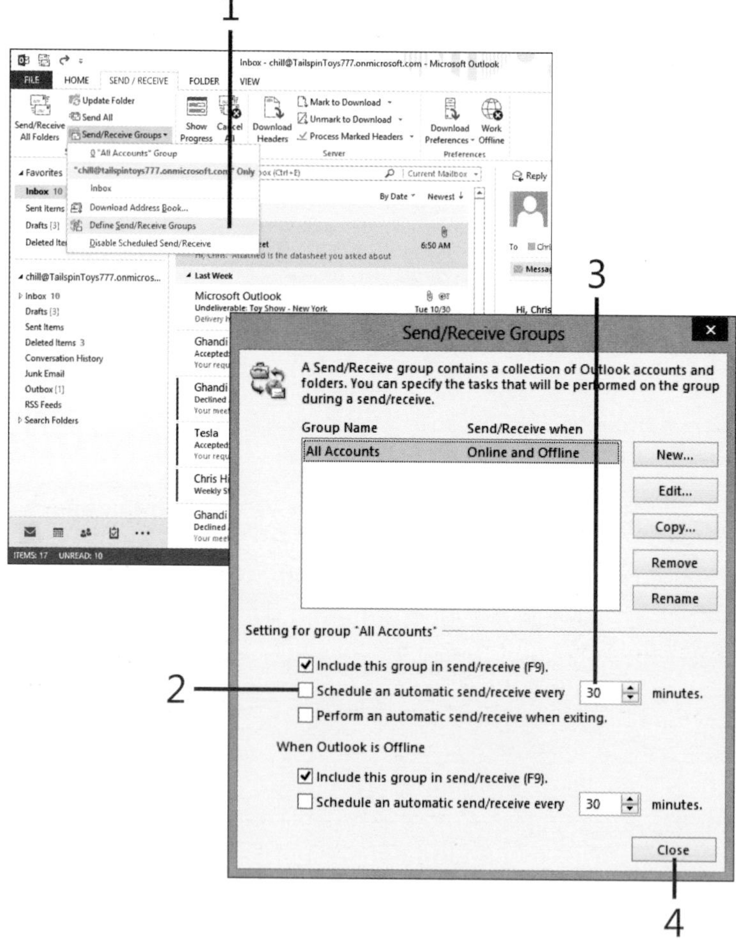

Retrieve email manually

1. On the Send/Receive tab, in the Send & Receive group, click Send/Receive All Folders.
2. At the bottom of the folder pane, click the Inbox icon to see your new messages.
3. Messages that have not yet been read are shown with a bold subject and a line to the left of the message header.

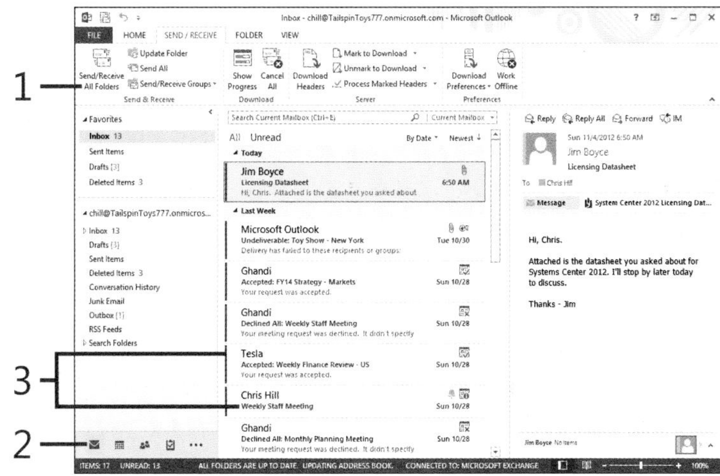

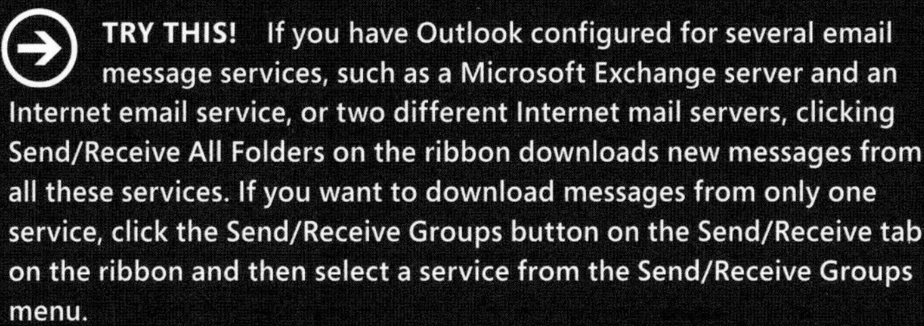

TRY THIS! If you have Outlook configured for several email message services, such as a Microsoft Exchange server and an Internet email service, or two different Internet mail servers, clicking Send/Receive All Folders on the ribbon downloads new messages from all these services. If you want to download messages from only one service, click the Send/Receive Groups button on the Send/Receive tab on the ribbon and then select a service from the Send/Receive Groups menu.

TIP The total number of email messages in your Inbox folder appears on the status bar along with the number of unread messages. The number of unread messages also appears next to the Inbox icon in the Folder pane.

Reading email

After you receive a message in your Inbox folder, you can preview it or read its contents. The Inbox folder displays the sender's name, the message subject, the date the message was received, the size of the message, and whether the message has an attachment.

Locate new messages

1 At the bottom of the folder pane, click the Mail button and open the Inbox.

2 On the ribbon, click the View tab. In the Layout group, click Reading Pane and then, on the drop-down menu that appears, choose Bottom.

3 Click the Received column to sort your new messages by the date you received them.

4 Messages you have not read appear in boldface.

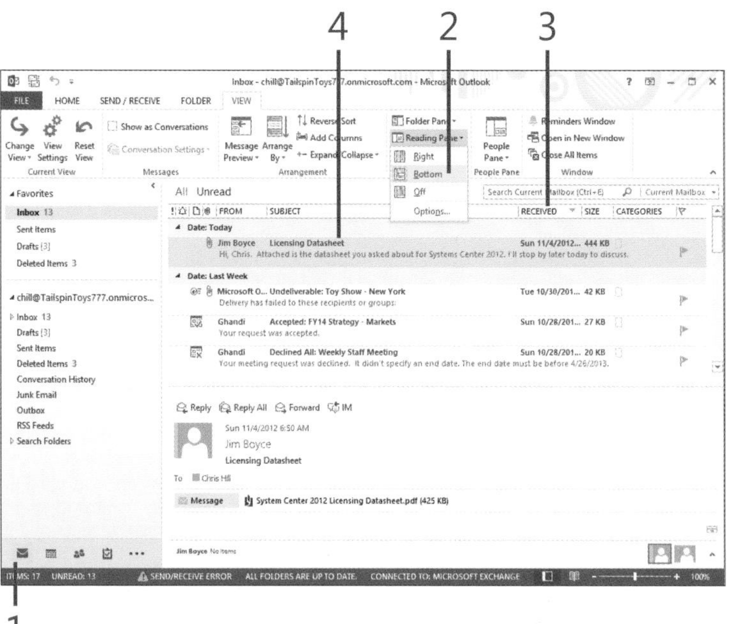

TRY THIS! Click the Received column once. If the most current date is at the top of the list, you're sorting from the most current date received to the earliest date received. Click the Received column again to reverse the order of sorting, from the earliest date to the most current.

TIP If the reading pane is displayed at the right, you can click Newest or Oldest to change the sort order for messages in the Inbox.

Open message items

1 In the Inbox, click the message that you want to read.

2 View its contents in the Reading pane.

3 Double-click the message to open it.

4 View the message in its own window.

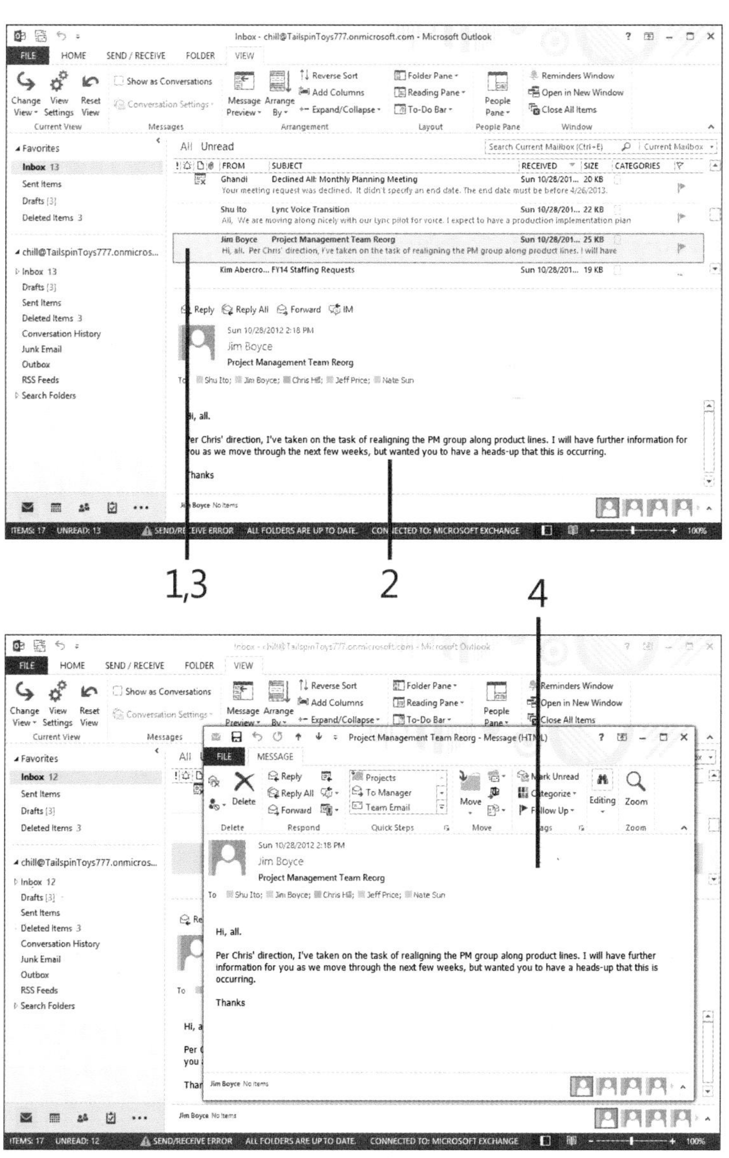

TIP To turn off the Reading pane, on the View tab, in the Layout group, click Reading Pane and then, on the drop-down menu that appears, click Off. To turn it back on, choose Right or Bottom from the Reading Pane menu.

TRY THIS! You can have Outlook display a few lines of each message by choosing Preview from the Change View button on the View tab on the ribbon. This shows the first few lines of the messages in the Inbox folder.

Managing the Inbox folder

Over time, your Inbox folder can quickly fill with hundreds of messages. This makes finding messages more difficult and takes up storage space on your device. You can reduce these problems by managing your Inbox folder. Some of the administrative tasks you can perform include deleting unneeded messages, saving important messages, and printing a copy of a message to read or store in hardcopy format.

Delete unneeded messages

1 Select the message(s) that you you want to delete.

2 On the ribbon, click the Home tab and then, in the Respond group, click the Delete button.

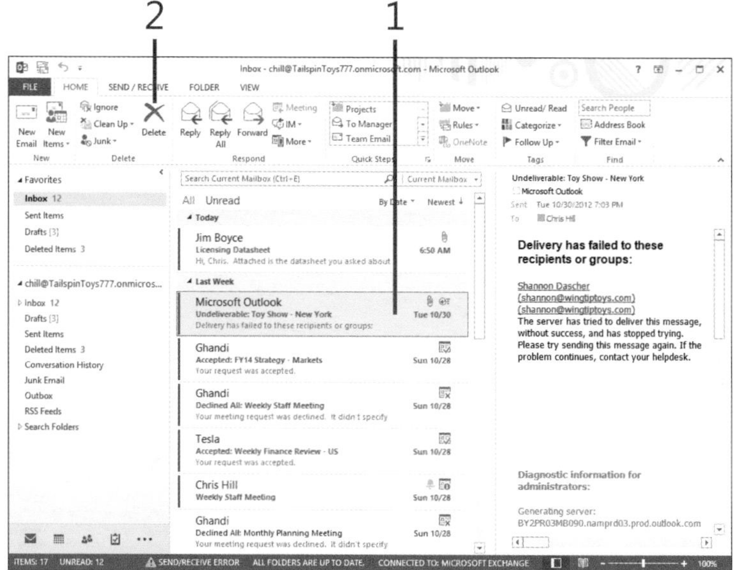

CAUTION Outlook does not ask whether you're sure you want to delete a message. Make sure that you want to delete the message before you press Delete or choose the Delete command. You can press Ctrl+Z to undo a deletion.

TIP Deleted messages are moved to the Deleted Items folder and can be moved back to your Inbox folder if necessary. If you delete messages from the Deleted Items folder, those items are generally gone for good (unless you had copied them to another folder). However, if you're using Exchange Server, you can recover deleted items up to a period of time set by the mail administrator.

Save important messages

1 Select the message(s) that you want to save.

2 On the ribbon, click the File tab to display the Backstage view and then click the Save As tab.

(continued on next page)

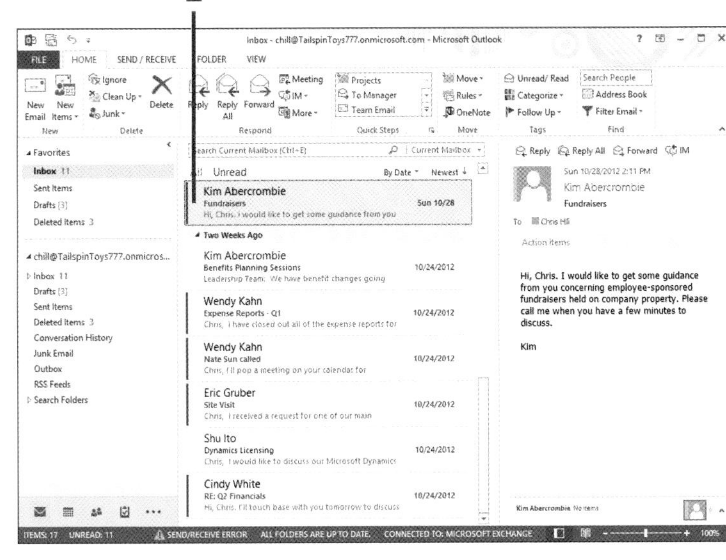

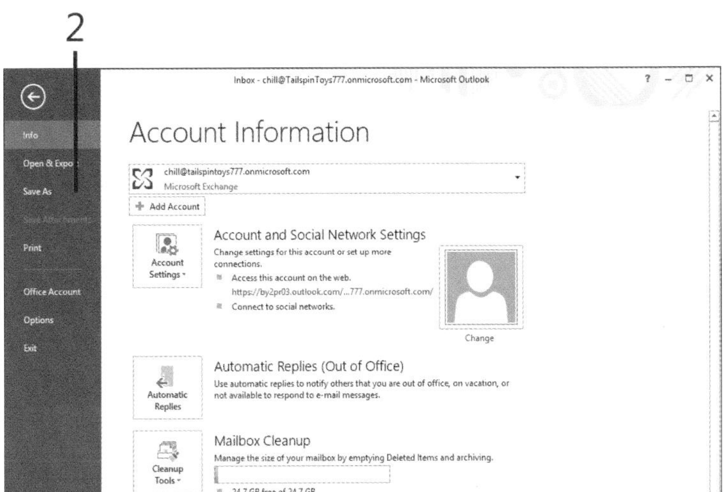

TIP To find a message from a specific sender, click the From column. This sorts messages alphanumerically, based on the sender's name.

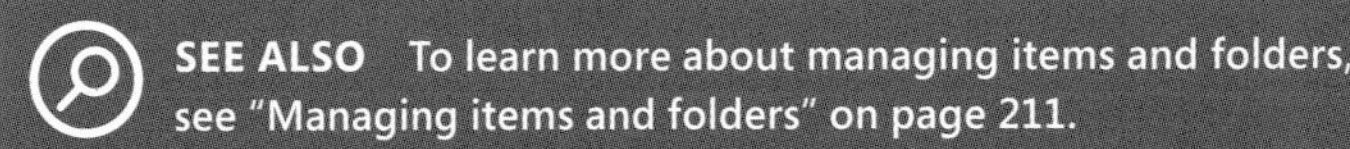

SEE ALSO To learn more about managing items and folders, see "Managing items and folders" on page 211.

Save important messages *(continued)*

3 In the Save As dialog box, choose a folder in which to store the message.

4 Optionally, type a new name for the message.

5 Choose the desired file type.

6 Click Save.

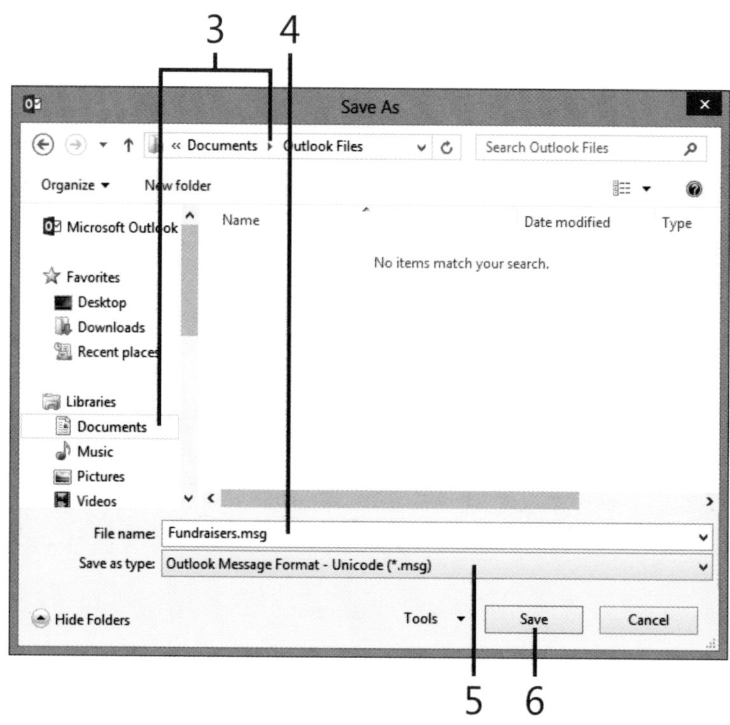

TIP To save the message in a format other than message format (.msg), click the Save As Type drop-down list and choose the format type. You can save messages in text, HTML, MHT, Outlook template, and two message formats. This makes it handy when you want to open the message in another application, such as a word processor or Internet web browser. Note that you can't save a plain text message in HTML.

CAUTION When you save a message in a format other than .msg, the formatting of the message itself might change. If this is the case, you might find it difficult to read the message without modifying it.

Print a copy of a message

1 Select a message. Then, on the ribbon, click the File tab to display the Backstage view and click the Print tab.

2 Click the Printer drop-down list and select the printer that you want to use.

3 Click the Print Style option that you want.

4 Click Print.

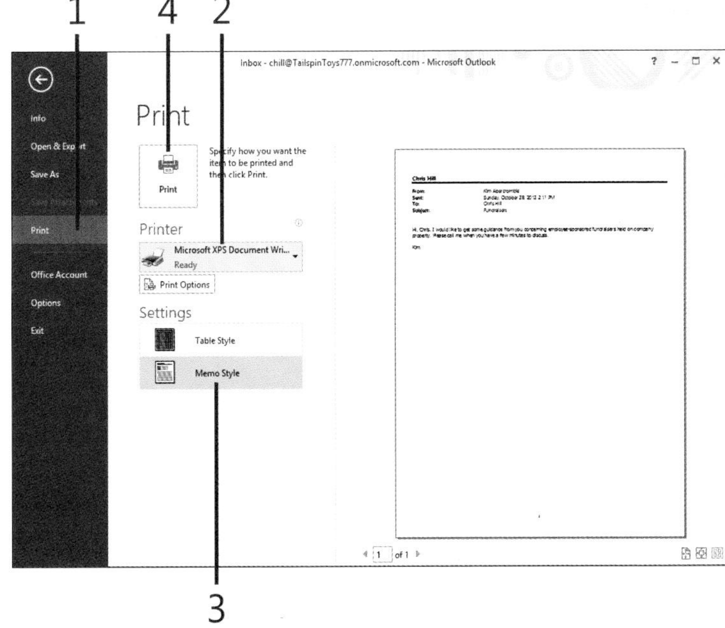

TIP With a message open, on the Quick Access Toolbar, click Quick Print to print to the default printer. If Quick Print does not appear on your Quick Access Toolbar, you can customize it to add that option. Use the buttons in the lower-right corner of the Print page to control print preview options.

Working with attachments

When you receive an email attachment, you can open it directly from the message, save it to devices storage medium and open it from there, or print it straight from the message to a printer. Messages that have attachments display a paper-clip icon to the left of the message author's name or below the message received date, depending on the location of the Reading pane and the width of the display.

Open an attachment

1 Click a message that has an attachment.

2 In the Reading pane, double-click the attachment.

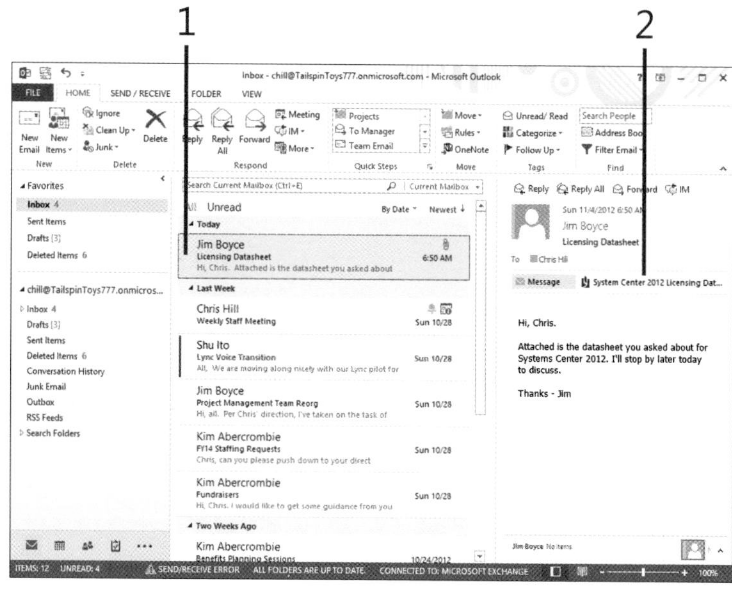

TIP To open an attachment, you must have an application that supports the attached file. For example, if you receive a Microsoft PowerPoint file (.ppt or .pptx), you must have PowerPoint, the PowerPoint Viewer, or some similar application installed on your system to view the file.

SEE ALSO For information about attaching files to messages you send, see "Sending a file by email" on page 56.

Save an attachment

1. Click the message that has the attachment.
2. In the Reading pane, in the Attachment field, right-click the attachment.
3. On the shortcut menu that appears, click Save As.
4. Choose the folder where you want to save the file.
5. Make any necessary changes to the file name.
6. Click Save.

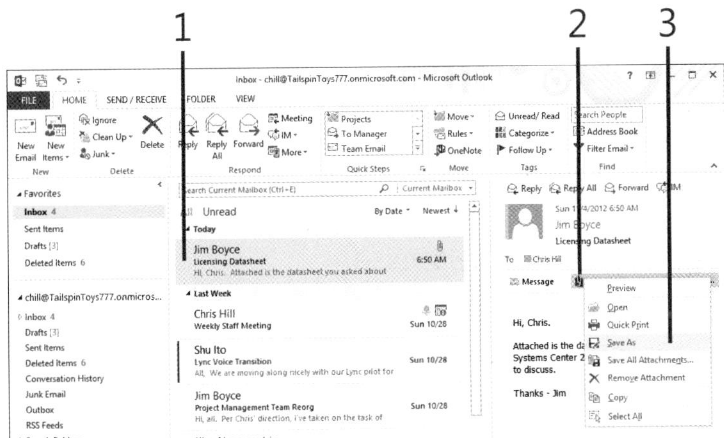

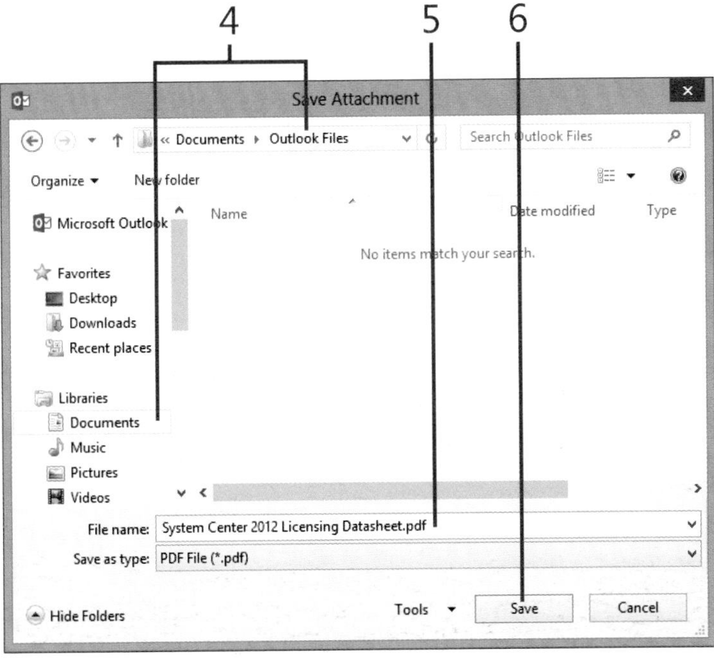

CAUTION Some files that you receive from another user, such as programs, webpages, and script files, can be infected with a computer virus. You should save all executable files to your system and run an antivirus program that checks the file for a virus before you open it. If you receive an attachment from an unknown sender (as happens a lot with junk email), you should never open it. Just delete the message.

Replying to and forwarding email

When you receive a message, you can reply directly to the sender. You can also forward the message or send a response to everyone who receives the message. When you reply to a message, Outlook 2013 keeps the original message text; you add your new text above it. The sender's name becomes the recipient name, and the subject line begins with "RE:" to denote that the message is a reply.

Reply to an email message

1 Click the message to which you want to reply.

2 On the ribbon, click the Home tab and then, in the respond group, click the Reply button.

3 Click in the space above the original message line and type your reply.

4 Click Send.

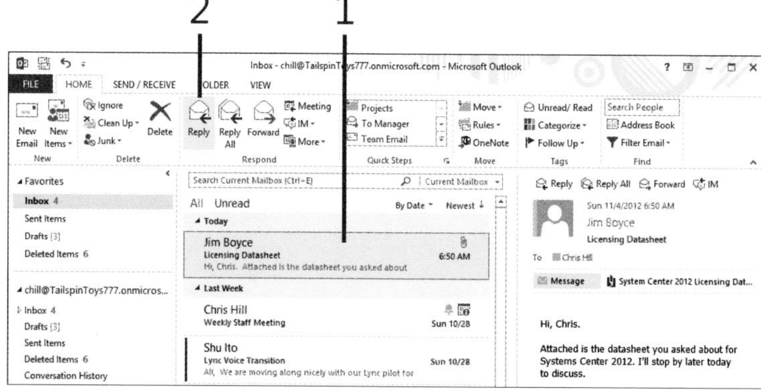

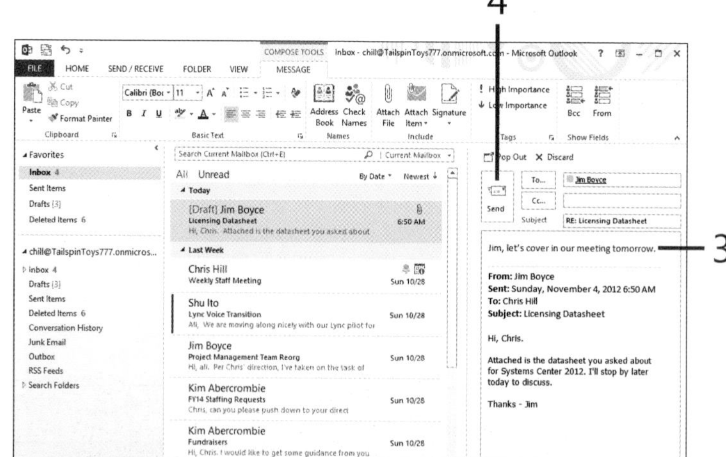

TIP When you reply to messages that have attachments, the reply message does not include the attached file.

TIP To reply to all recipients of a message, on the ribbon, on the Home tab, click Reply All. To open the draft message in its own window, above the Reading pane, click Pop Out.

Forward an email message

1 Click the message that you want to forward.

2 On the ribbon, click the Home tab and then, in the Respond group, click the Forward button.

3 Add the address to which you want to forward this message.

4 Optionally, you can click in the space above the original message line and type a message.

5 Click Send.

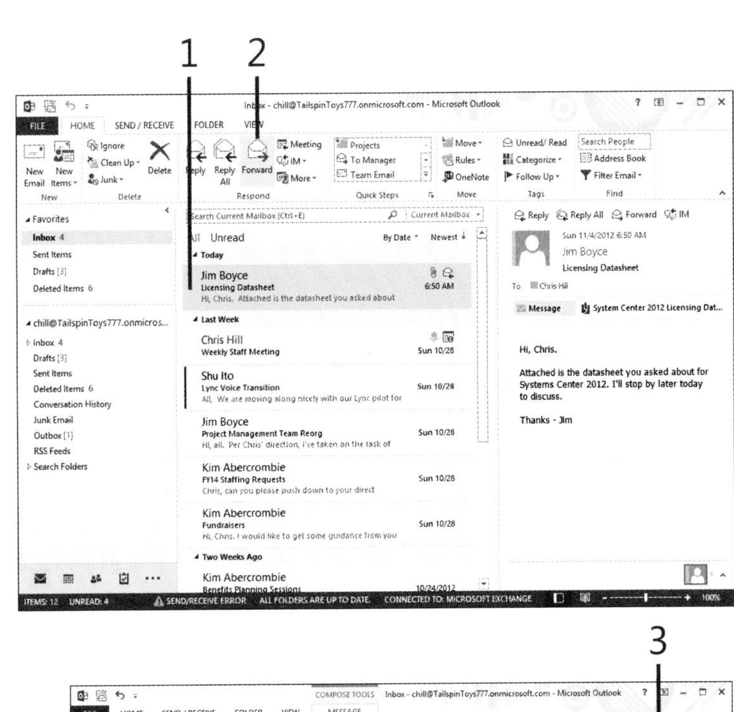

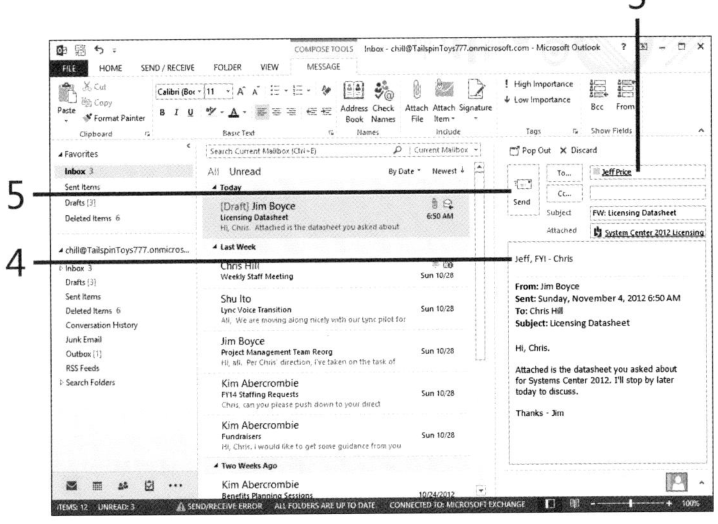

TIP When you forward messages that have attachments, the forwarded message includes the attached file.

SEE ALSO For information about addressing messages, see "Writing an email message" on page 36.

Handling junk mail

Just like the junk mail that you receive in your postal mailbox, you probably get too many junk email messages (also known as spam) in your Outlook 2013 Inbox. You can set up mail filters that can sort your incoming mail so that junk mail is moved to its own folder, flagged, or deleted. You can also turn on mail filters so that only specific messages are displayed in the Inbox.

Turn on junk email filters

1. On the Home tab, in the Delete group, click the Junk button.
2. On the drop-down menu that appears, click Junk E-mail Options.
3. In the Junk E-Mail Options dialog box that opens, choose a junk filtering level.
4. Choose other mail security options that you want.
5. Click OK.

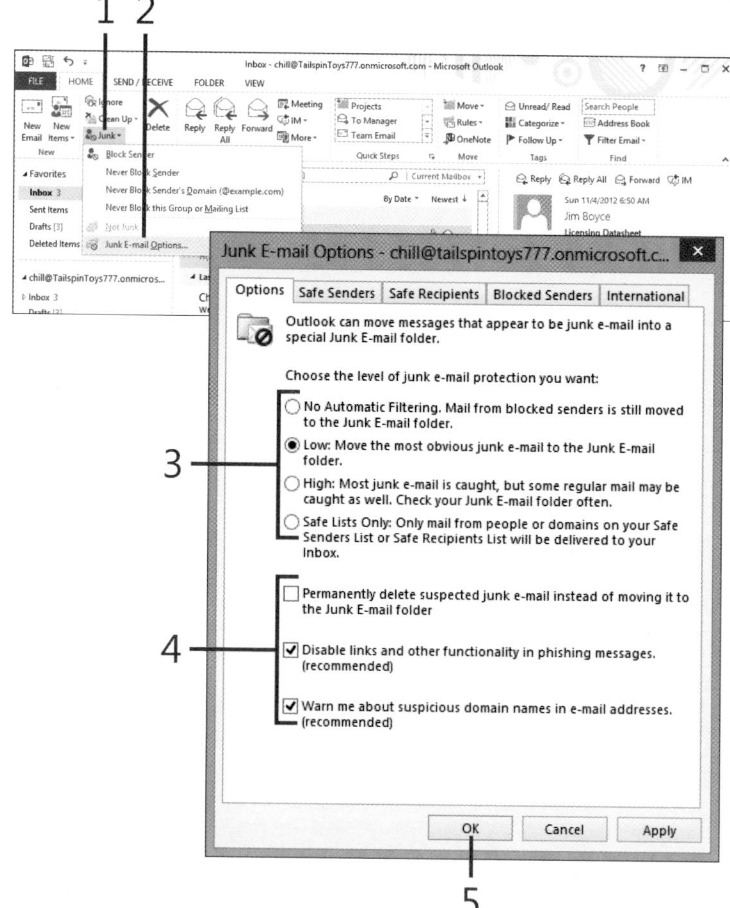

SEE ALSO For more information about setting rules and filters, see "Working with the Rules Wizard" on page 81.

Add to the junk mail senders list

1 In the Inbox folder, click a message from a sender that you want to add to the junk mail senders list.

2 On the ribbon, click the Home tab, and in the Delete group, click the Junk button.

3 On the drop-down menu that appears, click Block Sender.

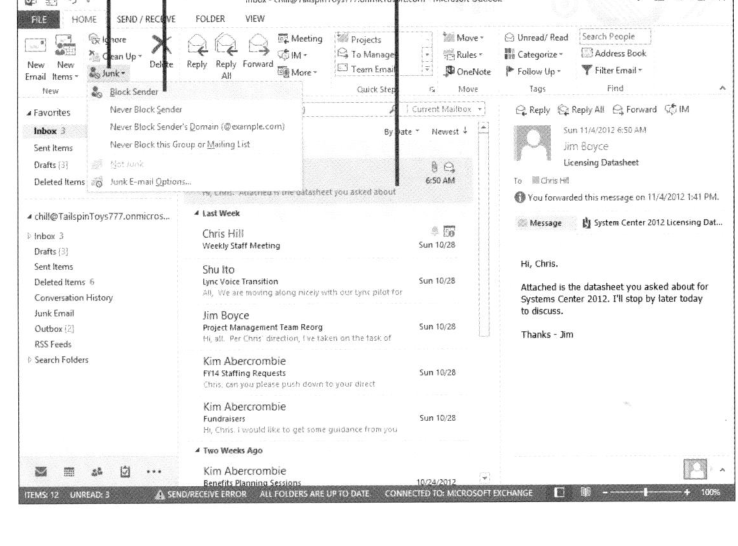

TIP One way that you can end up on a junk mail list is by filling out surveys and other online forms on websites. Usually these forms ask for your email address to process the form. To reduce the amount of junk email you get, limit the number of website surveys you fill out, or use a "junk" email account that you create just for this purpose.

CAUTION If you add a sender to the junk email list by accident, all messages from this sender might be deleted as soon as they're received by Outlook. If you think a legitimate sender is on your junk mail filter, see the next procedure for removing him from the list.

Fine-tune the junk mail filter

1. On the Home tab, in the Respond group, click Junk and then, on the menu that appears, click Junk Email Options.
2. In the Junk E-Mail Options dialog box, click the Blocked Senders tab.
3. To remove a sender from the Junk Mail list, select a name and click Remove.
4. To add a sender to the Blocked Senders list, click Add.
5. In the Add Address Or Domain dialog box, type the email address or domain of the junk mail sender.
6. Click OK to close the Add Address Or Domain dialog box.
7. Click OK to close the Junk E-mail Options dialog box.

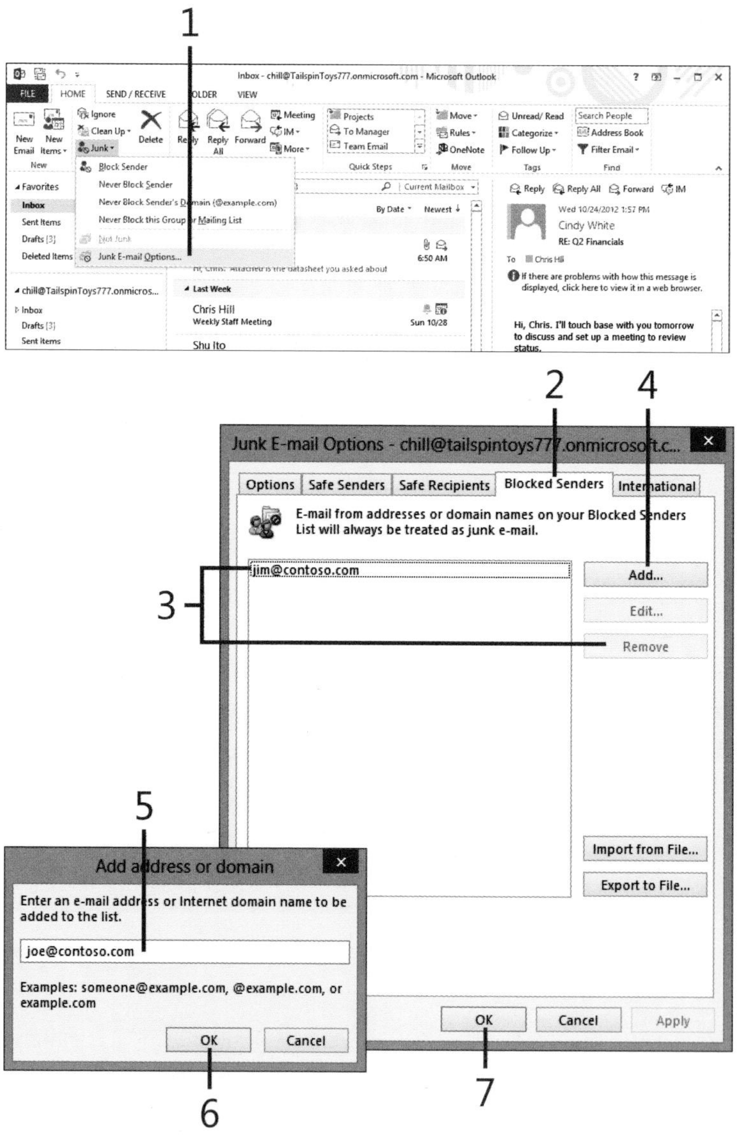

TIP You can block an entire domain, if needed. Blocking a domain blocks all messages from all addresses in that domain.

Working with the Rules Wizard

Rules are actions that Outlook performs on your messages to organize them. When you have Outlook rules set, many management tasks are taken care of automatically when your new messages arrive. To make setting up rules painless, Outlook includes a Rules Wizard that walks you through the process of creating a rule by referring to a message that you have already received. You can also create a rule from scratch.

Create a rule based on a message

1. In the Inbox folder, click the message on which you want to base the new rule.
2. On the ribbon, click the Home tab and then, in the Move group, click Rules. On the menu that appears, click Create Rule.

(continued on next page)

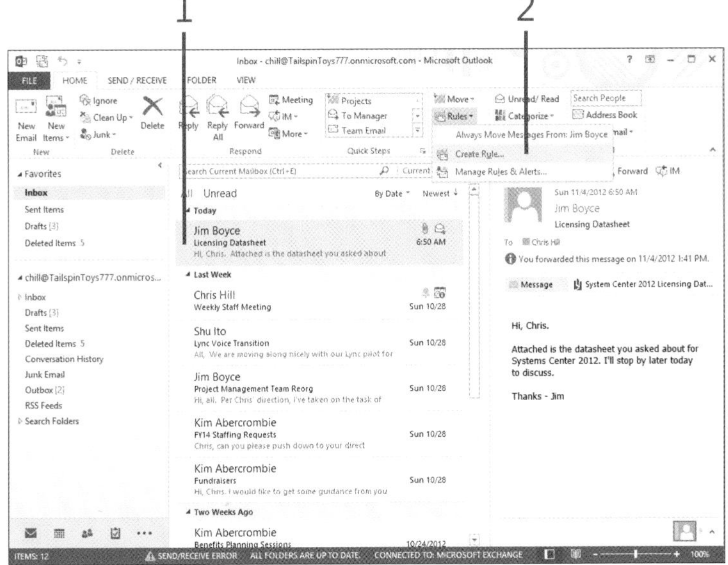

> **TIP** You can select multiple conditions under which your new rule is applied. However, when you do this, the rule isn't applied unless all the conditions are met.

Create a rule based on a message *(continued)*

3 In the Create Rule dialog box, choose the conditions to apply to the rule.

4 Choose the action you want Outlook to perform on messages that match the condition. For example, select the Move The Item To Folder check box.

5 Click Select Folder.

6 In the Rules And Alerts dialog box, choose the folder to which you want the messages moved.

7 Click OK to close the Rules And Alerts dialog box. Click OK again to close the Create Rule dialog box.

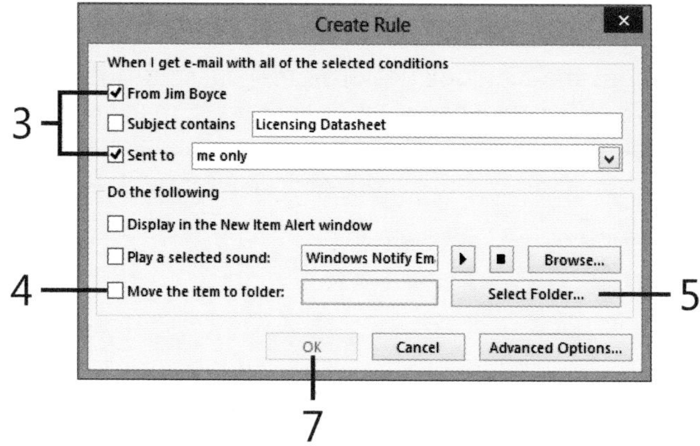

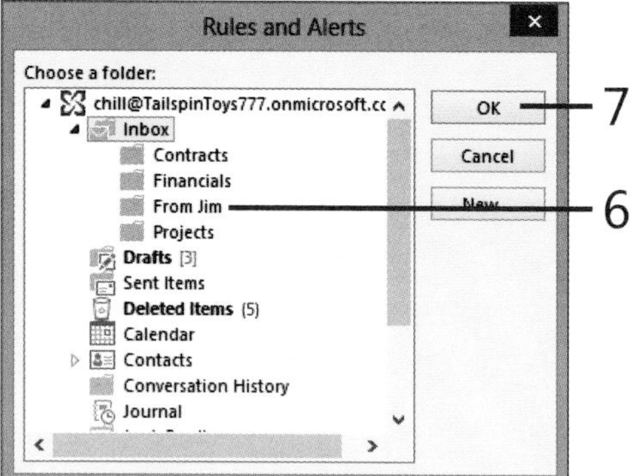

SEE ALSO For more information about setting rules, see "Working with the Rules Wizard" on page 81.

TIP The conditions and actions available in the Create Rule dialog box are just some of the ones you can use in Outlook. The Rules Wizard, which you access by clicking Rules on the Home tab on the ribbon and then clicking Manage Rules & Alerts on the drop-down menu, offers many additional conditions and actions for message-processing rules.

Create a rule from scratch

1 With the Inbox folder displayed, on the Home tab, in the Move group, click Rules. On the drop-down menu that appears, click Manage Rules & Alerts.

2 In the Rules And Alerts dialog box, click New Rule.

3 On the first page of the Rules Wizard, click Apply Rule On Messages I Receive under Start From A Blank Rule.

4 Click Next.

(continued on next page)

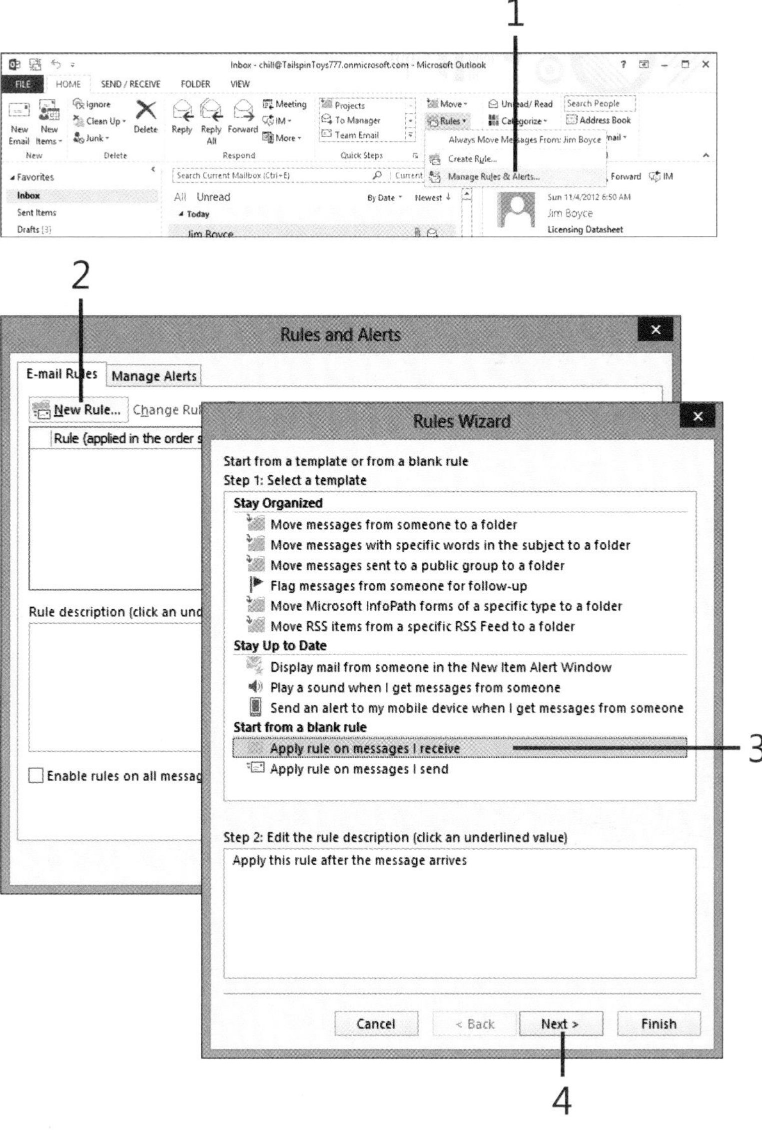

TRY THIS! To run rules manually, in the Rules And Alerts dialog box, click Run Rules Now. Select the rules you want to run and then click Run Now.

Create a rule from scratch *(continued)*

5 On the conditions page of the wizard, select the condition under which you want the rule applied.

6 If the condition requires additional configuration, click the link in the Step 2 field and enter the information.

7 Click Next.

(continued on next page)

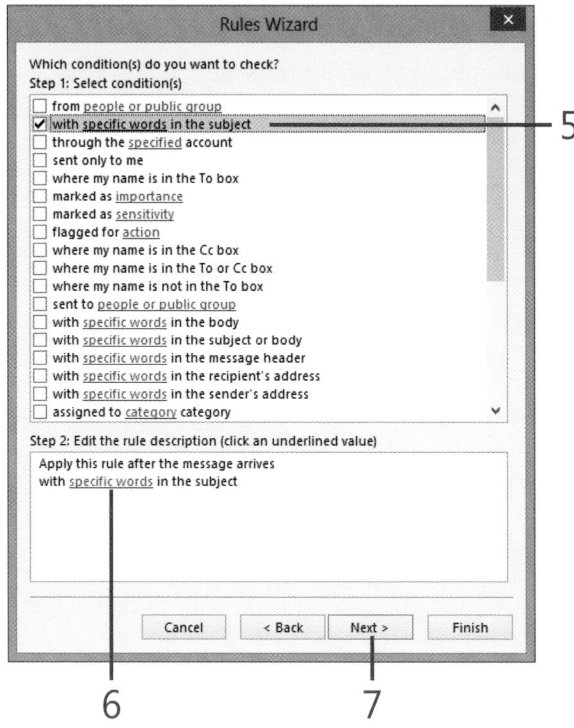

Create a rule from scratch *(continued)*

8 On the What Do You Want To Do With The Message? page of the wizard, select what you want to do with the message.

9 If the action requires further configuration, click the link in the Step 2 field and enter the required information.

10 Click Next.

(continued on next page)

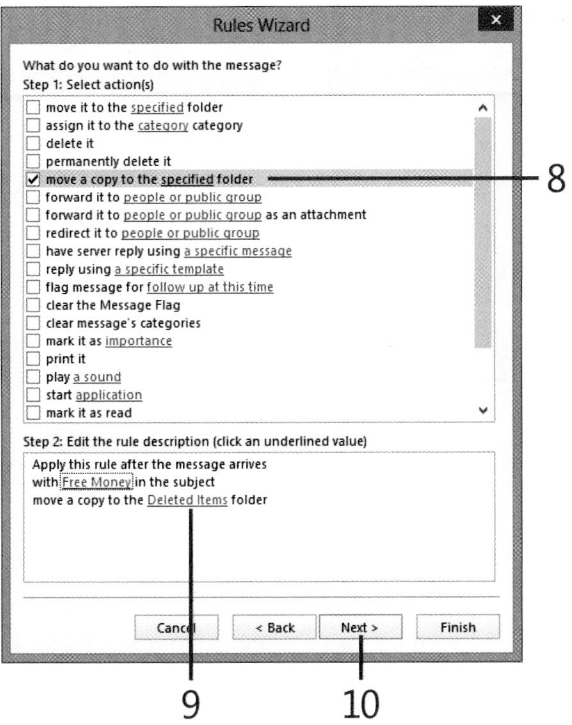

Create a rule from scratch *(continued)*

11 On the exceptions page of the wizard, select exceptions to the rule.

12 Click Next.

(continued on next page)

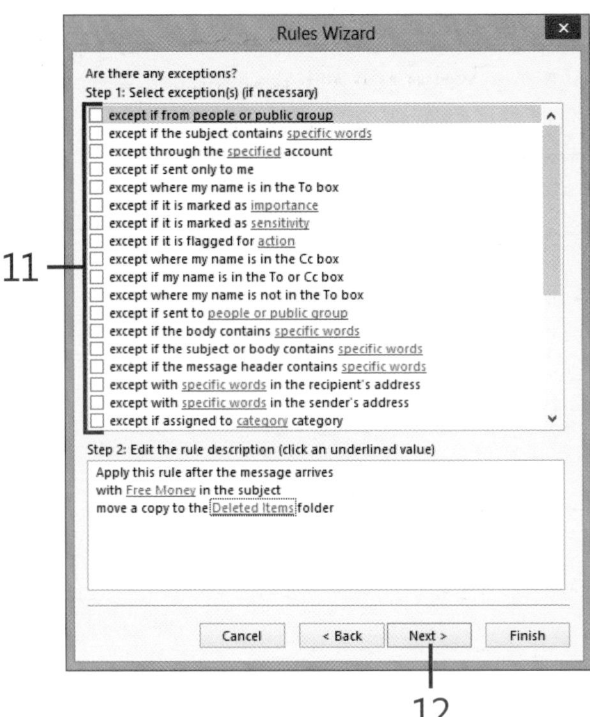

Create a rule from scratch *(continued)*

13 On the Finish page of the wizard, type a name for your rule.

14 Select the Turn On This Rule check box.

15 Click Finish.

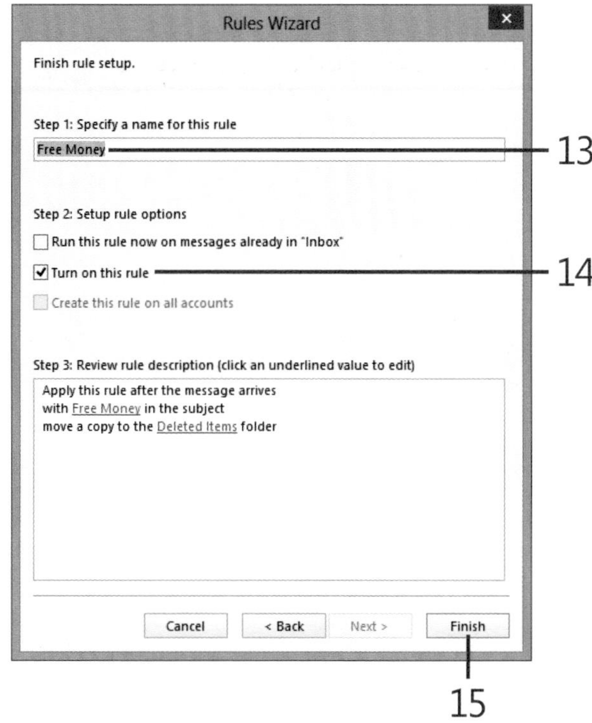

Following up on a message

When you receive a message, you might not have the time or the information you need to reply to it right away. In such cases, you can flag a message to remind yourself to follow up on it later. You can designate different types of follow-up, including reminders to reply by email, to forward the message to a third party, or to reply by telephone.

Flag a message for follow-up

1 In the Inbox pane, right-click the message on which you want to follow up.
2 On the shortcut menu that appears, click Follow Up.
3 On the submenu that appears, click the follow-up action, or click Add Reminder to open the Custom dialog box.
4 Select the Reminder check box.
5 Select a reminder date.
6 Set a time for the reminder, and then click OK.

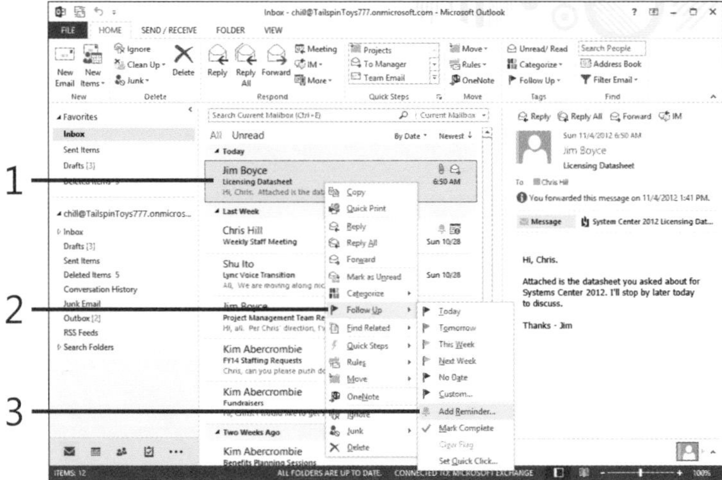

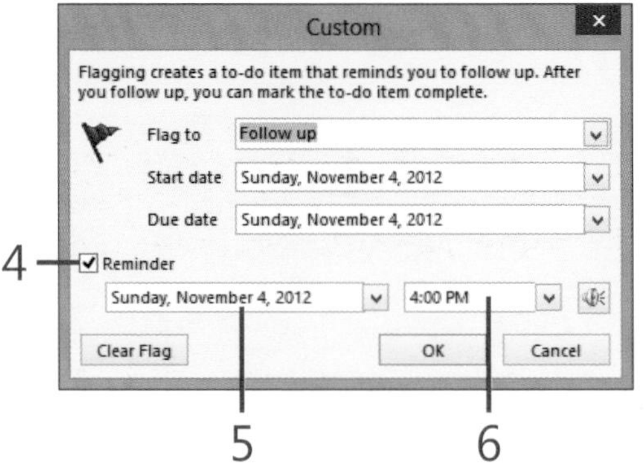

TRY THIS! In the Flag For Follow Up dialog box, set a flag that is due today at 30 minutes from the current time. When the time expires, Outlook displays a message prompting you to follow up on the message.

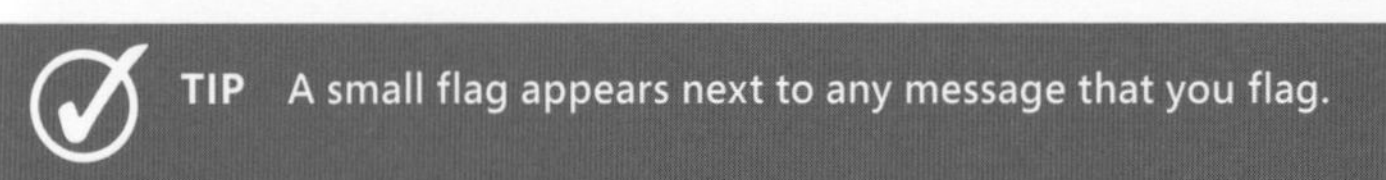
TIP A small flag appears next to any message that you flag.

Set follow-up flag status

1 In the Inbox pane, click the follow-up flag to clear or set the flag.

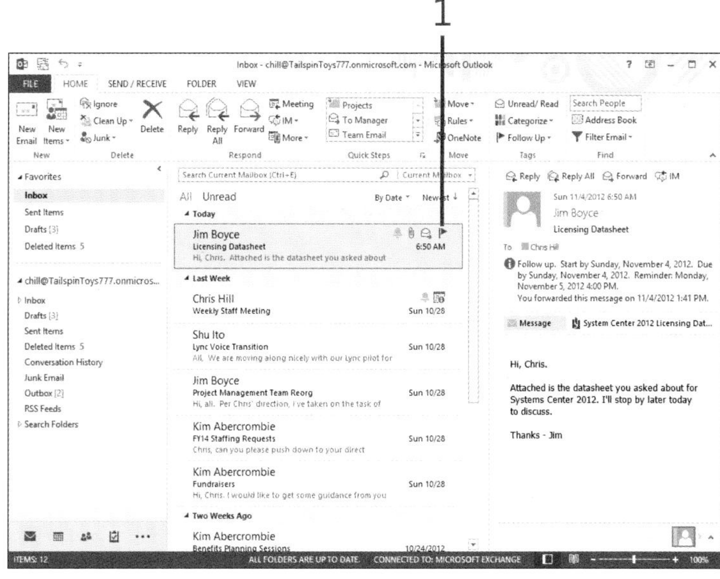

SEE ALSO For information about replying to email messages, see "Replying to and forwarding email" on page 76.

TIP When you clear a follow-up flag, a clear flag appears next to the message subject. If you later determine that you want to set the flag again, right-click the message, choose Follow Up from the shortcut menu, clear the Mark Complete option, and then click OK.

Working with the People Hub

6

Staying in contact with others is part of life and an important task in business. Whether it's your best friend from high school, a client you've worked with for years, or a new customer, you need a way to store all the information about each one of them.

You can use the People Hub in Microsoft Outlook 2013 to save personal and business contact information, including phone numbers, addresses, email addresses, website information, and personal data. Not merely a glorified card file, the Contacts folder is a full-featured database that lets you use automatic dialing to call a contact, import data from other contact managers or databases (such as Microsoft Access), create new messages to send to a contact, set up contact groups for contacts, and more. The People Hub also integrates your social networking accounts from Facebook, LinkedIn, and other networking sites so that you can work with your contacts in those accounts, as well.

This section explores the Contacts folder. You learn how to create and sort contacts and use them for a variety of tasks. You learn how to add social networking accounts, send email messages to contacts, work with contacts in your address book, add files to a contact, and organize and manage contacts.

In this section:

- Working with social networking accounts and contacts
- Adding a new contact
- Inserting items into a contact record
- Viewing your contacts
- Viewing contact status and activities
- Finding a contact
- Organizing your contacts
- Customizing People Hub and contact views
- Communicating with contacts

Working with social networking accounts and contacts

Outlook 2013 has built-in support for social networking accounts from Facebook, LinkedIn, and SharePoint. This capability is extensible, meaning developers for other social networking sites can build support for Outlook 2013. Adding a social networking account makes it possible for you you to work with your contacts from that account, such as your Facebook friends.

Add a social networking account

1 On the ribbon, click the File tab to display the Backstage view, click Account Settings and then, in the drop-down list that appears, choose Social Network Account.

(continued on next page)

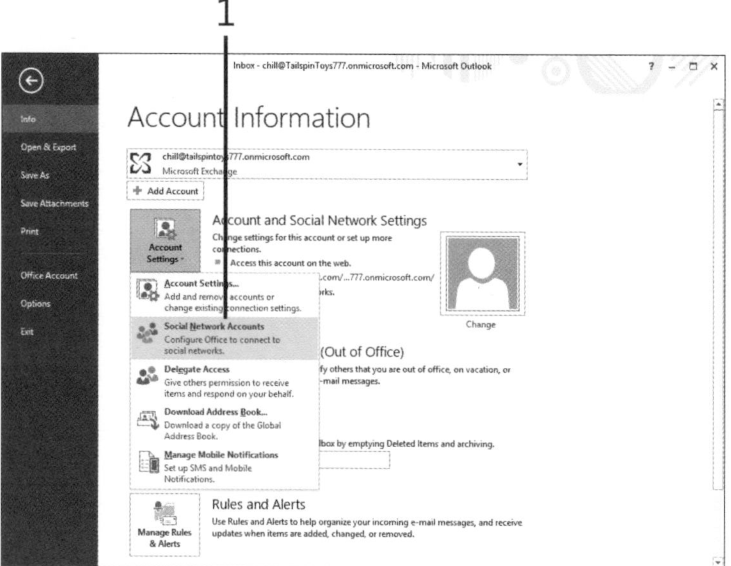

Add a social networking account *(continued)*

2 In the Social Network Accounts dialog box, select the appropriate check box for the account type you want to add.

3 Type your user name for the social networking service.

4 Type your password.

5 Select the check box if you want to automatically show photos and other information from the account in the People Hub.

6 Click Connect.

(continued on next page)

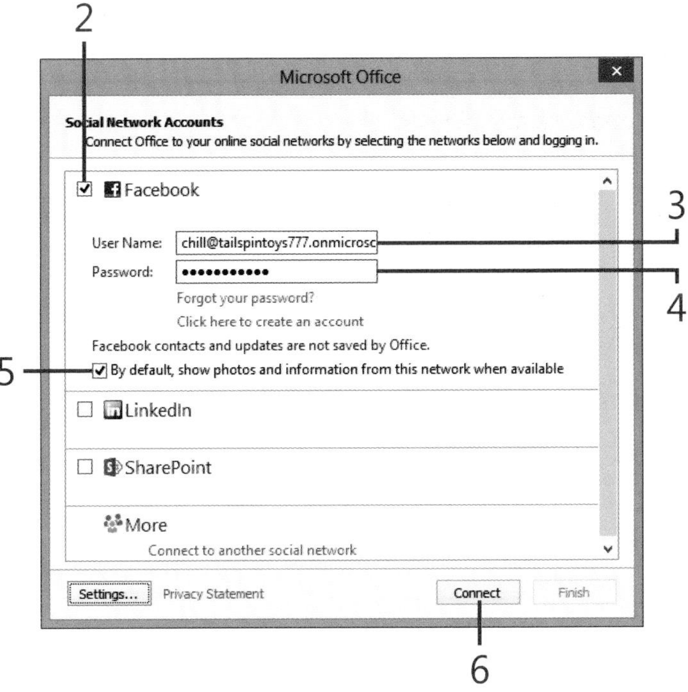

Add a social networking account *(continued)*

7 Click Finish.

8 Click Close.

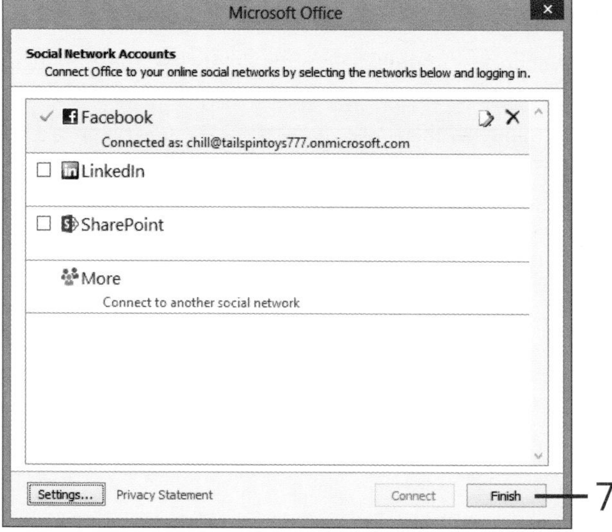

TIP After you add a Facebook account in Outlook, your Facebook friends will not automatically appear in Outlook. Instead, you must add a contact to Outlook using the same email address as the friend's Facebook account. After you add the contact, Outlook will sync the photo and other information from Facebook for that contact (subject to the permissions the friend has set on his data).

Add a Facebook friend to the People Hub

1. At the bottom of the Folder pane, click the People icon to open the People Hub.
2. On the ribbon, click the Home tab and then, in the New group, click New Contact.
3. Enter the friend's name.
4. Enter the friend's email address that is associated with his Facebook account.
5. Add other information as desired.
6. On the ribbon, click the Contact tab and then click Save & Close.

(continued on next page)

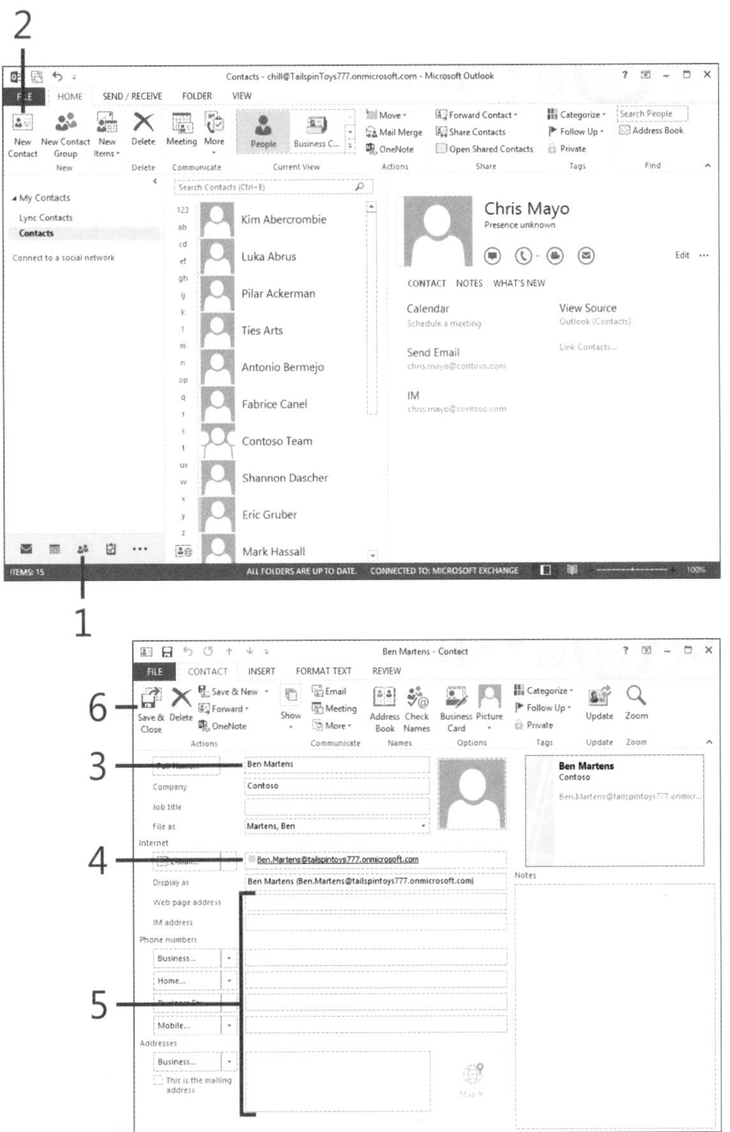

Add a Facebook friend to the People Hub *(continued)*

7 Click the newly created contact.

8 Note that the Facebook profile picture is added automatically.

9 Click the Facebook link to open Facebook and view the friend's profile.

10 Click What's New.

11 View the friend's latest post on Facebook.

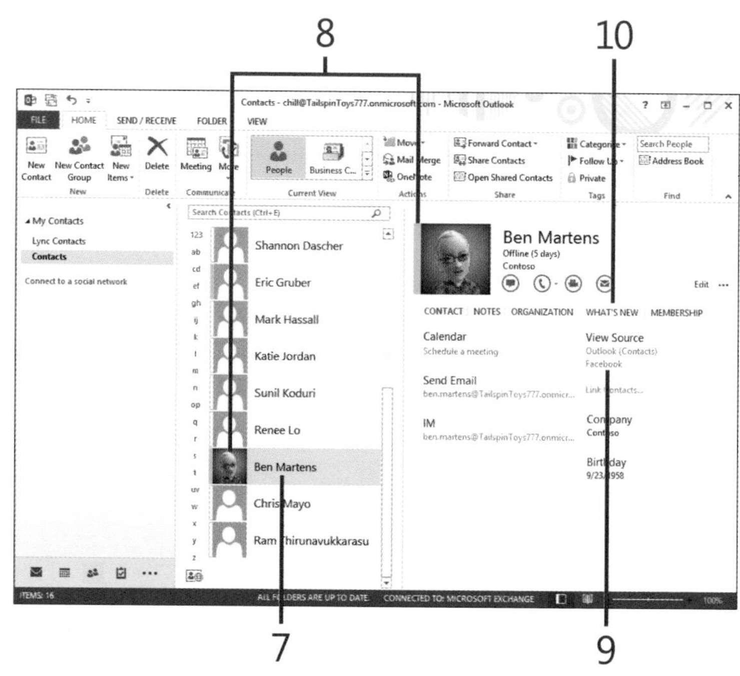

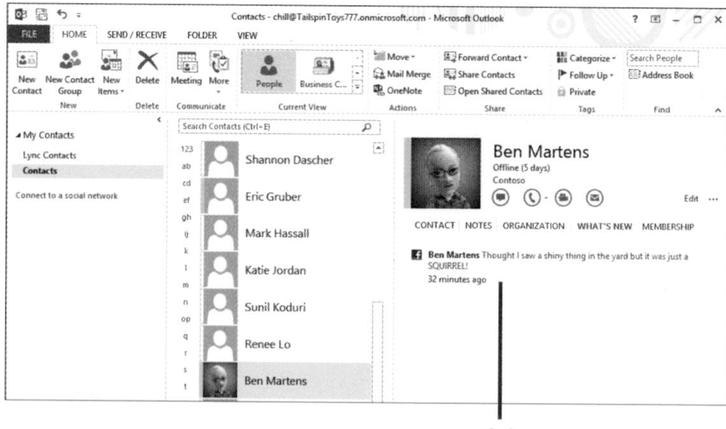

Adding a new contact

You can add contacts to Outlook's Contacts folder in three ways: by typing new information about someone into a Contacts form, by using information you've entered for another contact, or by using information from an email message. In the latter case, for example, you can quickly create a new contact by using the information from a message that you've received.

Create a contact from an email message

1 With the Inbox showing, select the message that has the contact information that you want to save. If you don't have the Reading pane displayed, open the message to access the From field.

2 Right-click the name or address that appears in the From field.

3 On the shortcut menu that appears, click Add To Outlook Contacts.

(continued on next page)

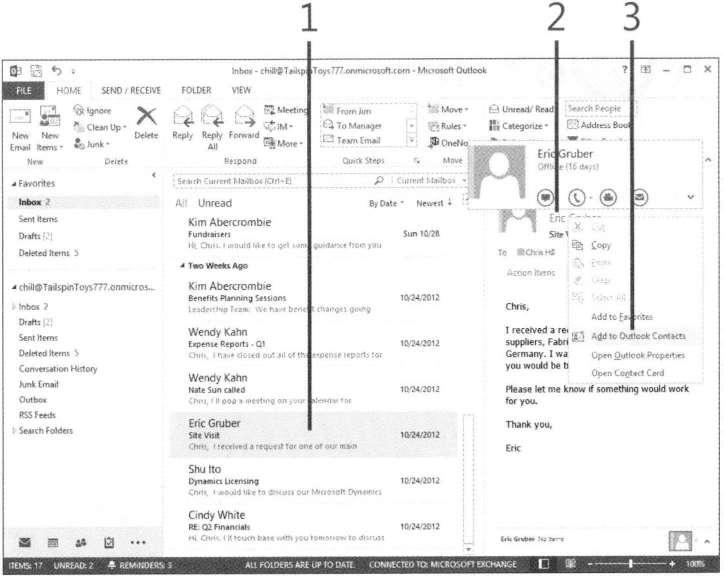

TIP Depending on how the From field is filled out in an email message, you might need to modify the Full Name field when you create a new contact from a mail message. For example, if the sender's name isn't complete or doesn't appear at all, you need to manually enter the information in the address card.

TIP If you want to keep the Inbox open and also open the People Hub, right-click People in the Folder pane and then, on the shortcut menu that appears, click Open In New Window.

Create a contact from an email message *(continued)*

4 Type the pertinent information into the remaining fields.

5 If a field isn't visible, click the + button to choose the field you want to add.

6 Click the Save button to save the contact information.

> **TIP** To add other fields not shown in the form or to modify other information for the contact, double-click a contact to open the contact form, where the additional fields are available for editing.

Use the contact form

1 At the bottom of the Folder pane, click the People icon to display the People Hub.

2 On the ribbon, click the Home tab and then, in the New group, click the New Contact button.

(continued on next page)

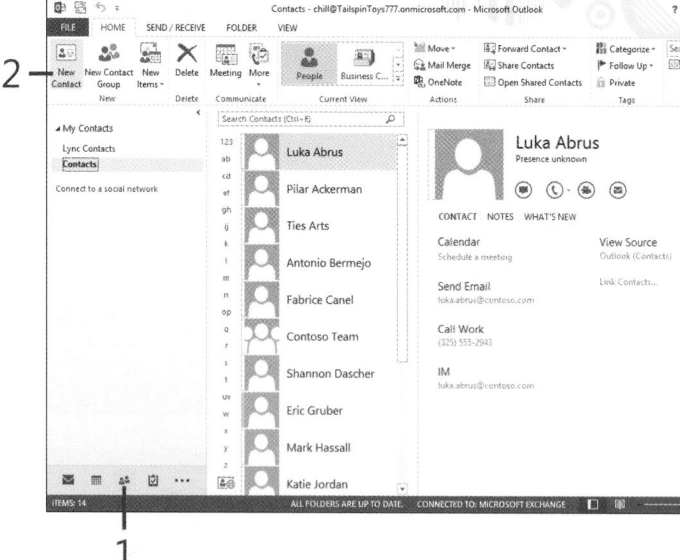

> **CAUTION** When you type a contact's email address, be sure you type it correctly. An incorrect address prevents your messages from being sent successfully. Take the time to double-check your spelling of an email address. You can change it later, but it's best to ensure that it's correct now.

Use the contact form *(continued)*

3 Type information about your contact in the appropriate fields.

4 From the File As drop-down list, select one of the ways in which Outlook can display the contact's name, such as last name first, first name last, and so on.

5 Type any additional useful information in the Notes box at the bottom of the address card.

6 On the ribbon, click the Contact tab and then click Save & Close to save your changes.

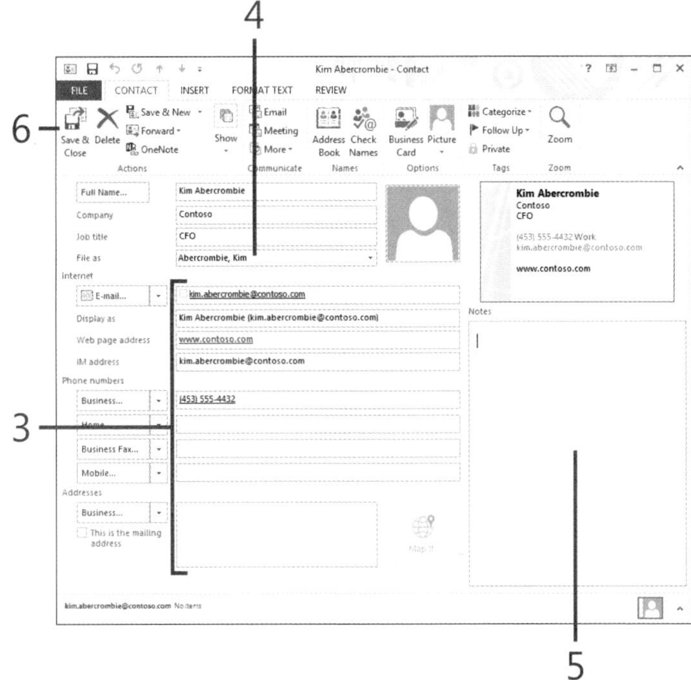

TIP To ensure that Outlook can dial the phone number for a contact, type phone numbers as numbers; don't use acronyms or letters.

TIP If the contact already exists in your Contacts folder, Outlook asks whether you want to update the information in the existing contact with the new information.

Inserting items into a contact record

You can add Outlook 2013 items, application and document objects, and files to a contact by using the Outlook Item button on the Insert tab on the ribbon. For example, you can add an email message to a contact for future reference, insert an attachment, or insert a Microsoft Excel worksheet. You can then access these items from the contact card. You can add a new, empty item and then modify it right in the Outlook item, or you can insert an existing document.

Add an Outlook item

1 Open the People Hub and choose any view other than People.
2 Open the contact in which you want to insert an item.
3 On the ribbon, click the Insert tab.
4 In the Include group, click Outlook Item.

(continued on next page)

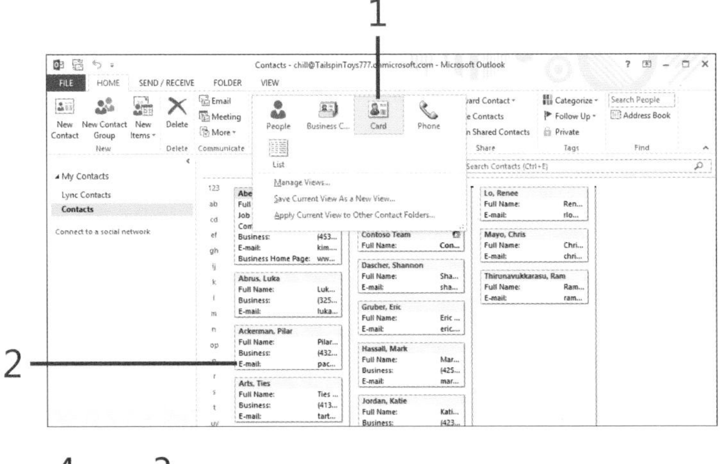

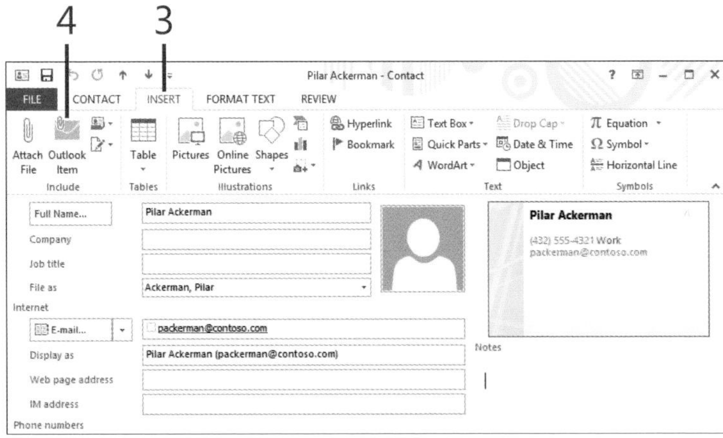

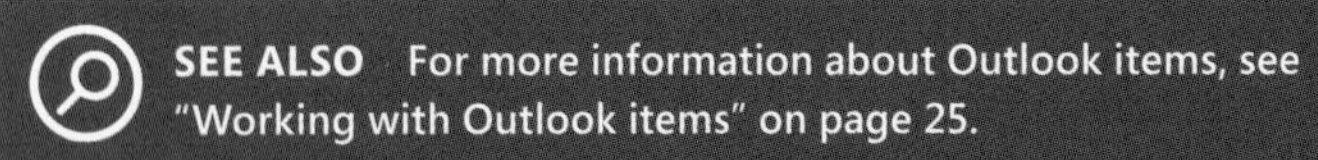

SEE ALSO For more information about Outlook items, see "Working with Outlook items" on page 25.

Add an Outlook item *(continued)*

5 In the Insert Item dialog box, click the Outlook folder in which the item you want to insert is located.

6 Select an item in the Items list.

7 Select the format of the item: Text Only, Attachment, or Shortcut.

8 Click OK to insert the item into the contact item.

9 The item now appears with the contact.

10 On the ribbon, click the Contact tab and then click Save & Close.

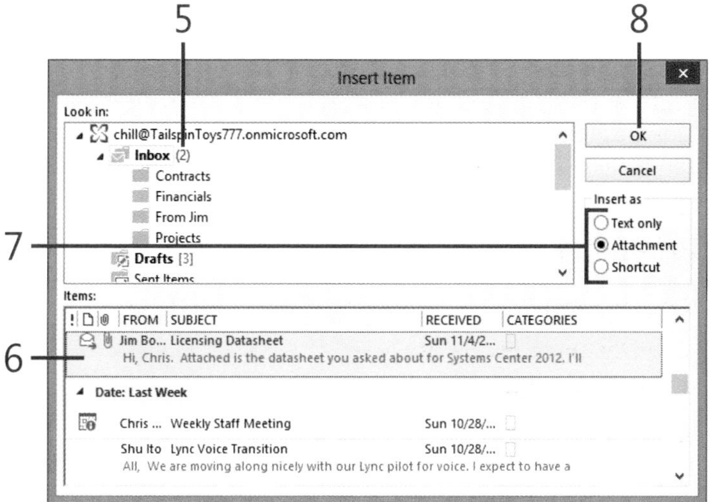

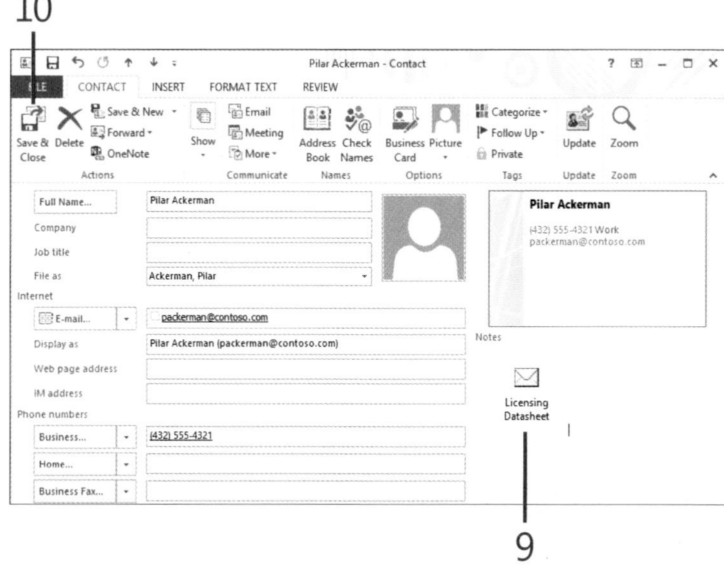

Add a file

1 Open a contact and then, on the ribbon, click the Insert tab.
2 In the Include group, click the Attach File button.
3 In the Insert Item dialog box, select the folder in which the file you want to insert is located.
4 Select the file that you want to insert.
5 Click Insert.

(continued on next page)

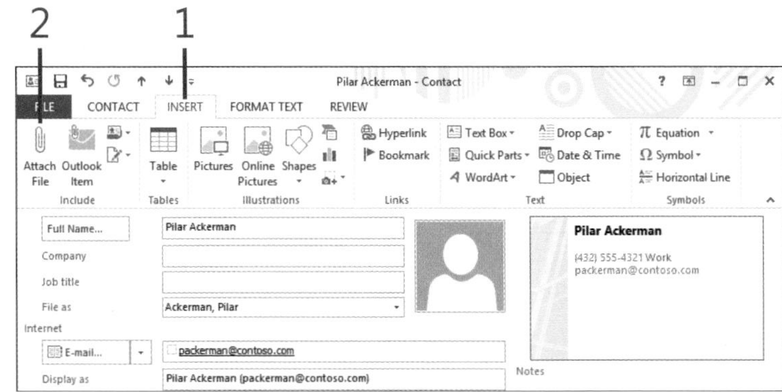

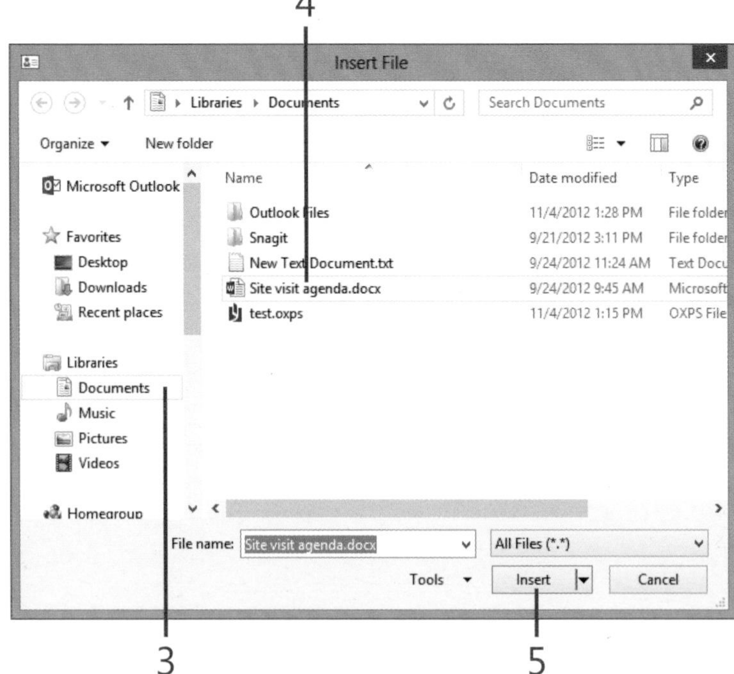

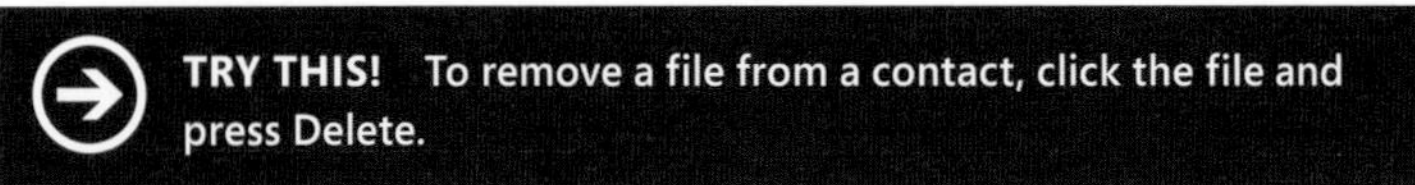

TRY THIS! To remove a file from a contact, click the file and press Delete.

Add a file *(continued)*

6 The file now appears with the contact.

7 On the ribbon, click the Contact tab and then click Save & Close.

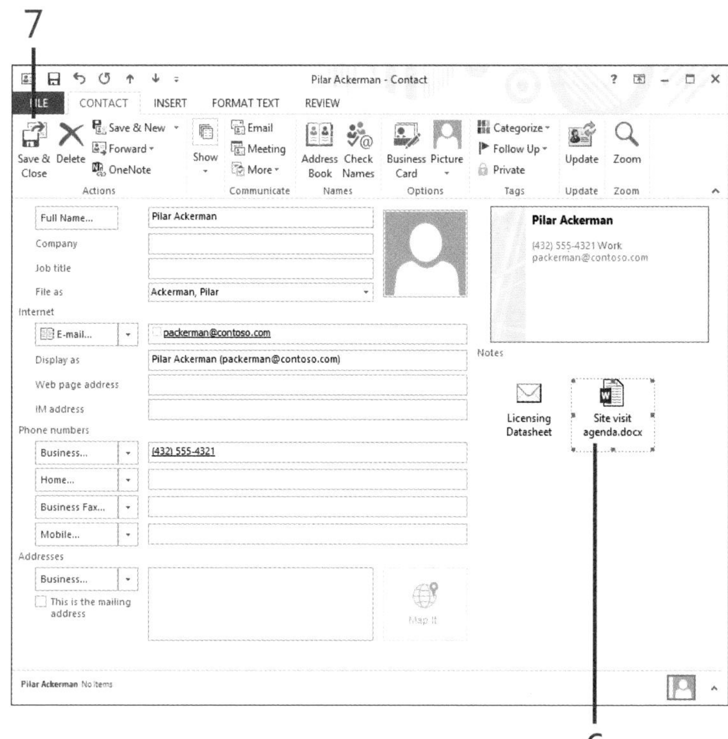

> **TIP** After you insert a file into a contact's card, you can open it to view, edit, or print it. To do this, double-click the file's icon in the contact item to launch the file within its associated application. Note that this edits the file embedded in the contact, not the original file.

> **CAUTION** As you add items, files, and objects to a contact, the size of that contact card increases. When you add several items, files, or objects to a contact, it takes longer for Outlook to open the contact. You should limit the number of attachments you add to a contact. To conserve space, you can insert links instead of items.

Viewing your contacts

You can view your Outlook 2013 contacts as a series of single address cards, or you can view them all at once, moving through your Contacts folder as if it were an electronic phone book or address book. Another way to look at your contact information is through the Outlook Address Book, which lists contacts alphabetically.

Choose a view of the People Hub

1 At the bottom of the Folder pane, click the People icon.

2 On the ribbon, click the Home tab. In the Current View group, click More if the view you want isn't shown.

3 Select the view type you want to use to view the contact information in the Contacts folder. You can choose from the following list:

- People
- Business Card
- Card
- Phone
- List

SEE ALSO One task that no one wants to face is typing in all their contacts a second time. This is why it's a good idea to set up a backup schedule to ensure that your contacts are backed up on a regular basis. For information about backing up and restoring Outlook Contacts, see "Backing up and restoring a data file" on page 237.

TRY THIS! To see how Outlook displays your contact information in different formats, select each of the views in the Change View drop-down list. When you see one that you like, such as the Phone view, keep it so that the next time you open the Contacts folder that view is showing.

View contacts in the Address Book

1 On the ribbon, click the Home tab and then, in the Find group, click Address Book.

2 In the Address Books dialog box, click the Address Book drop-down list and choose Contacts.

3 View or select contacts.

4 If desired, on the File menu, click the New Message command to start a new email addressed to the selected contact.

5 Close the Address Book when you're finished working with your contacts.

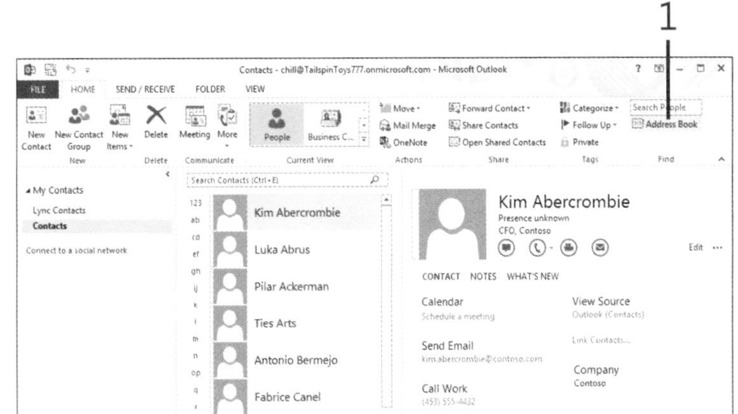

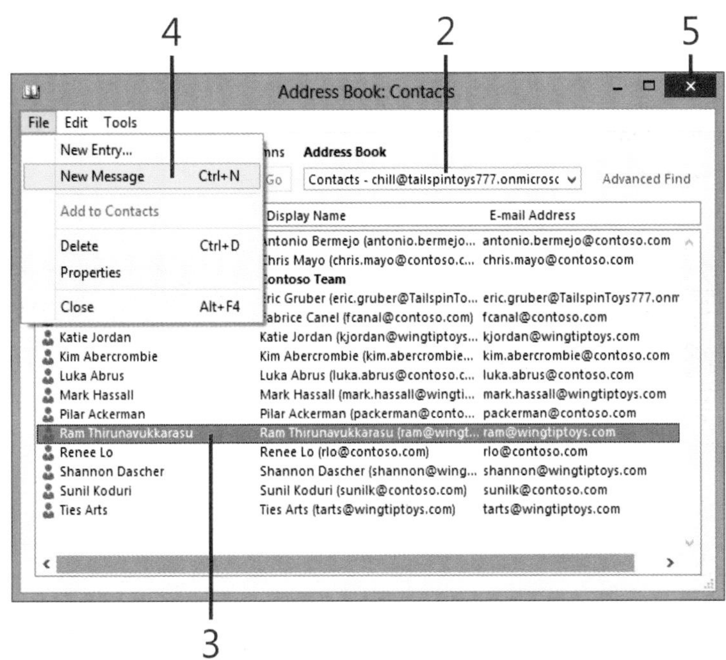

SEE ALSO You can also use the Address Book to add and modify contact information. See "Working with the Address Book" on page 38 for details.

TIP You can add contact groups to the Contacts folder by using the Address Book. Rather than clicking New Contact in the Select The Entry Type dialog box, click New Contact Group. The new contact group appears in the Contacts folder alongside individual entries.

Viewing contact status and activities

After you create a contact in Outlook 2013, you can view it in the People Hub or open it in its own contact form. In the People Hub, you can see the contact's name, company, title, selected phone information, email address, and selected other information. To see a contact's full set of information, you must display the contact form. For contacts that have associated social networking accounts or information feeds from Facebook, LinkedIn, or SharePoint, you can also view status and activity information.

View social network feeds and status

1 At the bottom of the Folder pane, click the People icon to open the People Hub.

2 Select a contact that has an associated social network account.

3 In the Reading pane, click What's New.

4 View the news feed content for the contact.

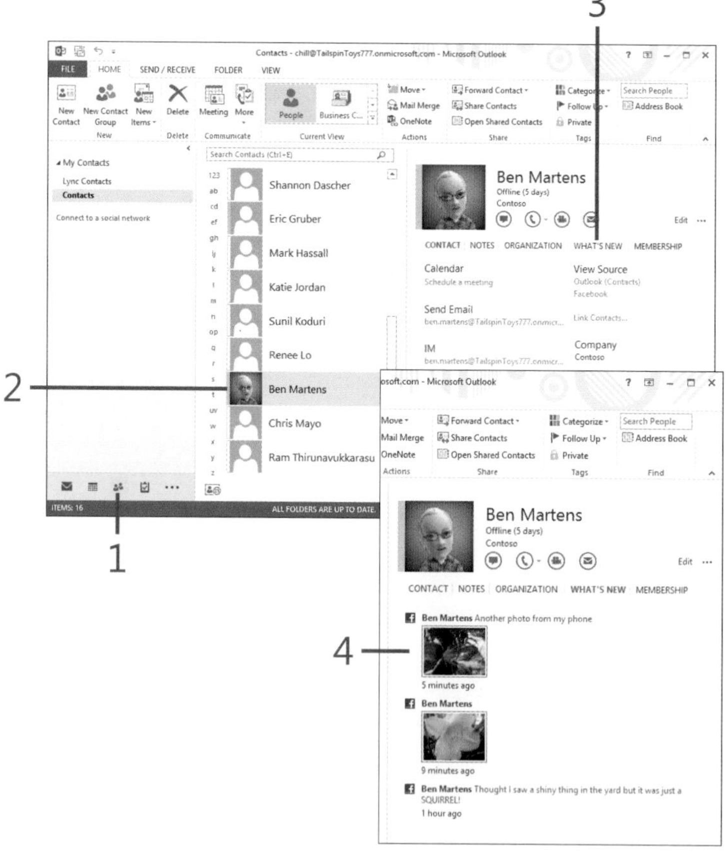

Use the Activities tab

1 At the bottom of the Folder pane, click the People icon to open the People Hub.

2 On the ribbon, click the View tab and then, in the Current View group, click the Change View button to choose a view other than the People view.

3 Double-click the contact name that you want to view.

(continued on next page)

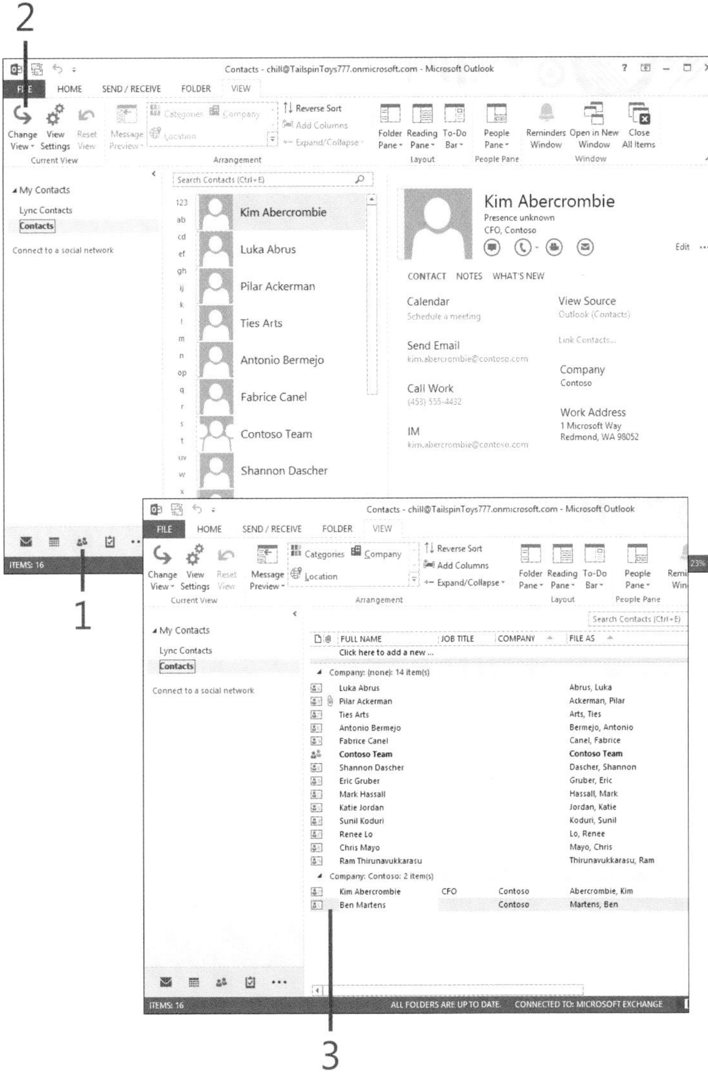

TIP The People pane must be open to show activities. If you don't see the list of activity categories, click the small up-arrow near the lower-right corner of the contact form to expand the People pane.

Use the Activities tab *(continued)*

4 Click to select the type of activities that you want to view.

5 Click or double-click to open an item (depending on its type).

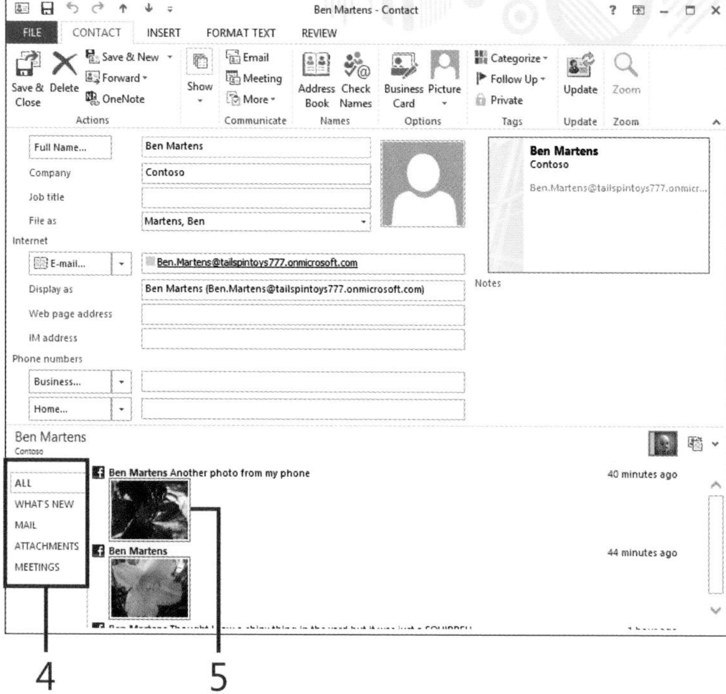

SEE ALSO For information about using contacts in email messages, see "Writing and sending email" on page 35.

TIP When you view contacts using the People, Business Card, or Address Cards views, you can click the letter buttons on the left side of the window to jump to contacts whose names start with that letter. For example, click the letter *m* to jump to contacts with the last names Mitchell, Mosley, and so on.

Finding a contact

You can search for contacts in Outlook 2013 by using Instant Search or the Find A Contact box—or simply by scrolling through the list of your contacts. You don't even have to know the complete name of the person you are looking for in Outlook because searching for part of a name brings up any name that matches that string.

Scroll through the Contacts folder

1. At the bottom of the Folder pane, click the People icon to open the People Hub.
2. In the People and Business Card views, use the scroll bar at the right side of the contact list to view other contacts.
3. On the ribbon, click the View tab and then, in the Current View group, click the Change View button to choose the Card view.
4. Move the scroll bar at the bottom of the window to scroll through your contacts.

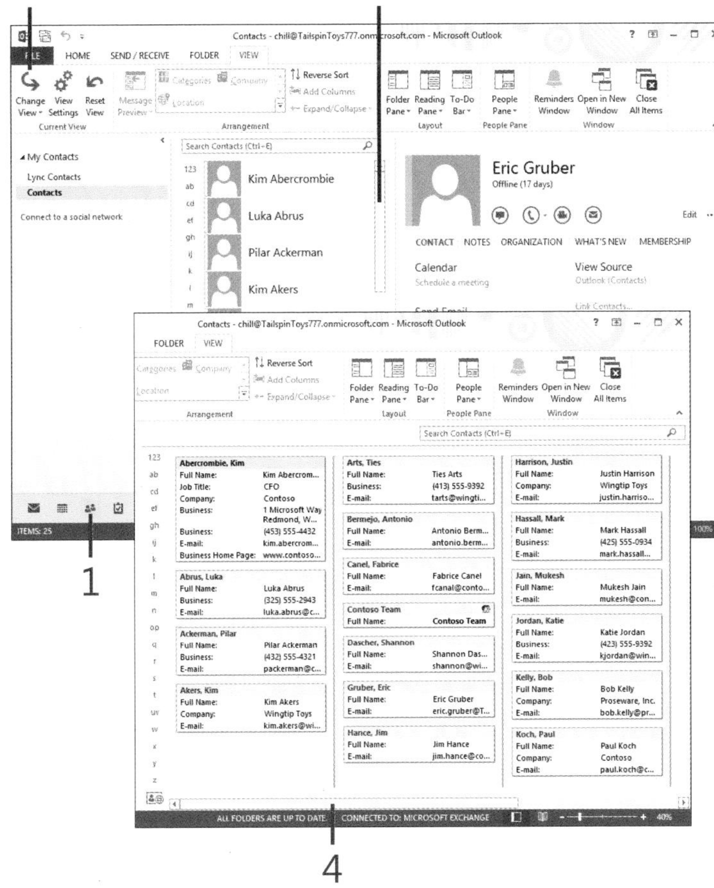

TIP If you press Delete after clicking a contact, you delete the contact. If this happens, press Ctrl+Z to undo the deletion.

TIP If your Contacts folder is really large, scrolling through the list of contacts isn't the most efficient way to locate a contact. Instead, use the Find A Contact box or Instant Search to locate the contact.

Use Instant Search

1. At the bottom of the Folder pane, click the People icon to open the People Hub.
2. Click in the Search box.
3. Type the name of the contact that you want to find.
4. Click the Search button.
5. View the contact.
6. Double-click the contact to open it.
7. Click X to clear the search.

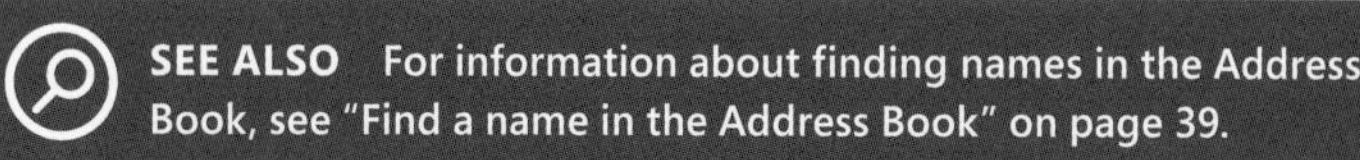

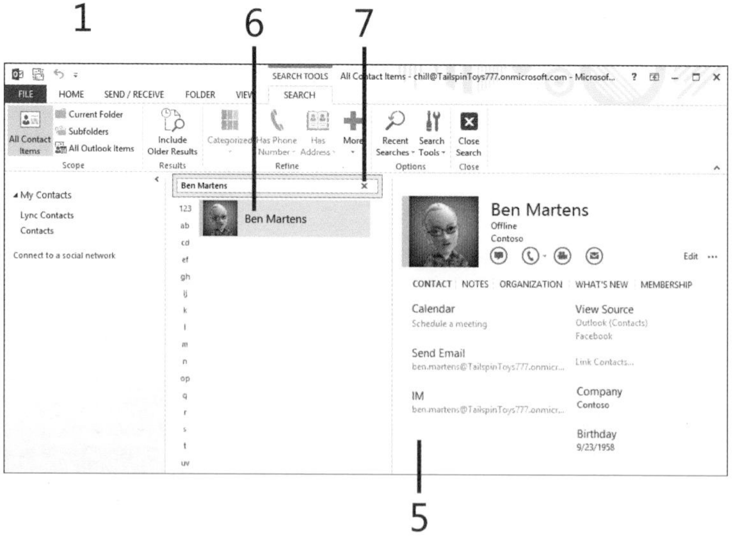

SEE ALSO For information about finding names in the Address Book, see "Find a name in the Address Book" on page 39.

TIP You don't have to click the Search button to see results. By default, Outlook is configured to show results as you type. You can turn this behavior on or off through Outlook's search options.

Use the Advanced Find dialog box

1 At the bottom of the Folder pane, click the People icon to open the People Hub.

2 Click in the Search box to display the Search Tools|Search contextual tab on the ribbon.

3 In the Options group, click the Search Tools button and then, on the drop-down menu that appears, click Advanced Find.

(continued on next page)

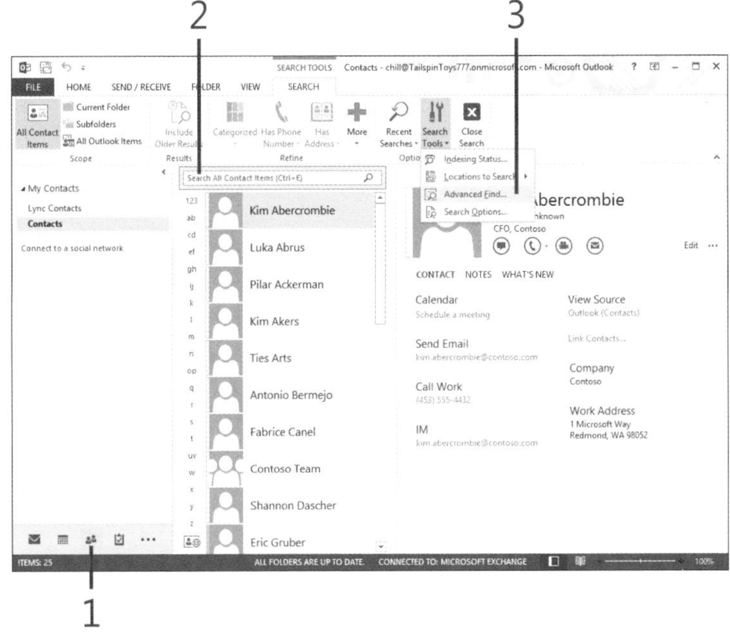

> **TIP** Click New Search to clear your search results so that you can begin a new one. Click OK when the prompt informs you that beginning a new search loses the results of the previous search. You can also use the Advanced Find dialog box to find contacts by using a number of search criteria. For example, you can search for contacts who have a specific email address or domain name in the email address. This is handy if you know that a contact has a domain name of @tailspintoys.com but aren't sure of her name or complete email address. Simply type **@tailspintoys.com** in the E-Mail field, and press Enter.

Use the Advanced Find dialog box *(continued)*

4 In the Advanced Find dialog box, type a word or phrase in the Search For The Word(s) field.

5 Select the fields in which to search.

6 Click Find Now to search for contacts matching the search criteria.

7 View the results of the search.

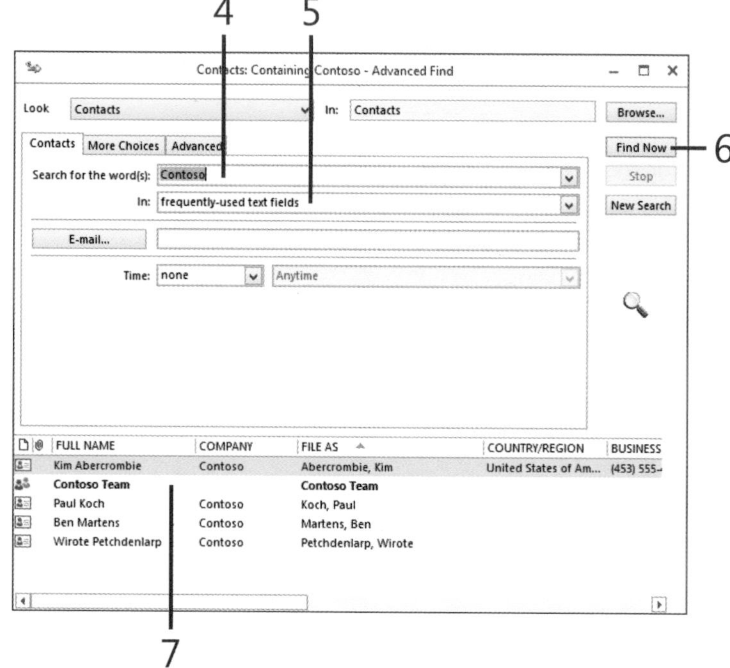

Map a contact

1 At the bottom of the Folder pane, click the People icon to open the People Hub. On the ribbon, click the Home tab and then, in the Current View group, click the Card or Business Card view.

2 Double-click the contact for which you want to display a map.

3 On the ribbon, click the Contact tab and then, in the Communicate group, click More and then click Map It. Or, click the Map It button to the right of the address field on the contact form.

(continued on next page)

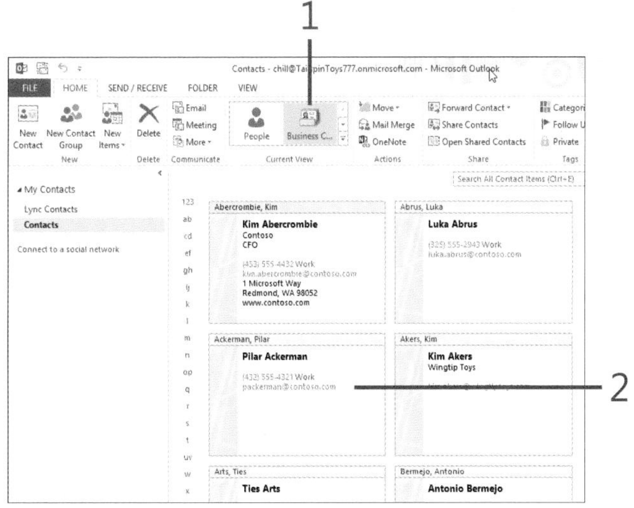

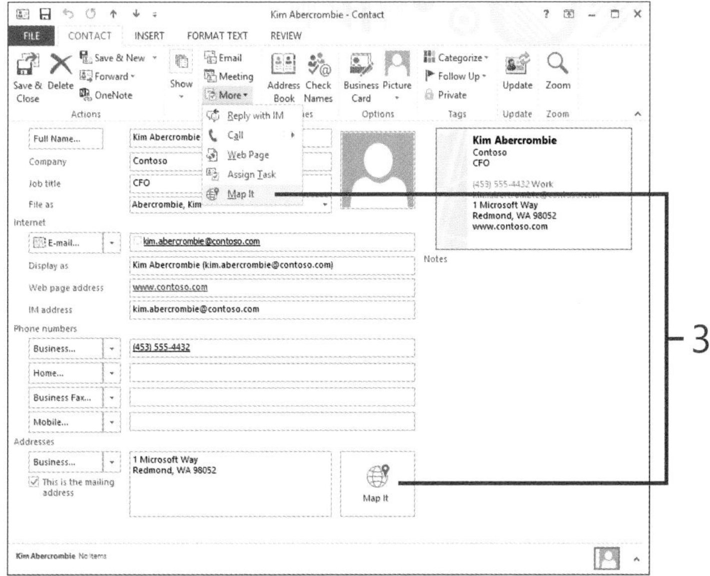

Map a contact *(continued)*

4 View the map in your web browser.

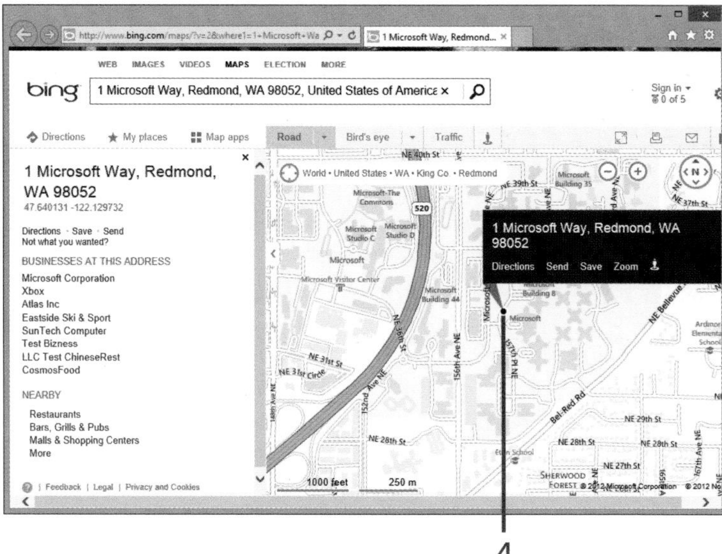

TIP To see a map for an address, you must have Internet access.

CAUTION Not all addresses are available from the Bing website. If you can't find the address you're looking for, modify the information you enter on the search webpage. Click the Search button to begin the search again.

Organizing your contacts

When you have only a few dozen or so contacts, finding and managing them is fairly easy. You can simply open the People Hub, scroll through the list, and find what you're looking for. However, after the Contacts folder grows, you need to organize your contacts to make them easier to find and update. Outlook 2013 gives you three ways to organize your contacts: you can use folders to store related contacts, use categories to set up relationships between contacts, or use views to sort contacts in ways that make sense to you.

Use folders

1. At the bottom of the Folder pane, click the People icon to open the People Hub.
2. Click the Folder tab.
3. Click New Folder.

(continued on next page)

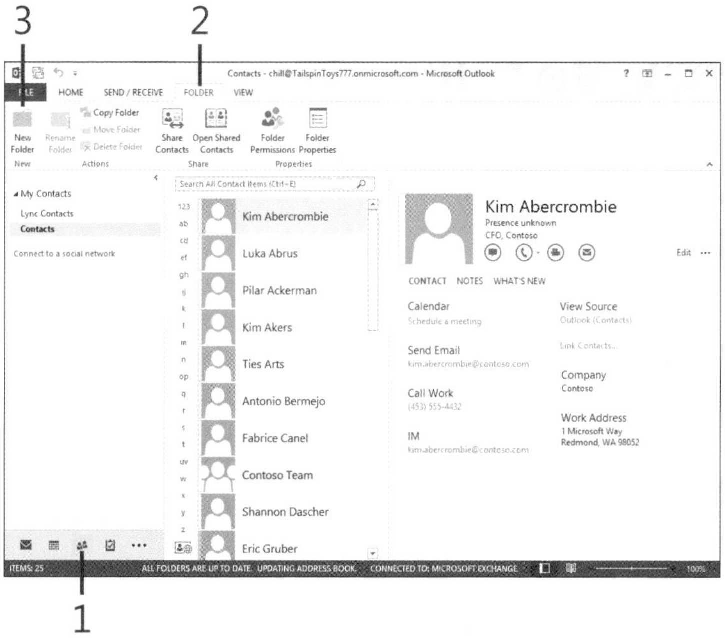

TRY THIS! After you create a folder for contacts, you can drag existing contacts to your new folder to organize them as necessary. For example, create a folder named "Project Team" in the Contacts folder. Open the Folder List in the folder pane so that you can see the new folder, but keep the focus on the Contacts folder. Drag members from your project team into the Project Team folder. You now can quickly see who is on your team by clicking this folder.

Use folders *(continued)*

4 In the Create A New Folder dialog box, type a name for the folder in the Name field.

5 Click the Folder Contains drop-down list and select Contact Items.

6 Choose the parent folder where the new folder will be created.

7 Click OK.

8 In the Folder pane, click the folder to view the newly created folder.

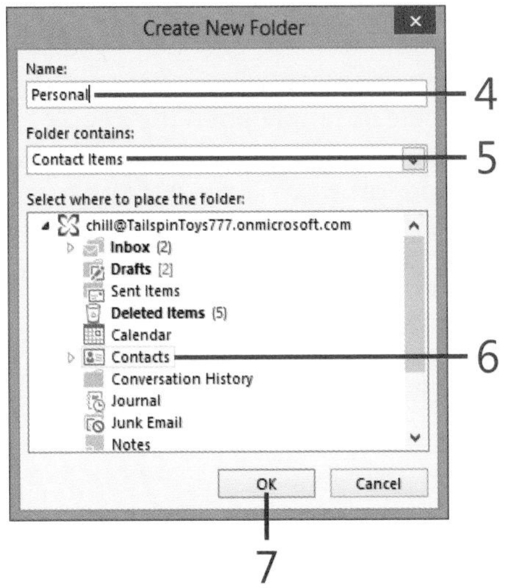

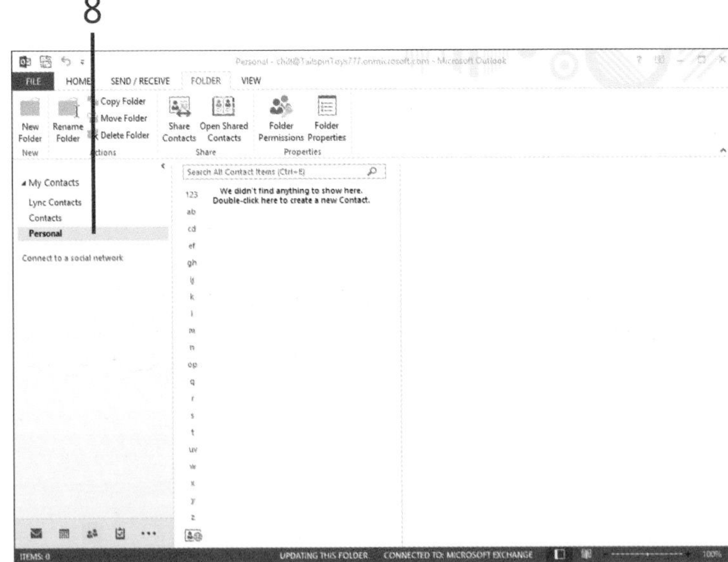

CAUTION When you create a new folder for contacts, ensure the Contact Items option is selected in the Folder Contains drop-down list.

TIP Your new contacts folder appears in the My Contacts area of the folder pane when you're in Contacts. You don't have to open the Folder List to access the additional contacts folders.

Use categories

1 At the bottom of the Folder pane, click the People icon to open the People Hub.

2 Right-click a contact and then, on the shortcut menu that appears, click Categorize.

3 Select the category to which you want the contact to belong.

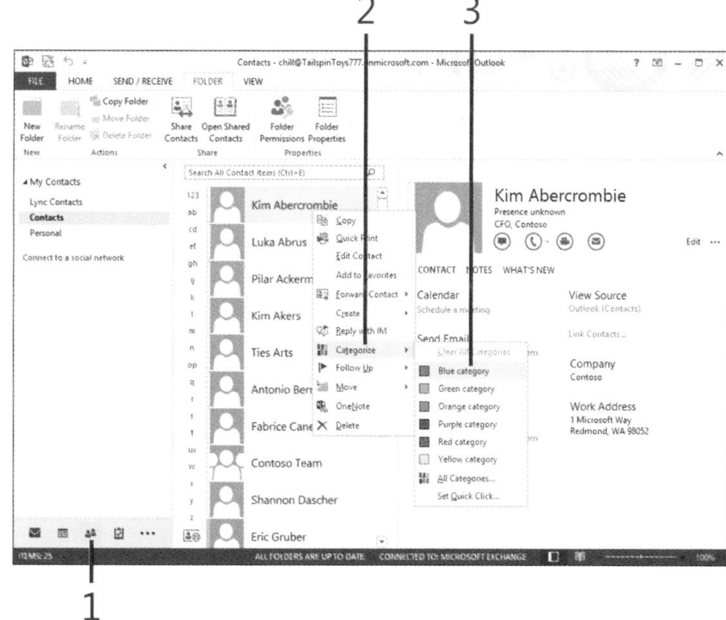

SEE ALSO For more information about Outlook Categories, see "Using categories" on page 212.

TIP You can add your own categories and modify existing ones. Choose Categorize from the Tags group on the Home tab and then choose All Categories to open the Color Categories dialog box, where you can add and modify categories.

Customizing People Hub and contact views

Outlook 2013 includes five different views of the People Hub. Each of these views gives you a different way to view your contacts. For example, the People view gives you a consolidated look at a contact's information, including data from social networking services such as Facebook, using a simplified form. The Card view displays your contacts as business cards and enables you to open the full contact item form. You can modify properties for each of these views to tailor the view to your needs.

Some views facilitate more customization than others, but the general process is the same. Common ways in which you can customize a view include adding a filter to define which contacts appear in the view, adding or removing fields, setting font characteristics, and using conditional formatting to make contacts appear with different fonts and colors, depending on criteria you specify.

Filter a view

1 In the People Hub, display the view that you want to customize.

2 On the View tab, in the Current View group, click View Settings.

(continued on next page)

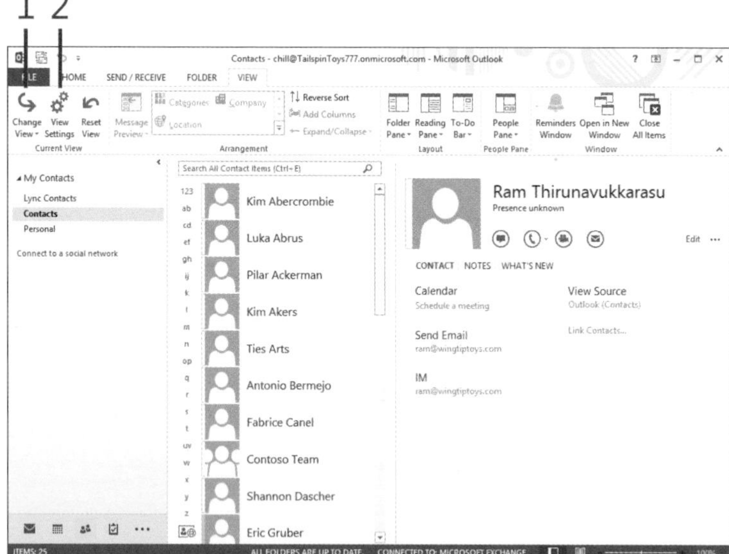

Filter a view *(continued)*

3 In the Advanced View Settings dialog box, click Filter to open the Filter dialog box.

4 Click in the Search For The Word(s) text box and type a search word or phrase.

5 Click OK to close the Filter dialog box.

6 Click OK to close the Advanced View Settings dialog box.

(continued on next page)

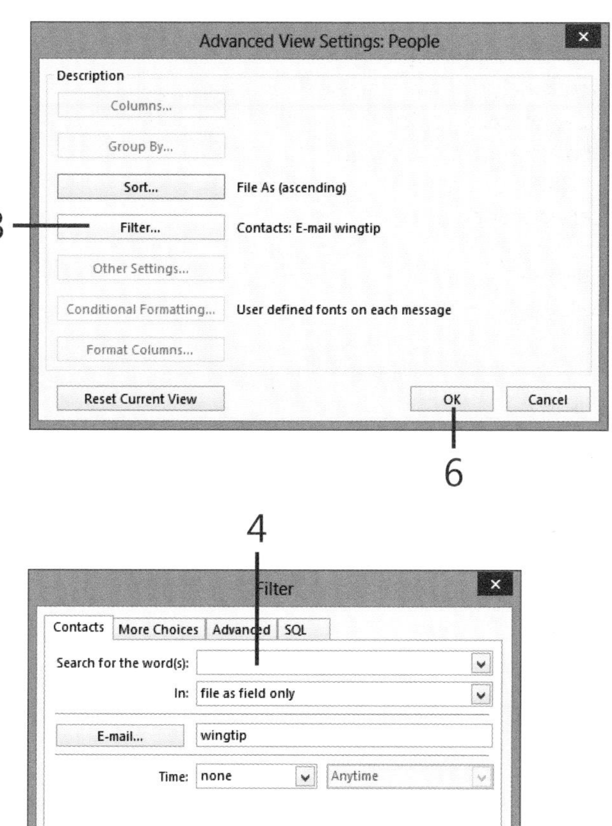

TIP To clear the filter on a view and restore its regular settings, click View Settings, click Filter, and then click Clear All. Then, click OK twice.

Filter a view *(continued)*

7 The view shows only items that match the filter criteria.

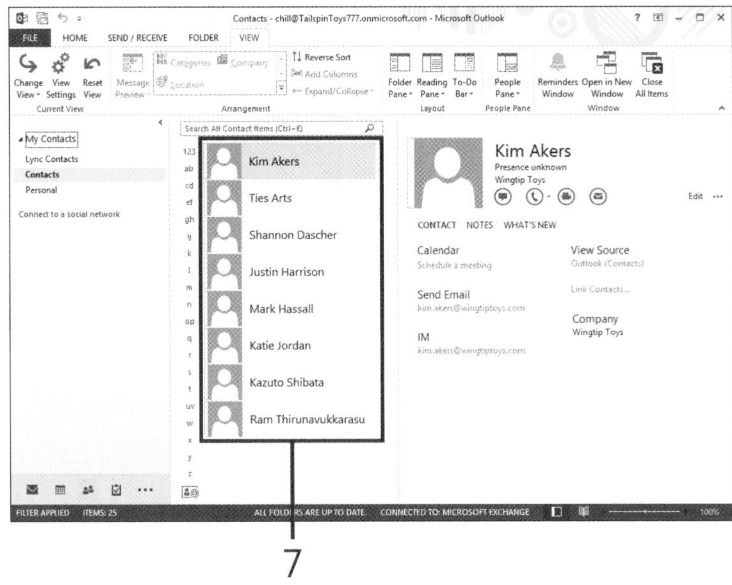

TRY THIS! Create a customized view by selecting Customize Current View from the Current View submenu. Click Filter and specify the filtering criteria for your custom view. For example, if you want Outlook to show only those contacts that have a specific email domain name, type that domain name in the E-Mail field.

View more fields in the contact form

1 Open the Card view from the Change View menu.

2 Double-click a contact to open its contact form.

(continued on next page)

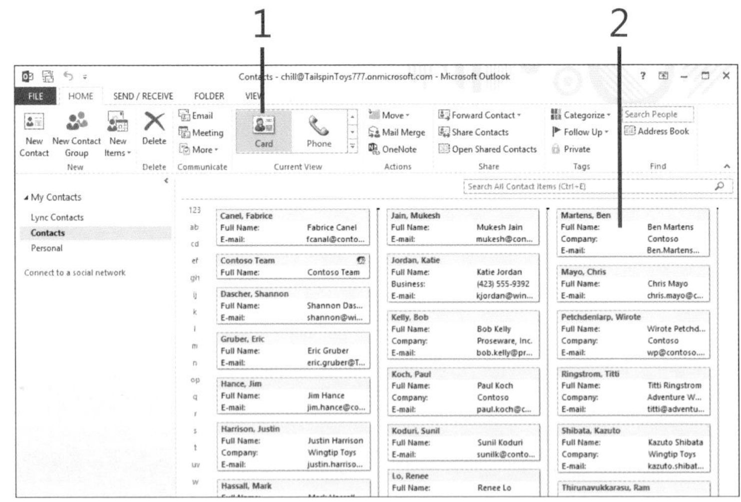

View more fields in the contact form *(continued)*

3 On the Contact tab, in the Communicate group, click the Show button.

4 In the drop-down list that appears, click Details.

5 Add content to other fields as desired.

(continued on next page)

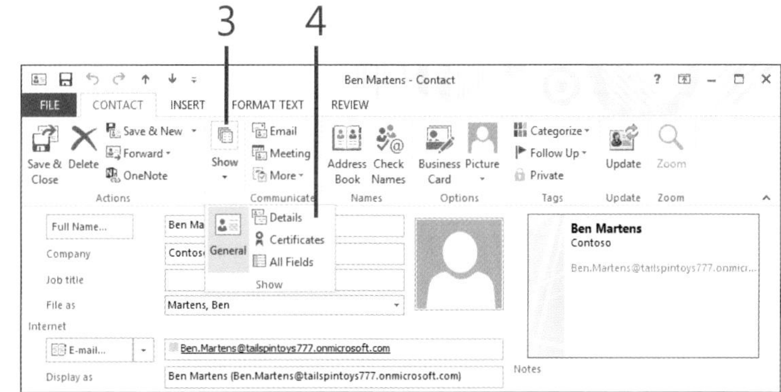

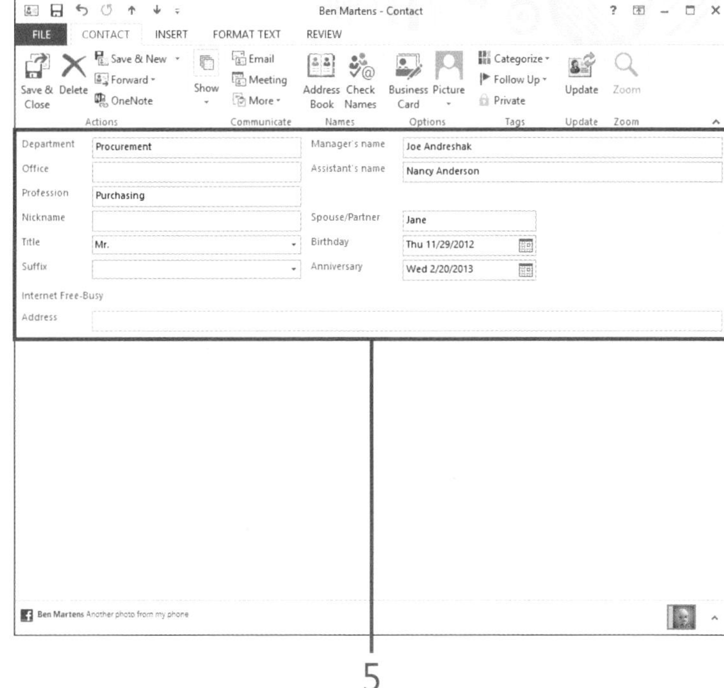

TIP You can create and use customized views in any Outlook folder, not just the Contacts folder.

View more fields in the contact form *(continued)*

6 Again, on the Contact tab, in the Communicate group, click the Show button and then, in the drop-down list that appears, choose All Fields.

7 In the Select From drop-down list, choose All Contact Fields.

8 Enter data in the resulting tabular view.

9 On the ribbon, click the Contact tab and then Save & Close.

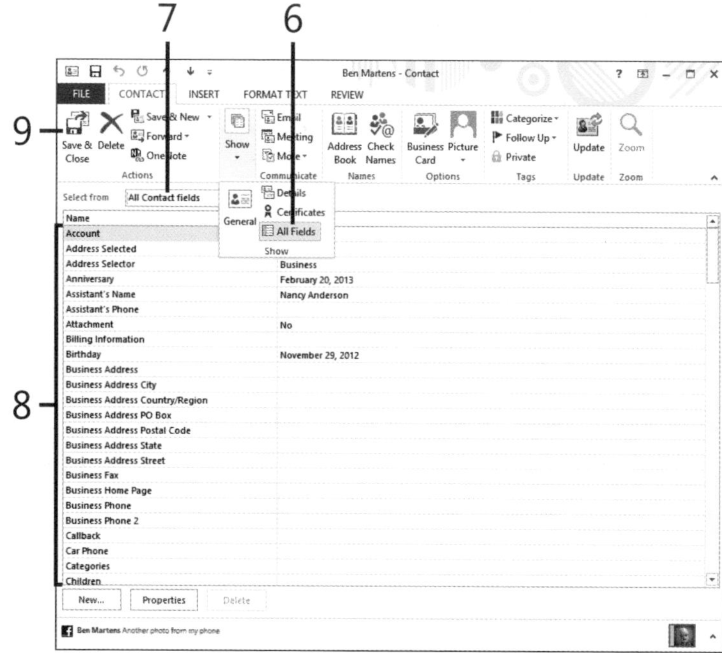

SEE ALSO For more information about sorting contacts, see "Organizing your contacts" on page 115.

TIP You can't view the Details or All Fields pages from the People view. Instead, you must open the contact from one of the other views and then choose the Details option from the Show menu on the ribbon.

Communicating with contacts

Outlook 2013 makes it easy to communicate with your contacts. You can open the Contacts folder and create a new email message while viewing a contact's address card, or you can use Outlook's phone dialing feature to call a contact. You can also initiate an instant message (IM) session with the contact if you have Microsoft Lync installed and running on your computer.

Send a contact by email

1. At the bottom of the Folder pane, click the People icon to open the People Hub.
2. If the Reading pane is not displayed, open it.
3. Click a contact.
4. In the Reading pane, click the Email button.

(continued on next page)

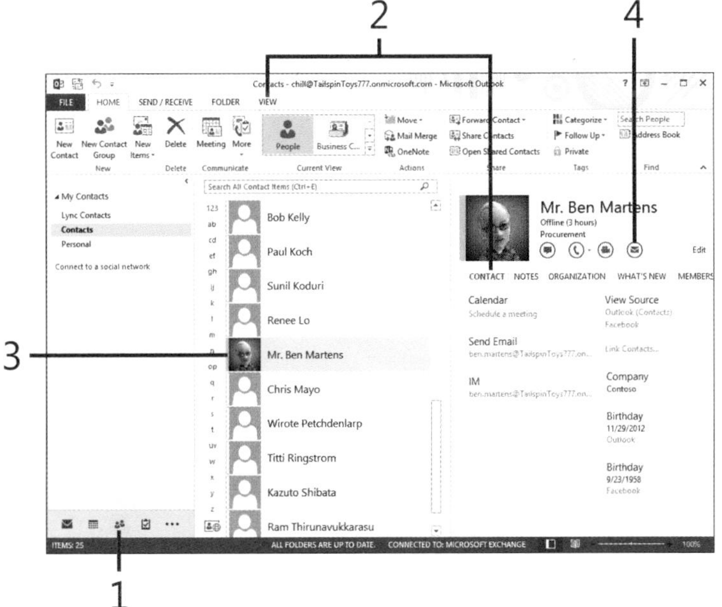

TIP To send a message to multiple contacts, press Ctrl as you click contact names in the Contact folder. Then, on the Home tab, click Email to open a new message for those contacts.

Send a contact by email *(continued)*

5 Type a subject in the Subject field.

6 Type your message.

7 Click Send.

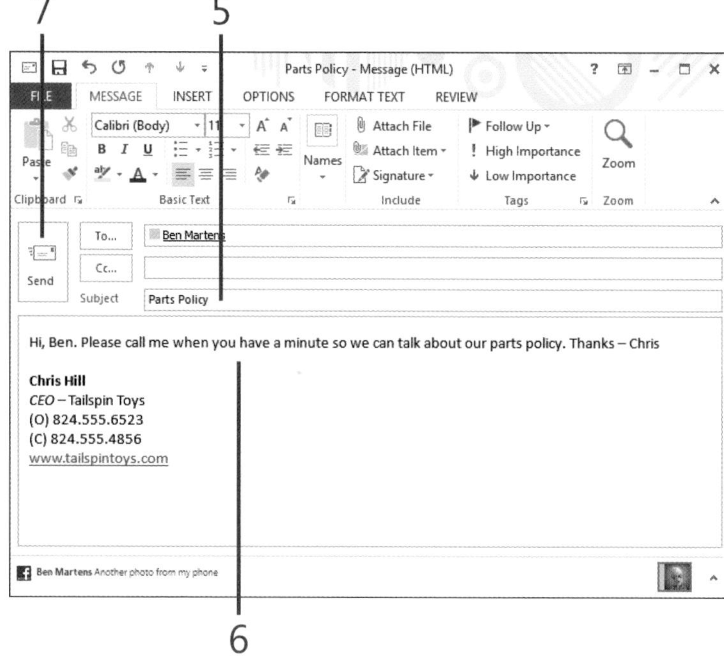

CAUTION If you select a contact that doesn't have an email address, you receive an error message that informing you of the problem or that another problem exists. You can click OK to continue, but you can't send the message to that contact until you provide a valid email address.

Phone or IM a contact

1 At the bottom of the Folder pane, click the People icon to open the People Hub.

2 Ensure that the Reading pane is displayed.

3 Click the contact that you want to call.

4 In the Reading pane, click the Phone button, or...

5 Click the small down-arrow beside the Phone button and choose a specific phone number to call.

6 Choose the number to call.

7 Select a person to whom you want to send an Instant Message, and note the green bar indicating that the contact is online.

8 In the Reading pane, click the Send An IM button.

(continued on next page)

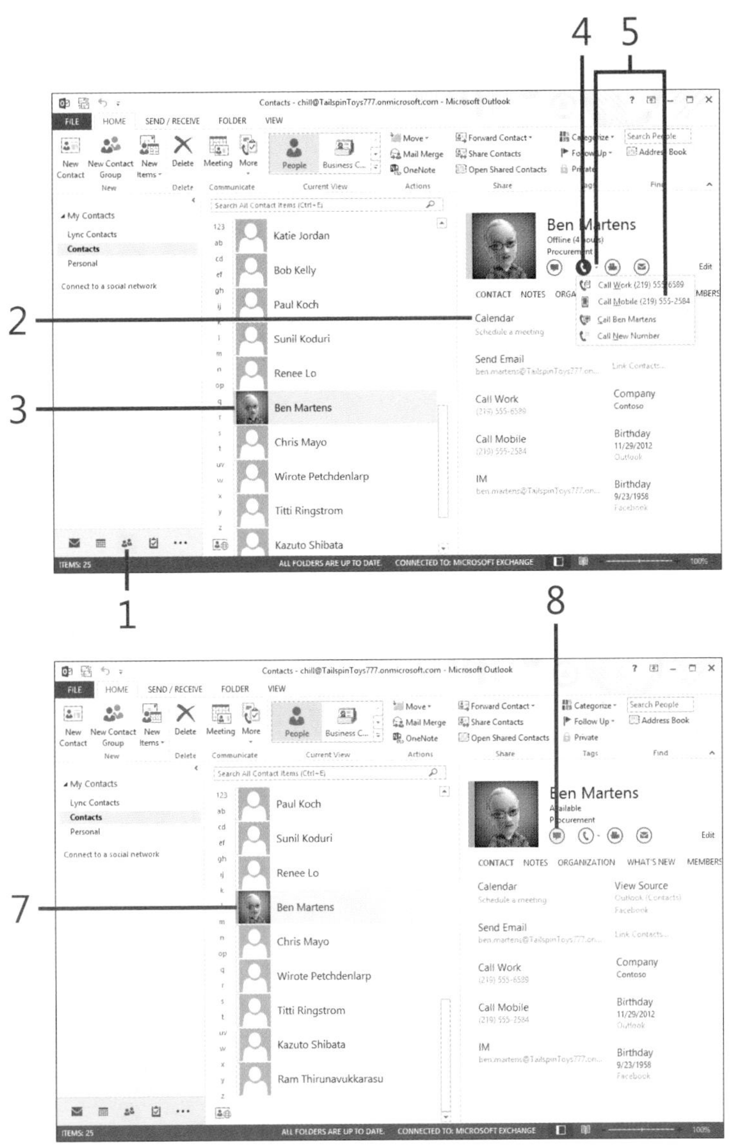

Phone or IM a contact *(continued)*

9 In Lync, type your message and press Enter.

10 View the response and continue the conversation.

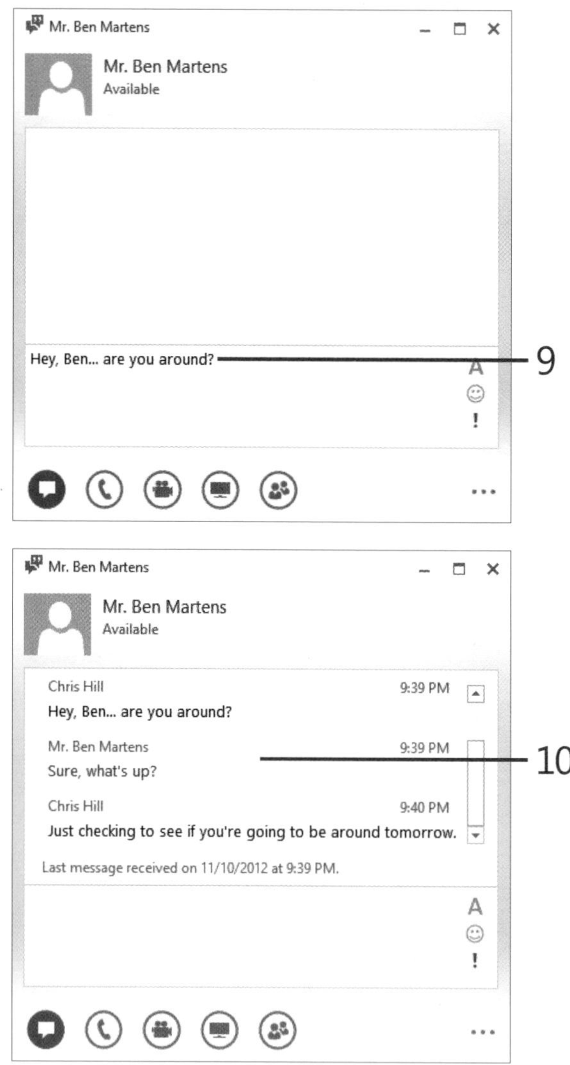

TIP If you are using Lync, configure your audio settings in Lync before you place a call through Outlook.

Managing a calendar

7

In this section:

- Viewing your calendar
- Using the To-Do Bar
- Adding appointments
- Adding and modifying events
- Adding meetings
- Modifying meetings and tracking responses
- Inserting Outlook items, documents, and Excel objects into calendar items
- Attaching a file or document to a calendar item
- Sharing calendar information
- Printing calendars

The Microsoft Outlook 2013 calendar simplifies the burden of keeping and maintaining a schedule of meetings, appointments, events, and tasks. At a glance, you can quickly see your agenda in daily, weekly, or monthly views. With Outlook, you won't have any excuses for missing a lunch date or forgetting a meeting.

You can use Outlook to keep track of recurring meetings or events so that you don't have to manually enter these items each time they take place. For example, you might have a weekly staff meeting that takes place every Friday from 9:00 to 10:00 A.M. Make it a recurring meeting, and Outlook blocks out that day and time. Similarly, if your PTA meets every third Tuesday of the month at 7:00 P.M., you can set Outlook to schedule that meeting, as well.

Outlook includes an alert that displays a message prior to your calendar meeting, appointment, or task so that you won't forget it. For example, you can set up Outlook to display a reminder of an upcoming meeting two or three days before its occurrence. If you need to prepare a presentation, document, or other item for the meeting, you give yourself ample time to do so. You then can "snooze" the reminder so that it gets your attention again later, but perhaps only three hours prior to the meeting.

Viewing your calendar

You can view your Outlook 2013 calendar in several different formats. Day view is an hour-by-hour view of your daily schedule, whereas Month view shows your schedule for the entire month. The Date Navigator is a small calendar with which you can navigate quickly to a specific day, week, or month. The To-Do Bar consolidates all of the features of task list, Date Navigator, and appointment list into one task pane.

Use the calendar views and Date Navigator

1 At the bottom of the Folder pane, click the Calendar icon.

2 View the week's meetings and appointments.

3 To display the current day in the current view, click Today.

(continued on next page)

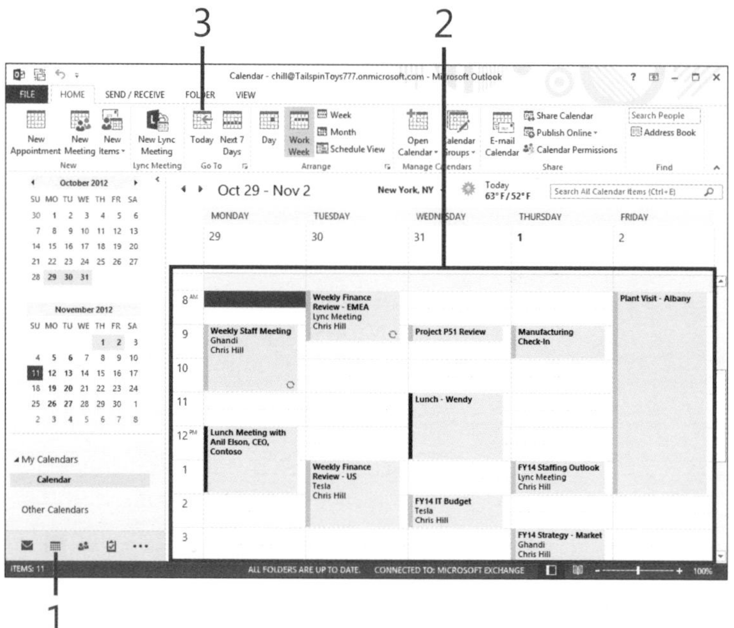

TIP You can access the current, last three, and next three months by clicking the month name in the Date Navigator. This is handy if you want to jump back a few months or jump forward a month or two.

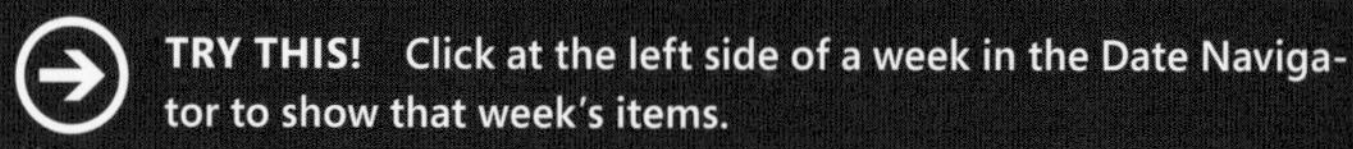

TRY THIS! Click at the left side of a week in the Date Navigator to show that week's items.

Use the calendar views and Date Navigator *(continued)*

4 In the Date Navigator, click a different date.

5 To view the selected day's appointments and meetings, click Day.

(continued on next page)

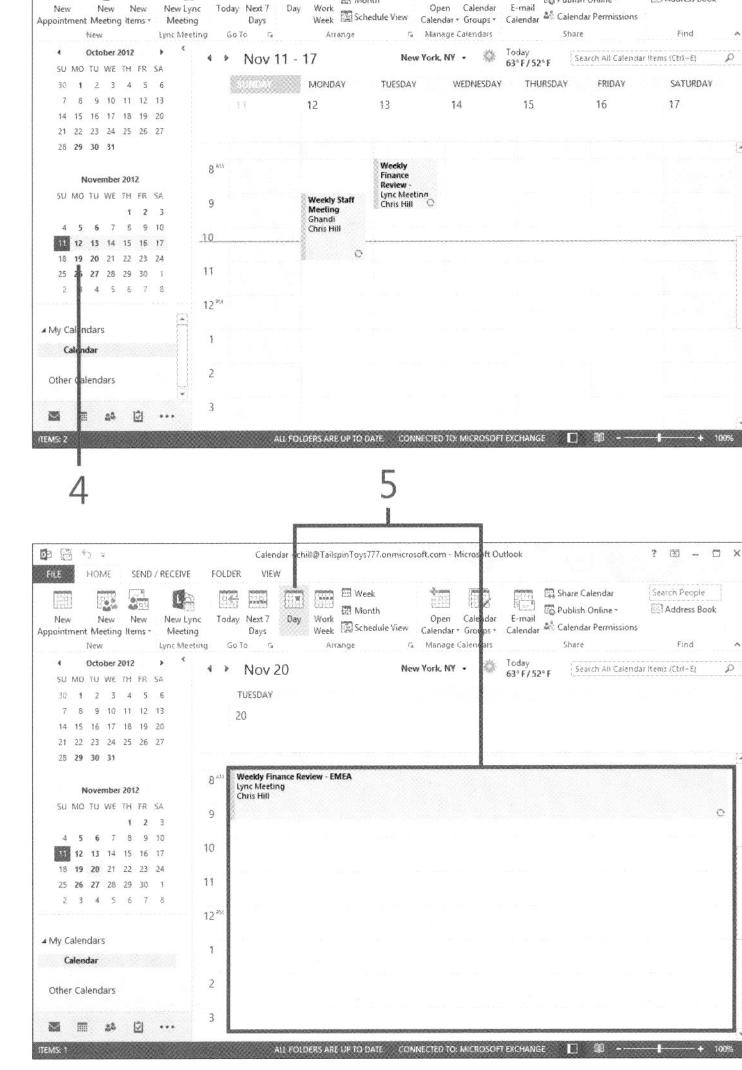

TIP You can make more room available for the Calendar pane on the screen by resizing or minimizing the Folder pane.

TRY THIS! To return to today's date, right-click inside a view and then, on the shortcut menu that appears, click Today.

Use the calendar views and Date Navigator *(continued)*

6 Click Month to see a month's schedule.

7 The displayed date range is highlighted in the Date Navigator.

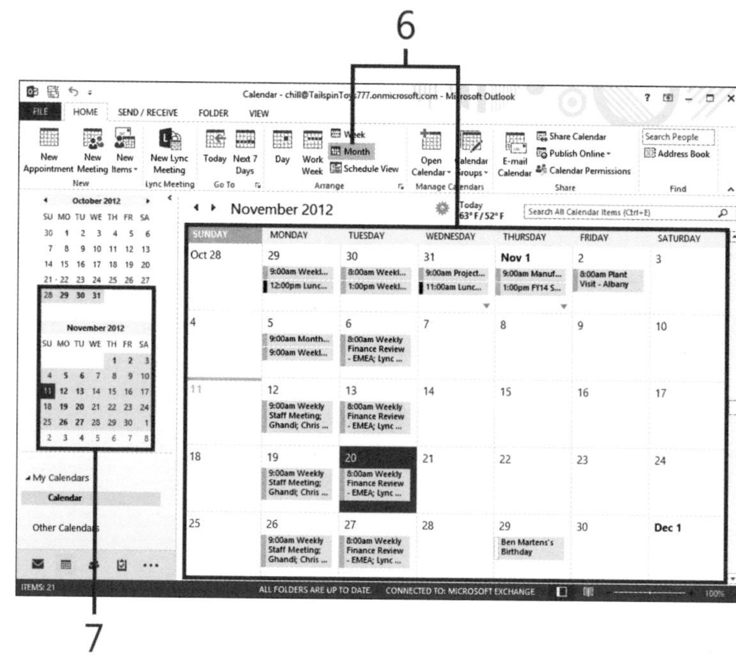

Using the To-Do Bar

The To-Do Bar lets you view other information in the Calendar view as well as calendar items. In addition to showing a small calendar, you can use to choose a day to view (in place of the Folder pane, for example). You can also view contacts that you have added to your Favorites as well as upcoming tasks.

Use the To-Do Bar

1 On the ribbon, click the View tab.
2 In the Layouts group, click To-Do Bar and then, in the drop-down list that appears, choose Calendar
3 Any items for the current day appear in the To-Do Bar.
4 Again, in the Layouts group, click To-Do Bar and then, in the drop-down list that appears, choose People.

(continued on next page)

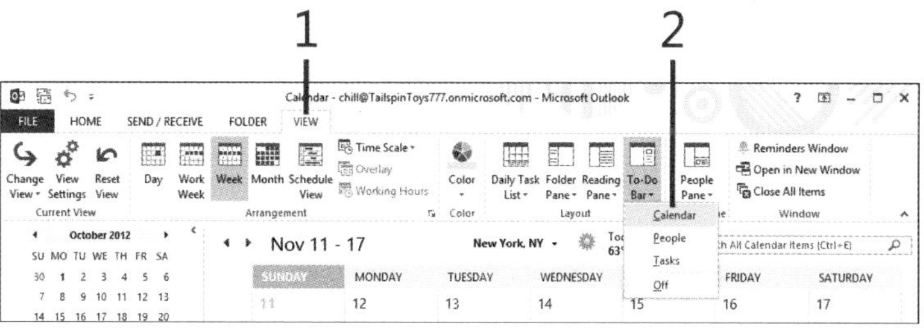

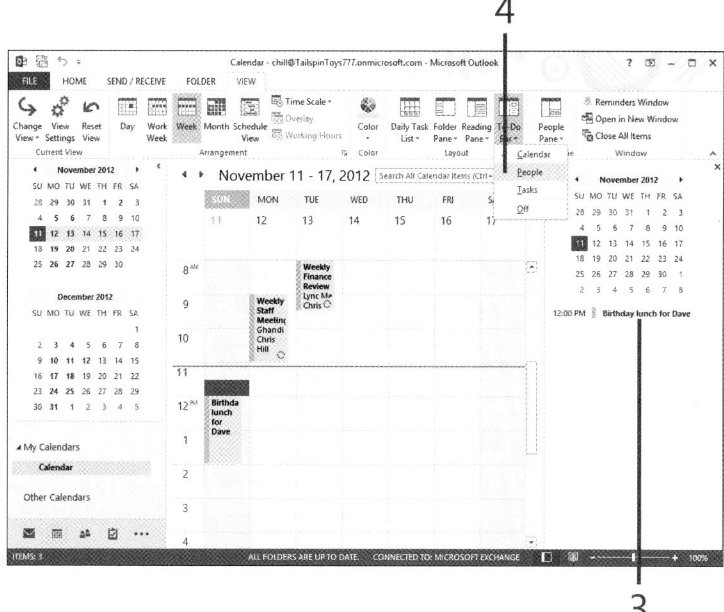

TIP Choose the Minimized option from the To-Do Bar submenu to make the To-Do Bar automatically hide at the edge of the Outlook window.

Use the To-Do Bar *(continued)*

5 People that you have added as favorites appear in the To-Do Bar.

6 Use the Search People text box to search for contacts.

7 In the Layouts group, click To-Do Bar and then, in the drop-down list that appears, choose Tasks.

8 Double-click a task to open it.

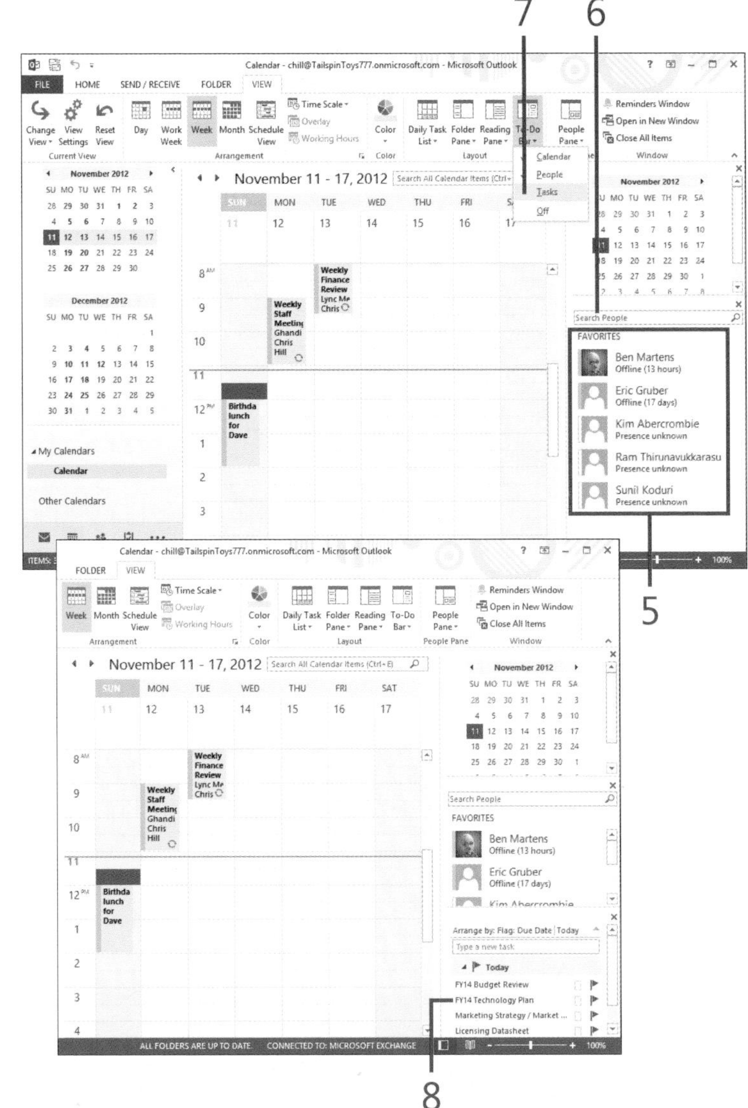

> **TIP** Depending on the options you set for the To-Do Bar, portions of the Appointments or Tasks areas of the To-Do Bar might be blank.

Adding appointments

An appointment in Outlook 2013 is an activity you enter for a specific time that, unlike a meeting, doesn't typically involve other people or resources. When you schedule an appointment, you block out a day, a time, and a location for that appointment to occur. As mentioned earlier, Outlook also lets you set a reminder that flashes on your screen and plays a sound to alert you to the appointment. To learn how to set a reminder, see page 164.

Add an appointment with the menu

1 Select a block of time for the appointment.

2 On the Home tab, in the New group, click New Appointment.

(continued on next page)

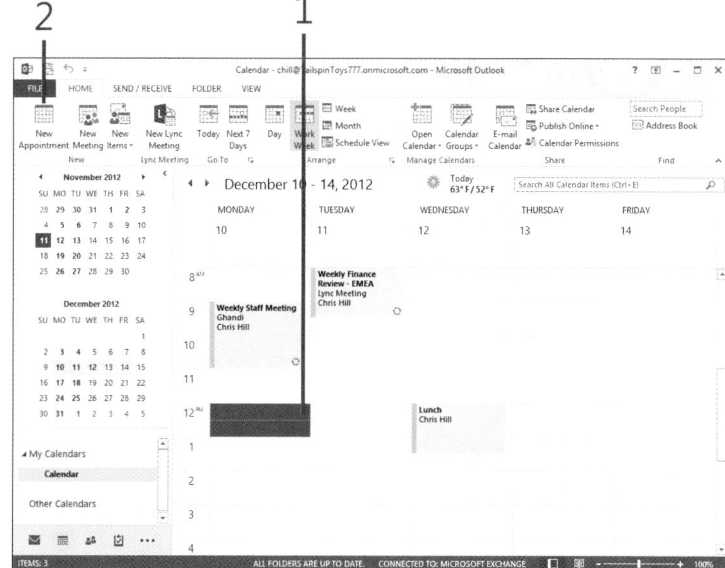

TIP Keep your appointment subjects as short as possible so that they're easy to read in the Calendar view.

Add an appointment with the menu *(continued)*

3 Type a subject.

4 Type the location of the appointment.

5 Adjust the date and times, if needed.

6 Add notes if you want.

7 Click the Save & Close button.

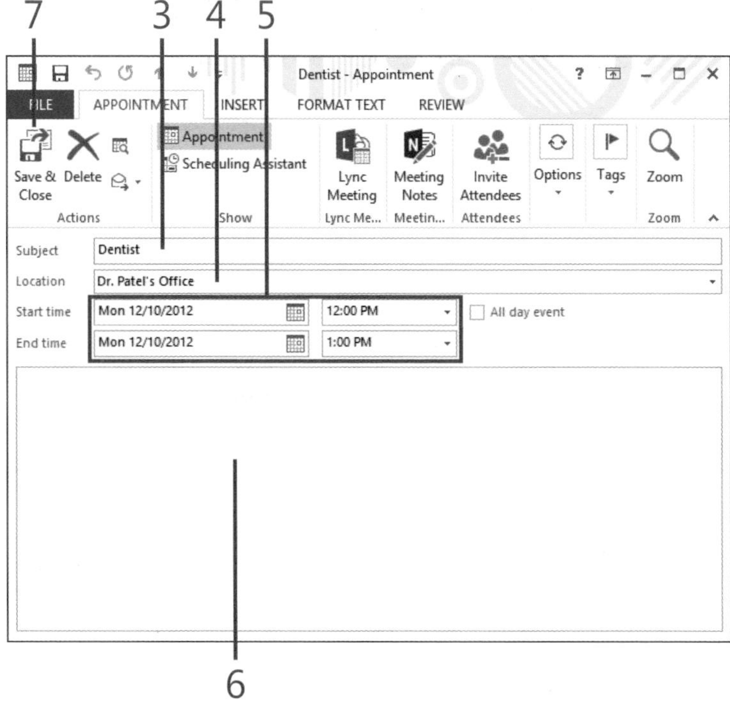

TRY THIS! If you'd like to add extended information about an appointment, click in the text area at the bottom of the Appointment window. Type a longer description here, such as directions to the appointment location, important information about the appointment, and so on.

Add an appointment right on the calendar

1 On the calendar, drag to select a block of time for the appointment.
2 Type the subject of the appointment and press Enter.
3 Double-click the appointment to open the appointment form.
4 Add the location, notes, and other information to the appointment.
5 Click the Save & Close button.

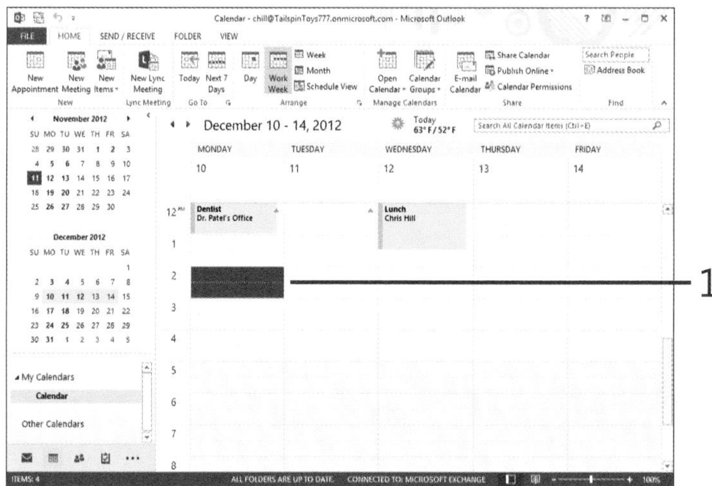

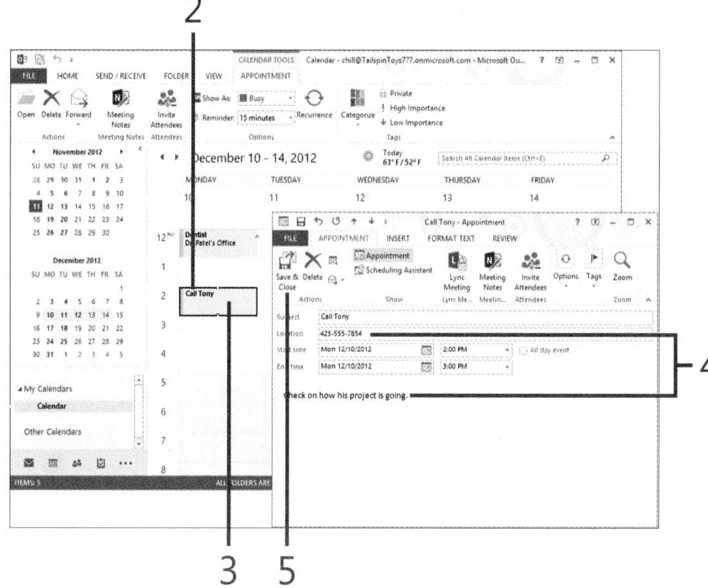

TIP If you use Outlook with a Microsoft Exchange Server account, others can easily see your free/busy time. They will know when you're busy and can schedule meetings with you based on this information.

TRY THIS! To categorize the appointment, right-click the appointment, point to Categorize, and then, on the submenu that appears, click a category.

Adding and modifying events

In Outlook 2013, an event is an activity that runs for 24 hours or longer. An example of an event is a weeklong conference or seminar that you attend. Events display as banners at the top of the day and run from midnight to midnight, so they don't take up blocks of time on the calendar. This display method leaves room in your calendar for you to show appointments or meetings that you might schedule during event days.

Add the event

1 On the Home tab, in the Arrange group, click Work Week.

2 On the calendar, select one or more days.

3 Type the subject for the event.

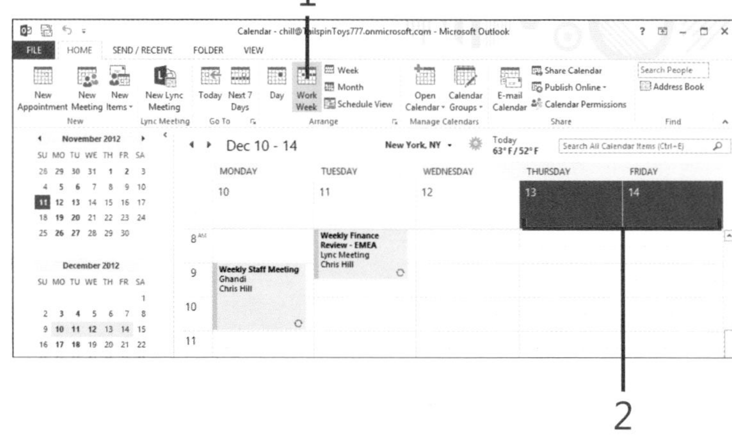

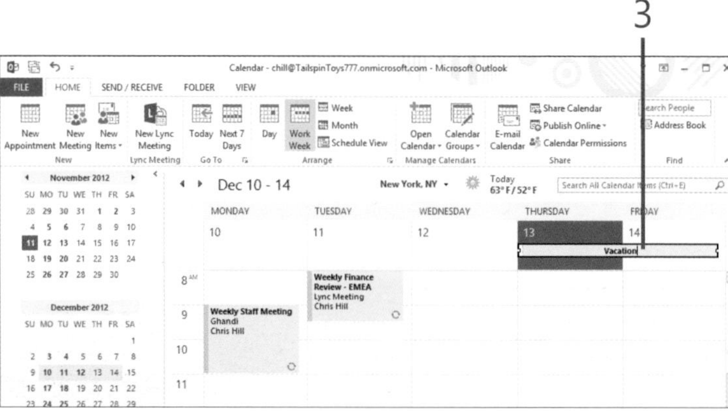

TIP To add an all-day event to a day other than the current day, display the week or month, right-click the day, and then, on the shortcut menu that appears, click New All Day Event.

TRY THIS! You can add more information about an event to the text area at the bottom of the Event window.

Modify an event

1. Double-click the event to open it.
2. Change details of the event as needed.
3. Choose a free/busy option.
4. Click Save & Close.
5. The selected days now show as Out Of Office (purple).

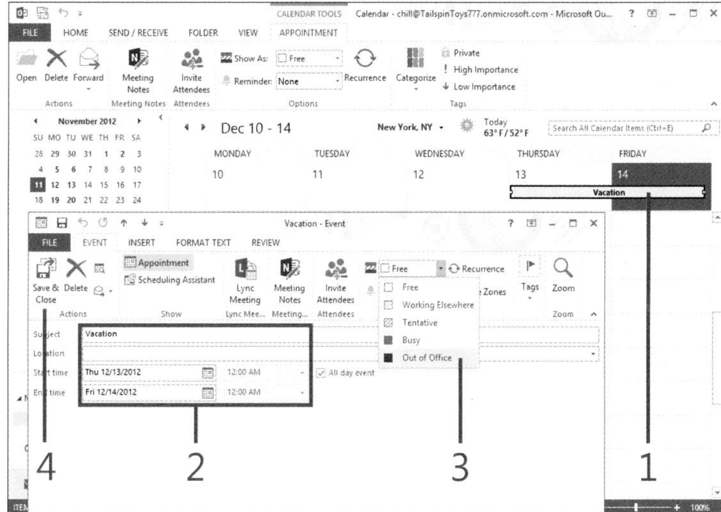

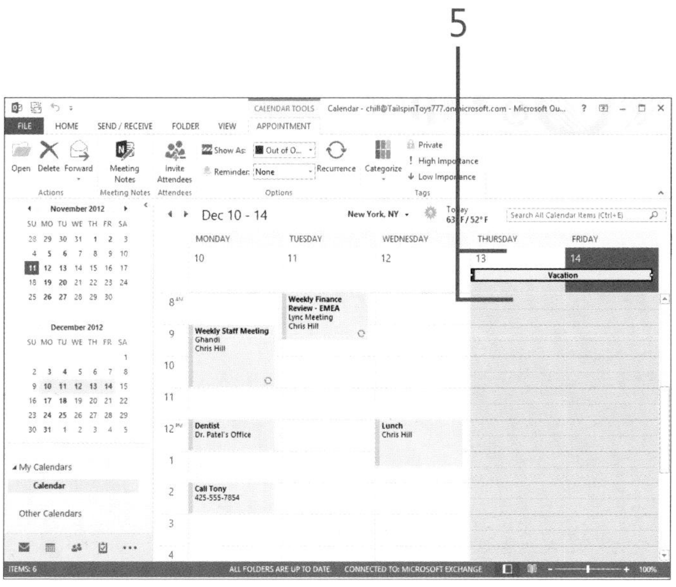

TIP You might already have events entered in your Calendar folder without even knowing it. When you create a new contact in the Contacts folder and include a birthday or anniversary for the contact, Outlook schedules that date as an event in the calendar.

SEE ALSO For information about setting up contacts, see "Working with contacts" on page 41.

Adding meetings

A meeting is an activity (often a physical meeting or conference call) that involves other people and sometimes resources. A resource can be a conference room, VCR, slide projector, telephones, laptop computer, or other equipment. Usually, a meeting involves you and at least two other people (but can certainly be just you and one other person). Outlook sends a meeting invitation to every person you designate, and they can accept or reject the request or propose a new time for the meeting.

Create a meeting

1 At the bottom of the Folder pane, click the Calendar icon to open the Calendar folder.

2 Select a date.

3 Select a block of time for the meeting.

4 On the Home tab, in the New group, click New Meeting.

(continued on next page)

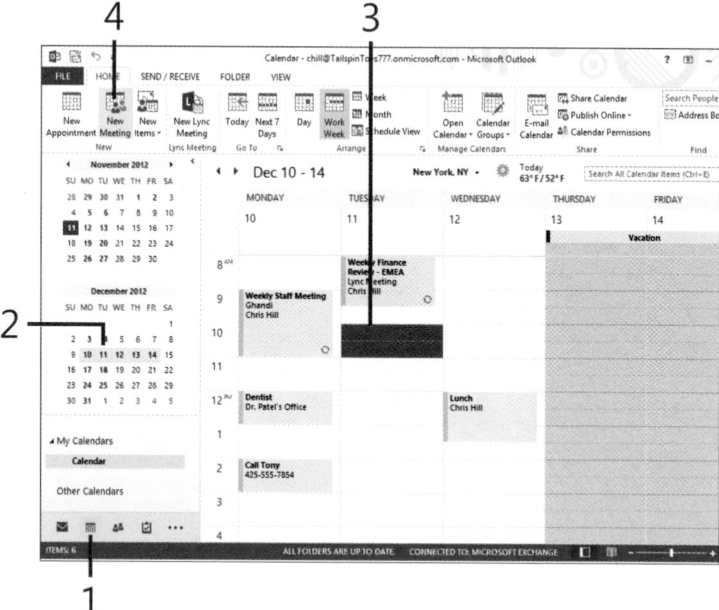

TIP You can use the Scheduling Assistant to help you find a time that is open for all invitees, and you can also identify available resources. To switch to the Scheduling Assistant view, on the Meeting tab, in the Show group, click Scheduling Assistant. Plus, as a follow-up, you can use the Tracking button on the Meeting tab to see which attendees have responded to your meeting request.

Create a meeting *(continued)*

5 Click To.

6 In the Select Attendees And Resources dialog box, choose the attendees and resources from the Address Book, or type the addresses manually.

7 If the invitee must attend, click Required.

8 If the invitee isn't required to attend, click Optional.

9 Click OK when you are done.

10 In the Subject box, type a description of the meeting.

11 Add notes, directions, or comments for the meeting as needed.

12 Choose a room, or type the location of the meeting in the Location box.

13 Click Send.

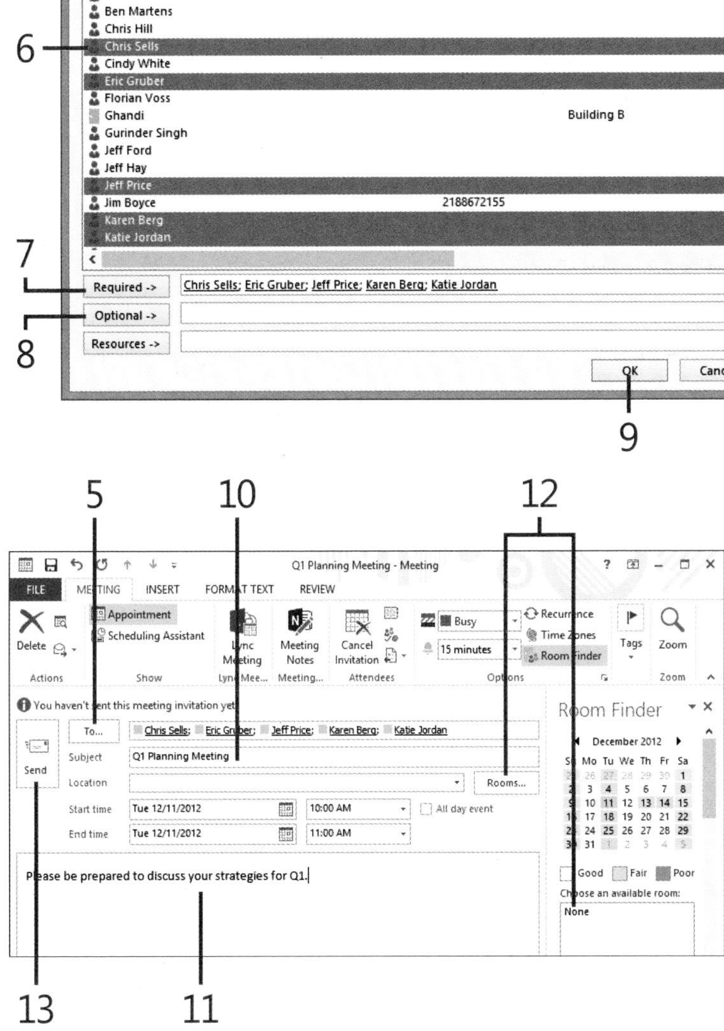

> **CAUTION** Make sure that your attendee list has correct email addresses. If you attempt to send the meeting request to someone not in one of your address books, Outlook informs you that the person can't be validated.

> **TIP** When you type your meeting subject, keep it short but descriptive. "Team Meeting" might not be enough if people are members of multiple teams. Use something specific like "Development Team Meeting" for your description.

Modifying meetings and tracking responses

After you create a meeting in Outlook 2013, you can add or remove attendees, add notes and attachments, change it to an online meeting, and make other changes. You can make these same types of changes with a new meeting invitation before you save it. You can also track which invitees have responded to your meeting invitation to find out who will attend.

Edit a meeting

1 Open an existing meeting.

2 Change attendees, subject, and location for the meeting, as needed.

3 Add notes or attach documents if needed.

4 Click Send Update to send an updated meeting invitation.

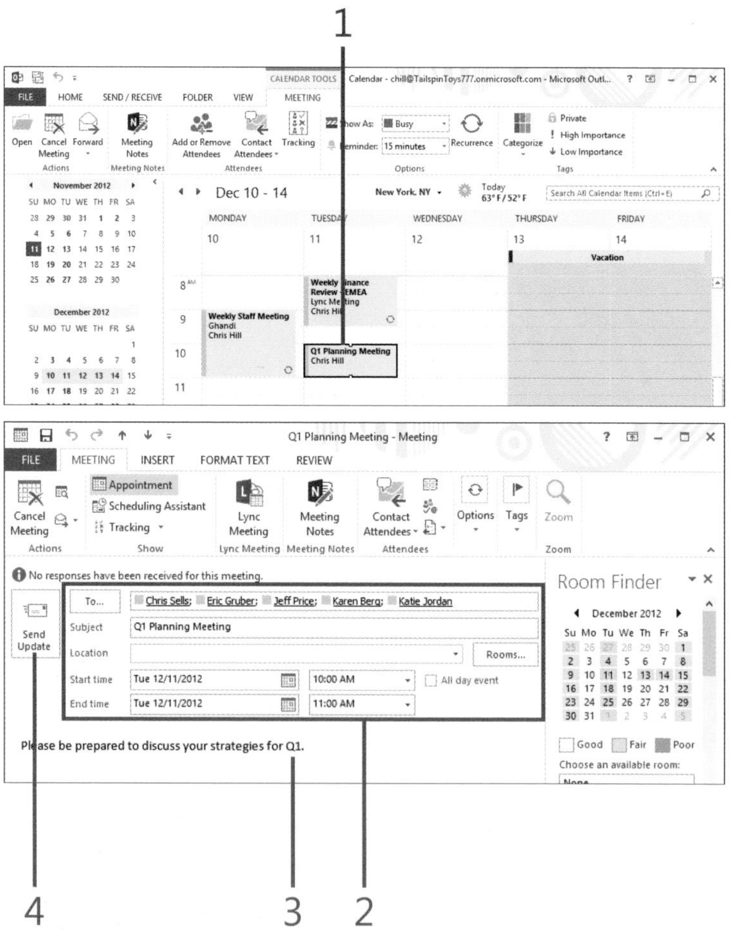

TIP You can reschedule a meeting simply by dragging it to a new location on the calendar. Regardless of the method you use to move the meeting, Outlook can automatically send an update to all attendees that includes a notice of the new day and time.

Track attendee responses

1. Open an existing meeting request. Then, on the Meeting tab, in the Show group, click Scheduling Assistant.
2. View attendees' free/busy times and adjust meeting day and time as needed.
3. Again, on the Meeting tab, in the Show group, click Tracking.
4. View response status for each attendee.
5. View online status.
6. On the ribbon, on the Meeting tab, click Appointment to return to the Appointment page, and then click Send Update.

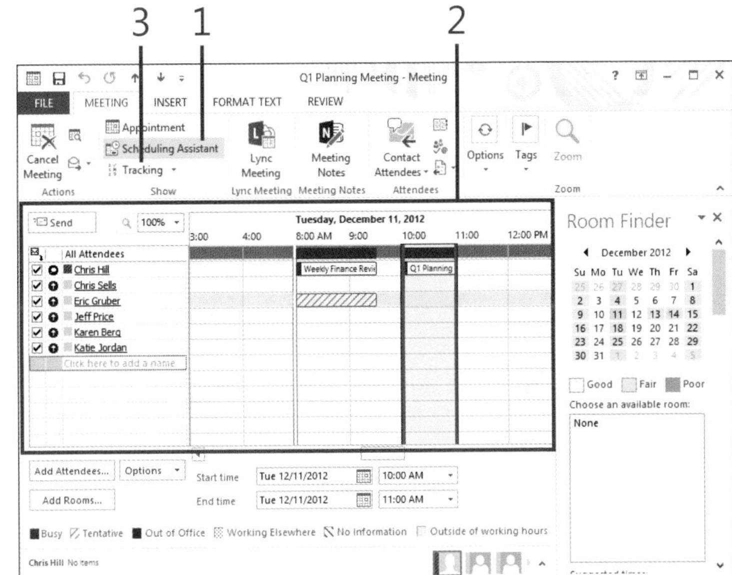

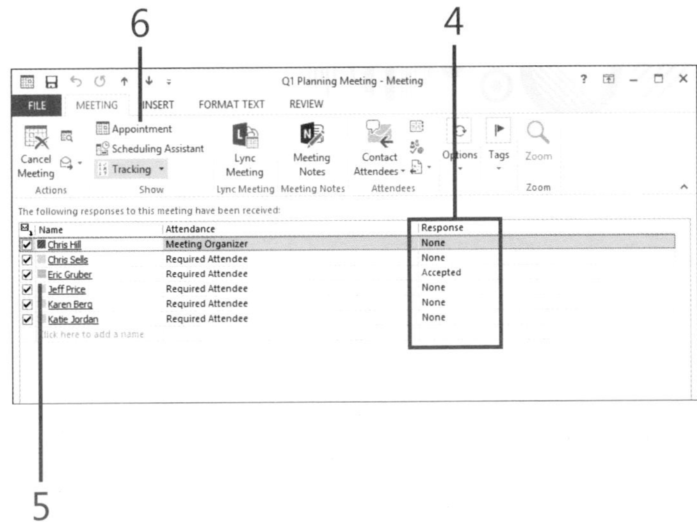

SEE ALSO For information about the Address Book and adding new contacts, see "Working with contacts" on page 41.

TIP Outlook provides the Scheduling Assistant to help you set up meetings with other people in your organization. The Scheduling Assistant lets you see other people's schedules if they have mailboxes in the same Exchange Server environment.

Inserting an Outlook item into a calendar item

In Outlook 2013, you can insert objects, files, and Outlook items into your calendar items. The capability to insert Outlook items means that you can insert contacts, email messages, and other Outlook items into an appointment, meeting, or event item. For example, if you are having a meeting to discuss a project with an outside partner, you can insert the partner's contact(s) into the meeting invitation so that other attendees will have them.

Add an Outlook item

1 With an appointment, meeting, or event open, on the ribbon, click the Insert tab.

2 In the Include group, click Outlook Item.

(continued on next page)

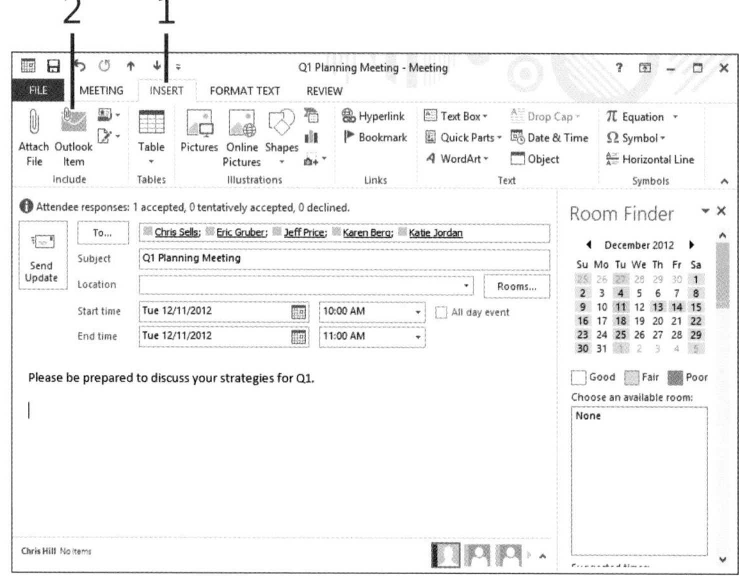

> **TIP** Outlook uses an item-specific icon to indicate the type of Outlook item that you can insert, such as a note icon for a note item or calendar icon for a calendar item.

Add an Outlook item *(continued)*

3 In the Insert Item dialog box, select the Outlook folder in which the item is stored.

4 Select the Outlook item thatyou want to insert from the Items list.

5 Click OK.

6 The selected item now appears in the comment field.

7 Click the Meeting, Appointment, or Event tab and then click Save & Close (for an appointment or event) or Send Update (for a meeting).

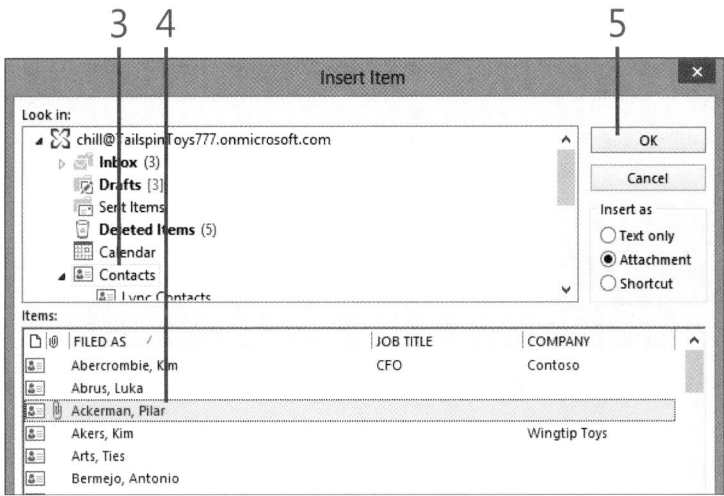

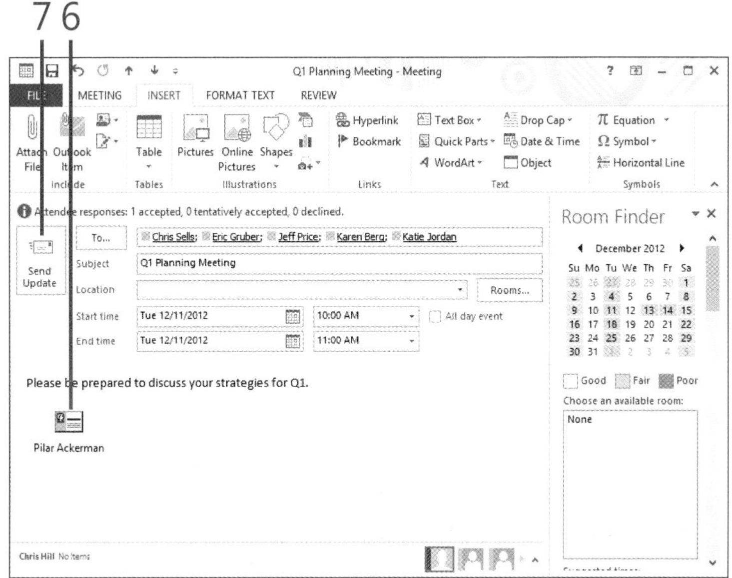

TRY THIS! To insert the text contained in a contact rather than the contact address card itself, in the Insert Item dialog box, select the Text Only option.

Attaching a file or document to a calendar item

In many situations, you might want to attach a document or other type of file to an Outlook 2013 calendar item. For example, if you are meeting to discuss a project, you might attach a project plan, financials from Microsoft Excel, or a report.

Attach a file

1 With an appointment, meeting, or event open, on the ribbon, click the Insert tab.

2 In the Include group, click the Attach File button.

3 In the Insert File dialog box, select a file location.

4 Select the file that you want to insert.

5 Click Insert.

(continued on next page)

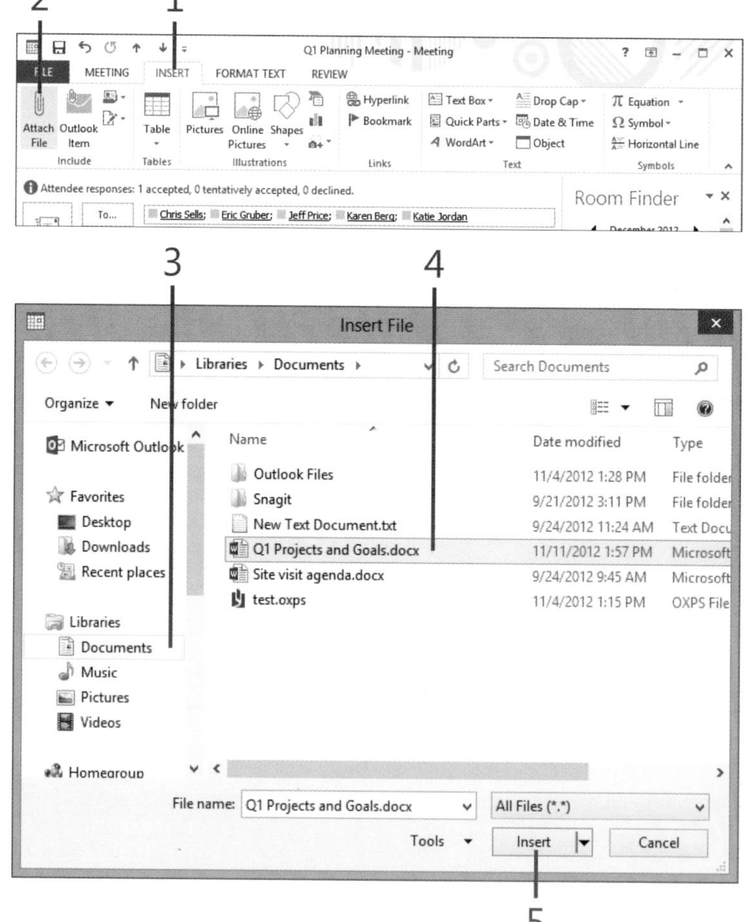

TIP To delete a file, item, or object from a calendar item, select the item and press Delete.

Attach a file *(continued)*

6 The added file appears in the comment field.

7 Click the Meeting, Appointment, or Event tab and then click Save & Close (or, for a meeting, click Send Update).

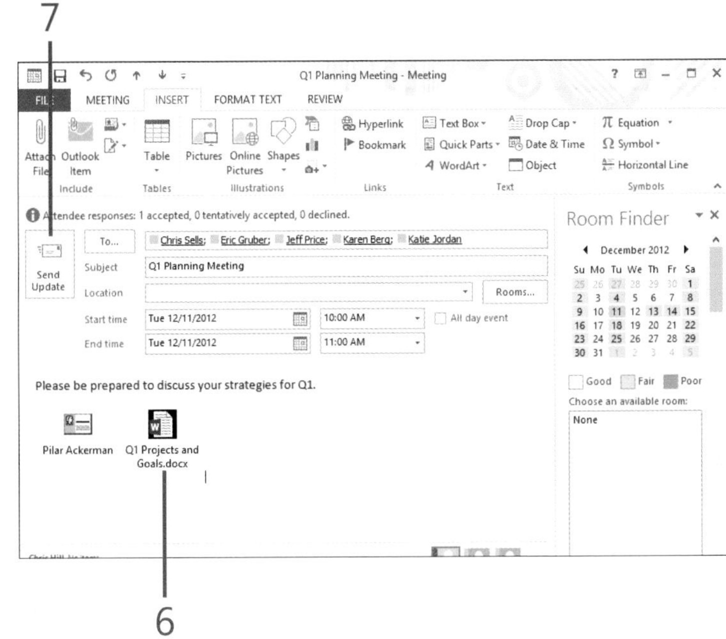

Inserting the contents of a document into a calendar item

Sometimes, you'll want to insert the contents of a document into an Outlook 2013 meeting or other calendar item, rather than attach the item to it. Inserting the contents into the calendar item makes it possible for you and others to view those contents without opening the attached source document.

Insert contents of a document

1 With an appointment, meeting, or event open, on the ribbon, click the Insert tab.

2 Click in the notes area of the item.

3 Back on the ribbon, in the Text group, click Object.

(continued on next page)

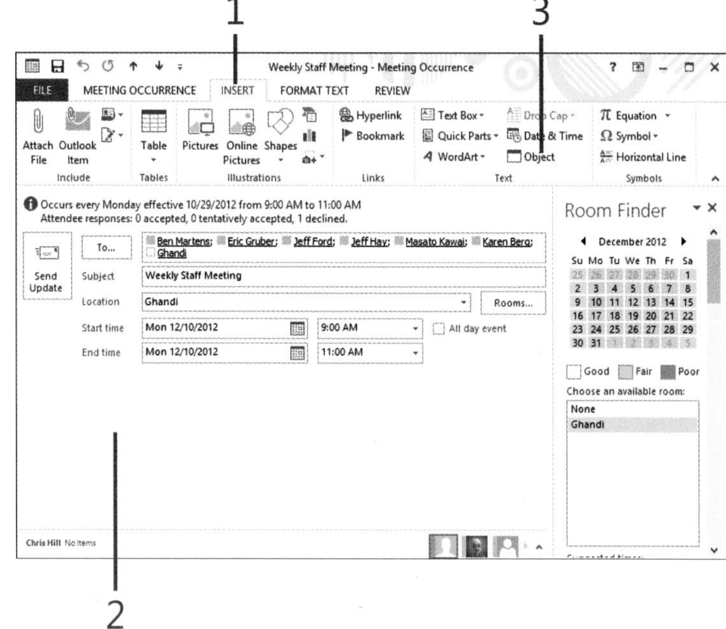

> **TIP** Because you can add objects from a file, you can also embed a portion of a spreadsheet or other type of document in the appointment item for reference. For example, if you are discussing a project issue list in a meeting, you might embed the issue list from an Excel spreadsheet in the meeting request so that the participants can review it before the meeting.

Insert contents of a document *(continued)*

4 In the Object dialog box, click the Create From File tab.

5 Click Browse.

6 In the Browse dialog box, locate and select the object that you want to add.

7 Click Insert.

8 In the Object dialog box, click OK.

(continued on next page)

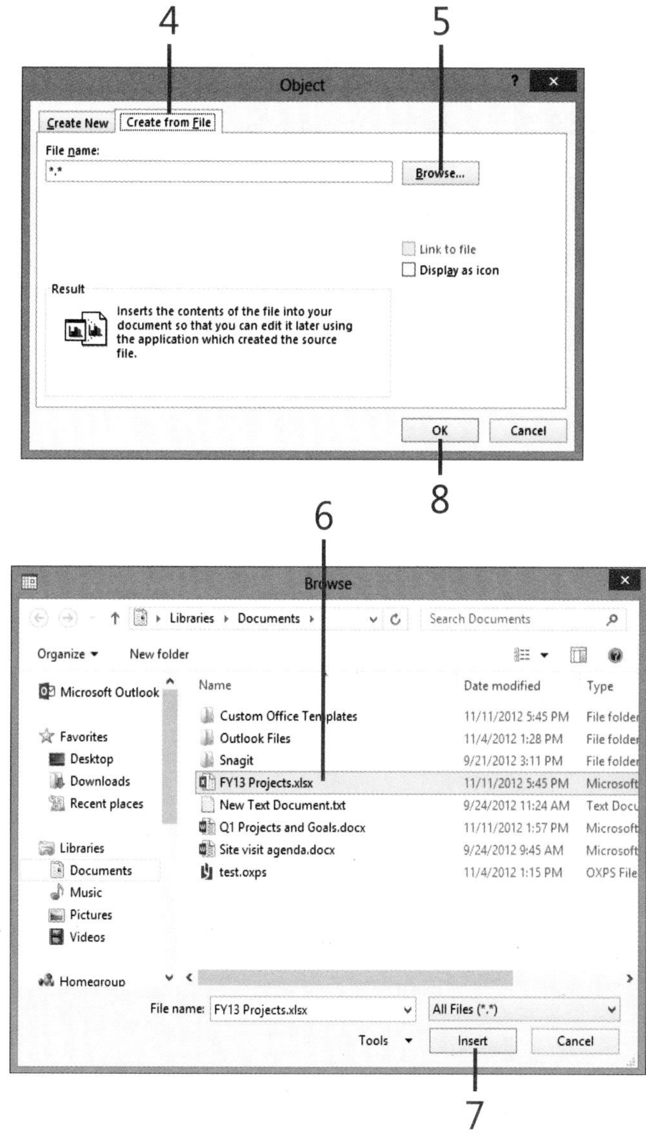

Insert contents of a document *(continued)*

9 Verify that the added object appears in the comment field.

10 Click Save & Close (or Send Update).

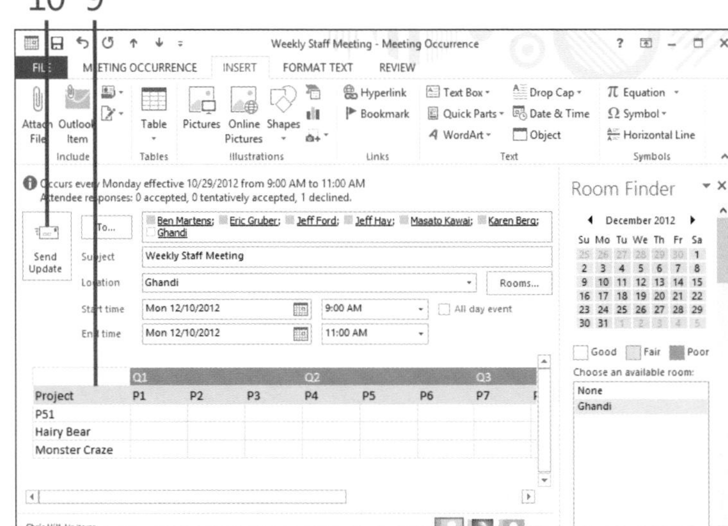

> **TIP** To create a new object, such as an Excel worksheet, in the Insert Object dialog box, select Create New. When you click OK to insert the object, you then create the new object in that object's native application (such as Excel).

Inserting an Excel object into a calendar item

You can insert a blank Excel object into a calendar item. This makes it possible for you to edit spreadsheet data within the calendar item itself. This capability is useful when you want to be able to enter values and calculate data that doesn't exist yet in an Excel file.

Insert a blank Excel object

1 With an appointment, meeting, or event open, on the ribbon, click the Insert tab.

2 Click in the notes area of the item.

3 Back on the ribbon, in the Text group, click Object.

(continued on next page)

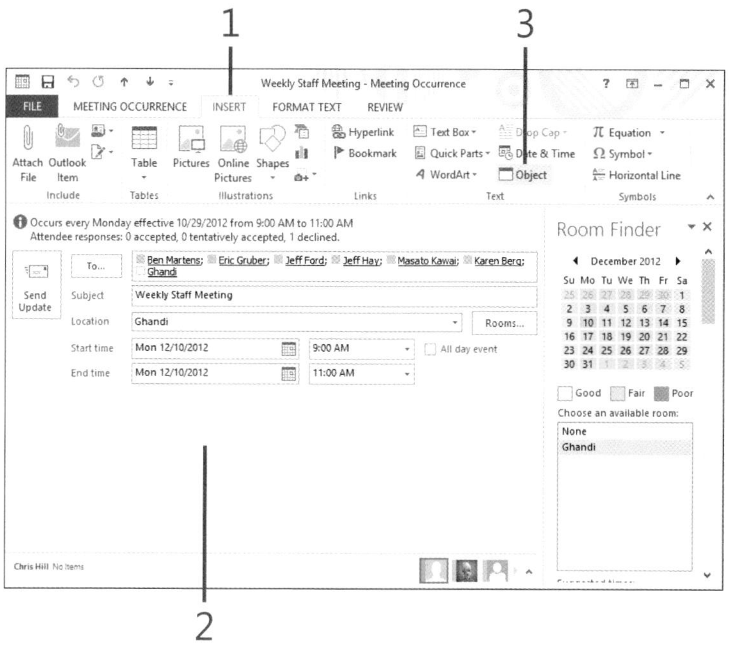

TIP Outlook adds a reminder to each meeting you create. The default is 15 minutes, but you can either change the default or change the reminder for a specific meeting. To change the reminder for one meeting, On the ribbon, on the Meeting Occurrence tab, click the Reminder drop-down list. To set the default reminder time, on the ribbon, click the File tab to display the Backstage view. Click the Options tab and then, in the Outlook Options dialog box, choose Calendar. In the Default Reminders drop-down list, select the desired reminder time.

Insert a blank Excel object *(continued)*

4 In the Object dialog box, click Microsoft Excel Worksheet on the Create New tab.

5 Click OK.

6 Add values and formulas as needed in the Excel object.

7 On the ribbon, on the home tab, use editing tools to modify or format the Excel data.

8 Click the Formulas tab to access additional Excel commands and features.

9 Click in a blank area of the notes field to stop editing the Excel object.

10 Click Send Update to send the meeting item with the embedded Excel object.

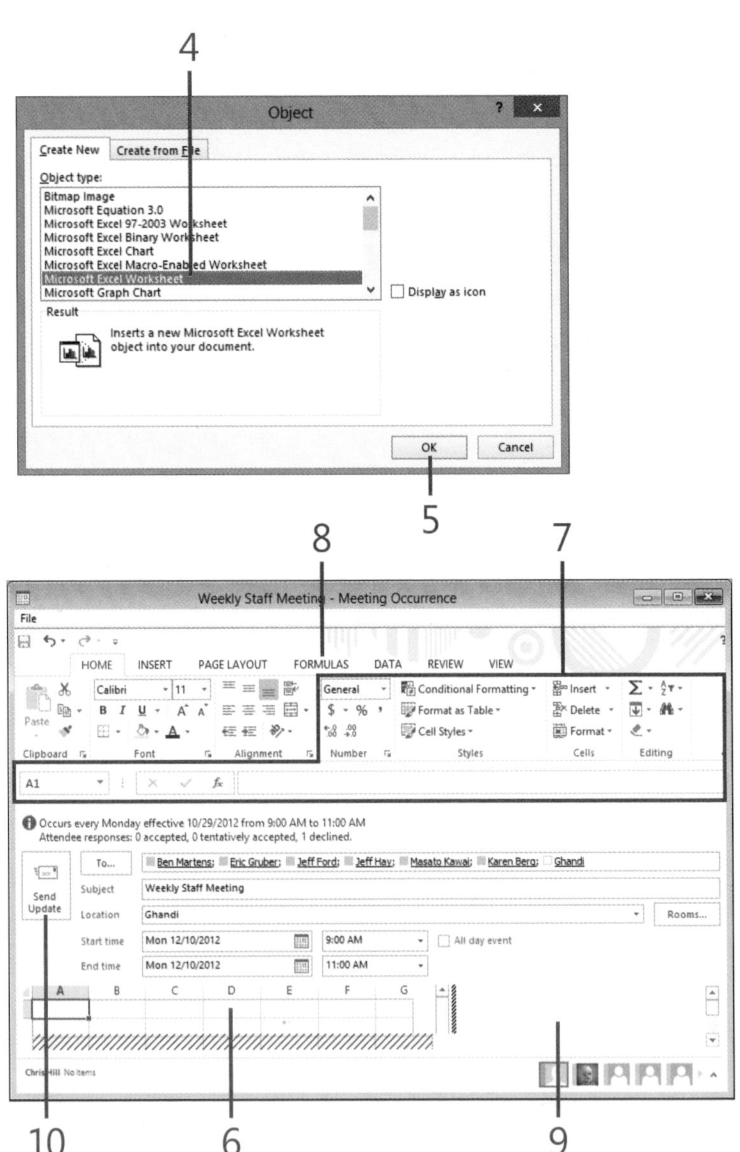

> **TIP** Reminders display even if the Calendar item is overdue. For example, if an event was set for Saturday and you didn't turn on your computer that day, the next time you start Windows the reminder for that event appears. You can dismiss the reminder at that point.

Sharing calendar information

With Outlook 2013, you can share Calendar information with others. You can forward a Calendar item by email to other Outlook users, or you can forward an iCalendar item to any user of any Internet-connected mail program. You should use iCalendar when you schedule meetings with people who don't use Outlook.

Forward a calendar item

1 Open an existing meeting item. On the Meeting Series tab, in the Actions group, click the drop-down arrow on the Forward button.

2 Choose Forward.

3 Add one or more recipients in the To box.

4 Click Send.

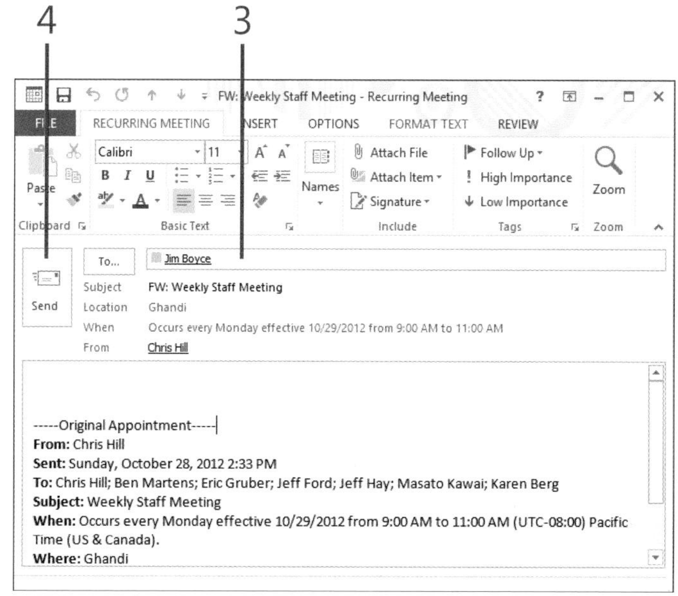

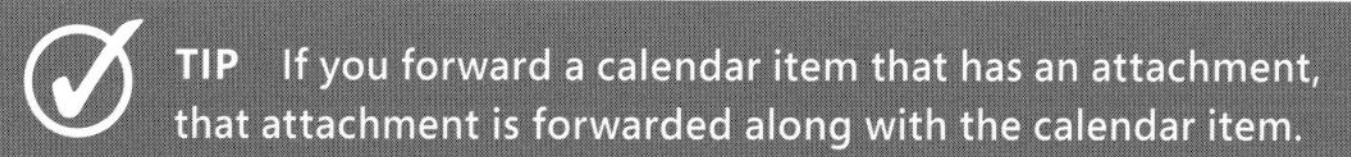
TIP If you forward a calendar item that has an attachment, that attachment is forwarded along with the calendar item.

Forward an item as an iCalendar item

1. Open an existing meeting item. On the Meeting Series tab, in the Actions group, click the drop-down arrow on the Forward button.
2. Choose Forward As iCalendar.
3. The iCalendar attachment appears in the Attached field.
4. Add one or more recipients in the To box.
5. Add notes as desired.
6. Click Send.

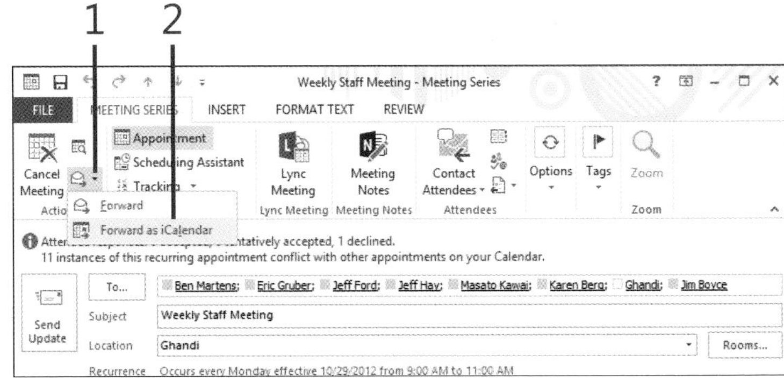

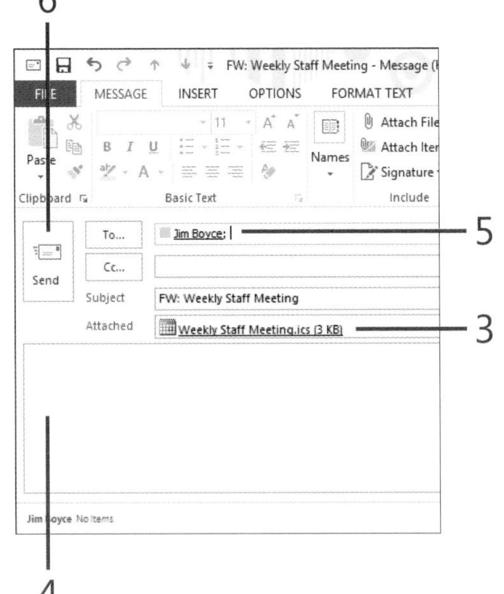

TIP iCalendar is for communicating with people who don't use Outlook. If you want to forward a calendar item to someone who uses Outlook, on the Actions menu, click the Forward command, or, in the Actions group on the meeting form's ribbon, click Forward.

Printing calendars

You can print your Outlook 2013 appointment calendar, such as your daily or weekly appointments, meetings, and events, or you can print an individual calendar item such as a meeting item.

Print your appointment calendar

1 Open the Calendar folder, click the File tab to display the Backstage view, and then click the Print tab.

2 In the Printer section, choose a printer.

3 In the Settings section, choose a calendar style.

4 Preview the results.

5 Click Print.

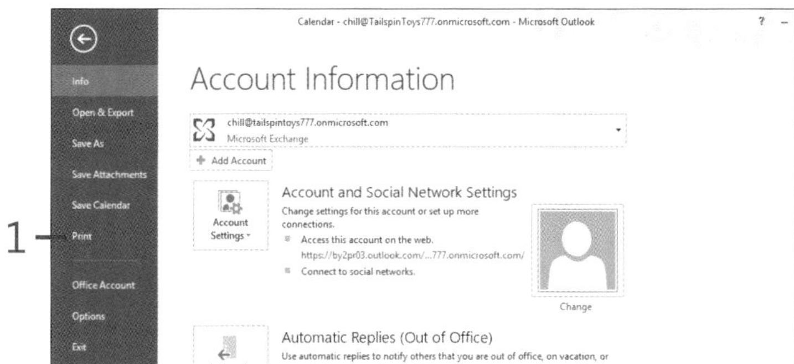

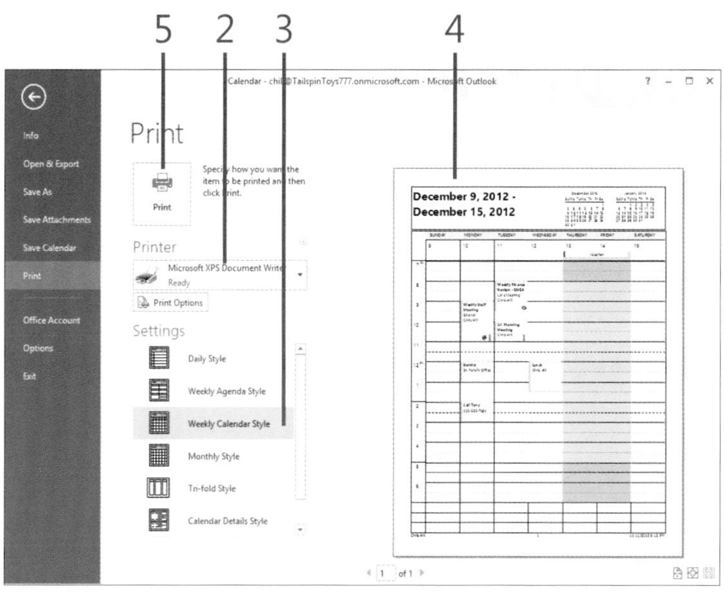

TIP You can print your calendars in Daily, Weekly, Monthly, Tri-fold, Calendar Detail, and Memo Style. Try printing your calendar in each one of these styles and then pick your favorite one.

TRY THIS! Print your appointment calendar at the beginning of each week so that you can keep track of all your upcoming events, appointments, and meetings. As schedules change, such as a meeting being delayed or canceled, make these changes on the hard copy as well as in Outlook. If too many changes occur, you might need to print a fresh calendar.

Print a calendar item

1 Open the calendar item that you want to print.

2 Click the File tab to display the Backstage view.

(continued on next page)

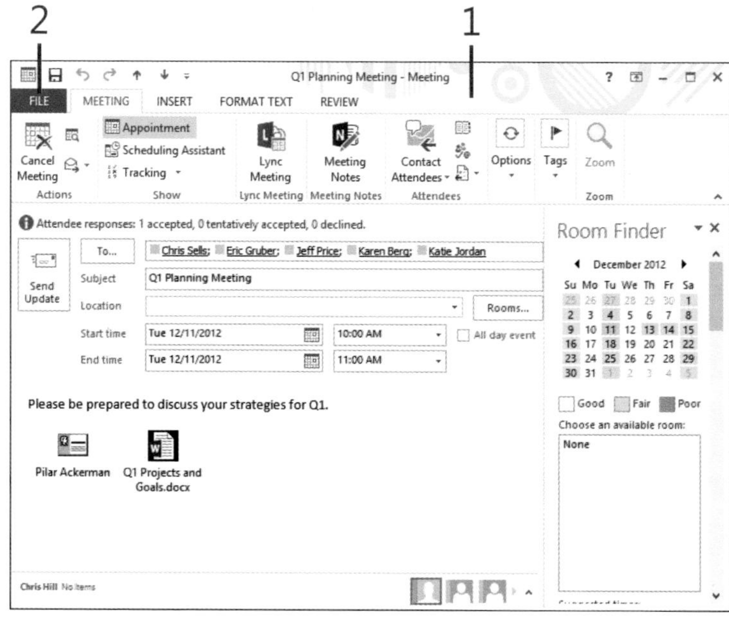

TIP If you want to print to a printer other than the default one, click the Printer drop-down list and select the printer.

Print a calendar item *(continued)*

3 Click the Print tab and then, in the Printer section, choose a printer.

1 4 Choose other print options such as printing attachments in addition to the meeting item.

5 Preview the results.

6 Click Print.

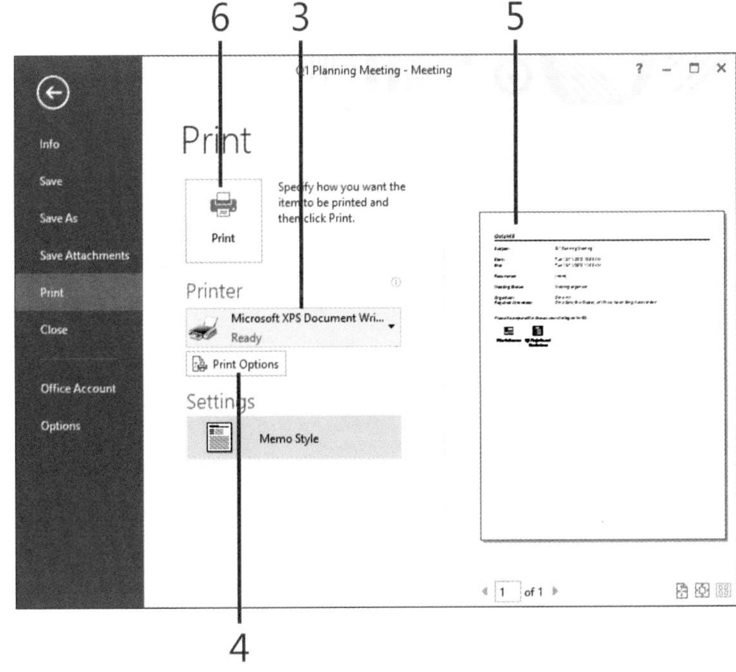

> **TIP** Attachments within an item will not print automatically, but you can use the Print Options button on the Print page to print the attachments.

Working with tasks

8

At one time or another, most of us have written a to-do list—a list of tasks that we need to perform. Maybe you put together a list of the improvements or repairs you want to make to your house. Maybe it's something simpler such as a list of errands to run. Whatever the case, having a list of the tasks can be valuable for keeping you on track.

Microsoft Outlook 2013 includes a feature to help you keep your pending tasks in mind. The Tasks folder stores your to-do list. You can create tasks for yourself, assign them a due date, and easily mark them as completed. You can create one-time tasks or recurring tasks. Outlook also lets you assign tasks to others and receive status updates on the tasks from the people to whom you assign them. This section explains how to use the Tasks folder to create and manage one-time and recurring tasks as well as how to assign tasks to others.

In this section:

- Working in the Tasks folder
- Viewing tasks
- Adding tasks
- Working with recurring tasks
- Modifying and updating a task
- Inserting an Outlook item into a task
- Inserting a file into a task
- Assigning a task to someone else
- Accepting or rejecting assigned tasks

Working in the Tasks folder

Outlook 2013 includes a Tasks folder that you can use to store your tasks as well as those that you assign to others. The Tasks folder offers a variety of ways to view and work with your tasks, including the daily task list that appears at the bottom of the calendar and the Tasks List in the To-Do Bar.

View and open tasks

1 In the Folder pane, click the Tasks icon (or word) to open the Tasks folder.
2 Click a task that you want to preview in the Reading pane.
3 Double-click a task to open the task's form (or double-click in the Tasks folder to start a new task).

(continued on next page)

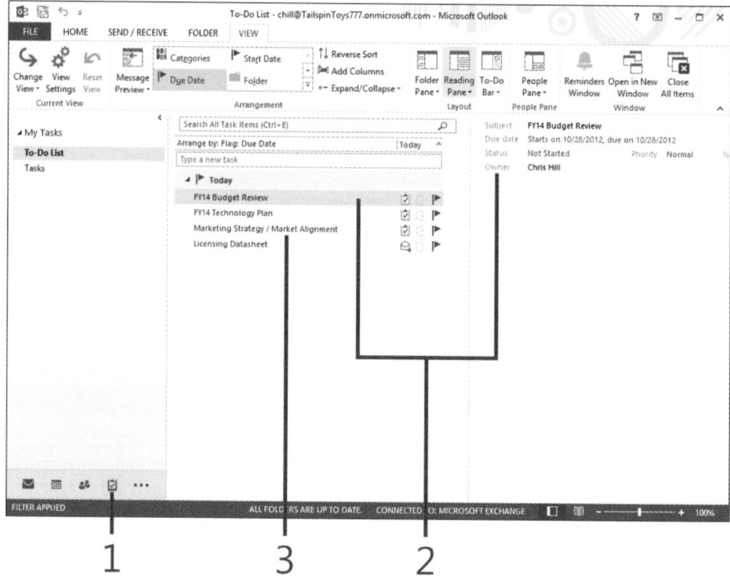

TIP Outlook provides several different views for the Tasks folder, and you can easily create your own views to suit your needs.

View and open tasks *(continued)*

4 Add notes or other information as needed.

5 On the Task tab, in the Show group, click Details.

6 Add other information on the Details page.

7 Back on the ribbon, in the Actions group, click Save & Close.

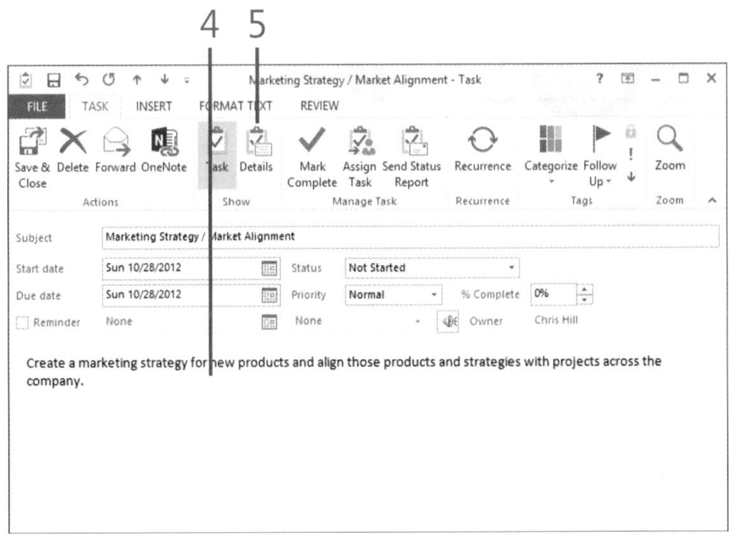

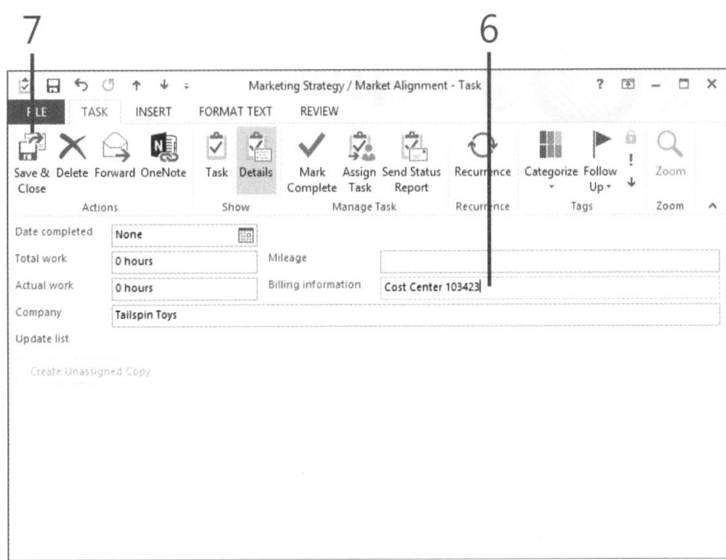

TIP When you create a task, Outlook doesn't set up a reminder for the task by default, but you can add one later. Open the task and then, on the ribbon, click the Task tab. In the Tags group, click Follow-Up and then click Add Reminder. In the Custom dialog box that opens, add a reminder. You can also select the Reminder check box on the Task form and set a reminder directly on the form.

Viewing tasks

With Outlook 2013, you can view your task list in various locations in Outlook so that you can not only access your task items to work on them, but also see a summary list of all your pending tasks, tasks due that day, and so on. You can view your tasks in the Tasks folder, or you can use the task list in the Calendar and To-Do Bar to view and work with tasks.

View tasks in the Tasks folder

1. At the bottom of the Folder pane, click the Tasks icon to open the Tasks folder.
2. Click a task that you want to preview in the Reading pane.
3. On the Home tab, in the Current View group, click Change View and then, in the gallery that opens, choose Simple List.
4. To sort the list by subject, click the Subject column.
5. To restore the default sort method, click Due Date.
6. To mark the task as complete, select the flag beside the task's subject.

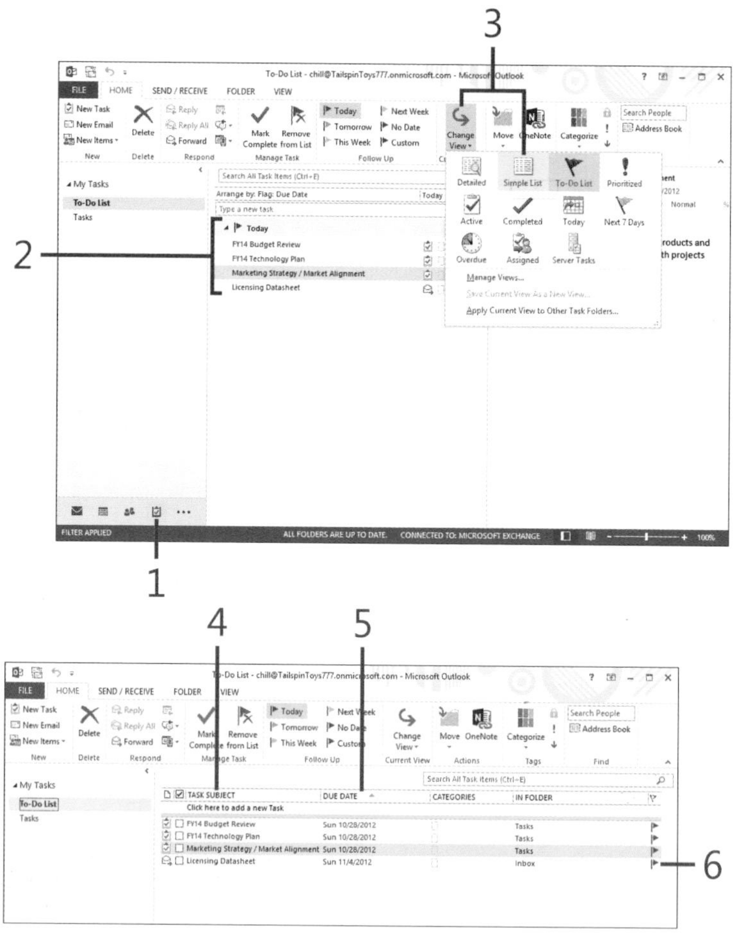

TRY THIS! You can add and remove columns from the task list to show the task data most important to you. Right-click the column header and then, on the shortcut menu that opens, click Field Chooser. In the Field Chooser dialog box, click a column and drag it to the column header. To remove a column, drag it from the column header to the Field Chooser dialog box. Note that you must widen some views or turn off the Reading pane to accomplish this with some views (such as the To-Do Bar).

TIP If you're using a view that includes the Complete check box, just select the check box to mark a task as complete.

View tasks in the To-Do Bar

1 At the bottom of the Folder pane, click the Calendar icon to open the Calendar folder.

2 On the Home tab, in the Arrangements group, click the Work Week button.

3 In the Layout group, Click the To-Do Bar button and then, in the drop-down list that appears, choose Tasks.

4 View the tasks in the task list.

5 Select the flag beside a task to mark it as complete.

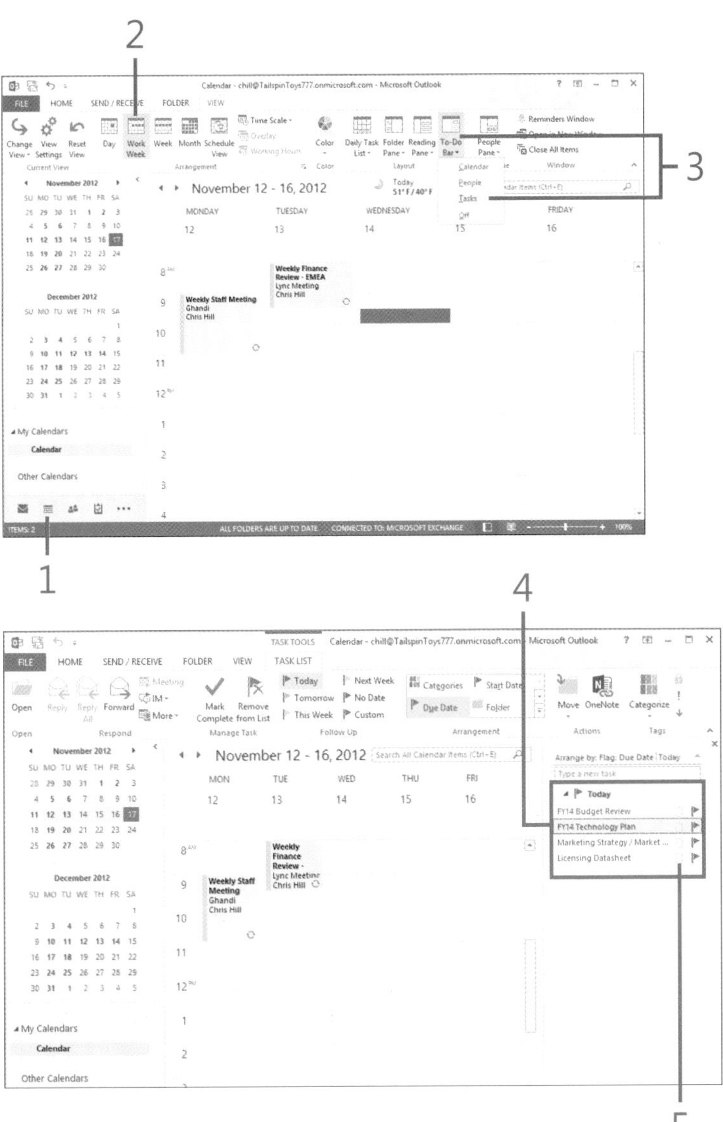

TIP If you don't see the To-Do Bar, on the ribbon, on the View tab, click To-Do Bar and choose Tasks.

TRY THIS! The Outlook Today view includes a simplified task list that shows the subject and completion status. You can click a task's subject to open the task to view its details or modify it. Select the check box beside a task to mark it as complete.

Adding tasks

Tasks can be added to your Outlook 2013 Tasks folder in one of two ways. You can create the task yourself, or you can accept a task that someone else assigns to you. If you create the task yourself, you can set it up by using the New Items button on the Home tab for any folder, or you can create it through the Tasks folder.

Create a new task

1 At the bottom of the Folder pane, click the Tasks icon to open the Tasks folder.
2 On the Home tab, in the New group, click the New Task button.
3 Type a subject for the task.
4 In the Priority list box, choose a priority.
5 On the Due Date drop-down calendar, choose a due date.
6 Click Save & Close.

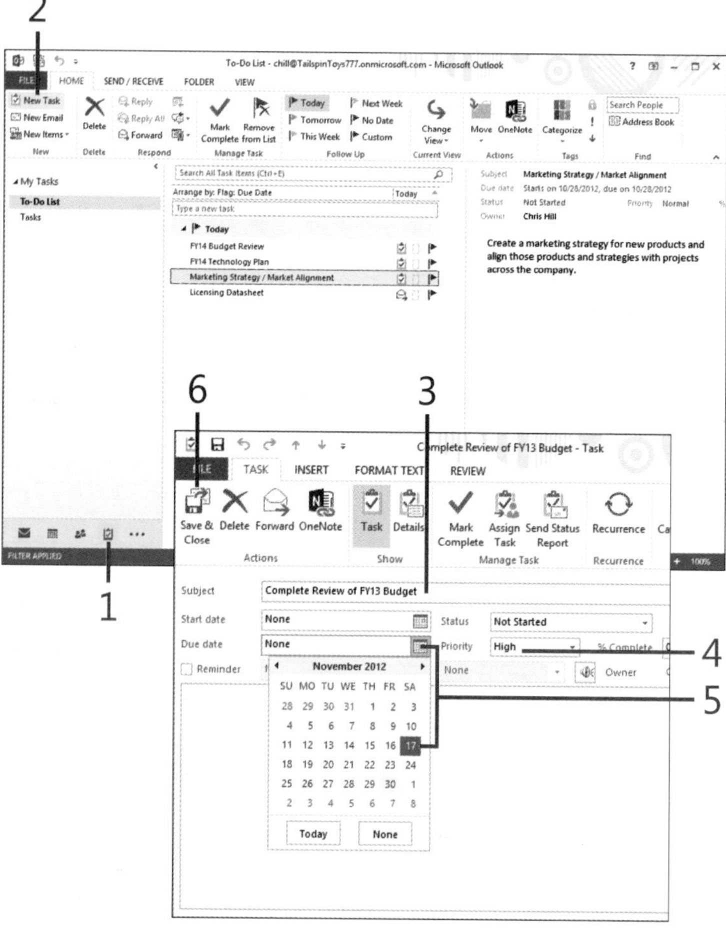

TRY THIS! With any folder open, you can use the New Items button on the Home tab to open a new task form and create the task. Click the New Items button and then, on the menu that appears, click Task to open the new task form.

TIP The Status and % Complete properties are connected. If you specify some percentage less than 100% in the % Complete field, Outlook changes the Status field to In Progress. Setting % Complete to 0 changes Status to Not Started. Setting % Complete to 100% causes Outlook to set Status to Completed. Likewise, setting Status to Completed sets % Complete to 100%.

Set or change task properties

1 Double-click the task that you want to change.
2 Set the task status.
3 Specify the current percent completion.
4 On the Task tab, in the Tags group, click the Categorize button to categorize the task.
5 Also in the Tags group, click the lock icon to mark the task as private.
6 Click the Zoom button to change the size of text in the notes field.
7 Click Save & Close to keep the changes.

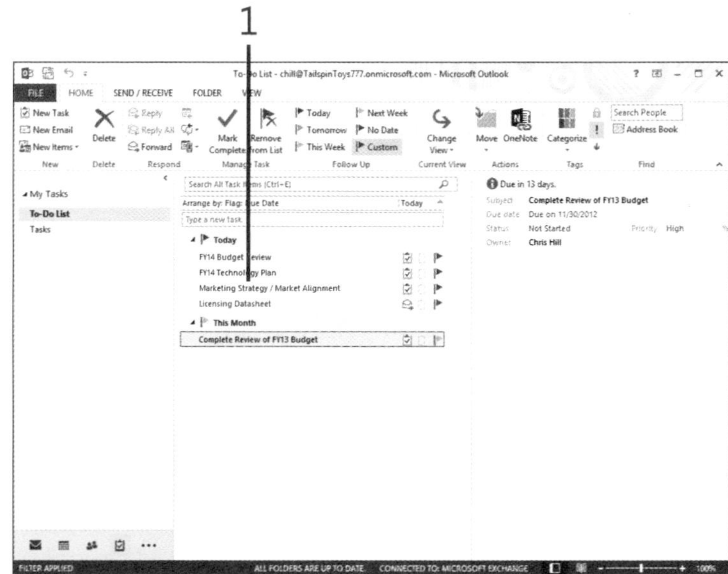

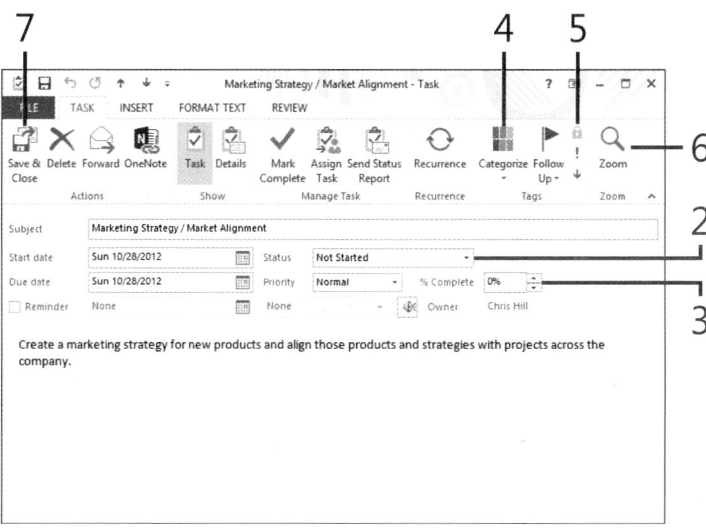

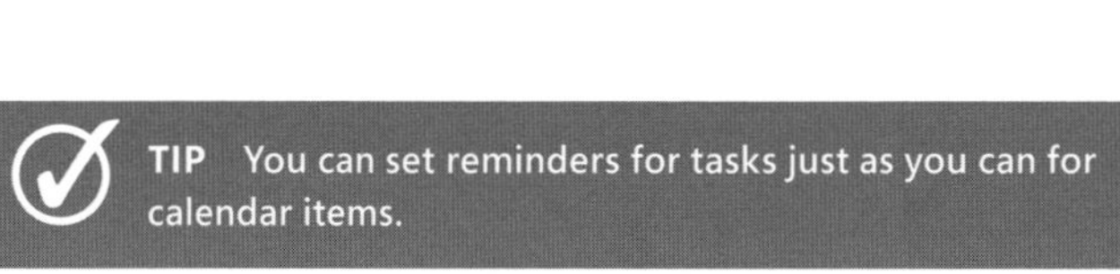

TIP You can set reminders for tasks just as you can for calendar items.

SEE ALSO For more information about working with reminders, see "Working with reminders" on page 182.

Working with recurring tasks

Some tasks that you create in Outlook 2013 are of a recurring nature—they repeat on a regular basis. For example, maybe you have to prepare a set of reports every Friday that summarizes the week's sales or other information. Or perhaps you need to back up your files every week. Although a recurring task shows up only once in the task list, it appears in the tasks lists in the calendar and on the To-Do Bar when the assigned due date falls in the list's range. If you set a reminder for the task, you receive the reminder for each recurrence of the task.

Create a recurring task

1 At the bottom of the Folder pane, click the Tasks icon to open the Tasks folder.

2 On the Home tab, in the New group, click the New Task button, or open an existing task.

(continued on next page)

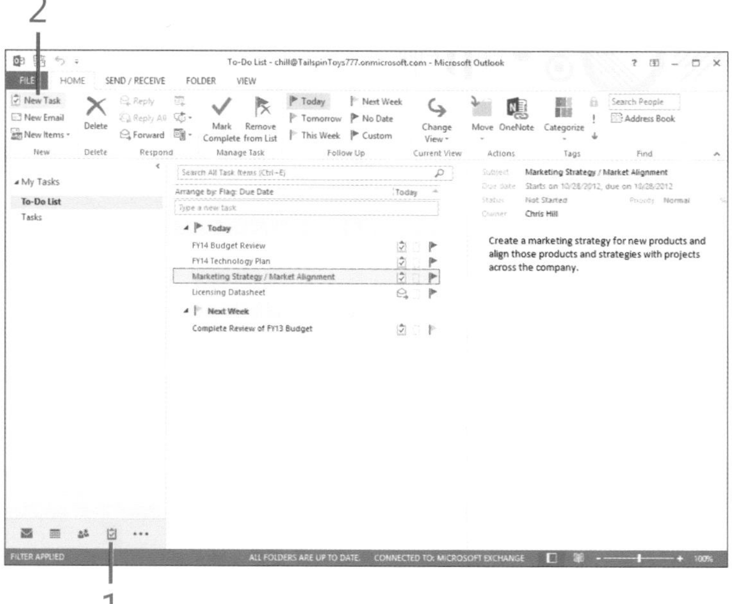

TRY THIS! On the ribbon, on the Tags tab, use the Private button in the Tags group to prevent your delegates from seeing the task in your task list.

TIP If you set a recurring task with no end date, you can still revise the task's properties to make it end after a specified number of occurrences or specified date. Just open the task's properties, click Recurrence to open the Task Recurrence dialog box, choose the end option that you want, and then click OK. Then, click Save & Close to save the changes.

Create a recurring task *(continued)*

3 Set the Subject, Start Date, and other information for the task.

4 On the Task tab, click the Recurrence button to open the Task Recurrence dialog box.

5 In the Recurrence Pattern section, select the type of recurrence.

6 Specify how often the task should recur.

7 In the Range Of Recurrence section, on the drop-down calendars, set the start and end of the recurrence period and click OK.

(continued on next page)

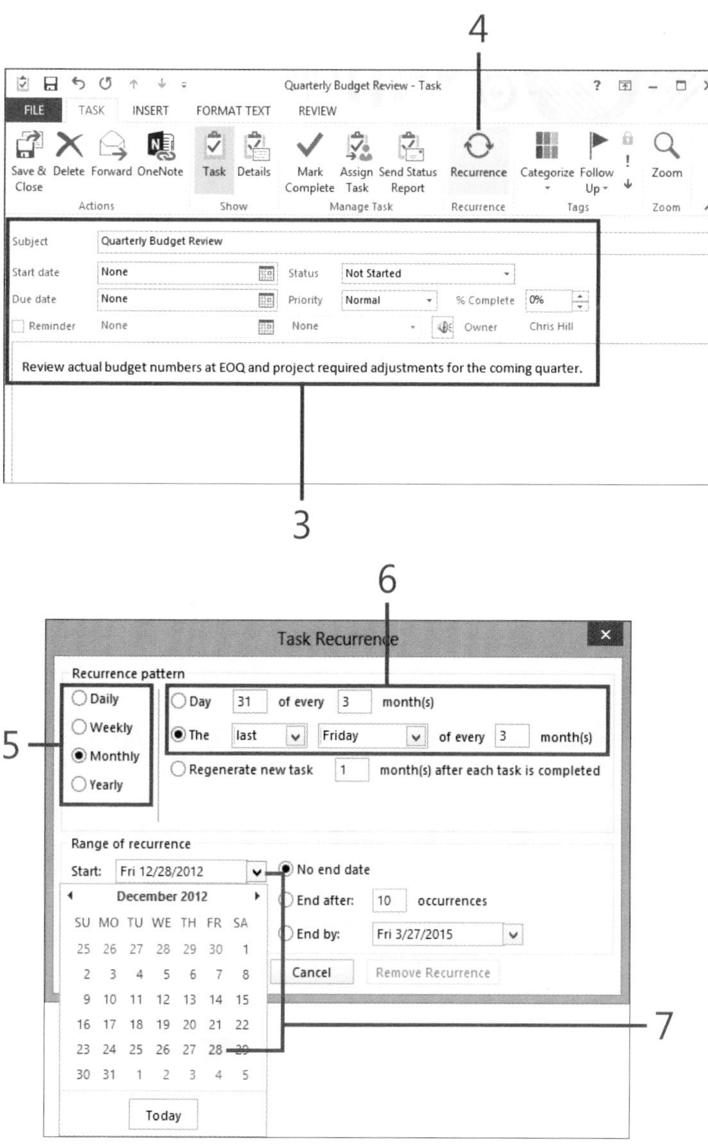

> **TIP** Select the Recur Every option in the Task Recurrence dialog box when you want the task to recur even if the previous occurrence hasn't been completed. Select the Regenerate New Task option if you want the task to recur only after the last occurrence is complete.

Create a recurring task *(continued)*

8 On the Task tab, in the Recurrence group, click Skip Occurrence to skip the current occurrence of the task.

9 Click Save & Close to close the task's form.

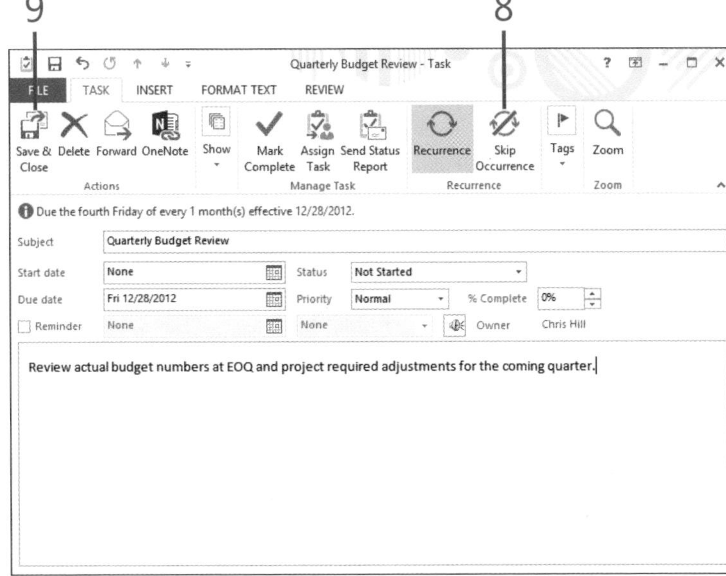

TRY THIS! You can make a recurring task nonrecurring by opening a task's form, clicking Recurrence on the toolbar to open the Task Recurrence dialog box, and then clicking Remove Recurrence.

Modifying and updating a task

You can modify a task in Outlook 2013 at any time to change any property, including subject, due date, recurrence, and so on. Another change you might want to make to tasks is to mark them as complete so that you can see at a glance the tasks that are finished and those that are not. You can also change the view of the Tasks folder to show only tasks that are complete, only tasks that are overdue, only those that are incomplete, and so on. In addition to marking tasks complete, you probably want to delete completed tasks and send status updates for tasks that are assigned to you.

Mark a task as complete

1. Select the task.
2. On the Home tab, in the Manage Task group, click the Mark Complete button.
3. Click Change View and then choose Simple List.
4. Outlook uses strikethrough to indicate that a task has been completed.
5. Select the check box to mark a task as complete.

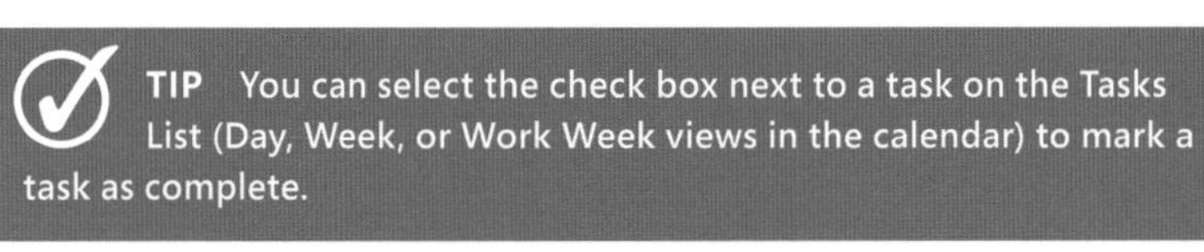

TIP You can select the check box next to a task on the Tasks List (Day, Week, or Work Week views in the calendar) to mark a task as complete.

TRY THIS! You can mark a task complete by setting its percent complete value to 100%. Open the task and use the arrow button beside the % Complete option to set the value to 100%. Outlook marks the task as complete.

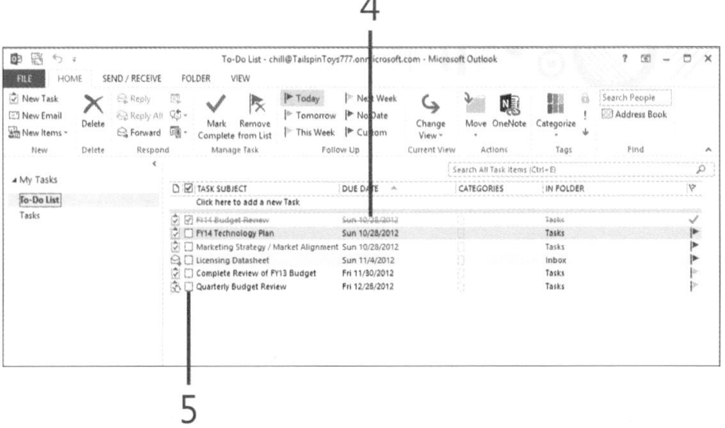

Send a status report for an assigned task

1 Double-click the assigned task to open its form.

2 Make changes to the task as needed and then, on the Task tab, in the Manage Task group, click Send Status Report.

(continued on next page)

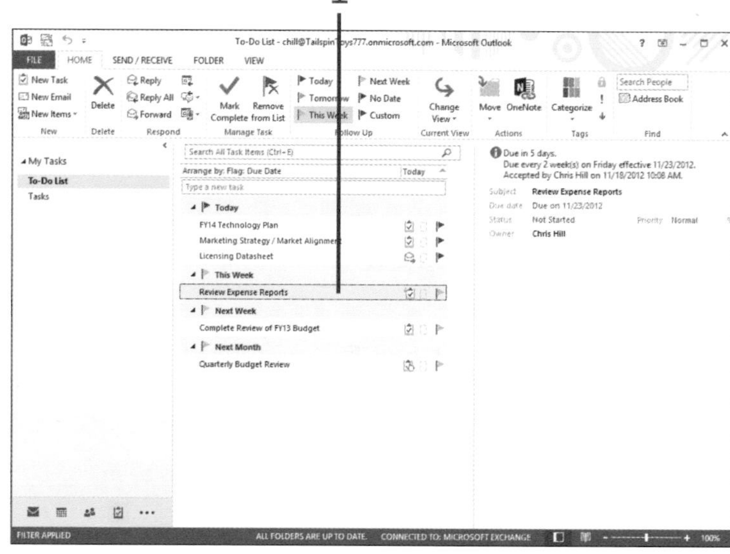

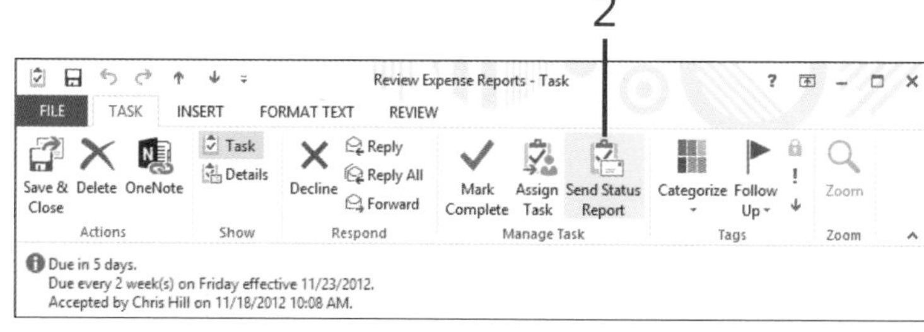

TIP To delete a task, select the task and then, on the Home tab, click Delete.

TRY THIS! You can send a copy of a status report to a person not on the update list without letting the people on the list know that you've copied that person. Just use the Bcc field to address the message to the other person. If Outlook isn't currently showing the Bcc field, on the Options tab, in the Show Fields group, click Show Bcc.

Send a status report for an assigned task *(continued)*

3 After Outlook adds the assigner's address, click To or Cc to add others if needed.

4 Add notes as needed.

5 Click Send.

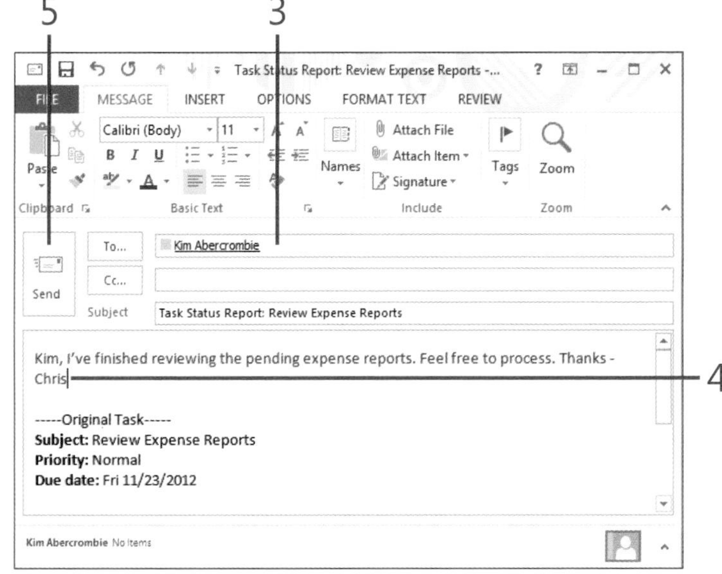

SEE ALSO For more information about assigning tasks to others, see "Assigning a task to someone else" on page 174.

TIP Outlook fills in the status information in the body of the update message for you. You can edit this text if you need to. Just highlight the text that you want to change and type the replacement text.

Inserting an Outlook item into a task

When you create a task in Outlook 2013—whether you create the task for yourself or assign it to someone else—you might want to add items to the task. For example, assume that you're going to assign a task to someone else, and that person needs a copy of a Microsoft Word document to perform the task. You can attach the document to the task. Or, perhaps you need to include some contacts with a task. Whatever the case, it's easy to insert Outlook items, objects, and files into a task.

Insert an Outlook item

1 Open a task and then, on the ribbon, click the Insert tab.

2 Click in the notes area of the task.

3 Back on the ribbon, in the Include group, click Outlook Item.

(continued on next page)

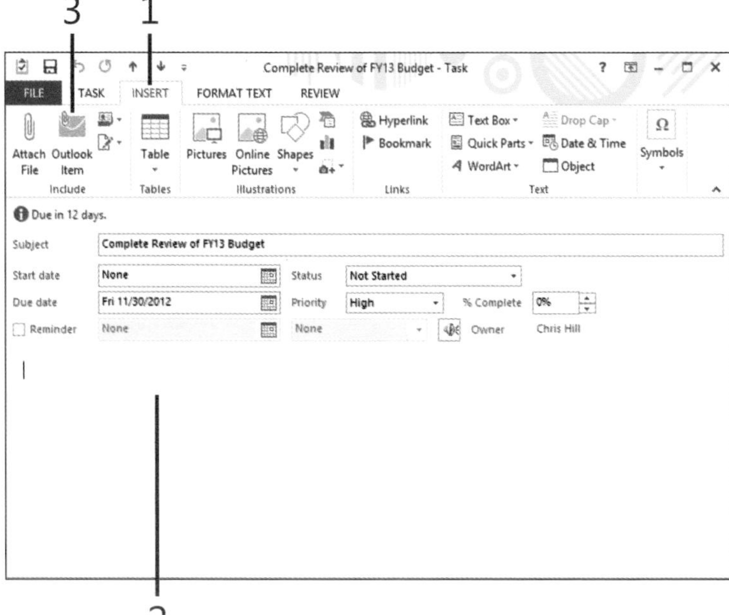

> **TIP** You can insert a file as a hyperlink rather than as an attachment, which makes it possible to open the task from its source rather than included in the task. The main benefit of this method is that you don't duplicate the document but instead create a shortcut to it. The limitation is that everyone who receives the message must have access to wherever the file is stored. To insert a hyperlink in a task, open the task and then, on the Insert tab, click Attach File. In the Insert File dialog box that opens, select the file, click the arrow beside the Insert button, and then choose Insert As Hyperlink.

Insert an Outlook item *(continued)*

4 In the Insert Item dialog box, select the Outlook folder that contains the object that you want to insert.

5 Select the item to insert.

6 Click OK.

7 Verify that the attached item appears in the notes area of the task.

8 Click the Task tab and change other task fields as needed.

9 Click Save & Close.

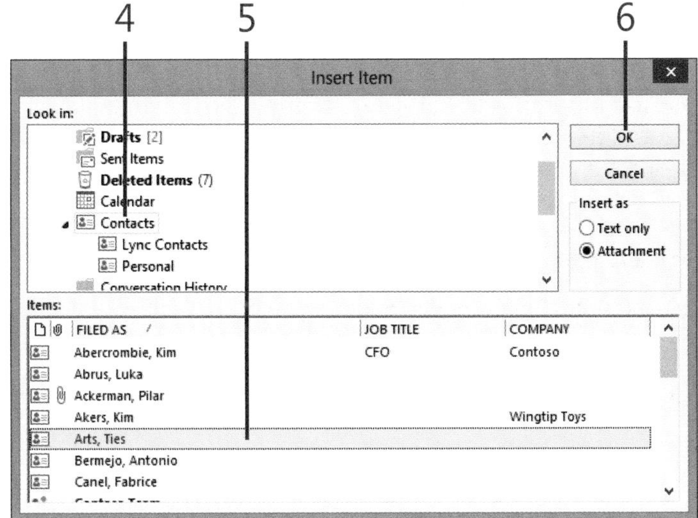

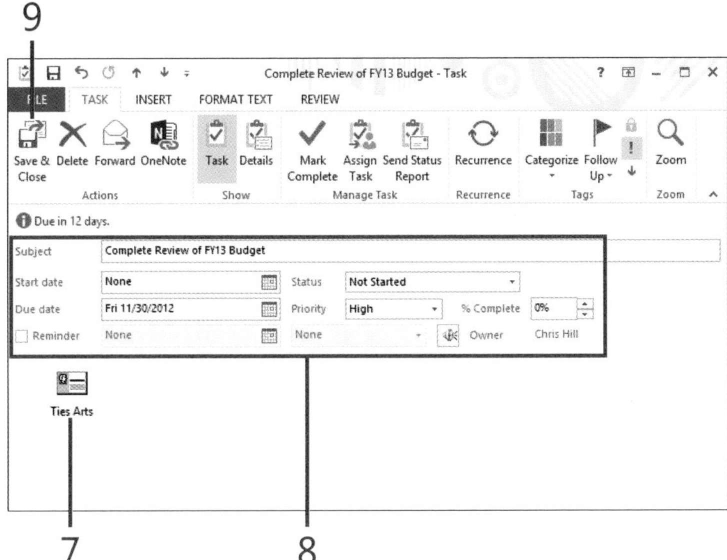

Inserting a file into a task

In addition to inserting Outlook items, you can insert documents and other types of files. For example, you might want to insert a project plan, report, or other document into a task so that when you're working on that task, you have the documents handy.

Insert a file

1 Open a task and then, on the ribbon, click the Insert tab.

2 In the Include group, click Attach File.

(continued on next page)

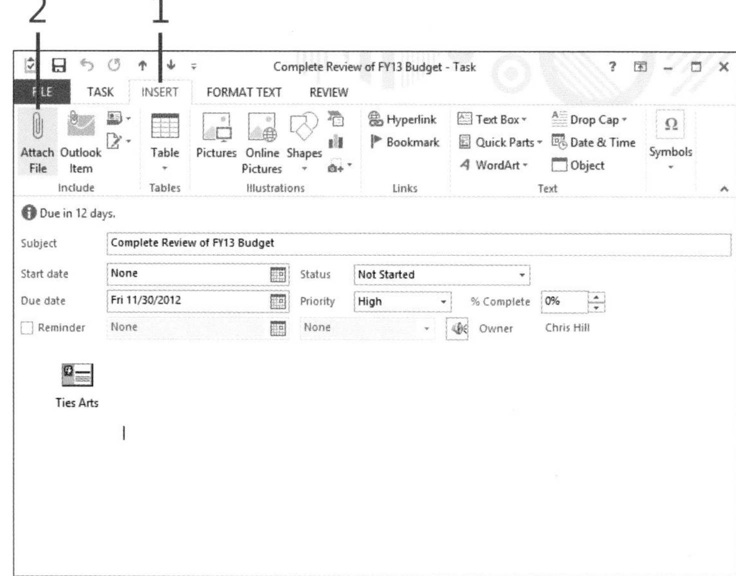

TIP When you insert a file as a hyperlink, Outlook inserts the path to the document. If you insert a file from your local computer, the path uses the local drive letter. This method works fine for creating hyperlinks to documents you use, but it doesn't work when you assign tasks to other people because clicking the link on their end causes Outlook to try to open the file from their computers. However, you can link files on network servers in tasks that you assign, as long as you view the server through a UNC path rather than a mapped drive. A UNC path takes the form *server**folder*, where *server* is the name of the server and *folder* is the name of the shared folder on the server on which the document is located. Likewise, you can link to a file on a SharePoint site by copying the URL for the SharePoint item into the task.

Insert a file *(continued)*

3 In the Insert File dialog box, select the file that you want to insert.

4 Click Insert to insert the file.

5 Notice that the file appears as an icon in the task.

6 Add other information to the task as you need to.

7 On the Task tab, in the Actions group, click Save & Close.

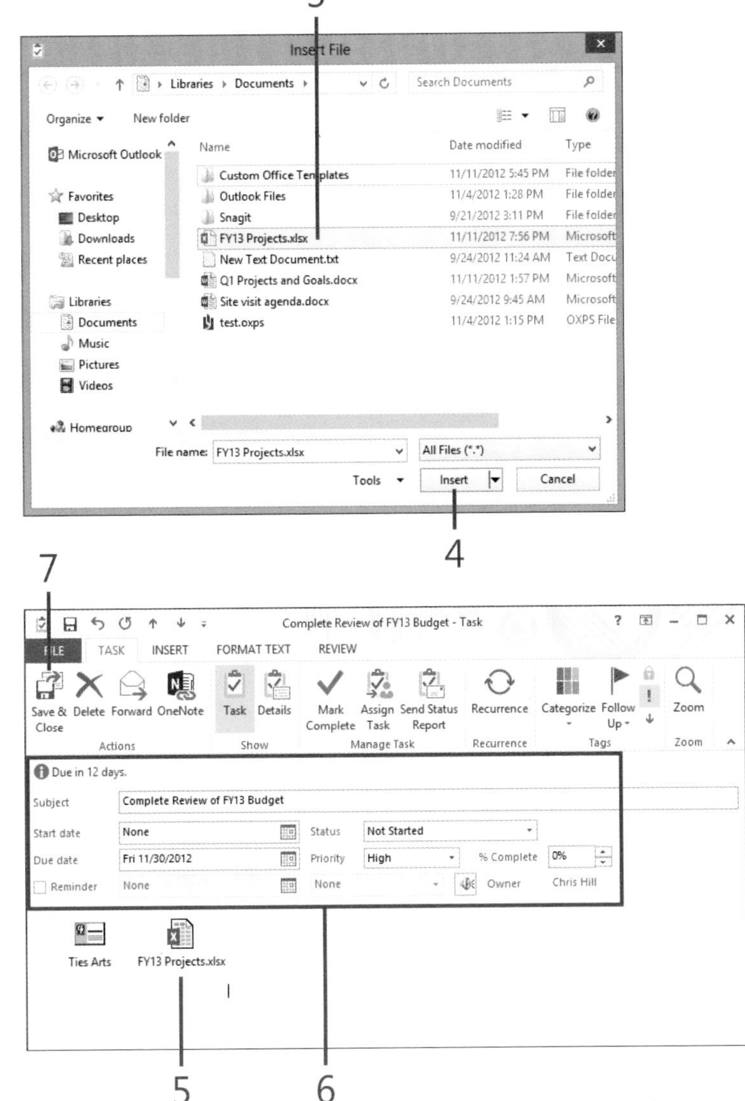

SEE ALSO For more information about attaching files to email messages rather than adding them to tasks, see "Sending a file by email" on page 56.

Assigning a task to someone else

If you manage others and use Outlook in your organization for email and collaboration, you probably want to assign tasks to others. Outlook 2013 sends the task assignment as an email message, and the assignee has the option of accepting or rejecting the task. When you assign a task, you define a status update distribution list. The people on that list receive status reports when the assignee makes changes to the task.

Assign a task

1 Create a new task and fill in task properties as needed.

2 On the Task tab, in the Manage Task group, click Assign Task.

(continued on next page)

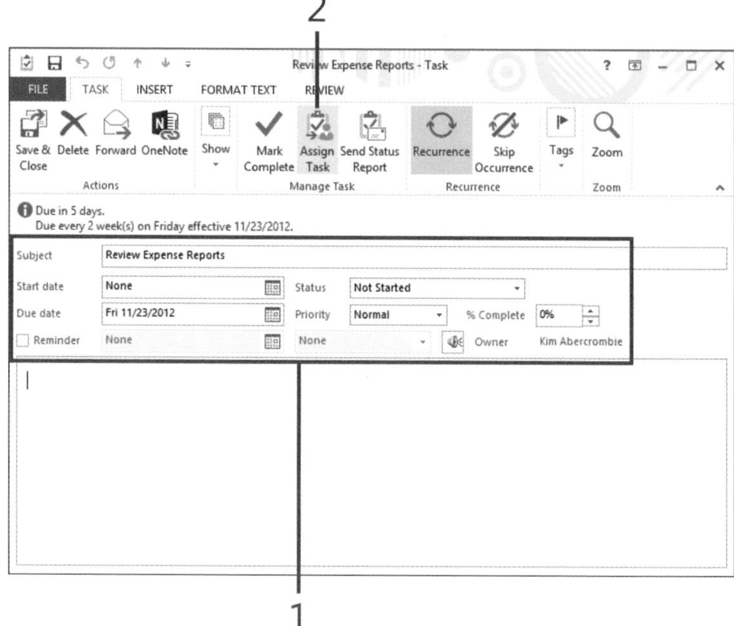

TRY THIS! If you want to pass the buck and reassign a task that was assigned to you to someone else, accept the task and open it. On the Task tab, in the Manage Task group, click Assign Task. Then, assign it by typing someone's name or by selecting a name from your address list.

SEE ALSO For information about how to include a document with a task you assign to someone else, see "Inserting items into a task" on page 100.

Assign a task *(continued)*

3 Specify the assignee.

4 Select the Keep An Updated Copy Of This Task On My Task List check box to have Outlook keep track of the assigned task with a copy on your own task list that updates as the assignee works on the task.

5 Select the Send Me A Status Report When This Task Is Complete check box to have Outlook send you a status report when the assignee completes the task.

6 Click Send.

7 Verify that the assignee appears as the owner of the task.

8 The status updates as the assignee sends back status reports.

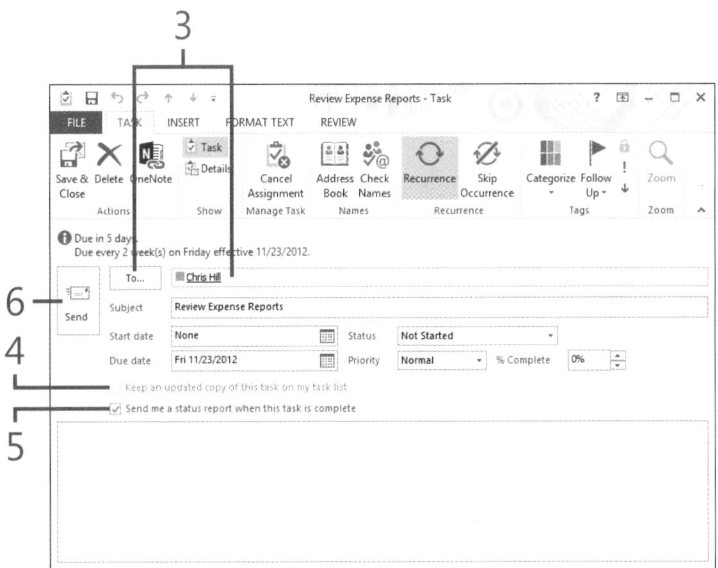

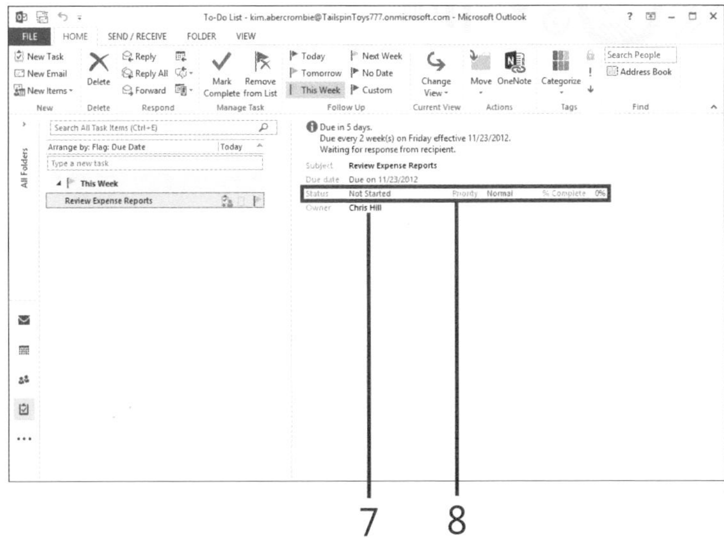

TIP When you assign a task to another person, a copy of the task request message goes into your Sent Items folder. If you open the message, its form shows a status message indicating that Outlook is waiting for a response from the assignee. This message changes after the assignee either accepts or rejects the task.

Accepting or rejecting assigned tasks

If someone assigns a task to you, the task assignment comes to you in the form of an email. You then must either accept or reject the task. Or, you can accept the task and then assign it to someone else.

Accept or reject an assigned task

1 At the bottom of the Folder pane, click the Mail icon and open the Inbox.

2 Click the Task Request message to select it. If the Preview pane is not open, double-click the message to open it.

3 Click Accept to accept the task (or click Decline to decline it).

4 In the Accepting Task dialog box, click OK.

5 The task now appears in the assignee's Tasks folder.

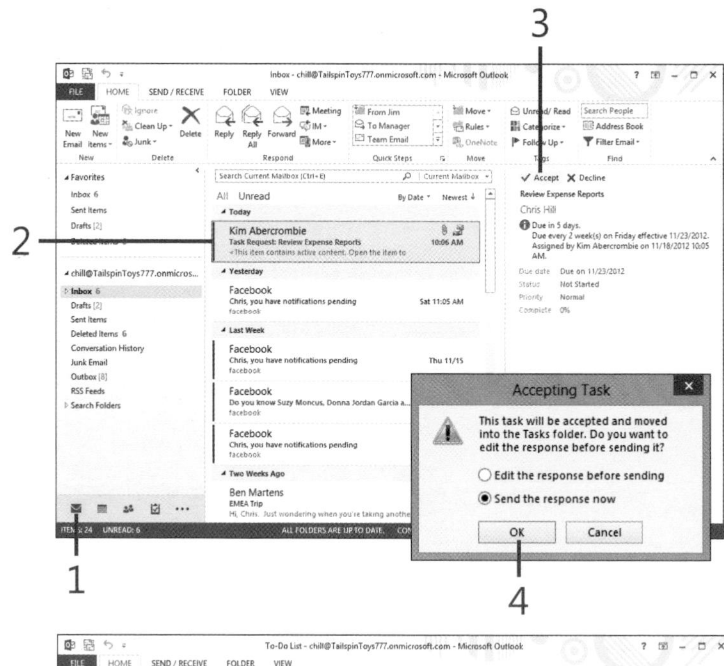

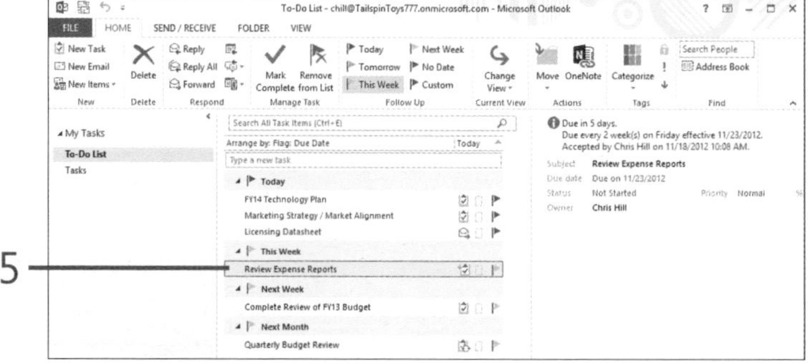

TIP When you reassign a task that someone has assigned to you and that third person accepts the task, Outlook sends an acceptance notice to you and to the task's originator. The status update list then includes the originator's address and yours, so you receive status updates along with the originator.

TIP When you accept or reject a task, Outlook deletes the task request message from your Inbox. You can't control this behavior to prevent Outlook from deleting the message. However, Outlook keeps copies in your Sent Items folder of task requests that you create.

Using alerts and mobile features

9

Microsoft Outlook 2013 offers some great mobility features to help you integrate it with your mobile devices. In particular, you can configure Outlook to send alerts to your cell phone when you receive important email or voice messages. Outlook can also send you reminders about appointments and meetings and a daily summary of your day's schedule. These features can help you arrive at your meetings on time and stay abreast of important email when you're out of the office.

In this section:

- Setting up your mobile phone in Microsoft Exchange
- Setting up calendar alerts
- Setting up mobile alerts for important messages

Setting up your mobile phone in Microsoft Exchange

Before you can receive alerts on your mobile device, you must configure your Exchange Server account settings to specify your mobile device number. (Note that your Exchange administrator might already have set it up.) If your Text Messaging page shows a Delete Settings button rather than a Turn On Notifications button, your mobile device is already configured for notifications through Exchange.

Add your mobile number

1 Click the File tab to display the Info page in the Backstage view, click the Account Settings buttons, and then, in the drop-down list that opens, click Manage Mobile Notifications.

(continued on next page)

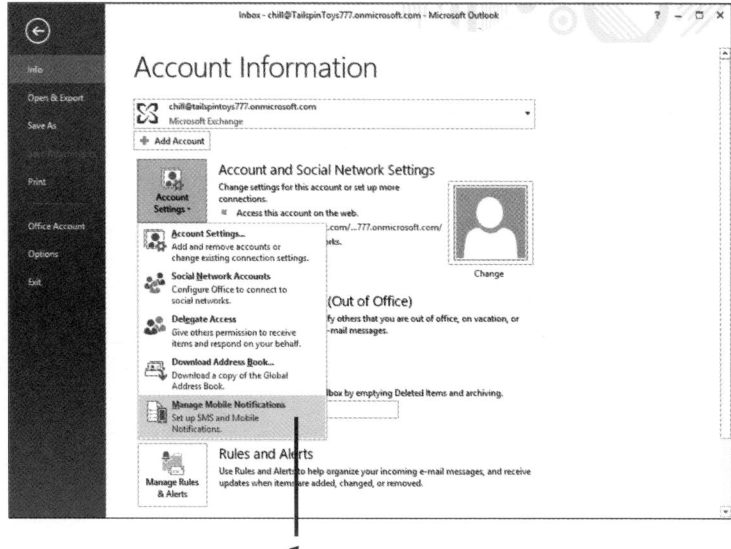

> **TIP** If the Manage Mobile Notifications option is missing from the Account Settings menu in Outlook, open Internet Explorer and browse to *https://YourMailServer/ecp*, where *YourMailServer* is the address of your Exchange Server. Then, log on using your domain credentials.

Add your mobile number *(continued)*

2 In the browser window that opens, in the Options section, click Phone.

3 Click Text Messaging.

4 Click Turn On Notifications.

5 In the Text Messaging Wizard that opens, choose your locale and cell provider and then click Next.

(continued on next page)

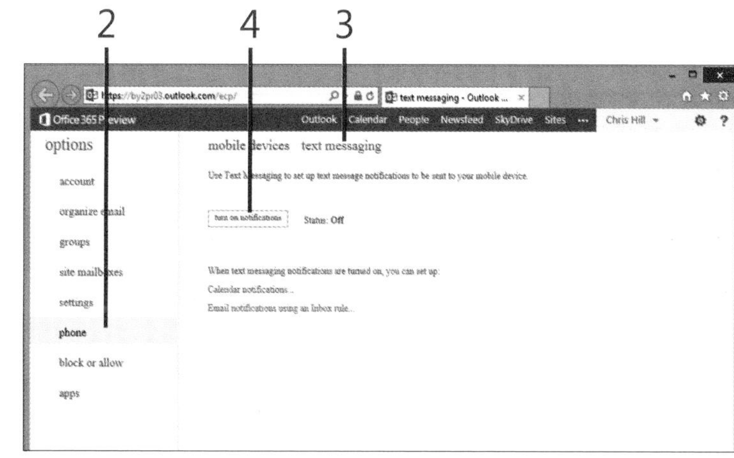

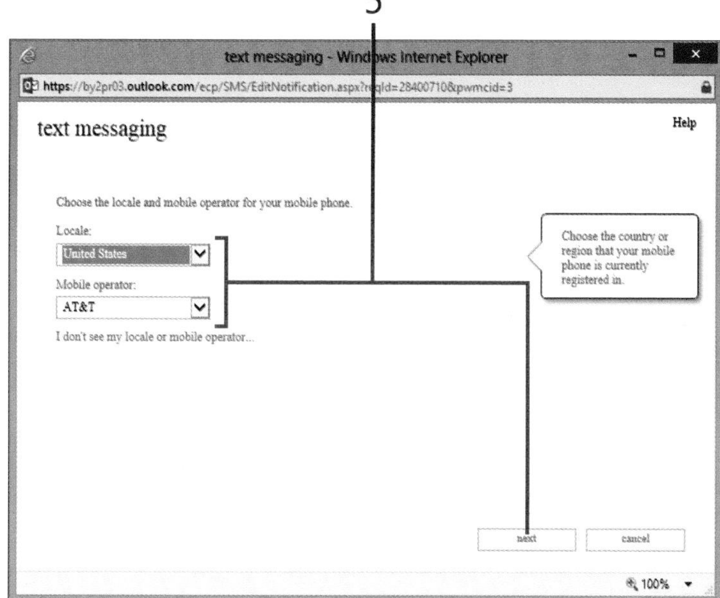

TIP The email and calendar alert features described in this chapter require an Exchange Server 2010 or later mailbox. The voice mail alerts also require that the mailbox user be enabled for unified messaging.

Add your mobile number *(continued)*

6 Enter your phone number and then click Next.

(continued on next page)

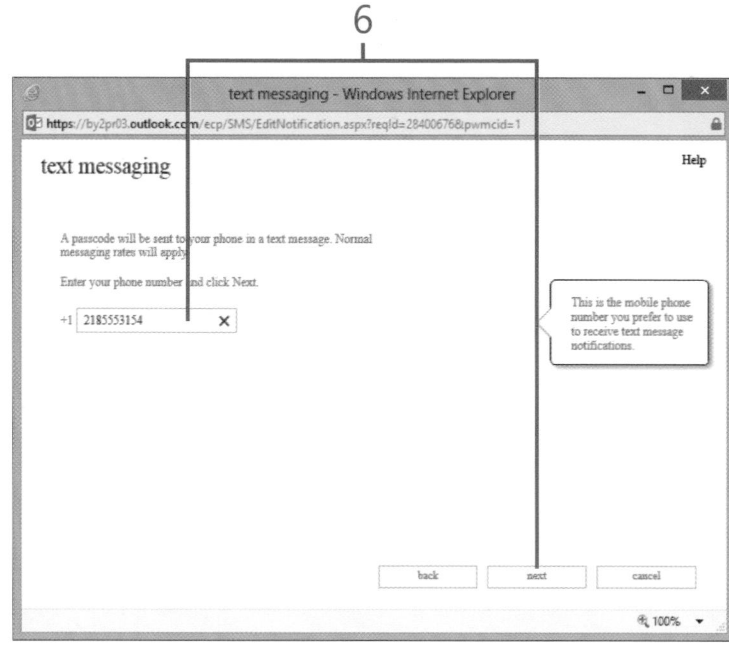

Add your mobile number *(continued)*

7 A passcode is sent to your phone; enter the passcode and click Finish.

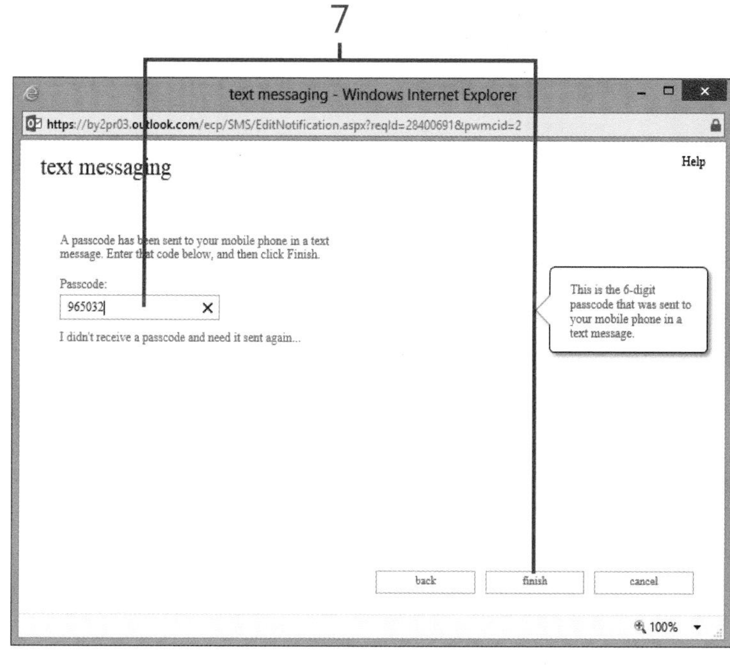

TIP Exchange Server sends a text message to your mobile device to let you know when you have successfully completed the alert setup process.

Setting up calendar alerts

Using calendar alerts, you can have Exchange Server send alerts to your mobile device when new items are added to your calendar or existing items are updated. This feature is particularly helpful when you're out of the office and an assistant is scheduling or accepting meetings for you. You can also have Exchange Server send reminders for meetings to your mobile device. In addition, you can configure your alert settings to have Exchange Server send a summary of your daily calendar agenda to your mobile device, giving you an easy reference to what's on your schedule for that day. These three features combined can keep you plugged into your schedule all day, even when you're away from your computer.

Add calendar alerts

1 Click the File tab to display the Info page in the Backstage view, click the Account Settings buttons, and then, in the drop-down list that opens, click Manage Mobile Notifications.

(continued on next page)

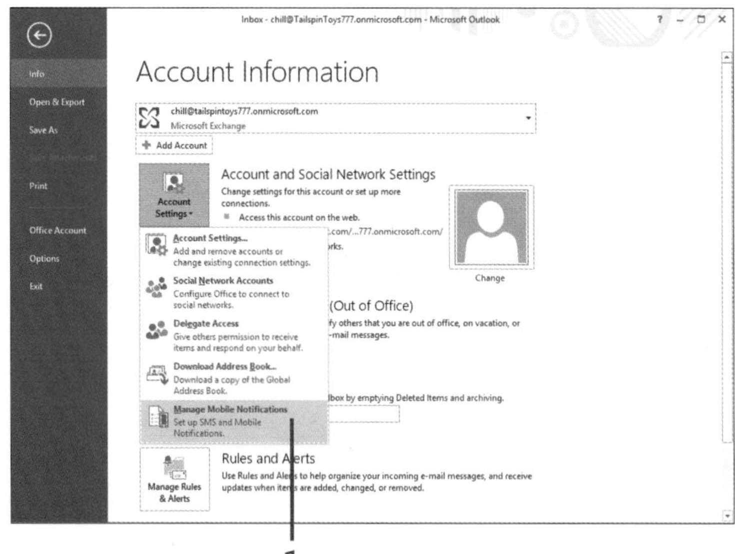

Add calendar alerts *(continued)*

2 In the browser window that opens, in the Options section, click Phone.
3 Click Text Messaging.
4 Click the Set Up Calendar Notifications link.
5 In the Text Messaging Notifications dialog box, optionally select to have Outlook send a notification when your calendar is updated.
6 Optionally select to have Outlook send you notifications for meeting reminders.
7 Optionally select to have Outlook send you a calendar summary at the specified time.
8 Click Save.

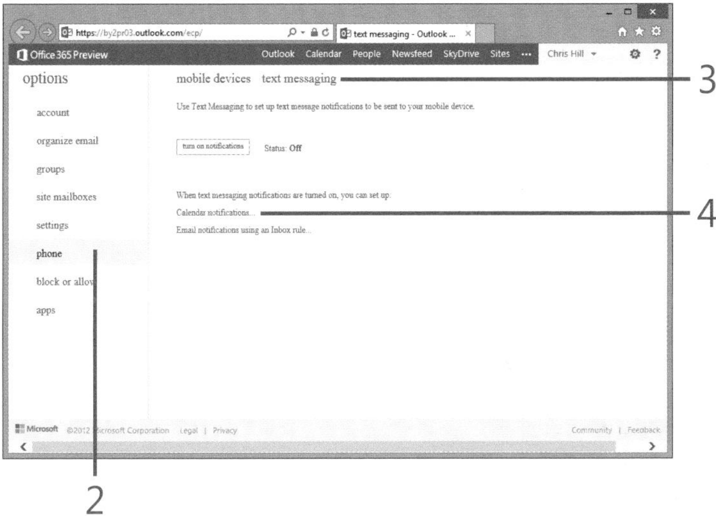

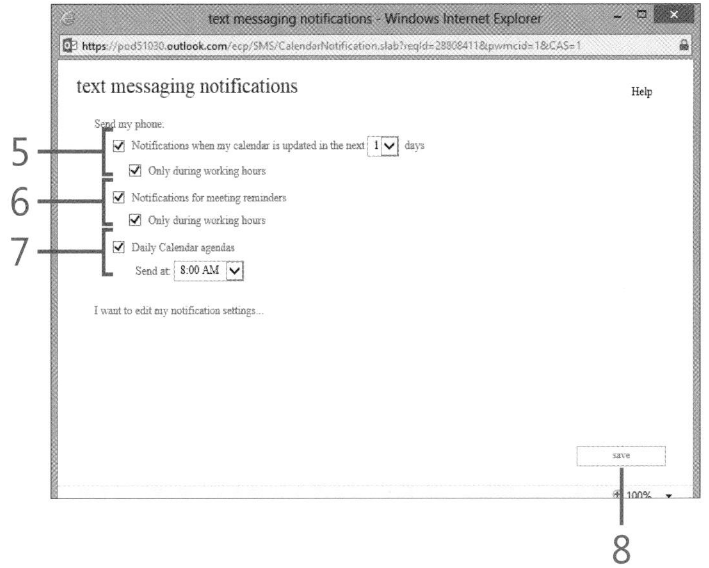

TIP If your schedule changes frequently, you might want to use the drop-down control on the Text Messaging Notifications dialog box to specify how many days ahead of its date you want to be notified or reminded of a new or changed calendar item. For example, choose 2 if you want to receive alerts about changes that affect your calendar over the next two days.

Setting up mobile alerts for important messages

If you have a mobile device that synchronizes your mailbox to your mobile device, you likely receive email on the device all day long. If not, you might want to configure Exchange Server to send an alert to your mobile device when you receive certain types of messages. For example, you might want it to send you an alert when you receive an email from your manager or an incident management system, or if you get an email that contains specific words in the subject, related to a particular project.

Set up mobile alerts

1 Click the File tab to display the Info page in the Backstage view, click the Account Settings buttons, and then, in the drop-down list that opens, click Manage Mobile Notifications.

2 In the browser window that opens, in the Options section, click Phone.

3 Click Text Messaging.

4 Click the Email Notifications Using An Inbox Rule link.

(continued on next page)

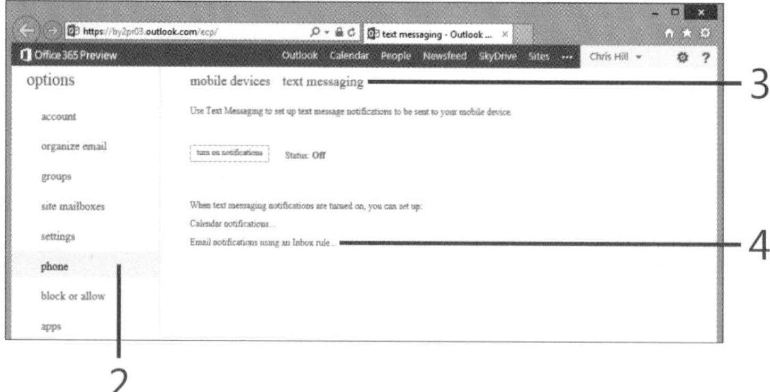

TIP Even if your mobile device synchronizes with your Exchange mailbox and you receive all email on your mobile device, you might still want to set up alerts. If you receive a lot of email during the day, you probably have configured your mobile device not to alert you when you receive an email. You can create the alert for the types of messages for which you do want to receive notification, and then you can configure your mobile device to notify you with a sound or vibration when you receive a text message. When you get the alert from Exchange Server, you can scroll through the email you've already received to find the one for which you received the alert.

Set up mobile alerts *(continued)*

5 In the New Inbox Rule dialog box, type a name for the rule.

6 Choose a condition for the rule.

7 Click to further define the condition (such as choose a sender).

8 Choose Send A Text Message To.

9 Click to select your mobile device.

10 Click Save.

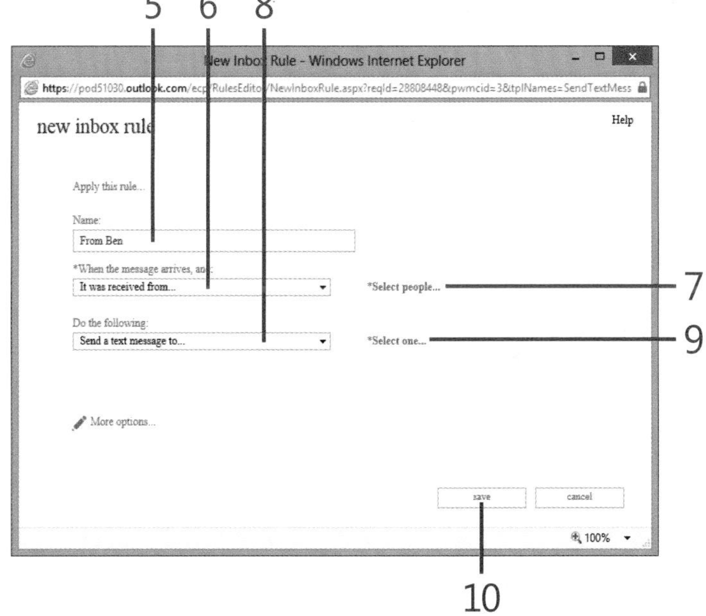

TIP You can click More Options to expand the dialog box to show options that let you add exceptions to the rule. For example, you might add an exception if the message is marked as low priority so that you don't receive alerts for those messages. Or, you might add an exception for messages for which your name is in the Cc field so that you receive alerts only for messages that were sent directly to you.

Using Outlook with SharePoint

10

Microsoft SharePoint is a leading solution for collaboration. Users can share documents, calendars, contacts, and other information among teams or across entire organizations. When you add SharePoint's process automation and business intelligence features, SharePoint becomes a rich framework for portals, dashboards, records management, and other collaboration features. Although many people work with SharePoint content from their web browsers, that's not the only way to interact with that content. You can use Microsoft Outlook 2013 to work with shared calendars, contacts, and other SharePoint content; you can integrate that content into the application that you probably use much of your day. This section shows you how to integrate SharePoint and Outlook.

In this section:

Using SharePoint calendars with Outlook

Outlook 2013 offers great features for managing your schedule. Its ability to display and even overlay multiple calendars is very handy for viewing schedules for multiple people or projects. If you use SharePoint to maintain shared calendars for time off, projects, team deliverables, and so on, you can open those calendars right in Outlook and work with them as if they were your own calendars. Updates that you make in Outlook are synchronized to SharePoint, and vice versa. The first step is to connect the SharePoint calendar to Outlook.

Connect a SharePoint calendar to Outlook

1 Open the calendar in SharePoint. On the ribbon, click the Calendar tab.

2 In the Connect And Export group, click Connect To Outlook.

3 In the Internet Explorer dialog box, click Allow.

(continued on next page)

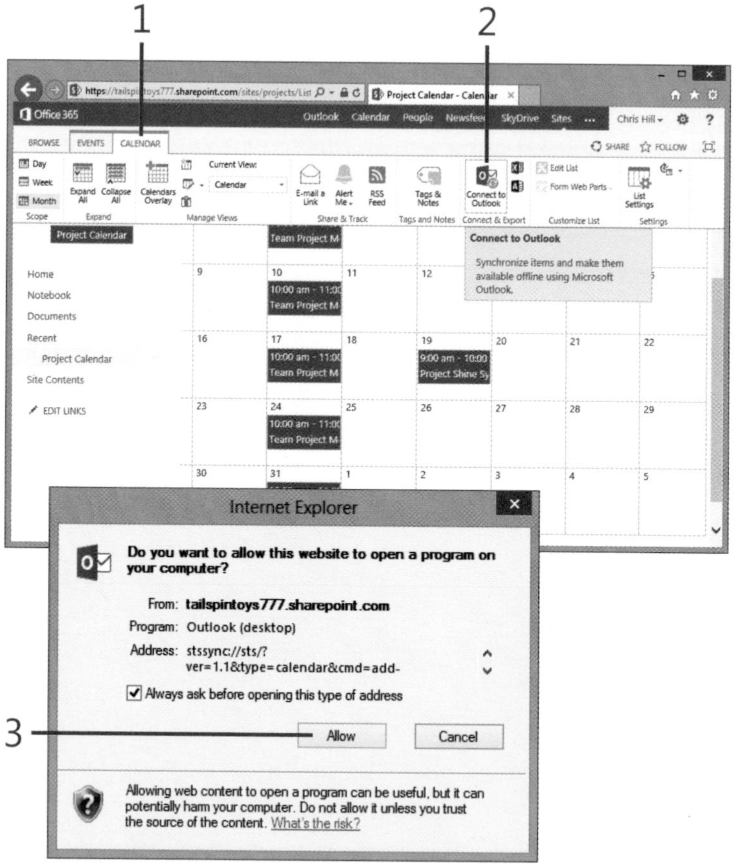

TIP The process for connecting a SharePoint calendar to Outlook is very similar for SharePoint 2007, 2010, and 2013. Look on the Actions menu on the calendar for the Connect To Outlook command.

Connect a SharePoint calendar to Outlook *(continued)*

4 In the Microsoft Outlook dialog box, click Yes. Enter your credentials for the SharePoint site, if you're prompted.

5 The SharePoint calendar appears in Outlook.

6 The calendar appears in the Folder pane.

7 Click the arrow icon to overlay the SharePoint calendar on your own calendar.

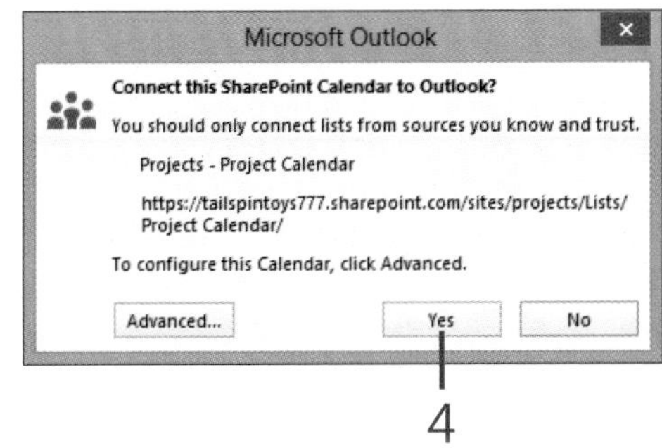

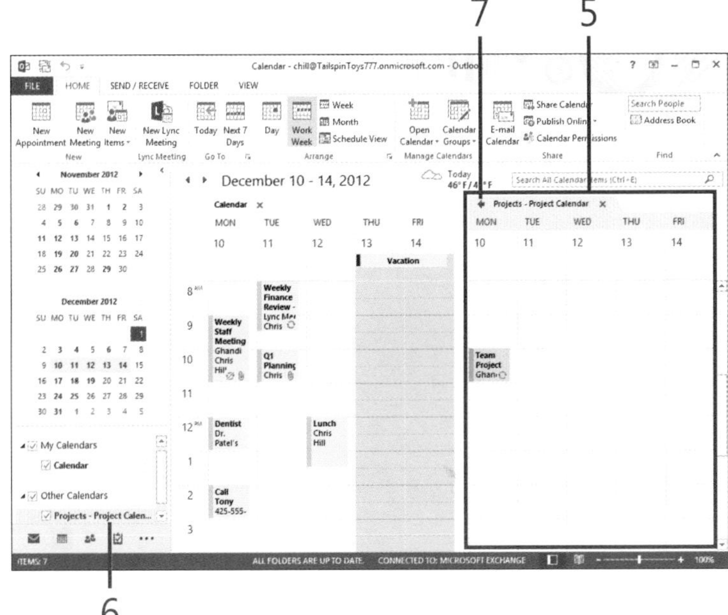

TRY THIS! To view details of an item in a SharePoint calendar, just click the item in SharePoint to open a form that shows those details.

TIP Use Alerts to have SharePoint notify you when a calendar changes.

Create and edit SharePoint calendar items from Outlook

1. At the bottom of the Folder pane, click the Calendar icon to open the Calendar folder.
2. Choose the SharePoint calendar that you want to view.
3. Optionally, clear the check box for your default calendar to remove it from the view.
4. Select a time range in the calendar.
5. On the Home tab, in the New group, click New Meeting.
6. Add attendees and other details as needed.
7. Click Send.
8. In the pop-up message box that appears, click Yes.

(continued on next page)

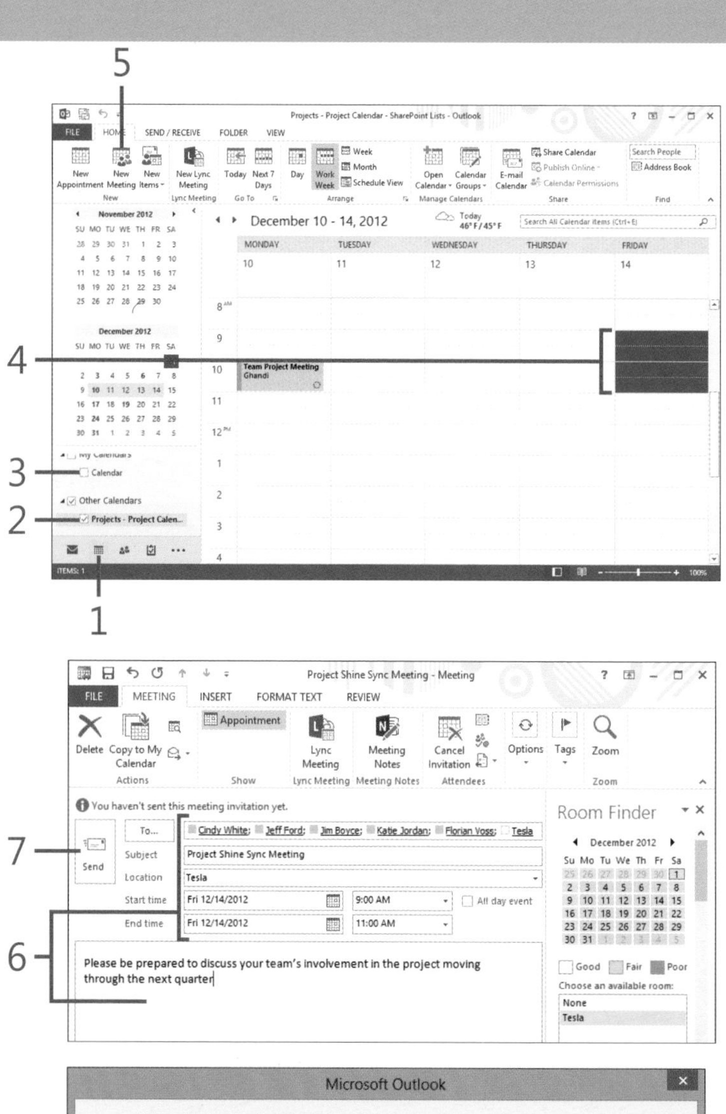

Create and edit SharePoint calendar items from Outlook *(continued)*

9 The new item appears in Outlook.

10 The new item also appears in SharePoint.

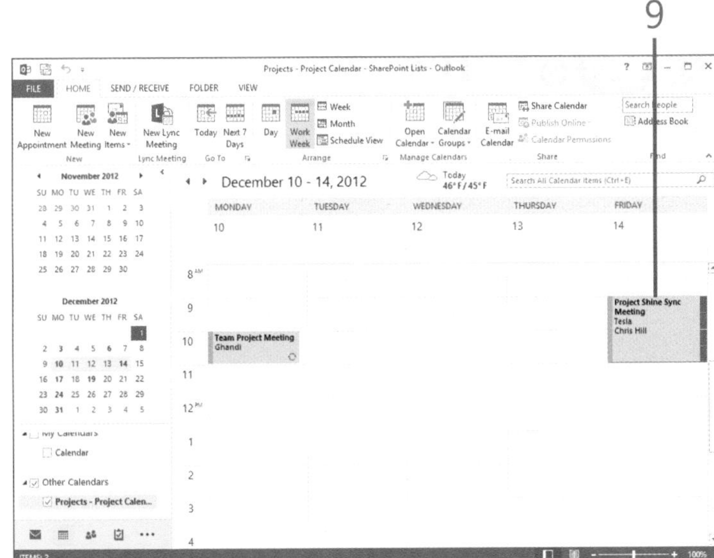

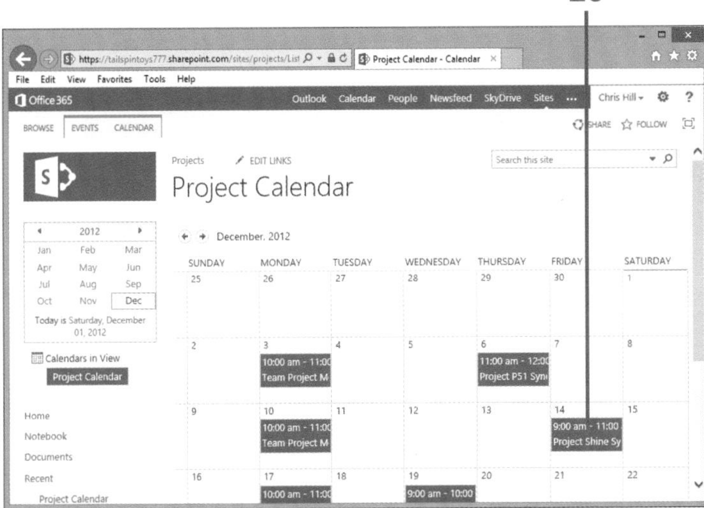

TIP You can create meetings in a SharePoint calendar, but you won't receive a tally of responses from requested participants. To receive tallies, you must create the meeting in your local Outlook Calendar folder.

TRY THIS! Use a different color in Outlook for each calendar that you overlay so that you can easily see which items are on each calendar.

Using SharePoint contacts in Outlook

If you use Exchange Server, your Global Address List (GAL) lists the people who have mailboxes in your organization and can also include other contacts added by the Exchange Server administrators. If you need to share other types of contacts—such as vendors or customers—with a team or even across your entire organization, you can turn to SharePoint as the place to share those contacts. Everyone can then connect that SharePoint contacts list in Outlook 2013 to work with the contacts, adding and updating them according to their SharePoint permissions for the shared list.

Connect a SharePoint contact list to Outlook

1 Open the SharePoint site in your web browser and navigate to the shared contacts list.
2 On the ribbon, click the List tab.
3 In the Connect & Export group, click Connect To Outlook.
4 In the Internet Explorer dialog box, click Allow.

(continued on next page)

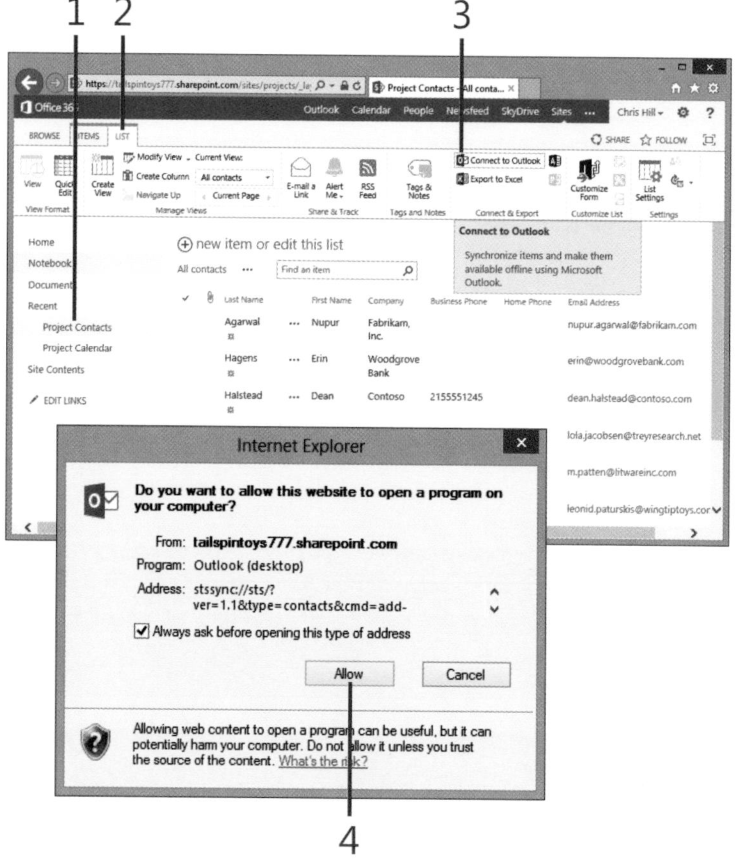

Connect a SharePoint contact list to Outlook *(continued)*

5 In the Microsoft Outlook dialog box, click Yes.

6 The shared contacts appear in Outlook.

7 The SharePoint list shows up in the Folder pane.

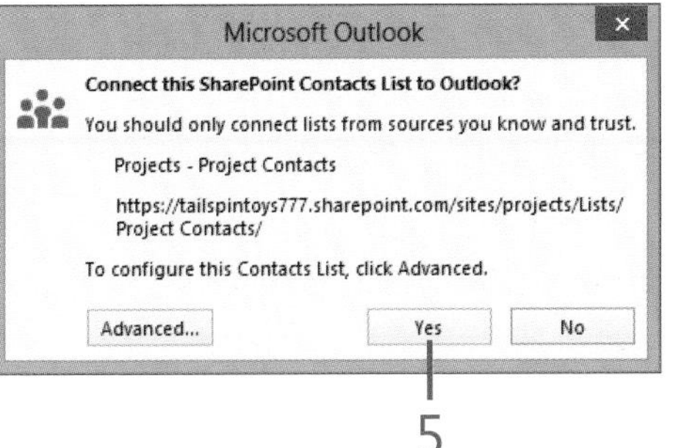

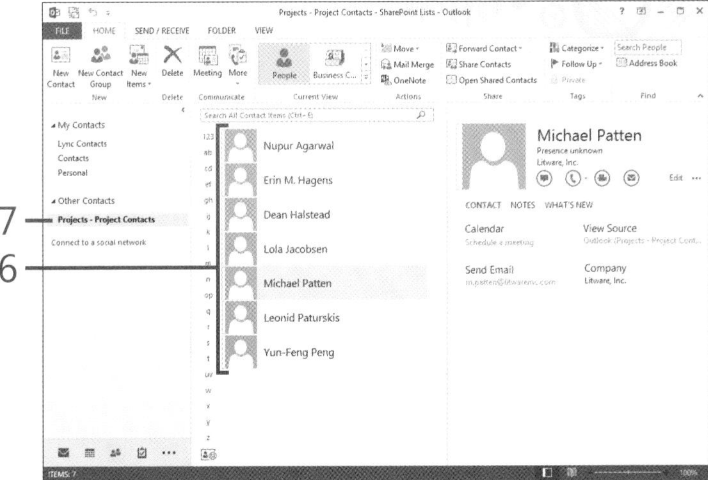

Create contacts in a SharePoint list from Outlook

1. In the folder pane, click the SharePoint contact list. Choose a different view, if you want.
2. On the Home tab, in the New group, click New Contact.
3. Enter the name and other details for the new contact.
4. Click Save & Close.

(continued on next page)

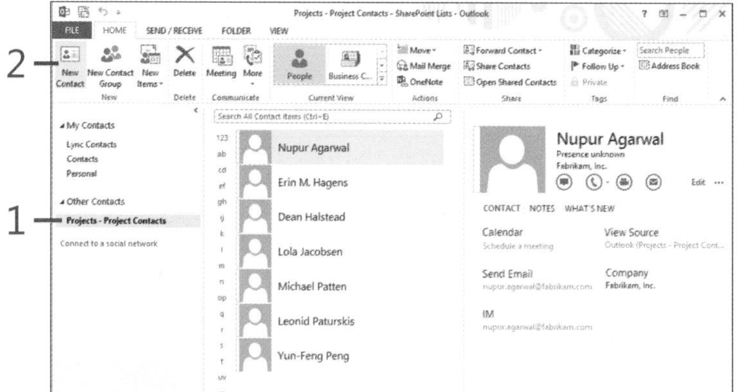

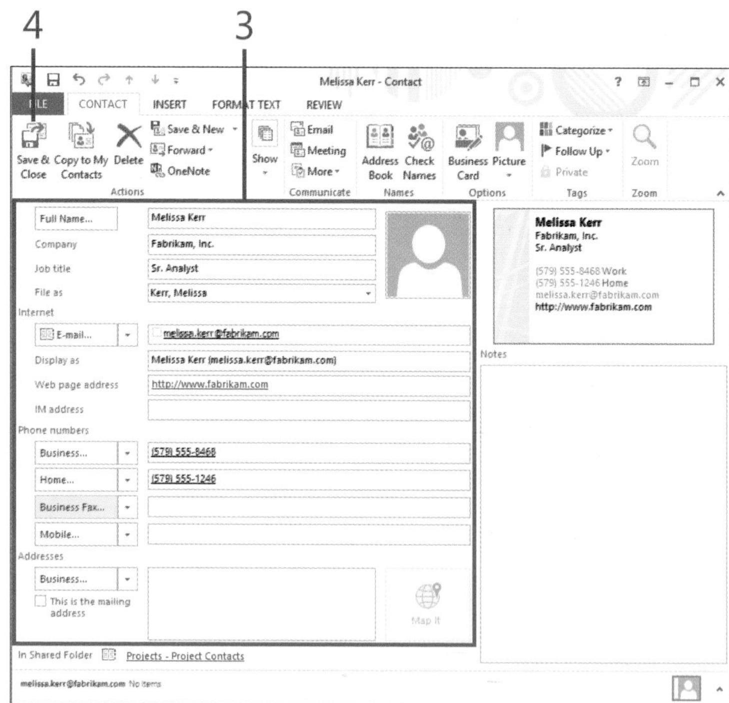

Create contacts in a SharePoint list from Outlook *(continued)*

5 The new contact appears in the list in Outlook.

6 The new contact also appears in the SharePoint list.

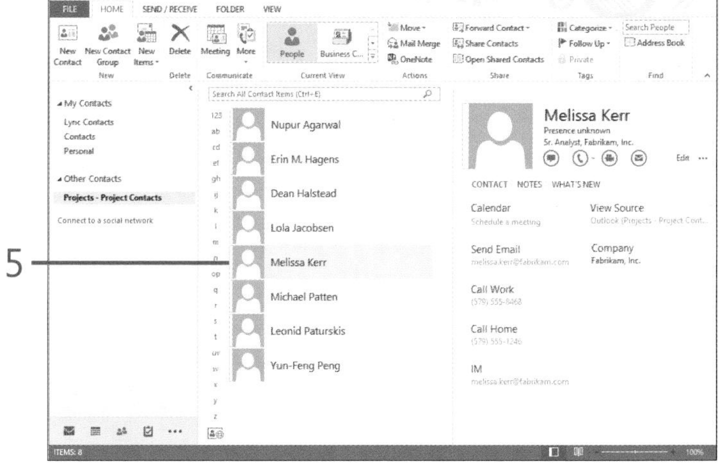

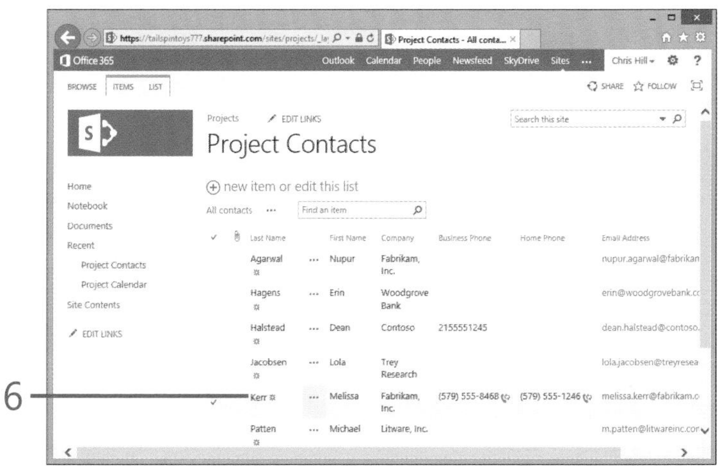

> **TIP** It's relatively easy to copy your Outlook contacts to a SharePoint list to share them with others. Just create the shared contacts list in SharePoint and then connect it to Outlook. Then, simply copy the contacts from your Contacts folder to the SharePoint folder in Outlook.

Using SharePoint document libraries in Outlook

SharePoint calendars and contacts are particular types of lists in SharePoint. You can connect other types of lists to Outlook 2013, as well. For example, you can connect a document library. When you do so, Outlook creates a cached local copy of the documents on your computer.

Connect a document library to Outlook

1 Open the SharePoint document library. On the ribbon, click the Library tab.

2 In the Connect & Export group, click Connect To Outlook.

3 In the Internet Explorer dialog box, click Allow.

4 In the Microsoft Outlook dialog box, click Yes.

(continued on next page)

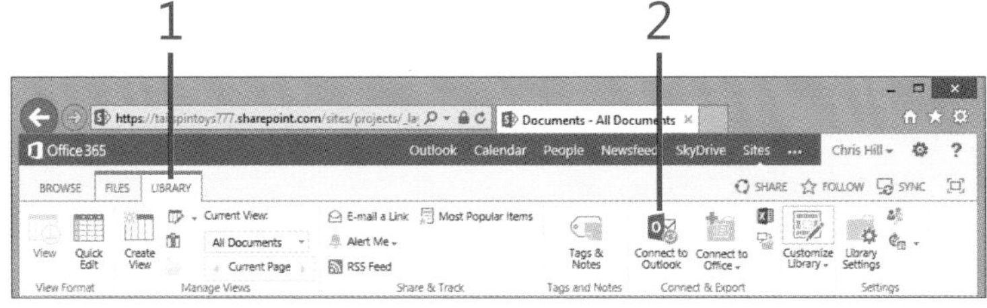

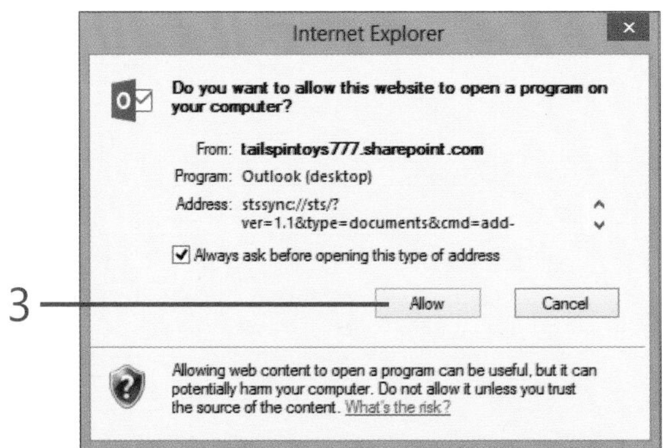

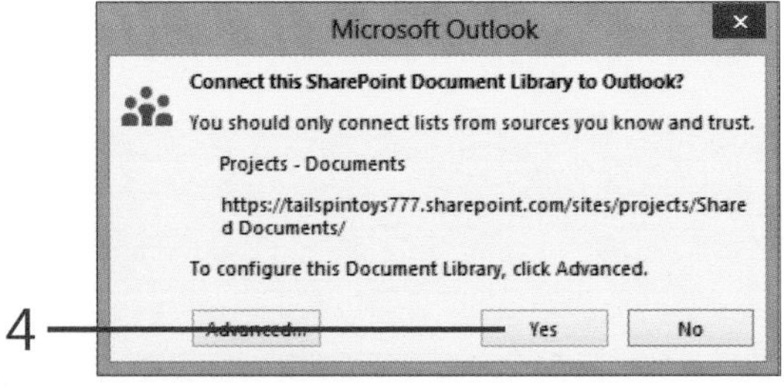

TIP Connecting a SharePoint document library to Outlook creates a synchronized version of all of the documents in the library. If the library contains a large number of documents or if the documents themselves are large, it could take some time to download them to Outlook. It can also consume a large amount of local disk storage.

Connect a document library to Outlook *(continued)*

5 The documents appear in Outlook.

6 The Documents library appears in the Folder pane.

7 Preview the document in the Reading pane.

8 Double-click a document to open it.

9 Click Edit Offline to edit the offline copy of the document. After you save your changes, Outlook synchronizes the updated copy to SharePoint.

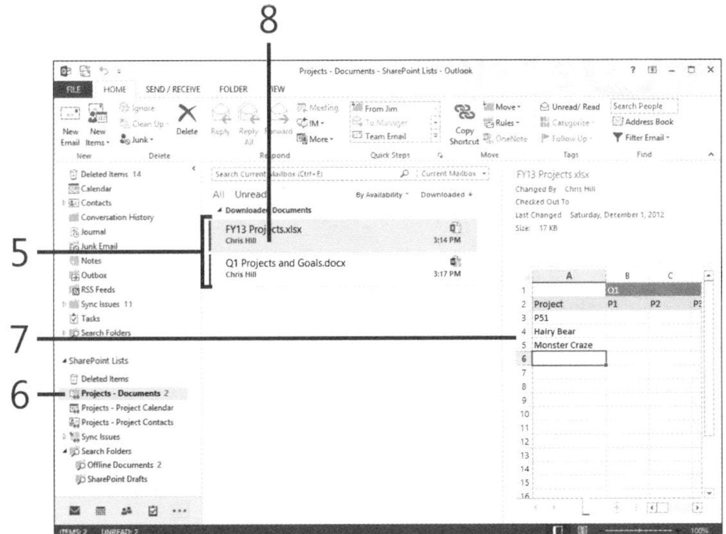

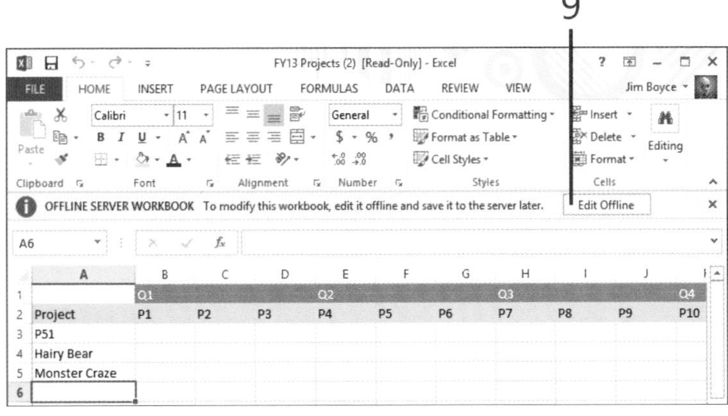

TIP Consider SharePoint Workspace as an alternative to working with document libraries offline in Outlook. SharePoint Workspace makes it possible for you to work with SharePoint content offline without connecting the content in Outlook, and it gives you greater control over what is synchronized and when.

Using Lync with Outlook

11

Microsoft Lync is a unified communications platform that provides capabilities for instant messaging, audio and video conferencing, and voice calling. In environments in which Lync is deployed, Microsoft Outlook 2013 can integrate with the Lync client to simplify communication. This section helps you to understand and use the core features of Lync within Outlook.

In this section:

- Creating and joining Lync meetings
- Setting Lync meeting options
- Starting an instant message conversation
- Starting voice and video calls

Creating and joining Lync meetings

If you have Lync deployed in your environment (or you are using Microsoft Office 365), you can use Lync to hold online meetings with others. In the meeting, you can use audio, video, and desktop sharing to communicate and collaborate. The first step in using Lync for online meetings is to create an online meeting in Outlook 2013.

Create an online meeting

1 Open the Calendar and choose a time for the meeting.

2 On the Home tab, in the Lync Meeting group, click New Lync Meeting.

(continued on next page)

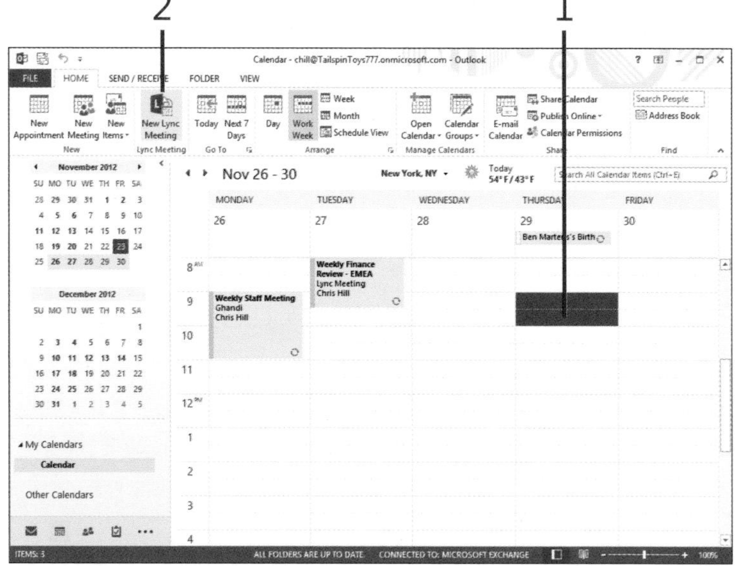

> **TIP** You can change a non-Lync meeting to a Lync meeting easily. Just open the meeting, and click Lync Meeting on the ribbon.

Create an online meeting *(continued)*

3 Add meeting attendees.

4 Add a meeting subject.

5 Add notes or attachments.

6 Note the Lync Meeting link in the invitation.

7 Click Send.

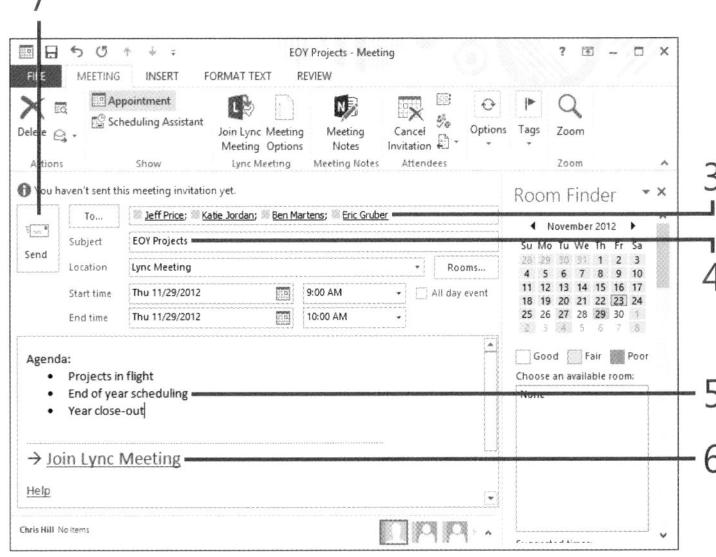

SEE ALSO There are several options you can configure for an online meeting. For details, see "Setting Lync meeting options" on page 203.

Join a Lync meeting

1 In the Calendar, click to select the Lync meeting.

2 On the Home tab, in the Lync Meeting group, click Join Lync Meeting.

3 In the Join Meeting Audio dialog box, click the Use Lync option to use Lync's audio.

4 Alternatively, click the Call Me At option to have Lync call you back at a specified phone number.

5 Alternatively, click the Don't Join Audio option if you don't want to use Lync for audio (for example, you're dialed in via phone).

6 Click OK.

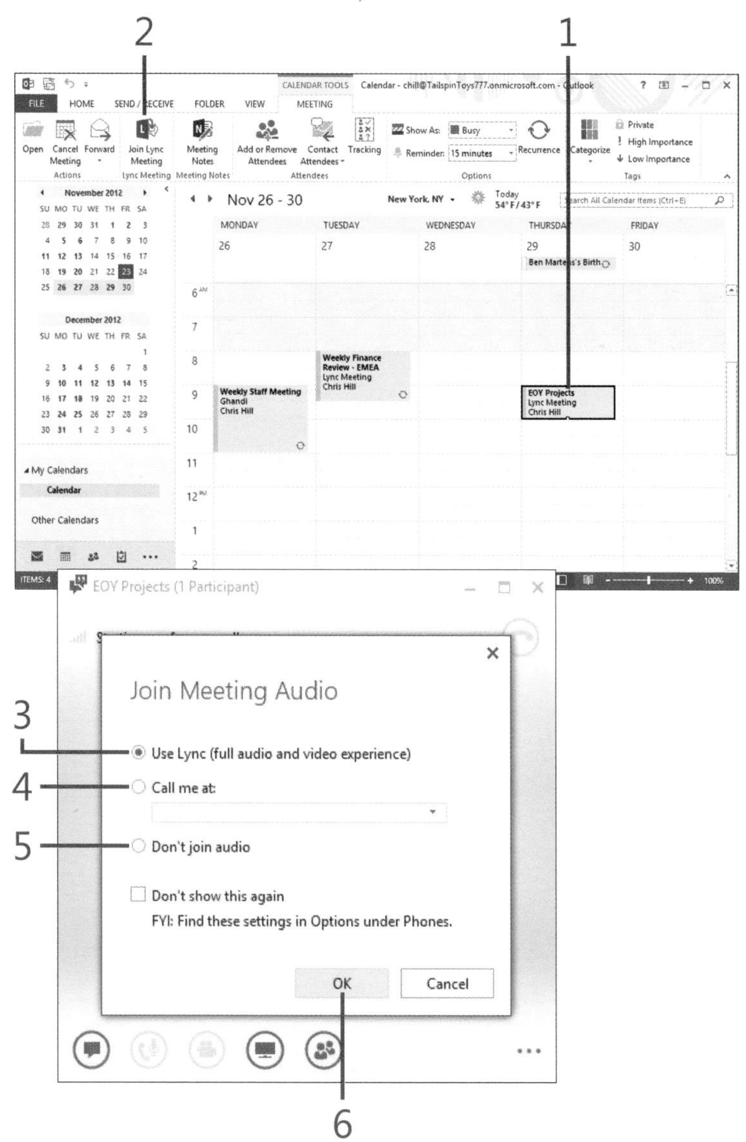

TIP Use the Call Me At option and specify a call-back number to have Lync call you. For example, if you're having problems with your computer's audio, you can have Lync call your office phone or cell phone.

TRY THIS! Hover your mouse pointer over the phone icon in the Lync client to display a dial pad for dialing a conference ID number.

Setting Lync meeting options

You can set several options for a Lync meeting to specify who can join the meeting automatically and who needs to wait in the virtual lobby and be admitted. You can specify which participants can act as presenters for the meeting (for example, sharing their applications for others to see). You can even set up the meeting so that only the organizer can speak, muting all other participants. You can set these options when you create the meeting, or you can edit the options for an existing meeting.

Set Online meeting options

1 Create a new Lync meeting or open an existing one.

2 On the Meeting tab, in the Lync Meeting group, click Meeting Options.

(continued on next page)

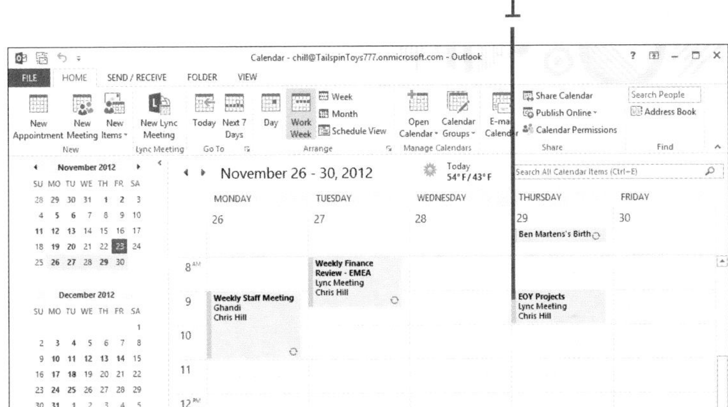

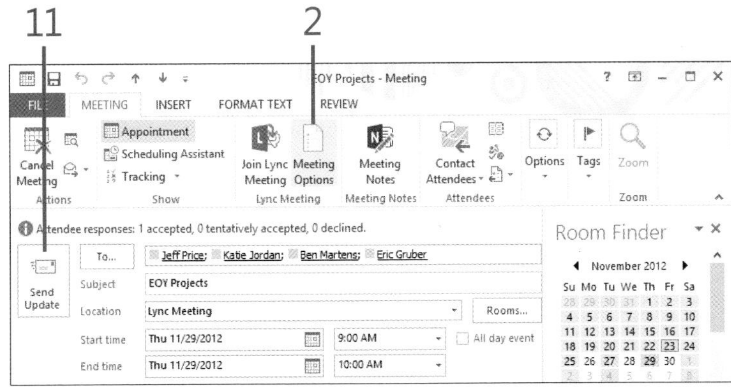

TIP The Don't Join Audio option is useful when you are using a conference phone or other audio device to call into the meeting and don't want to use your computer's audio for the call.

Set Online meeting options *(continued)*

3 In the Lync Meeting Options dialog box, specify which attendees can enter the meeting without waiting in the lobby.

4 Choose an option to specify which attendees can be a presenter.

5 Click Choose Presenters to assign specific people as presenters.

6 In the Meeting Options Presenter dialog box, select a person from the Attendees list, and then click Add to add that person as a presenter.

7 Click OK.

8 Select whether to mute all attendees and whether to block attendees' video.

9 Click Remember Settings to save the settings for your other Lync meetings.

10 Click OK.

11 Make other changes as needed, and then click Send Update (refer back to the screenshot on the previous page).

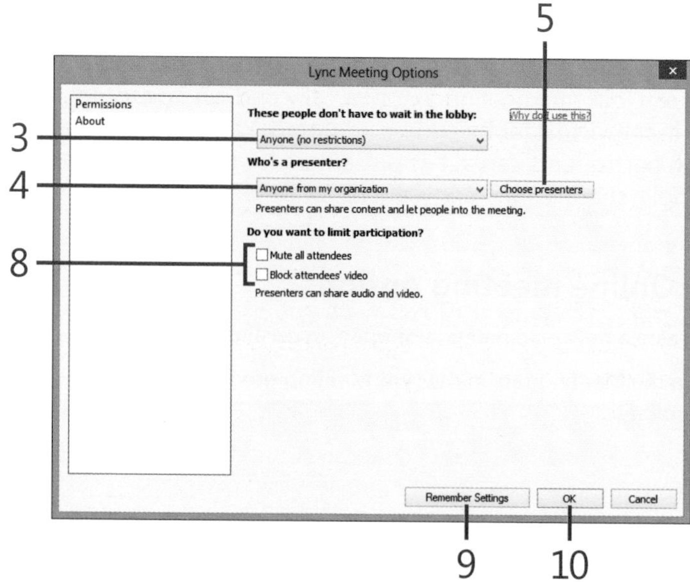

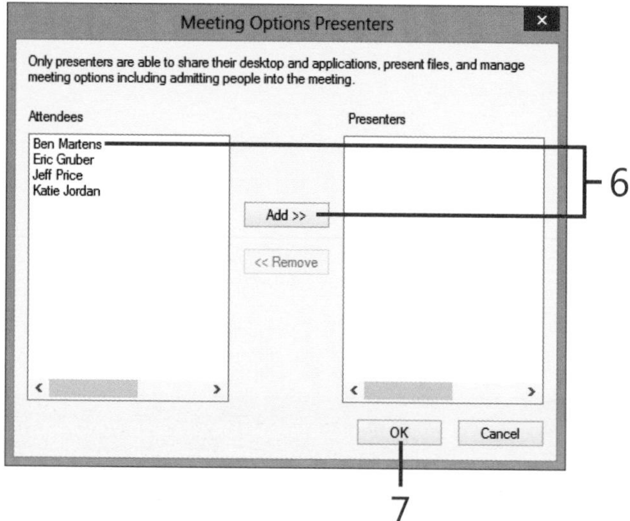

Starting an instant message conversation

You can easily use Lync to start an instant messaging (IM) conversation with others through Outlook 2013. To facilitate this feature, Outlook shows the online status of others (called presence), by which you to tell at a glance whether a person is online and available.

Start an IM conversation from an email

1 Open the Inbox and select a message with the desired contact as a recipient or sender.

2 In the Reading pane or the People pane, hover the mouse pointer over the person's name or picture.

3 On the menu that appears appears, click the Send An IM button.

(continued on next page)

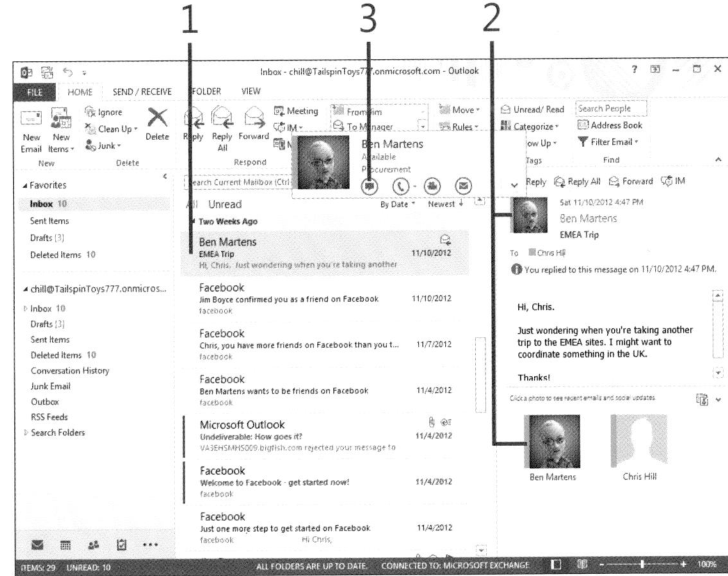

TRY THIS! Click the Font button (represented by a capital letter A) in the Lync IM window to change the font used for your IM conversation.

Start an IM conversation from an email *(continued)*

4 In the Lync client window, type your message and press Enter.

5 To invite others to the same conversation, at the bottom of the Lync client window, click the Invite More People button.

6 Choose an individual (or individuals).

7 Click OK.

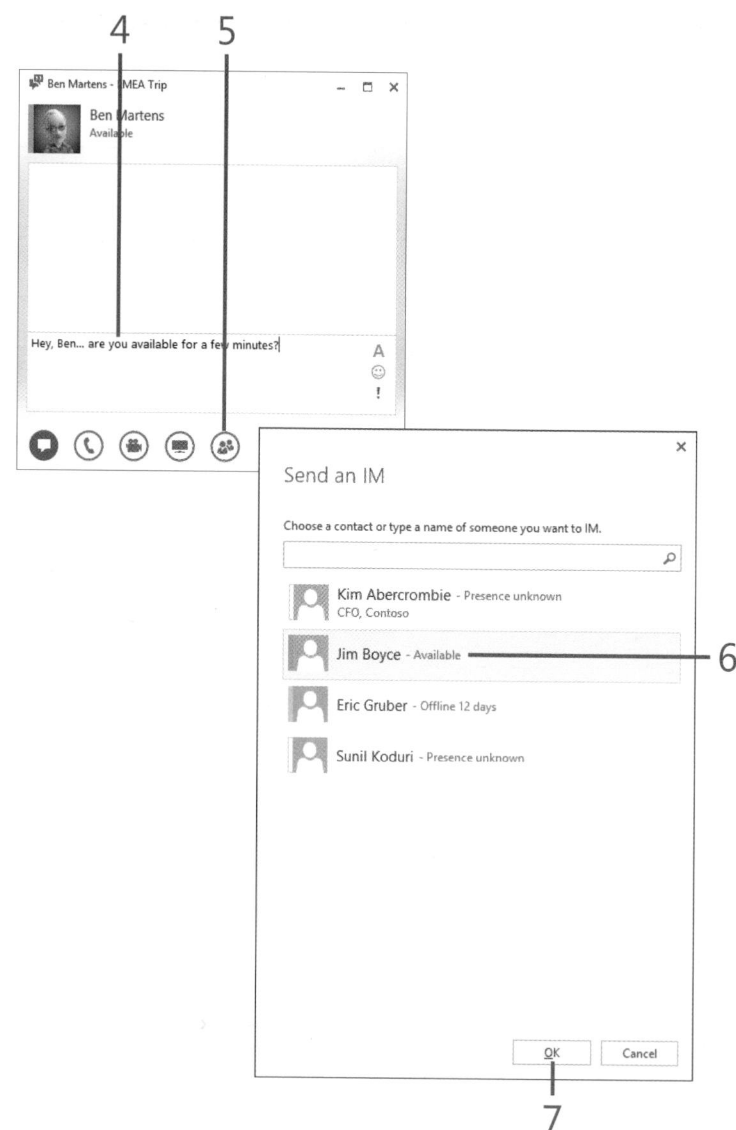

TIP Click the Set High Importance button (represented by an exclamation mark) in the Lync IM window to mark your message as important. Lync will display an exclamation mark to the left of the message in the recipient's Lync IM window.

Start an IM conversation from the People Hub

1. At the bottom of the Folder pane, click the People icon to display the People Hub.
2. Locate a contact whose presence shows as online.
3. In the Reading pane, click the Send An IM button.
4. After the Lync IM window appears, type your message and press Enter.

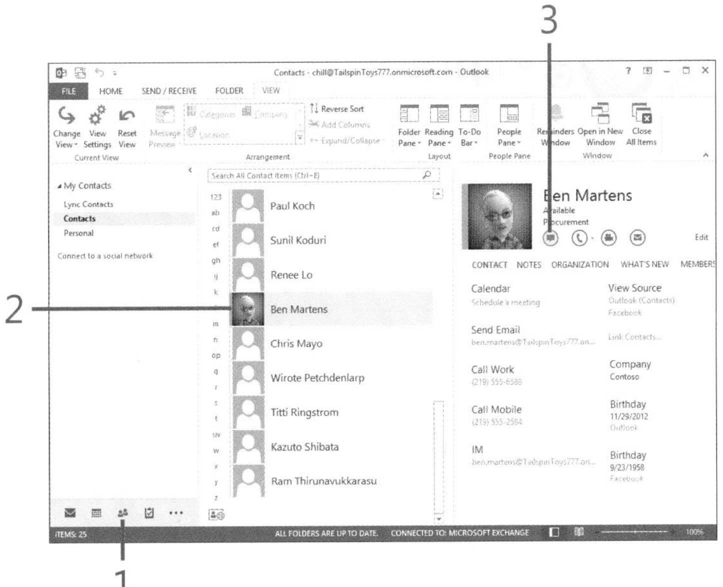

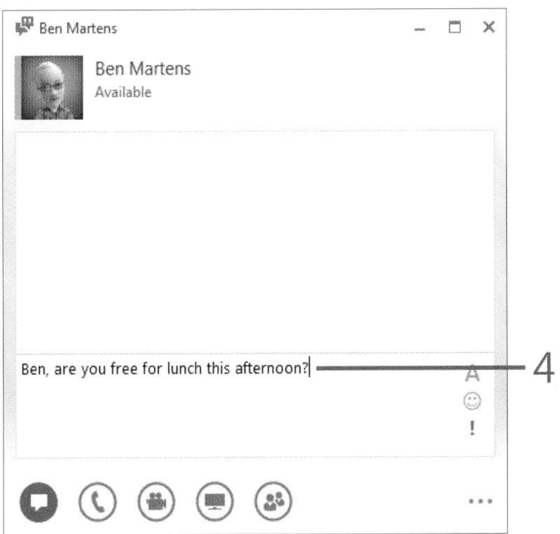

TIP The presence indicator isn't always an exact representation of another person's status. For example, the person might in fact be online and at her computer but has set her status as Away to reduce interruptions.

TRY THIS! You can quickly start a voice call from an IM window. Just click the Call button at the bottom of the IM window and choose which number to call.

Starting voice and video calls

You can easily start a Lync voice call from Outlook 2013, in much the same way you start an instant message. Anywhere you see presence information for a person in Outlook, you can start a voice call simply by clicking the Call button in that individual's contact card. Similarly, if you have a webcam connected to your computer (or built in), you can use Lync to make and receive video calls. The other participant will see your video, and if they also have a camera and have it enabled for the call, you'll see their video. Although the examples in this section start voice and video calls from the People Hub, you can also start calls from any location in Outlook that shows presence, such as the Inbox.

Start a voice call

1 At the bottom of the Folder pane, click the People icon to display the People Hub.

2 Select the contact whom you want to call.

3 In the Reading pane, click the Call button.

(continued on next page)

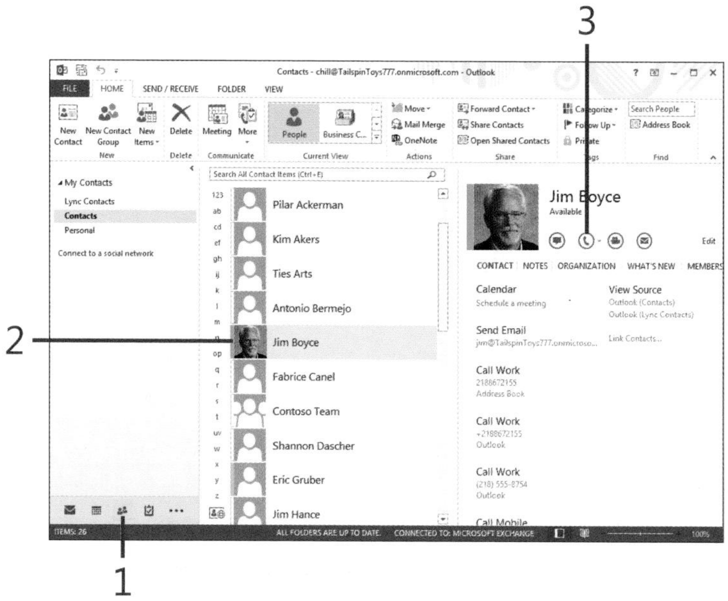

TIP You can merge together two calls. After you call and connect to the first person, call the second person. Lync will put the first call on hold. Then, in the lower-right corner of the Call window, click the ellipsis button. On the menu that appears, click Merge This Call Into and then choose the other call. Lync will join the calls into one.

Start a voice call *(continued)*

4 Track the length of time the call is active.

5 Click to mute.

6 Click to disconnect the call.

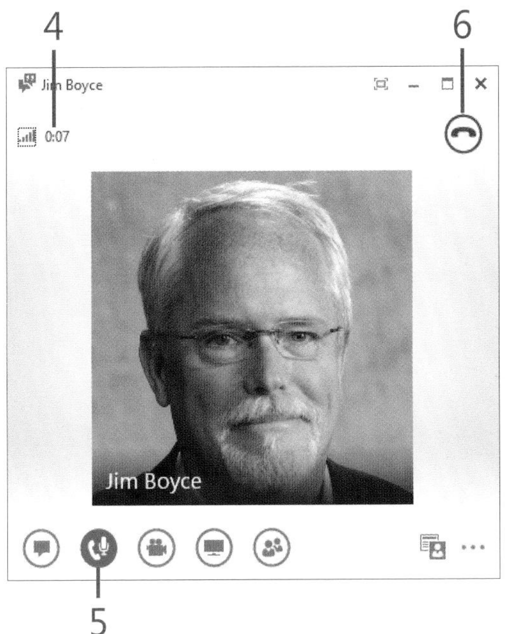

TRY THIS! Clicking the microphone button in the Call window mutes and unmutes your microphone. Hover the mouse pointer over the microphone button to display a dial pad that you can use to enter numbers in the call. For example, you might use the dial pad to dial a conference number after you have connected to the conference call main number.

Start a video call

1 In the Folder pane (shown collapsed), click the People icon to display the People Hub.

2 Select the contact whom you want to call.

3 In the Reading pane, click the Start Video Call button.

(continued on next page)

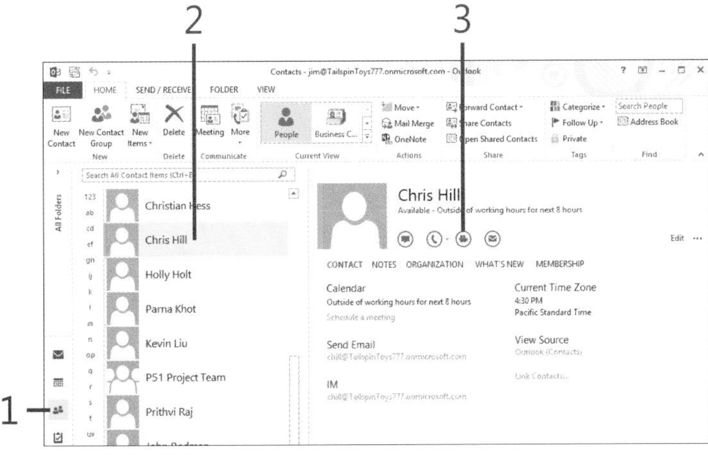

Start a video call *(continued)*

4 Lync shows your video preview.

5 Lync shows call status.

6 After the other person accepts the video call, you see his video.

7 Click to disconnect the call when finished.

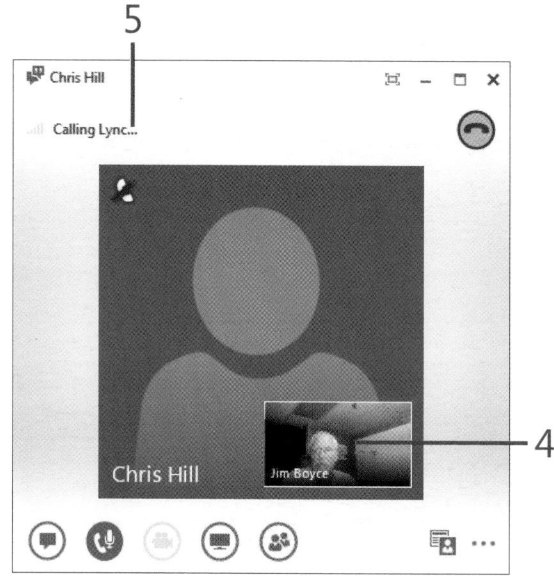

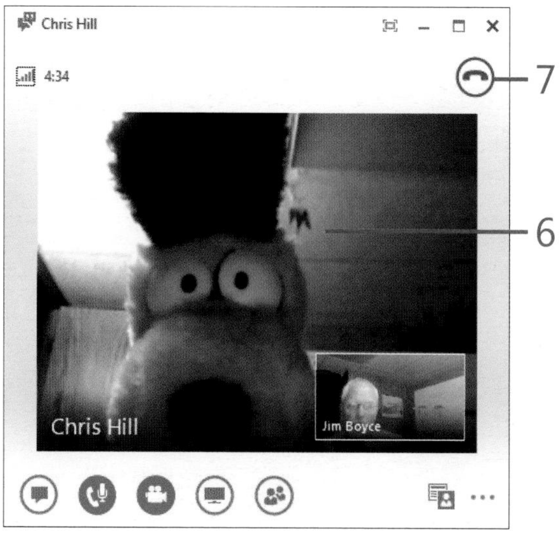

Managing items and folders

12

In this section:

- Using categories
- Adding your own categories
- Renaming and deleting categories
- Creating search folders
- Organizing with folders
- Cleaning up folders
- Deleting items

Microsoft Outlook 2013 gives you several ways to manage your Outlook items and folders, including organizing items in categories, creating and using folders to store items, and using the Mailbox Cleanup tool.

Outlook's abilities to help you manage message threads (conversations) have improved, as well. You can group messages into conversations so that you can view all messages in the thread, regardless of the folder in which they're stored. You can also use some new cleanup features to eliminate duplicate messages from a conversation.

Quick Steps are another new feature in Outlook 2013. Quick Steps are a little like rules except that they don't have conditions. Instead, they're actions that you define and that you can apply to messages selectively. For example, you might create Quick Steps to move messages to specific folders.

This section covers how to manage your items and folders in Outlook 2013. It covers how to categorize items, organize folders, delete items, and clean up folders.

Using categories

Categories use color indicators with associated keywords or phrases that help you to manage Outlook 2013 items, such as contacts, email messages, journal entries, and meetings. With categories, you can set up relationships between items stored in different places in Outlook. For example, you can categorize a piece of email and a meeting reminder as business items. Then, when you sort, filter, or search for all your business-related items, that email message and meeting reminder appear.

Categorize an item

1. Select an item.
2. On the Home tab, in the Tags group, click Categorize.
3. In the list that appears, choose a category to assign to the item.
4. A color category indicator appears in the Categories column and in the header.

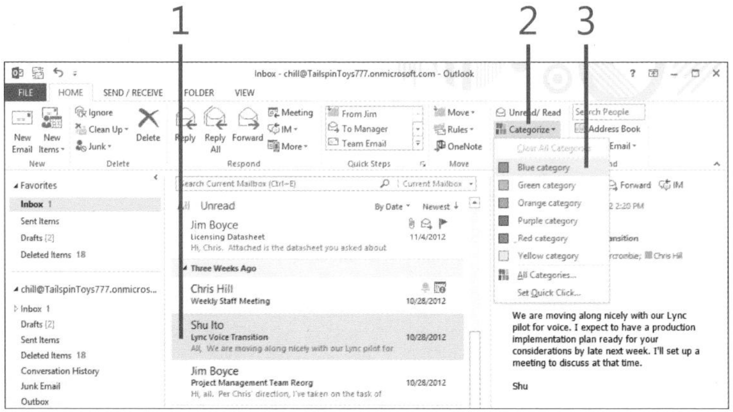

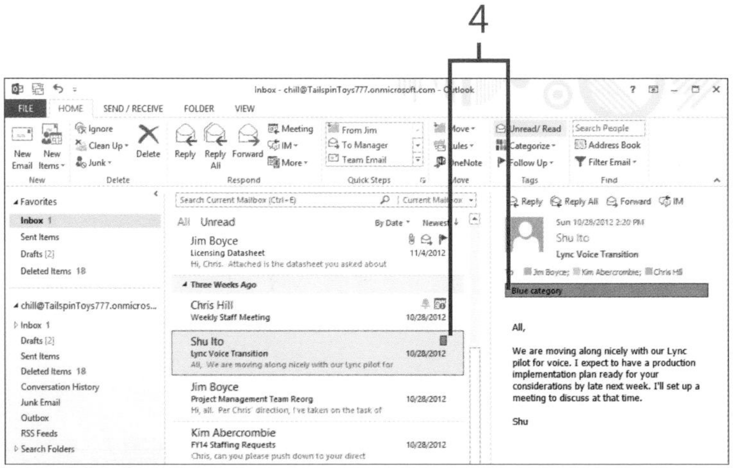

TIP You can associate an item with as many categories as you like. The more categories with which you associate an item, the easier it is to find that item when you conduct searches. The first time you have used the category, Outlook asks if you want to change the color. For now, just click No. You learn about changing category properties later in this section.

Assign multiple categories

1 Select an item.

2 On the Home tab, in the Tags group, click Categorize.

3 In the list that appears, choose All Categories.

4 In the Color Categories dialog box, select each category that you want to assign to that item.

5 Click OK.

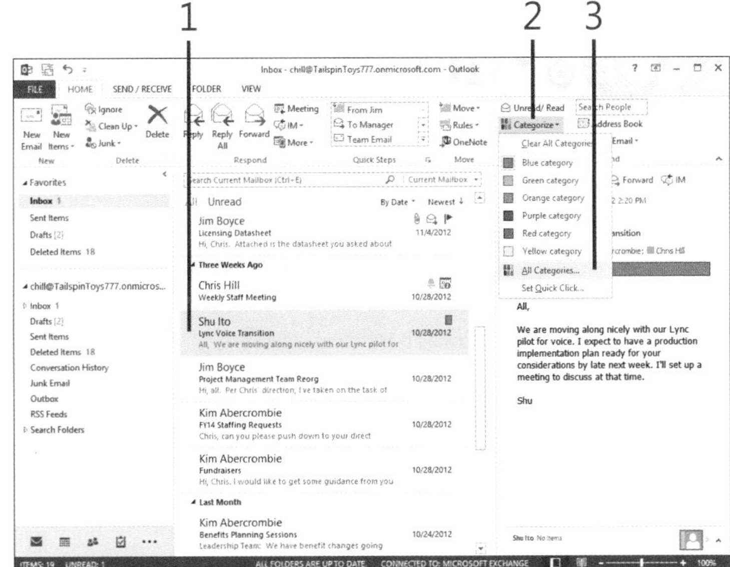

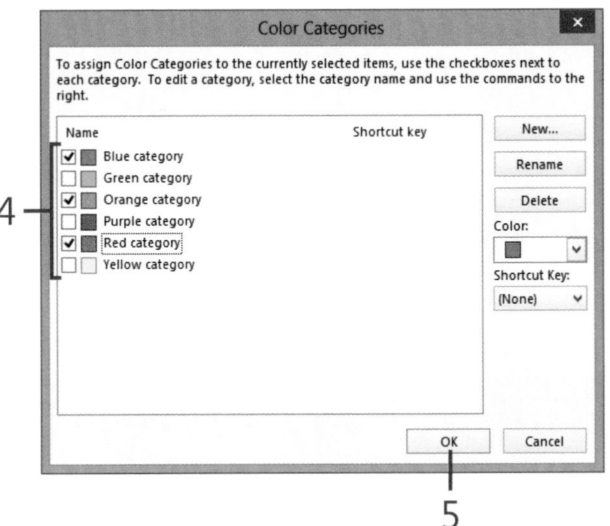

Adding your own categories

Outlook 2013 includes a small selection of predefined categories. You can easily add other categories as needed to help you organize your Outlook data in a way that makes sense to you. For example, you might create categories for projects, teams, and other specific items and groups that you work with regularly.

Add categories to your category list

1 Select an item. On the Home tab, in the Tags group, click Categorize and then, in the list that appears, click All Categories.

2 In the Color Categories dialog box, click New.

(continued on next page)

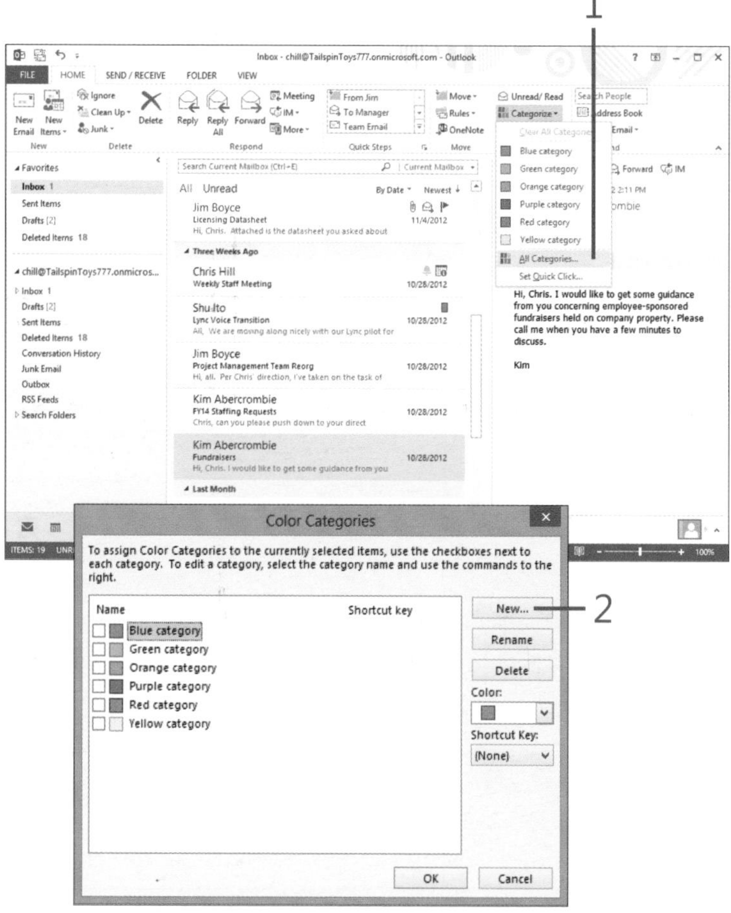

> **TIP** If you assign a category to an item and then delete the category from the Master Category List, the category isn't deleted from any items to which it is assigned. You can still sort, view, or filter items based on deleted categories.

Add categories to your category list *(continued)*

3 In the Add New Category dialog box, in the Name text box, type a name for the new category.

4 In the Color list, select a color.

5 Optionally, in the Shortcut Key list, choose a shortcut key.

6 Click OK.

7 The new category appears in the Color Categories dialog box.

8 Clear the check box if you want only to create the category but not assign it yet.

9 Click OK.

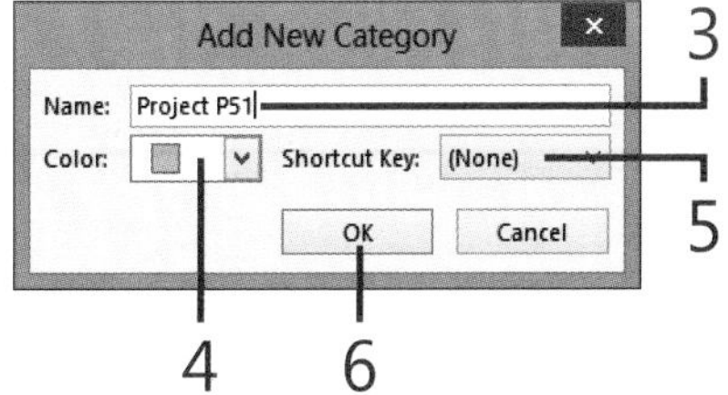

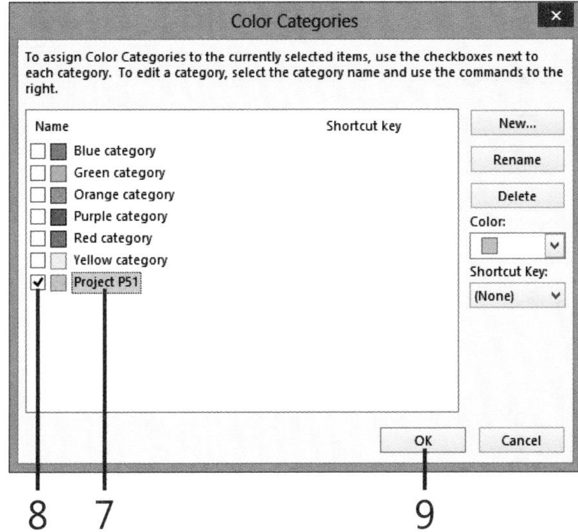

Renaming and deleting categories

You can easily rename a category. Doing so causes all items to which that category is assigned to be updated with the new name. You can also delete categories. Deleting a category from the Master Category List in the Color Categories dialog box removes the category only from the list; it does not remove the category from any items to which it is assigned.

Rename a category

1 On the Home tab, in the Tags group, click Categorize and then, in the list that appears, click All Categories.

2 In the Color Categories dialog box, click the category that you want to rename.

3 Click Rename, type a new name, and then press Enter.

4 Click OK.

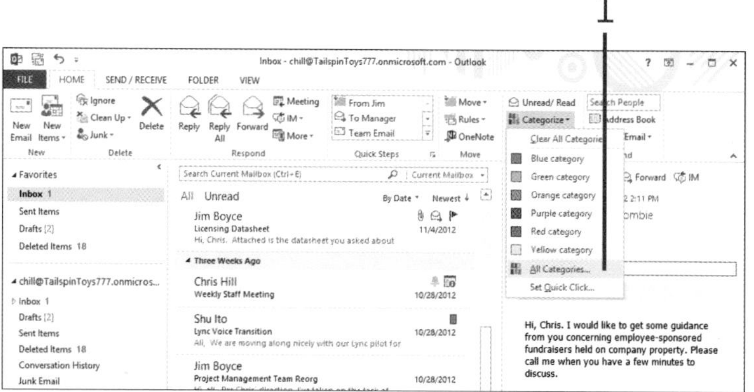

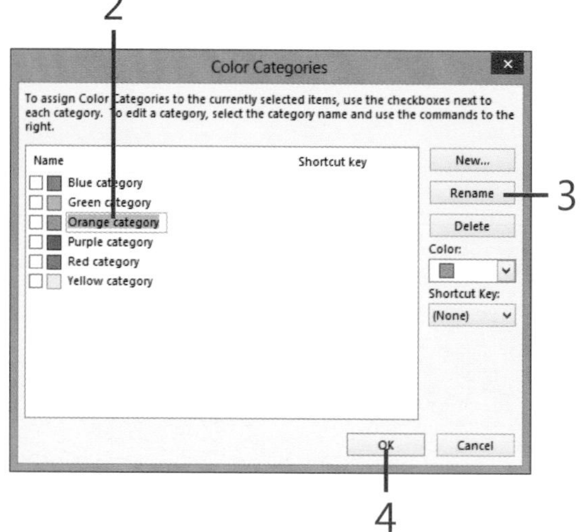

Delete a category

1 On the Home tab, in the Tags group, click Categorize and then, in the list that appears, click All Categories.

2 In the Color Categories dialog box, click the category that you want to delete.

3 Click Delete. In the pop-up message box that asks you to confirm the deletion the category, click Yes.

4 Click OK.

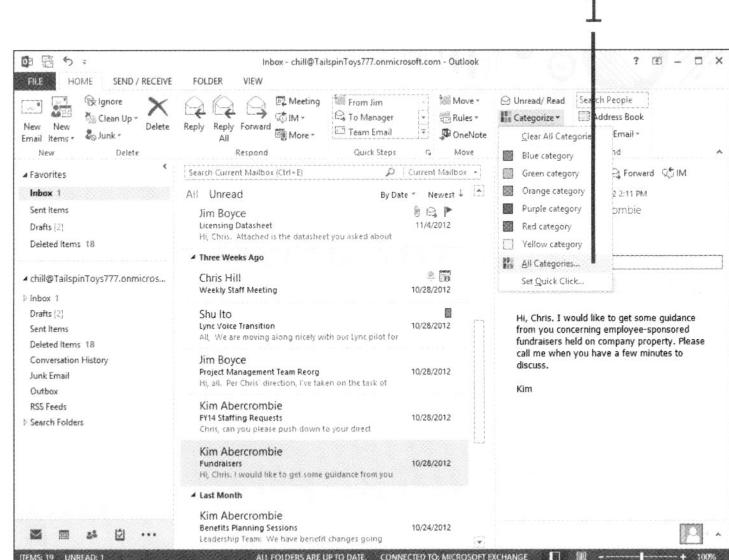

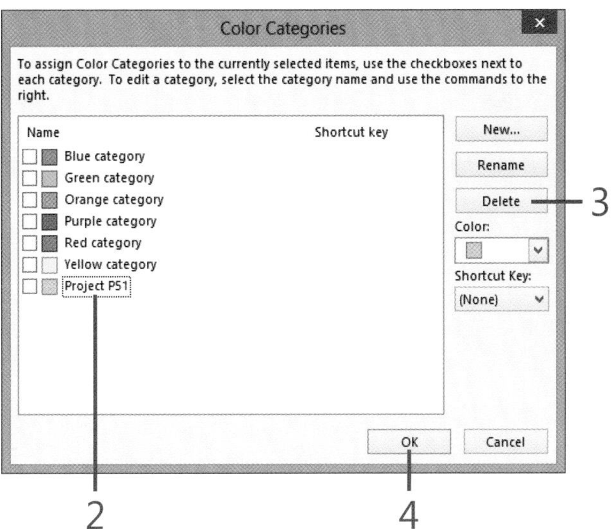

TIP Deleting a category that's in use clears the color only from the category. To remove the category altogether, you must clear the category from all items to which it's assigned.

TRY THIS! If you want to clear a category from all items to which it's assigned, arrange the view by category. Locate the grouped category that you want to remove, select all of the items in the group, right-click an item in the group, click Categorize, and then click the category that you want to remove.

Creating search folders

Using search folders, you can quickly locate messages anywhere they exist in your Outlook 2013 data store. Although a search folder looks and behaves like any other Outlook folder, the search folder is really a special way to display search results. When you create the search folder, you specify the search conditions. Outlook then displays the results of the search in a folderlike way. However, the items that appear in the search folder actually reside in other locations—the search folder is just a way to group those messages together in one viewing location.

Create a custom search folder

1 Open the Inbox, right-click Search Folders, and then click New Search Folder.

2 In the New Search Folder dialog box, scroll to the bottom of the list and click Create A Custom Search Folder.

3 Click Choose.

(continued on next page)

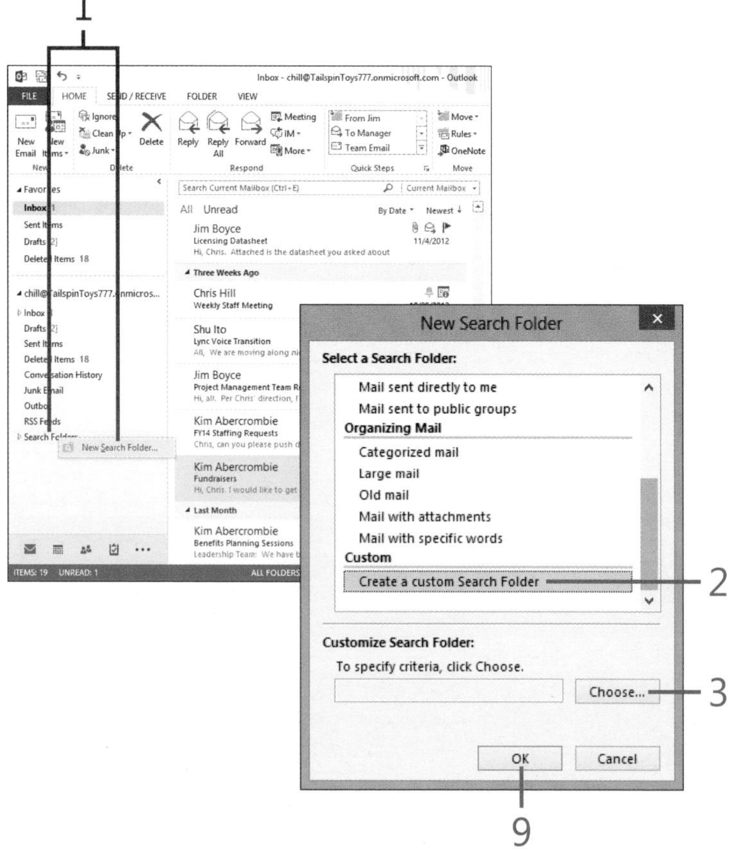

TIP The options in the Search Folder Criteria dialog box give you a wide array of conditions to use in defining the search. For example, on the Messages tab, you can search for words or phrases, specify that the message is from a particular sender or sent to a particular recipient, and set a time frame in which the message was sent or received (as well as other time options).

TRY THIS! To modify a search folder, right-click the search folder in the Folder pane and then, on the shortcut menu that appears, click Customize This Search Folder.

Create a custom search folder *(continued)*

4 In the Custom Search Folder dialog box, in the Name text box, type a name for the search folder.

5 Click Criteria.

6 In the Search Folder Criteria dialog box, click From and choose a contact or type an email address in the text box.

7 Click OK to save the changes and dismiss the Search Folder Criteria dialog box.

8 Click OK to save the changes and dismiss the Custom Search Folder dialog box.

9 Click OK to save the changes and dismiss the New Search Folder dialog box (refer back to the screenshot on the previous page).

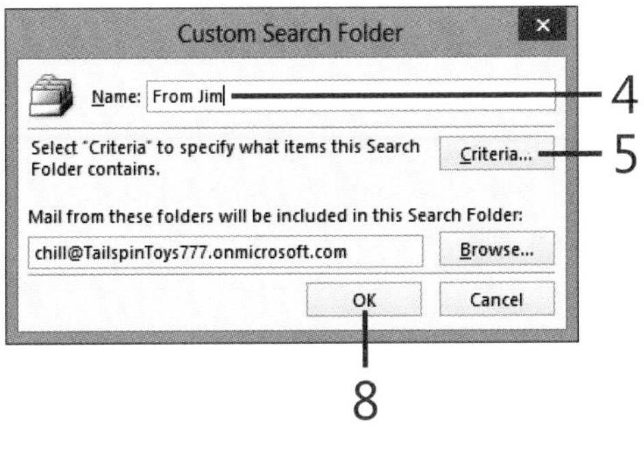

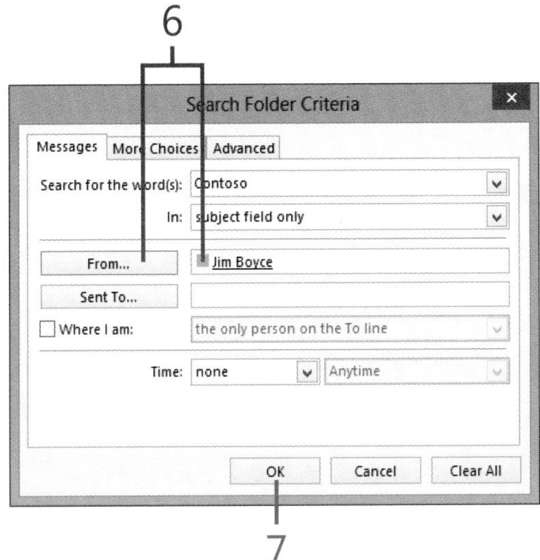

TIP The Unread Mail search folder shows all unread messages, including those in folders other than the Inbox. Likewise, the Categorized Mail search folder shows all messages that have a category assigned from all folders in your mailbox. The Categorized Mail search folder shows only messages with a category assignment (uncategorized messages are excluded).

Organizing with folders

Outlook 2013 uses folders to let you store items, such as email messages and notes. Outlook folders are similar to the folders you can create and modify in Windows Explorer in that they help organize items. For example, the Inbox folder is the default location for your incoming email messages, whereas the Outbox folder stores your outgoing email messages until you send them.

You can use the existing folders created automatically by Outlook, but you can also create your own folders to help you organize your items in a way that makes the most sense for the way you use Outlook. You can move items simply by dragging them to a folder in the Folder pane.

Create a new folder

1 On the ribbon, click the Folder tab.

2 In the New group, click New Folder.

3 In the Create New Folder dialog box, in the Name text box, type a name for the new folder.

4 In the Folder Contains list, select the type of item that the folder is to contain. For example, if you want a folder to store messages, select Mail And Post Items.

5 Select the location where you want the new folder to be placed.

6 Click OK.

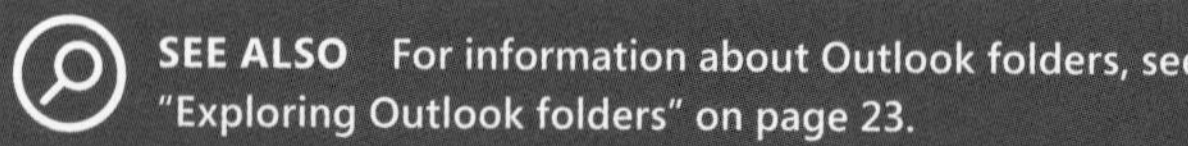

SEE ALSO For information about Outlook folders, see "Exploring Outlook folders" on page 23.

TRY THIS! You can move more than one item at a time. Select multiple items by holding down the Ctrl key while clicking the items that you want to move. Then, perform the move by using any of the methods described here. Also, if the destination folder is a subfolder that's not open in the folder list, drag the message and hold it on the parent folder until that parent folder opens to reveal the target folder.

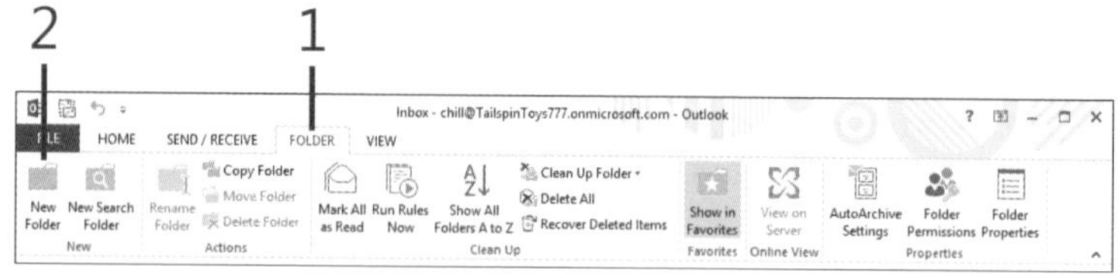

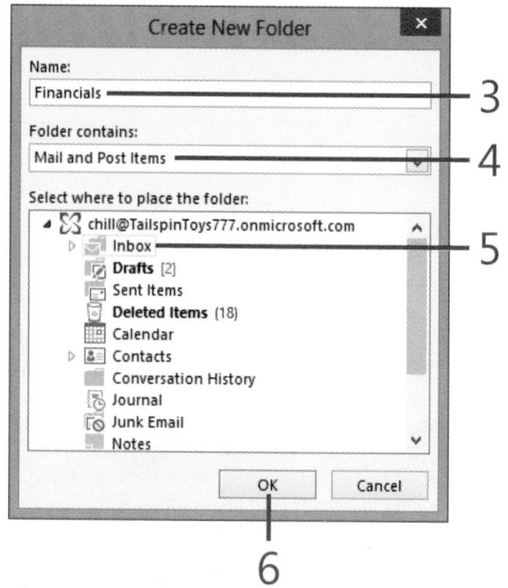

Move items

1. Select the message that you want to move.
2. On the Home tab, in the Move group, click Move and then, in the list that appears, choose the folder to which you want to move the item. If the folder isn't visible in the list, perform steps 3, 4, and 5 of this exercise.
3. Click Other Folder.
4. In the Move Items dialog box, click the target folder.
5. Click OK.

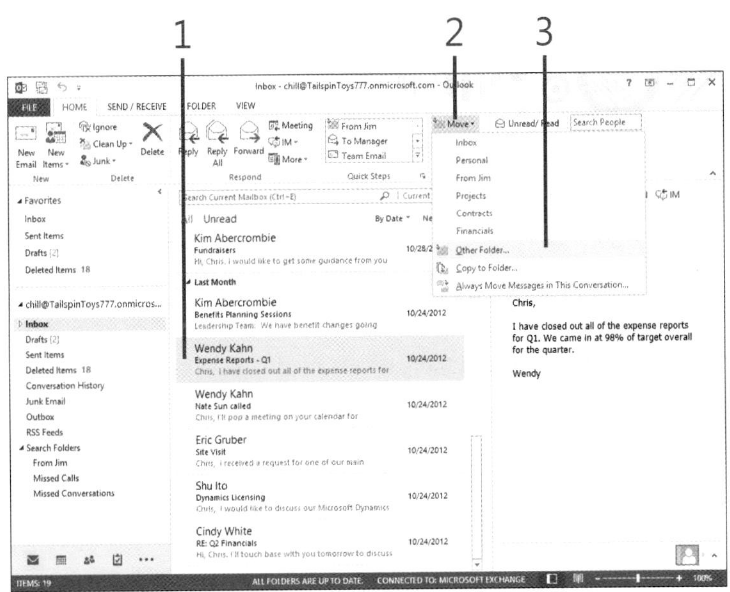

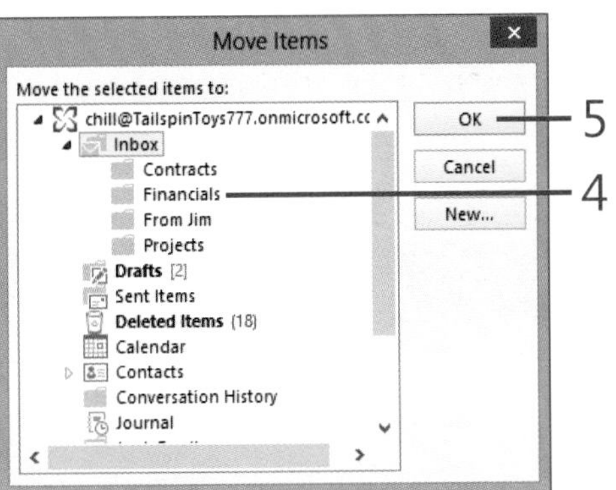

CAUTION Sometimes when you move an item, you might drag it into the wrong folder. If you do this, don't panic. Press Ctrl+Z immediately after you move the item. Outlook returns the item to its original location.

SEE ALSO To learn how to move messages to other folders automatically with rules, see "Working with the Rules Wizard" on page 81.

Cleaning up folders

You should get in the habit of cleaning out unwanted email messages, old contacts, and other items by deleting them or moving them to other folders. Outlook 2013 provides the Mailbox Cleanup tool to help you manage your mailbox. This tool helps you reduce the size of your mailbox to increase Outlook's performance and to make managing mailbox items easier.

Use the Mailbox Cleanup tool

1. On the ribbon, click the File tab to display the Backstage view.
2. Click Cleanup Tools and then, on the menu that appears, click Mailbox Cleanup.

(continued on next page)

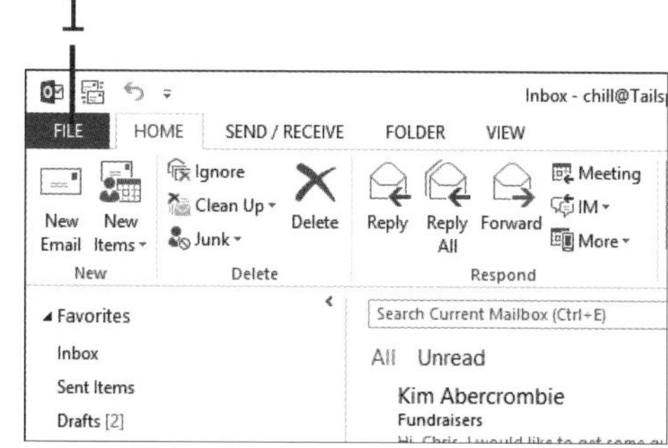

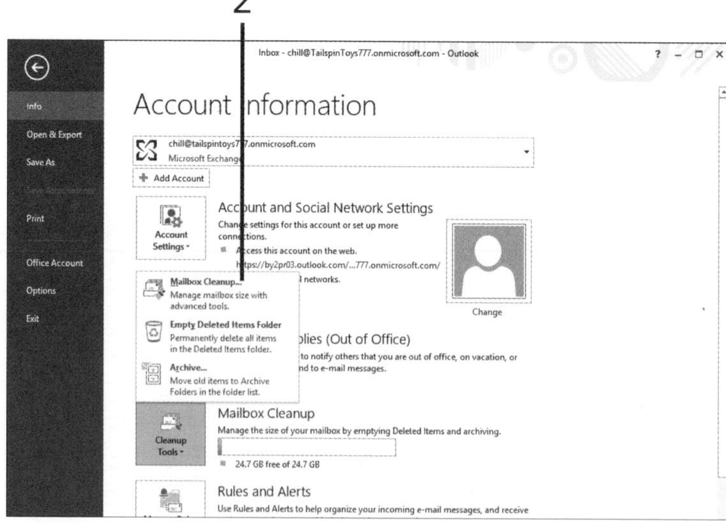

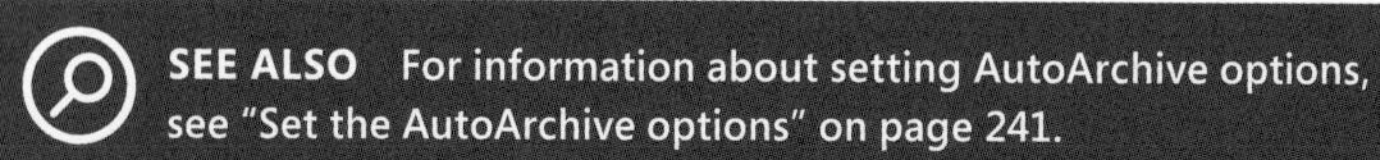

SEE ALSO For information about setting AutoArchive options, see "Set the AutoArchive options" on page 241.

CAUTION Depending on the AutoArchive options set for a folder, messages older than a specific date might be removed from your current folders and placed in the Archive Folders. If you want to access a message that has been moved to these folders, open the folders from the Folder pane and view the message in the main Outlook window.

Use the Mailbox Cleanup tool *(continued)*

3 In the Mailbox Cleanup dialog box, click View Mailbox Size to display the Folder Size dialog box.

4 Review the size of your mailbox and other Outlook folders.

5 Click Close.

6 Click AutoArchive to begin immediately archiving items based on the settings you have defined for AutoArchive. The Mailbox Cleanup dialog box closes automatically while your mail is being archived.

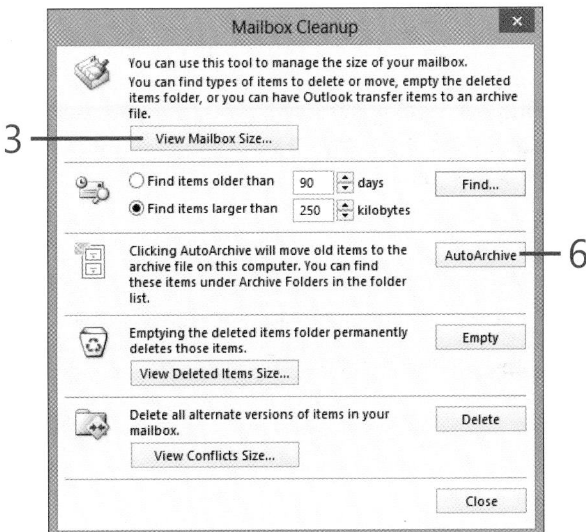

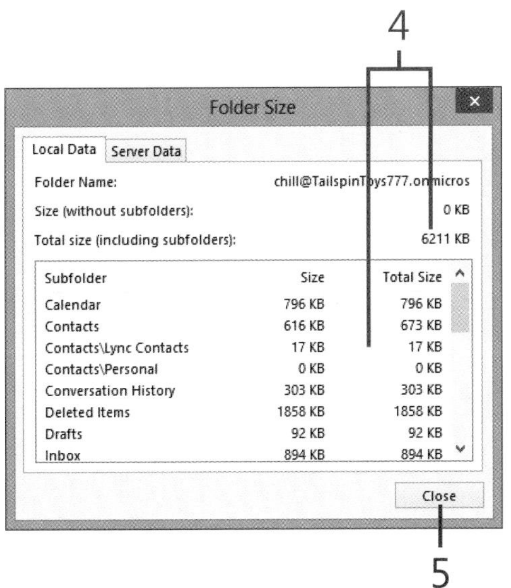

TIP You can use the two search options in the Mailbox Cleanup dialog box to search for messages that are older than a specified age or that are larger than a specified size. In the resulting search results window, you can select items and delete them from your mailbox. To delete these items, first select them in the Results pane, right-click the items, and then, in the shortcut menu that appears, click Delete. Or, alternatively, simply select the items and press the Delete key on the keyboard.

TRY THIS! Click View Deleted Items Size to view the amount of space taken up by your Deleted Items folder. Click Empty to permanently delete all items in the Deleted Items folder.

Deleting items

Over time, your Outlook 2013 folders fill up and can seem unmanageable. Outlook makes it possible you to delete items when you no longer need them. When you delete an item, the program removes it from its current folder and places it in the Deleted Items folder.

Delete an item

1. In an Outlook folder, choose the item that you want to delete.
2. On the Home tab, in the Delete group, click the Delete button.
3. To view deleted items, in the Folder pane, click Deleted Items.
4. The item you just deleted appears in the list.

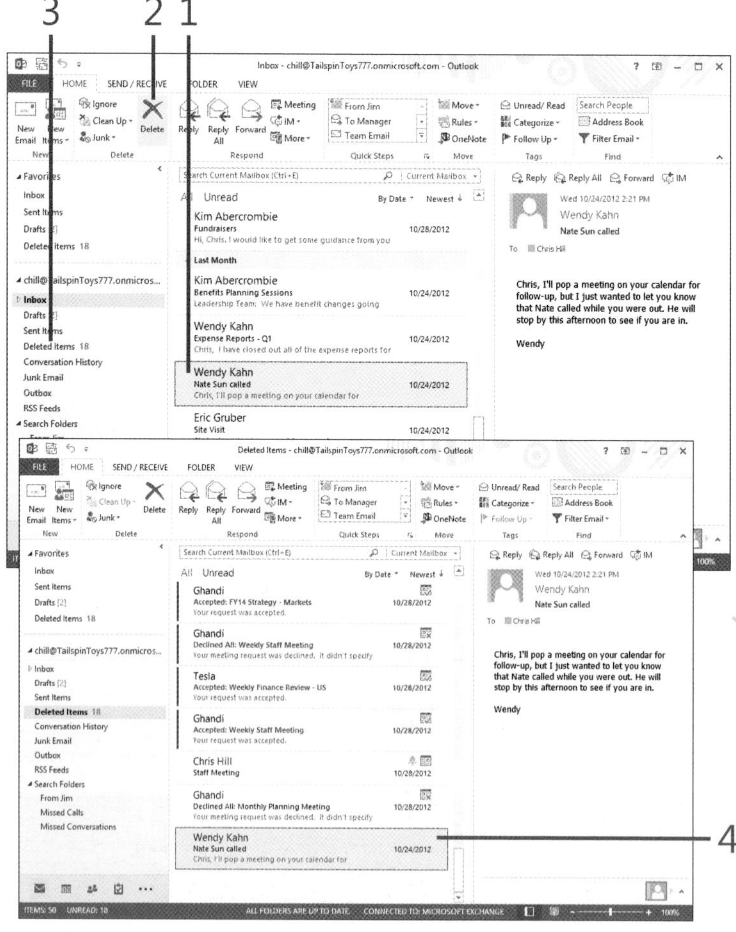

CAUTION When you delete an item from within Outlook, no prompt appears asking whether you're sure you want to delete the item. Outlook immediately moves it to the Deleted Items folder. If you delete an item by mistake, press Ctrl+Z before continuing with any other tasks. You can also open the Deleted Items folder and drag the deleted item back to its original location.

TIP Outlook does not list items in the Deleted Items folder in the order in which they were deleted; instead, deleted emails are listed by the date they were sent or received.

Empty the Deleted Items folder

1 In the Folder pane, right-click the Deleted Items folder.

2 On the menu that appears, click the Empty Folder.

3 In the pop-up message box asking you to confirm the deletion, click Yes to empty the Deleted Items folder.

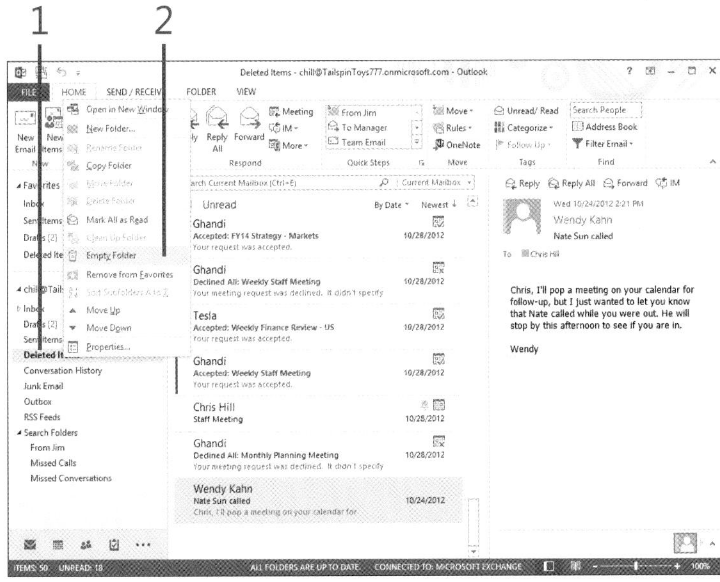

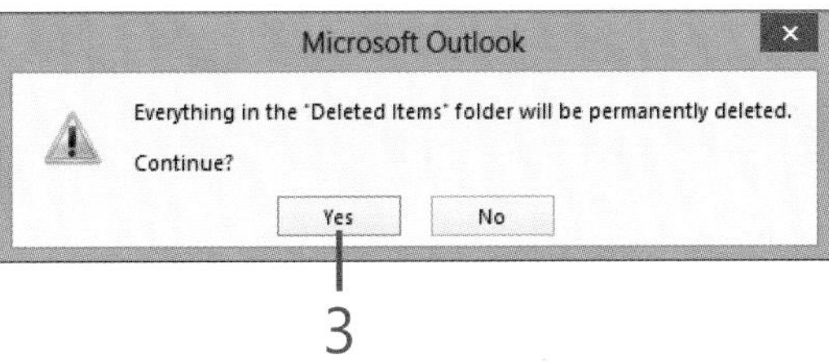

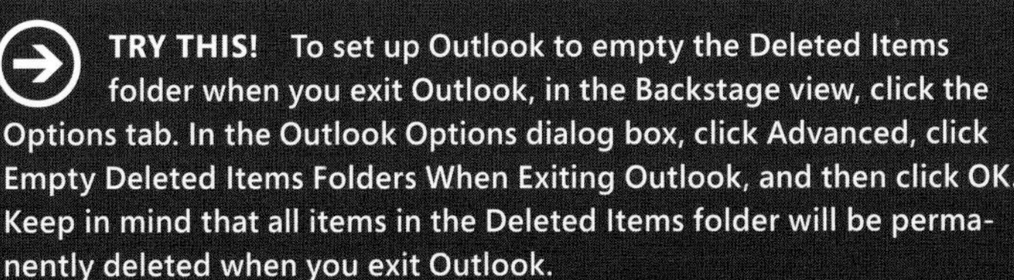
TRY THIS! To set up Outlook to empty the Deleted Items folder when you exit Outlook, in the Backstage view, click the Options tab. In the Outlook Options dialog box, click Advanced, click Empty Deleted Items Folders When Exiting Outlook, and then click OK. Keep in mind that all items in the Deleted Items folder will be permanently deleted when you exit Outlook.

SEE ALSO For information about managing the Inbox folder, including deleting unneeded messages, see "Managing the Inbox folder" on page 70.

Managing your Outlook files

13

When used without Microsoft Exchange Server, Microsoft Outlook 2013 stores your data—including all of your default and custom folders—in a personal folder file, or PST file. When used with Exchange, your mailbox resides on the server rather than on your computer. When you open Outlook, the program contacts the server to display your data.

Sometimes your computer can't communicate with the server because the server is offline or because you are unable to connect to the network. In these situations, Outlook can use a set of offline folders stored in an offline folder file, or OST file. Outlook stores data in the OST file and synchronizes the changes with the mailbox the next time it connects to the server.

This section explains how to perform several tasks with your Outlook data files, including how to add new data files, use an existing file, and import and export items. The section also explains how to back up and restore your Outlook data in a PST file and how to archive items.

In this section:

Working with Outlook data files

Unless your only email account is on an Exchange Server, Outlook 2013 creates a local data file for you when you set up your profile. You can easily create a new PST file and then add or remove folders to it as needed. When Exchange Server is the only account, Outlook stores all items in your Exchange Server mailbox.

Create a new personal data file

1 On the ribbon, click the File tab to display the Backstage view. Click the Account Settings button and then, on the menu that appears, click Account Settings

2 In the Account Settings dialog box, on the Data Files tab, click Add to open the Create Or Open Outlook Data File dialog box.

(continued on next page)

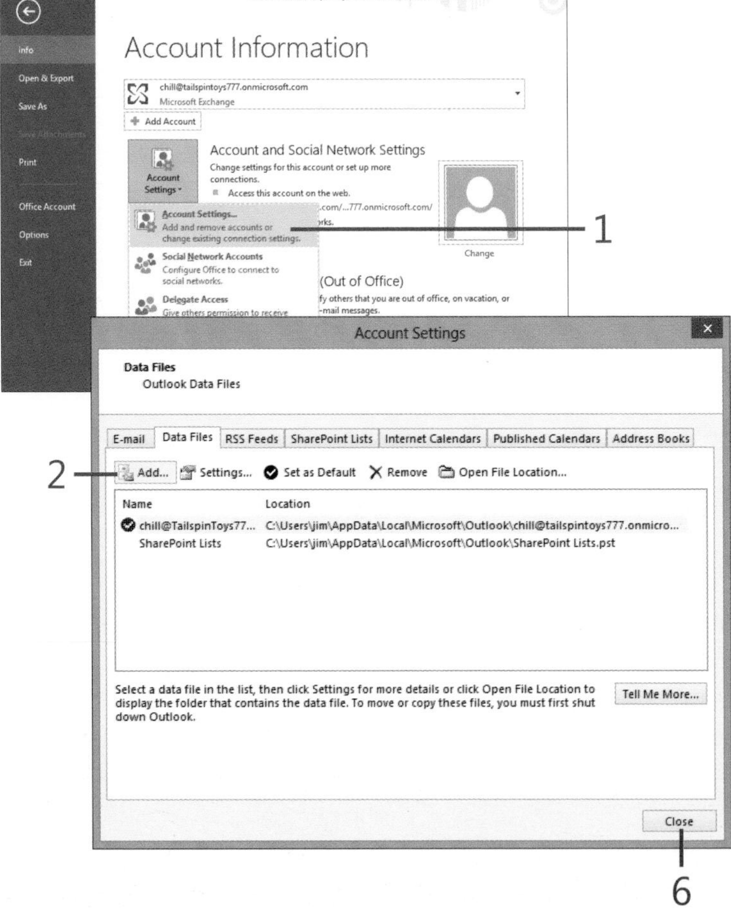

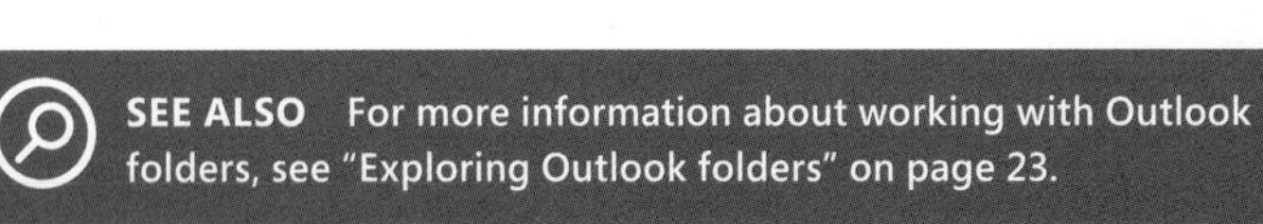

SEE ALSO For more information about working with Outlook folders, see "Exploring Outlook folders" on page 23.

TIP You can select an existing PST file in the Create Or Open Outlook Data File dialog box rather than create a new one. This method is good for moving a PST file from one computer to another. To do so, copy the PST to the new computer, open Outlook, and add the existing PST to your profile. You can then access all of the items in the old PST.

Create a new personal data file *(continued)*

3 In the Create Or Open Outlook Data File dialog box, browse for the location you want (if other than the default location).

4 In the File Name text box, type a name for the PST file.

5 Click OK to save the changes and dismiss the dialog box.

6 Click Close (refer back to the screenshot on the previous page).

7 The new set of folders appears in your folder list.

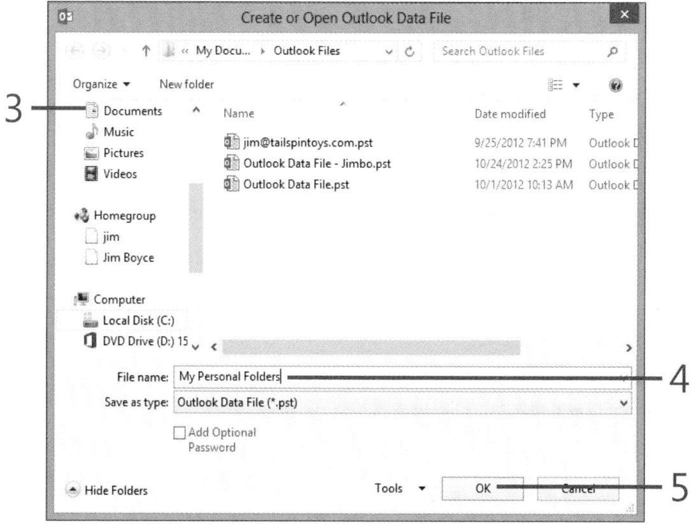

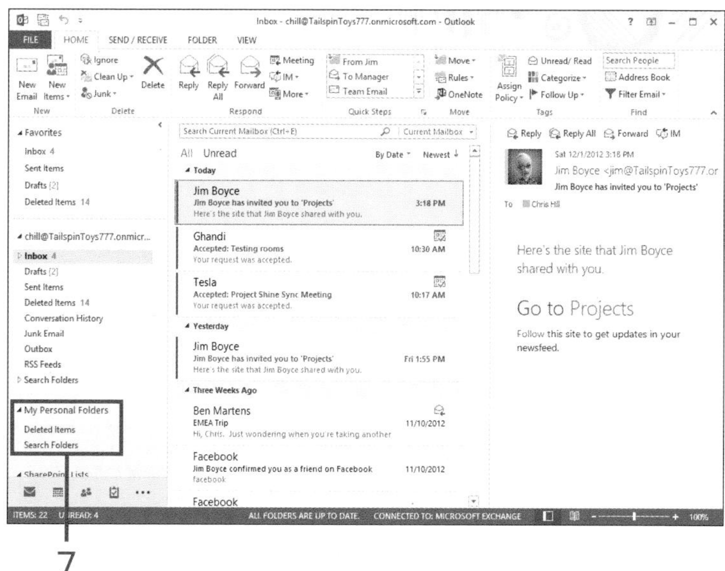

> **TRY THIS!** You can easily add folders to your new set of personal folders. Open Outlook, right-click in the folder list and then, on the shortcut menu that appears, click New Folder. Select a location in the new folder set, specify a name for the new folder, select the folder type, and then click OK to create the new folder.

Configure Outlook for Cached Exchange Mode

1. On the ribbon, click the File tab to display the Backstage view. Click the Account Settings button and then, on the menu that appears, click Account Settings.
2. In the Account Settings dialog box, on the E-Mail tab, click the Exchange Server account.
3. Click Change.

(continued on next page)

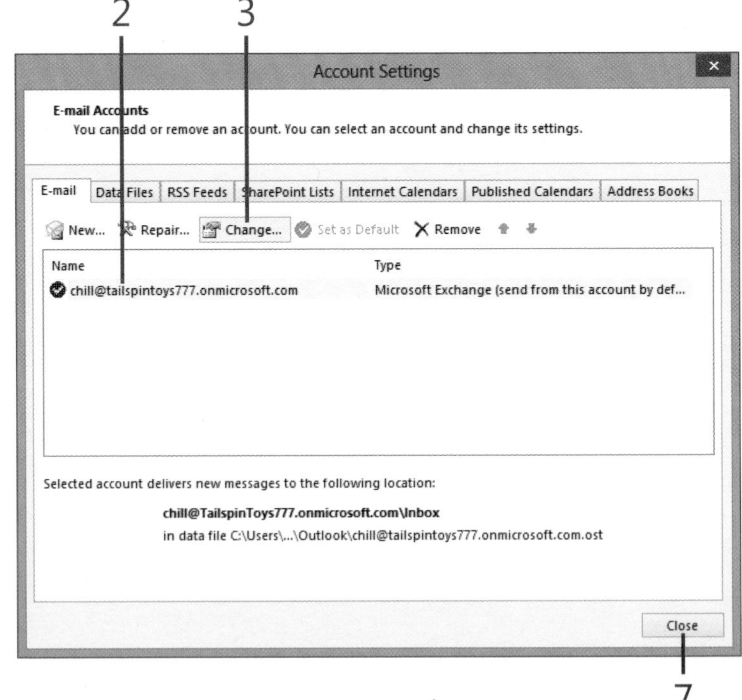

TIP Outlook 2013 automatically synchronizes your folders when using Cached Exchange Mode. It detects when the server is available and then synchronizes your folders for you in the background.

Configure Outlook for Cached Exchange Mode *(continued)*

4 In the Change Account dialog box, select the Use Cached Exchange Mode check box.

5 Choose how many months of data to cache locally.

6 Click Next and then click Finish.

7 Click Close, and then close and restart Outlook.

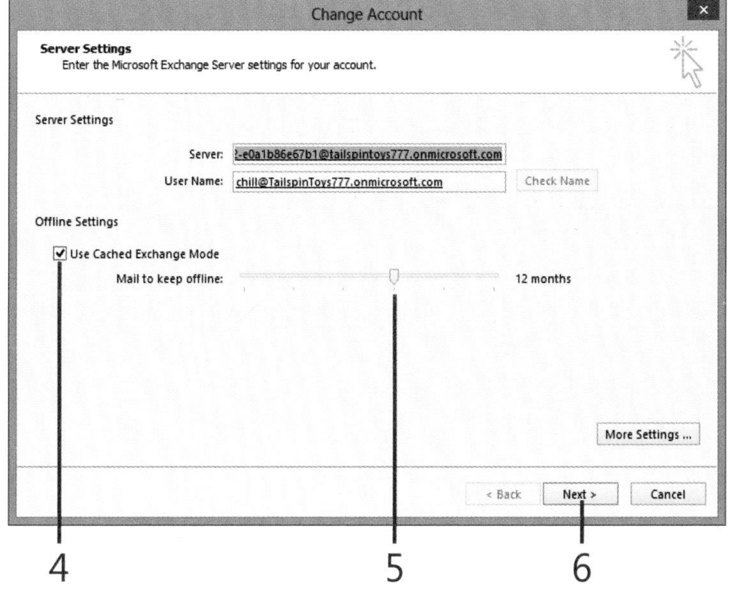

CAUTION Your computer must be connected to the Exchange Server the first time you start Outlook with Cached Exchange Mode to enable Outlook to create a locally cached copy of your mailbox.

Importing and exporting items

Although you probably do much of your work in Outlook 2013, occasionally you might want to move data into Outlook from other programs or export data from Outlook to another program. Outlook makes it easy to import and export items. This section shows how to import and export items to and from PST files.

Import items into Outlook

1 On the ribbon, click the File tab to display the Backstage view and then click the Open & Export tab.

2 Click Import/Export.

3 On the first page of the Import And Export Wizard, select Import From Another Program Or File, and then click Next.

(continued on next page)

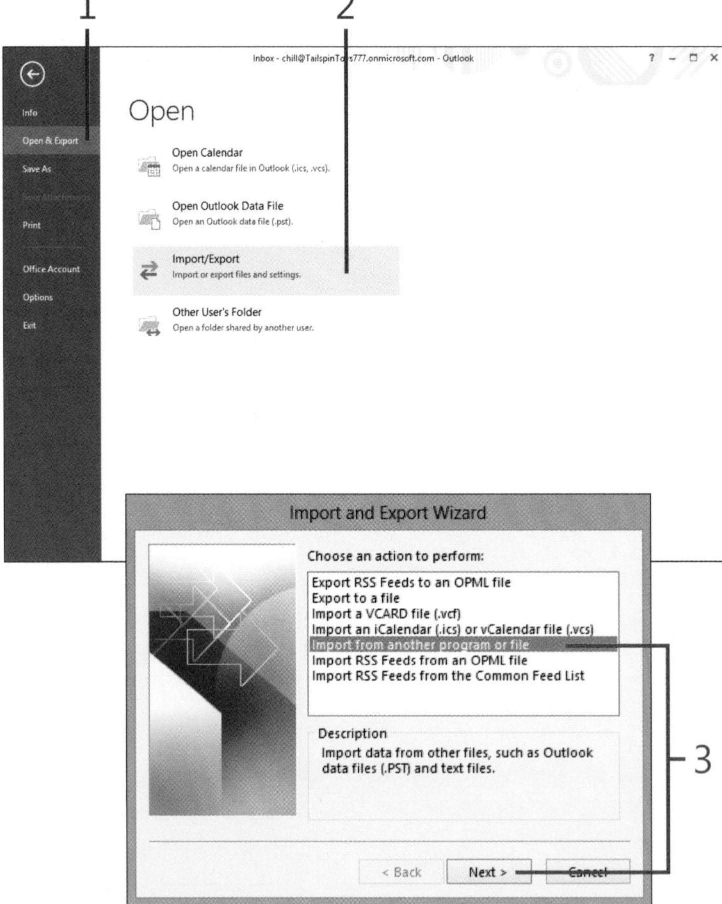

Import items into Outlook *(continued)*

4 On the Import A File page of the wizard, select Outlook Data File, and click Next.

5 On the first Import Outlook Data File page in the wizard choose the PST file from which you want to import.

6 Click one of the options to specify how you want duplicate items to be handled.

7 Click Next.

(continued on next page)

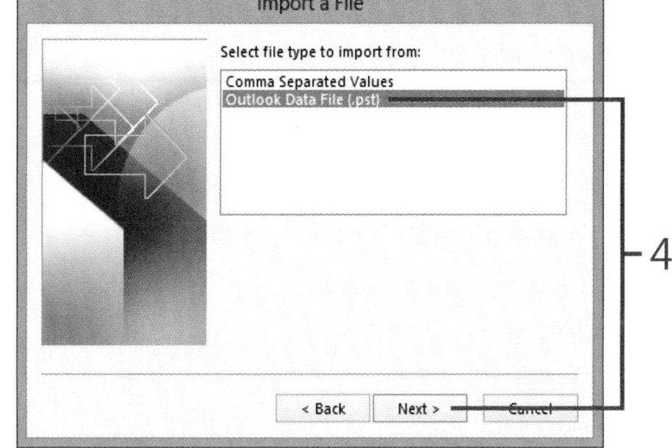

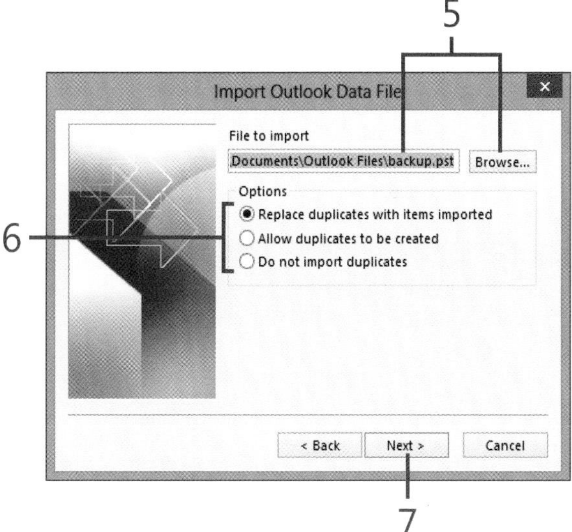

TIP You can use the import feature in Outlook to import messages and other items from other PST files, bring contacts from a Microsoft Access database or Microsoft Excel spreadsheet to your Contacts folder, and move other types of information from their original locations to other folders.

Import items into Outlook *(continued)*

8 On the second Import Outlook Data File page in the wizard, select the folder from which you want to import items.

9 Click Filter to open the Filter dialog box.

10 Specify options that define (filter) the data that Outlook will import.

11 Click OK to save the changes and dismiss the dialog box.

12 Click Finish to close the wizard.

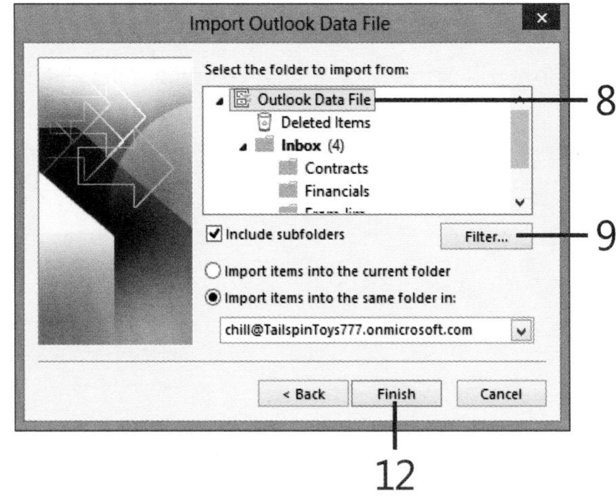

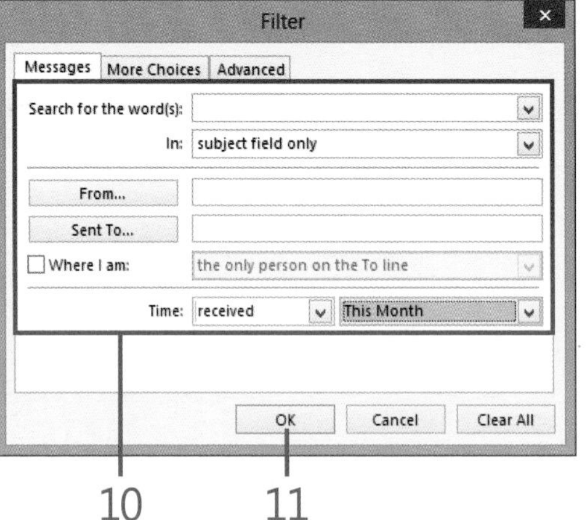

TRY THIS! Importing selected items from a PST file gives you an easy way to selectively copy Outlook items from one computer to another. Simply copy the PST file from the source computer to the destination computer, and then use the import feature to import only those items that you want on the destination computer.

TIP You can use the Filter dialog box to selectively import items. For example, perhaps you want to import only items that have the category Personal assigned to them. Or, maybe you want to import only messages that came from specific senders or only contacts that work for a particular company. Whatever the case, the Filter dialog box lets you control which items are imported.

Export items from Outlook

1. On the ribbon, click the File tab to display the Backstage view and then click the Open & Export tab.
2. Click Import/Export.
3. On the first page of the Import And Export Wizard, select Export To A File, and then click Next.
4. On the Export To A File page of the wizard, select Outlook Data File (.pst), and click Next.

(continued on next page)

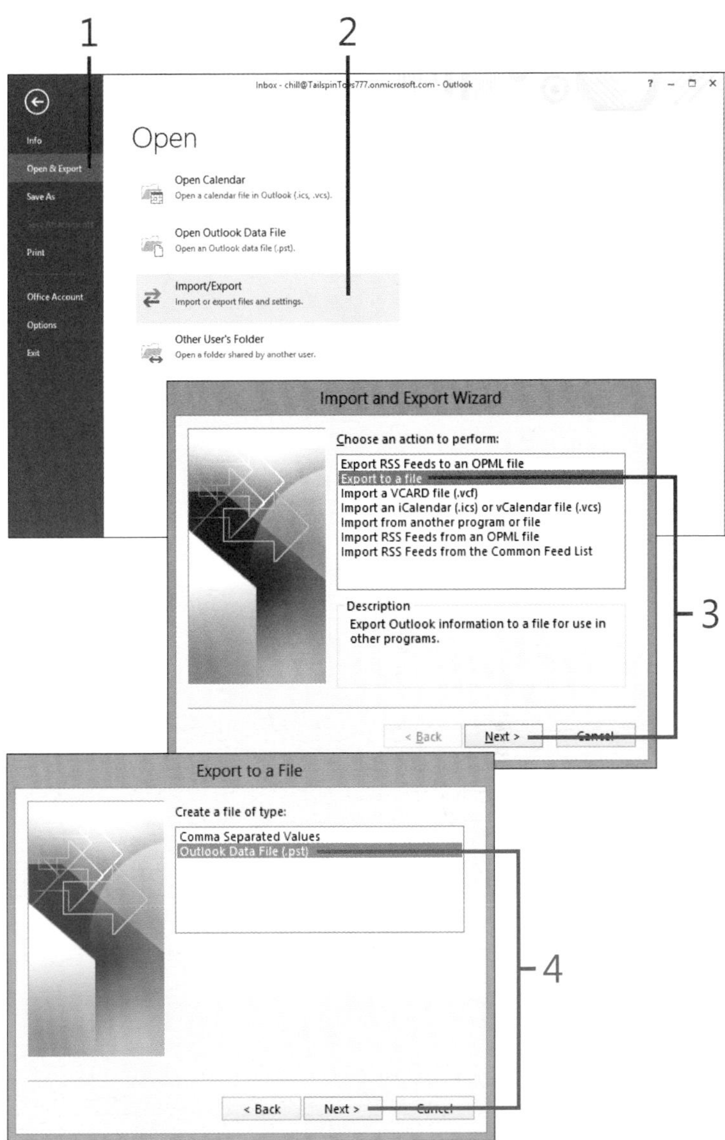

TIP You don't have to export to a new PST file. You can export items to an existing PST file. This method gives you a handy means of selectively backing up or archiving specific items. For example, you might back up selected items from your Exchange Server mailbox to a PST file on your local computer for archival.

SEE ALSO For more information about creating and using Outlook files, see "Working with Outlook data files" on page 228.

Export items from Outlook *(continued)*

5 On the first Export Outlook Data File page in the wizard, select the folder from which you want to export items, select the Include Subfolders check box if you want to include subfolders of the selected folder, and then click Next.

6 Specify the path and name of the file to which you want to export, or click Browse to select a file.

7 Click one of the options to specify how you want duplicate items to be handled.

8 Click Finish.

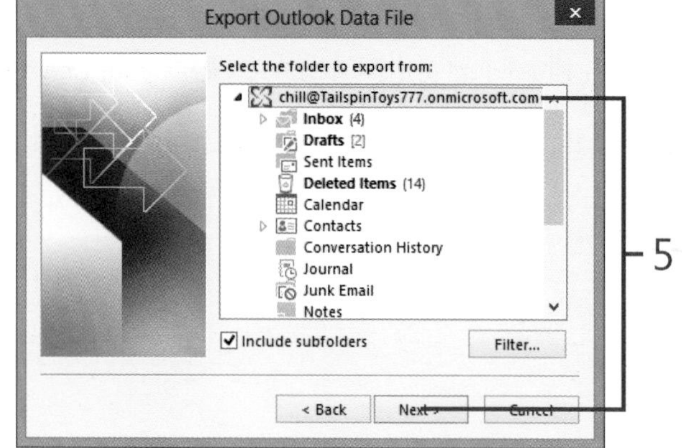

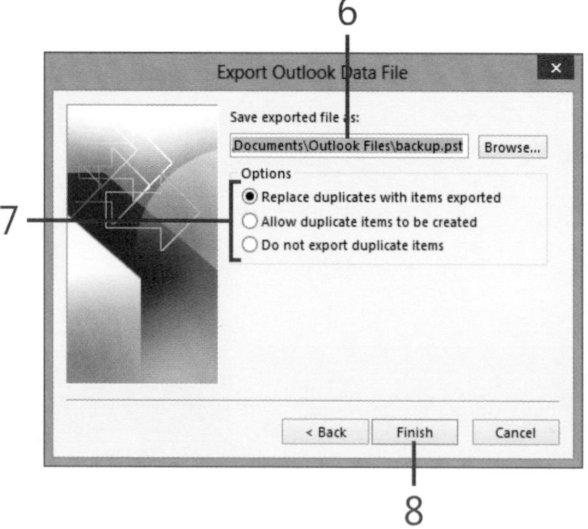

TIP If you specify a file in step 6 that doesn't exist, Outlook displays the Create Outlook Data File dialog box after you click Finish. Simply click OK to create the file and complete the export process.

Backing up and restoring a data file

If you use a set of personal folders in a PST file as your only data store or in addition to an Exchange Server mailbox, back up that PST file so that your data is still available if your computer experiences a problem, such as a failed hard disk. Having the PST file backed up allows you to restore the file and recover your data.

Back up Outlook data

1 On the ribbon, click the File tab to display the Backstage view. Click the Account Settings button and then, on the menu that appears, click Account Settings.

(continued on next page)

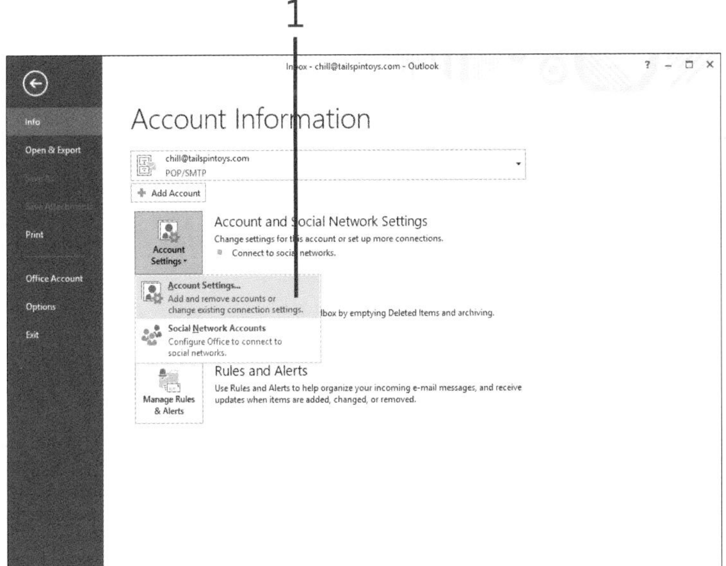

CAUTION Don't back up your PST file to the hard disk it's currently on. If that hard disk fails, you lose both copies of the file. Instead, back up the file to another hard disk, if your computer has more than one, or to another backup unit, network location, or flash drive.

TIP Set up a regular backup schedule for your PST file, and ensure that you back it up frequently to avoid losing any data.

Back up Outlook data *(continued)*

2 In the Account Settings dialog box, click the Data Files tab, and then note the full path to the PST file.

3 Click Close, and then exit Outlook. Open the file's location and copy the file to a backup location, such as a USB flash drive.

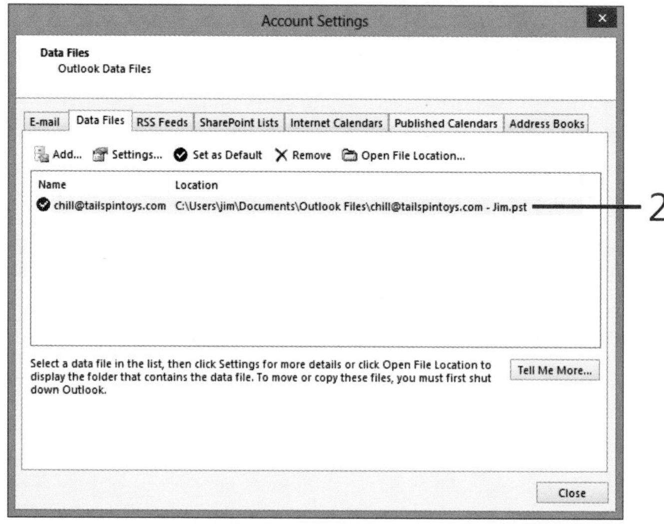

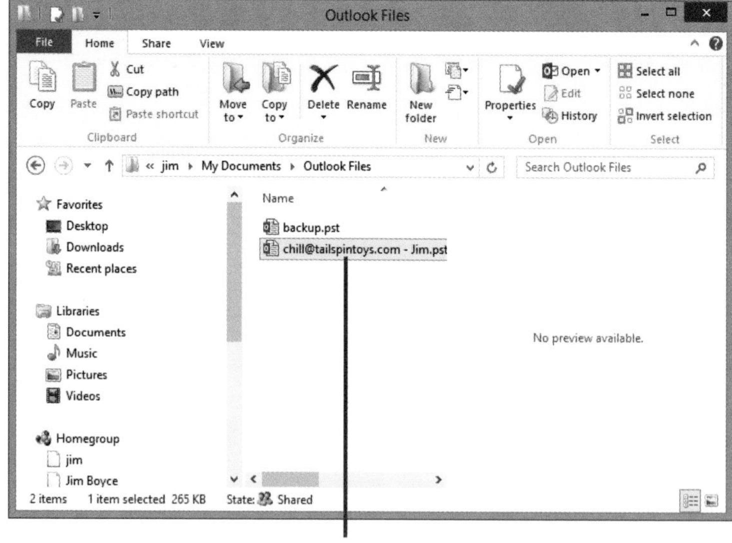

CAUTION Make sure that you close Outlook before making a backup copy of your PST file.

Restore Outlook data

1. Exit Outlook. In Windows Explorer, open the folder that contains the backup file.
2. Right-click the backup file and then, on the shortcut menu that appears, click Copy.
3. Open the original location for the file.

   This location is the one recorded in the Personal Folders dialog box for the file, as described in the previous procedure.
4. Right-click and then, on the shortcut menu that appears, click Paste.

(continued on next page)

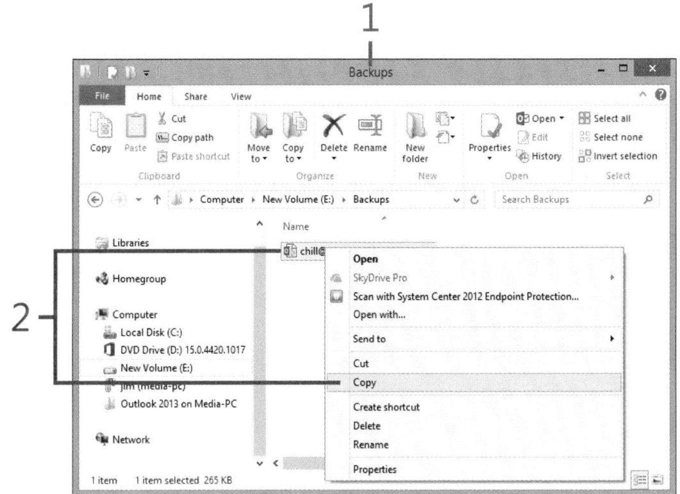

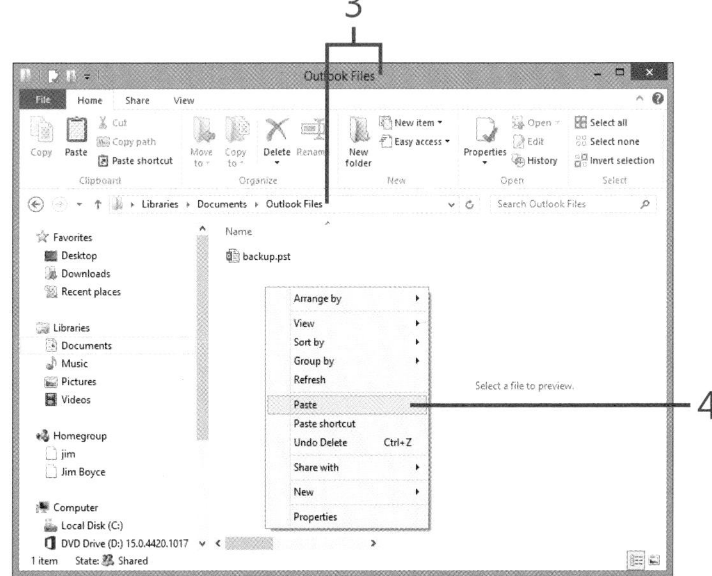

Restore Outlook data *(continued)*

5 Start Outlook and verify that your data items are intact.

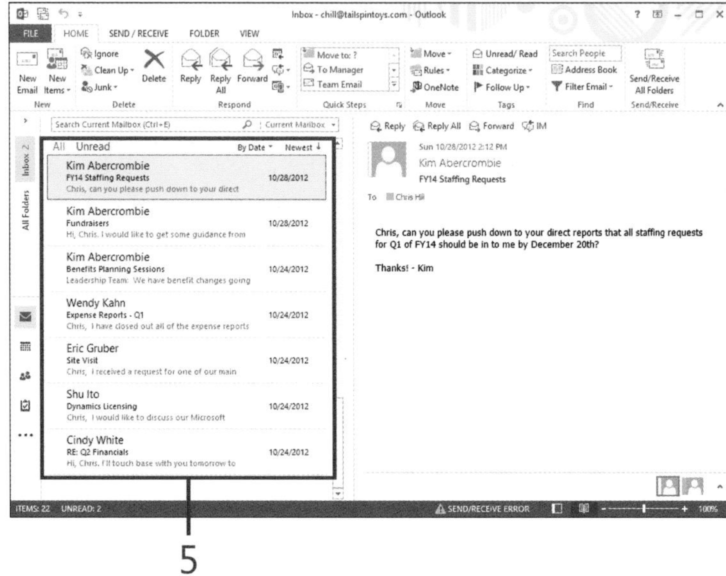

Archiving Outlook data files

Old messages, tasks, and other items have a tendency to pile up unless you clean them out. Outlook 2013 provides an AutoArchive feature with which you can specify how often Outlook should clean out old items, where it should place those items (or whether it should delete them), which items to move, and so on.

If you choose to archive items rather than delete them, Outlook places them in a PST file of your choosing. You can then recover them by opening that set of folders and copying the items back to your regular folders or by using the import feature in Outlook to import from the archive file.

Set the AutoArchive options

1 On the ribbon, click the File tab to display the Backstage view and then click the Options tab.

(continued on next page)

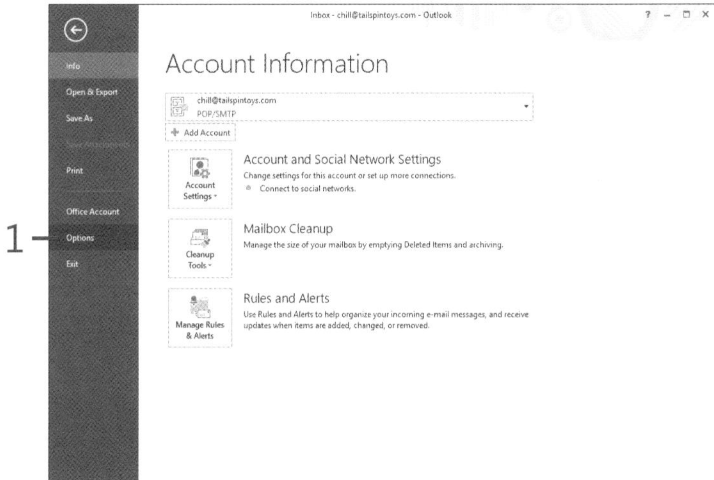

TIP A network administrator can set retention policies that control your AutoArchive settings. Be aware that this might prevent certain archive operations you might otherwise configure through your AutoArchive settings.

Set the AutoArchive options *(continued)*

2 In the Outlook Options dialog box, in the pane on the left, click Advanced.

3 Click AutoArchive Settings.

4 In the AutoArchive dialog box, select the Run AutoArchive Every check box. Specify how frequently you want Outlook to automatically archive items.

5 Select your preferred options to specify how Outlook will archive items.

6 Specify the location of the archive PST file.

7 Click OK to save the changes and dismiss the dialog box.

8 Click OK to close the Outlook Options dialog box.

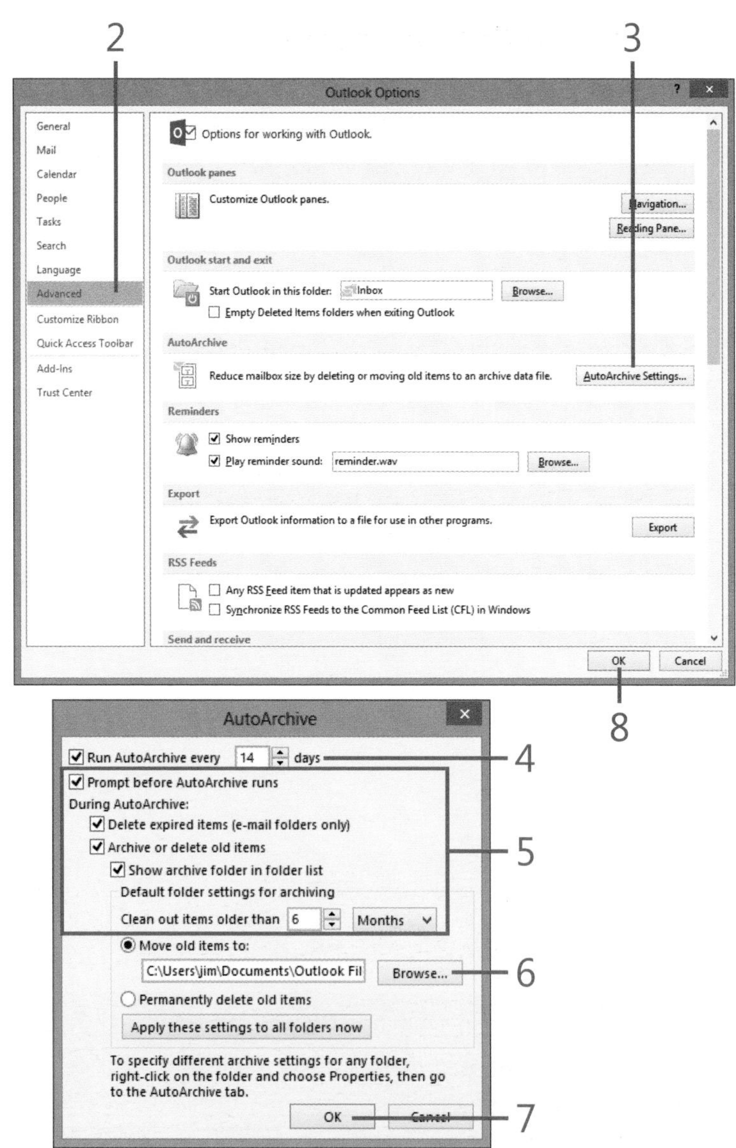

CAUTION Select the Prompt Before AutoArchive Runs check box if you want to control whether Outlook archives items. If you don't select this option, Outlook performs the archive operation without warning you.

TIP Back up your archive file each time you back up your PST file to ensure that you can recover archived items if a system or drive failure causes you to lose your regular archive file.

Archive to an Outlook data file

1. Click File to display the Backstage view, scroll down, click Cleanup Tools, and then, on the menu that appears, click Archive.
2. In the Archive dialog box, if you want to archive all folders by using the AutoArchive settings, click the Archive All Folders According To Their AutoArchive Settings option.
3. Alternatively, click the Archive This Folder And All Subfolders option if you want to archive only the selected folder and its subfolders.
4. If the option described in step 3 is selected, select the folder from which you want to archive items.
5. Specify how old items must be to be archived.
6. Select the Include Items With "Do Not AutoArchive" Checked check box to archive items that would otherwise be skipped because you have configured them not to AutoArchive.
7. Select the file in which you want to store the archived items.
8. Click OK to archive the items.

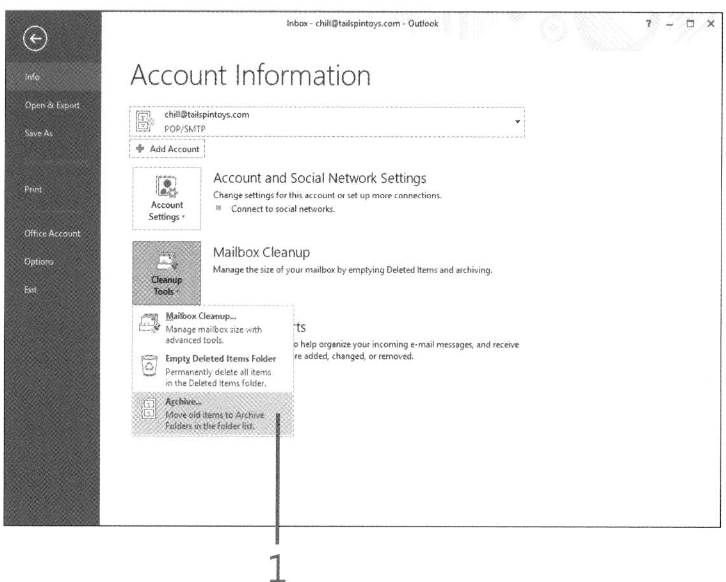

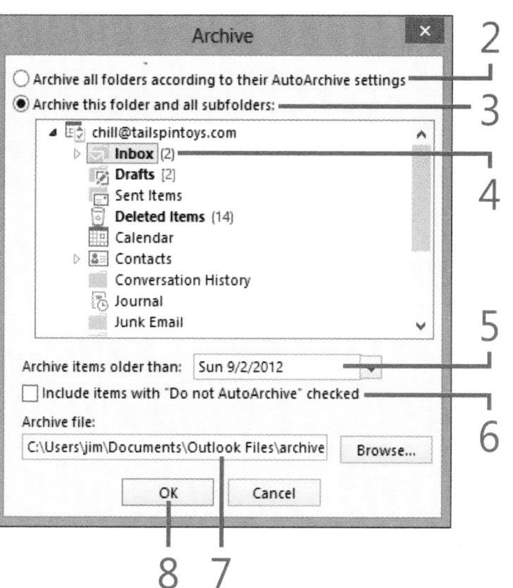

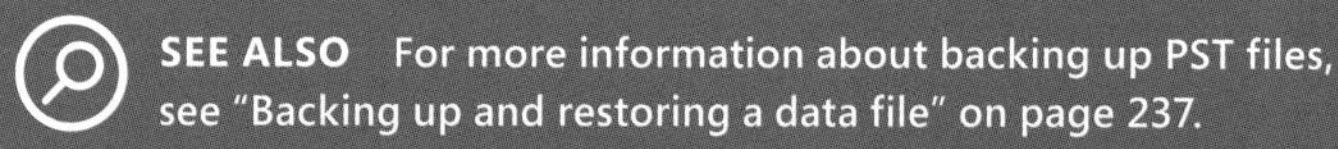

SEE ALSO For more information about backing up PST files, see "Backing up and restoring a data file" on page 237.

TRY THIS! Test your ability to recover archived items. Open the AutoArchive dialog box, and note the location of your archive file. Review the "Import items into Outlook" task earlier in this section, and import a selection of items from your archive PST file.

Customizing Outlook

14

In this section:

- Using read and delivery receipts
- Choosing message formats
- Setting Calendar options
- Customizing the Folder pane
- Customizing the Outlook ribbon
- Customizing the Quick Access Toolbar

Although you can use Microsoft Outlook 2013 out of the box, one of its finest features is its ability to let you tailor it to look and work the way you want. You can customize Outlook in a number of ways. You can choose formats for messages to personalize outgoing mail messages. Using Calendar, you can set up holiday schedules to match those recognized by your business or organization and specify your workweek. For example, if your workweek differs from the traditional 8:00 A.M. to 5:00 P.M., Monday through Friday, you can change Outlook's Calendar views to match the days and hours that you work, at least in most cases.

In addition, you can customize the ribbon and Quick Access Toolbar to suit the way you use Outlook and make frequently used features easily accessible. Outlook offers yet many other ways to adapt to your preferences. These topics and others related to customizing your Outlook experience are covered in this section.

Using read and delivery receipts

Outlook 2013 can help you manage your email messages by keeping track of when those messages are delivered and read by their recipients. This is handy when you send a time-sensitive email and you want to know when the recipients received and read the message. A delivery receipt confirms delivery of the message to the recipient's Inbox, while a read receipt confirms that the recipient has viewed the message.

Use read and delivery receipts on individual messages

1 Open the Inbox and then, on the Home tab, in the New group, click New Email to start a new email message.

(continued on next page)

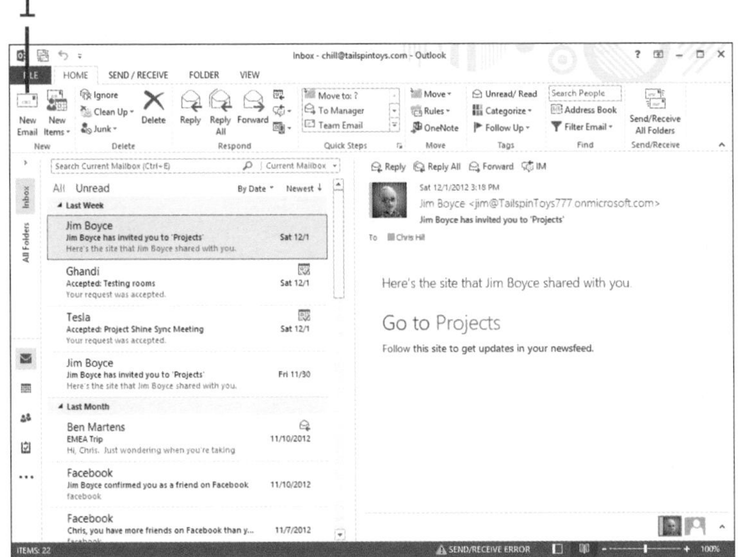

> **TIP** In the Properties dialog box for the message, you can set priority levels for an email message. Click the Importance drop-down list and select Low, Normal, or High. Low or High importance messages are sent at the same speed as Normal, but the recipient sees a symbol that indicates the message's importance.

Use read and delivery receipts on individual messages *(continued)*

2 On the ribbon, click the Options tab.

3 Select the Request A Delivery Receipt check box.

4 Select the Request A Read Receipt check box.

5 Compose the email as you normally would and then click Send. Outlook sends you a delivery receipt when the message is delivered to the user's mailbox (although not all mail servers send delivery receipts).

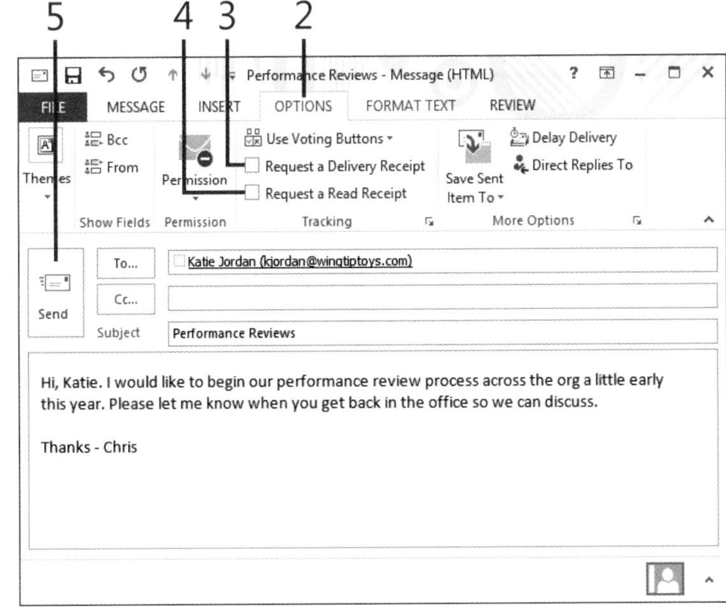

TRY THIS To set Outlook so that all messages have a delivery and read receipt, click the File tab to display the Backstage view, click the Options tab, and then, in the Outlook Options dialog box, click Mail. Scroll down to the Tracking group and select Read Receipt Confirming The Recipient Viewed The Message and Delivery Receipt Confirming The Message Was Delivered To The Recipient's Email Server.

Choosing message formats

When you create new email messages in Outlook 2013, you can specify the format in which the message should be created. The format you choose must be supported by the email program used by the recipient of the message. You can also set up your environment so that all your messages use the same format. You can choose from Plain Text, Rich Text, or HTML as the default. If you want to embed graphics or format text in a message, you must use Rich Text or HTML.

Select a format for a single message

1 Create a new message.

2 On the ribbon, click the Format Text tab.

3 In the Format group, choose a format for the message:

- To create a message without formatting, choose Plain Text.
- To create a message with HTML support, such as embedded tables, inserted pictures, and live hyperlinks, choose HTML.
- To create a message with rich text formatting support, such as embedded objects, font specifications, and colored text, choose Rich Text.

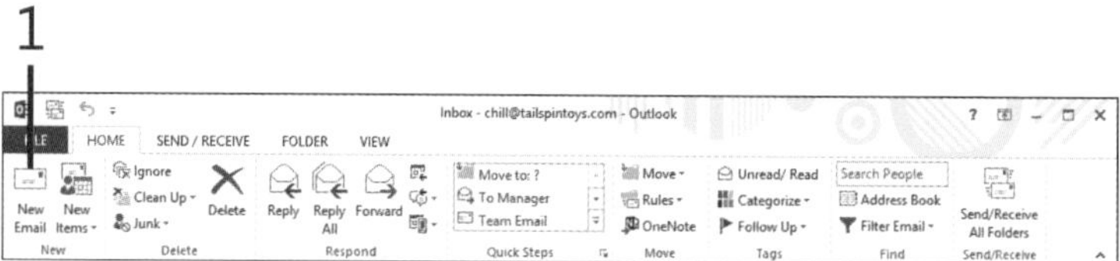

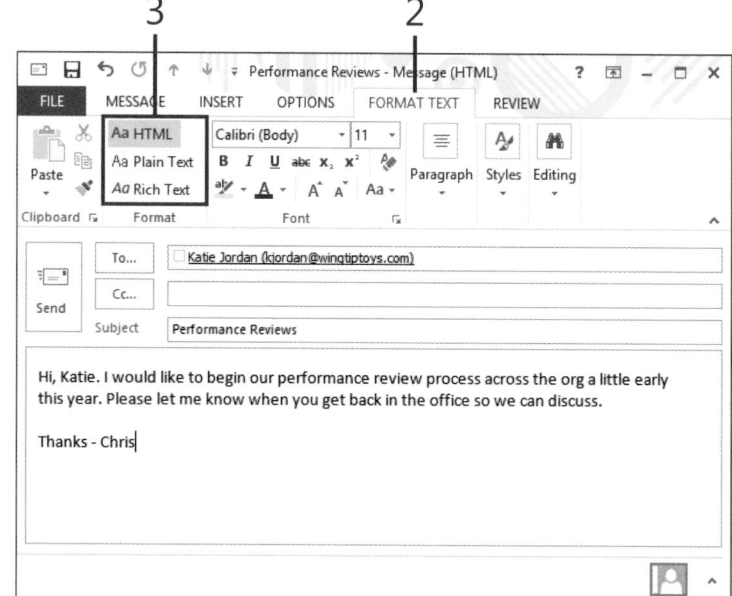

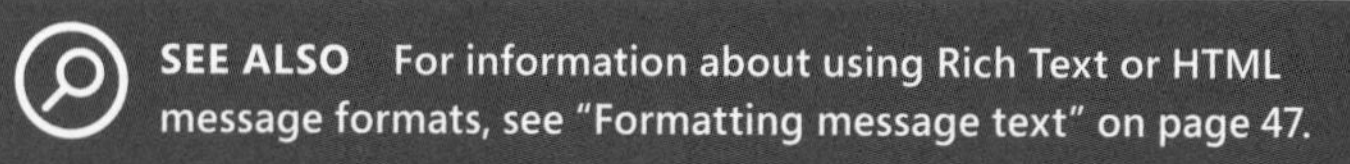

SEE ALSO For information about using Rich Text or HTML message formats, see "Formatting message text" on page 47.

TIP If you aren't sure of the format that your recipient can read, use the Plain Text option. This ensures that nothing is lost in the translation if your recipient's email program doesn't support Rich Text or HTML messages.

Select a default message format

1 On the ribbon, click the File tab to display the Backstage view. Then, click the Options tab.

2 In the Outlook Options dialog box, in the column on the left, click the Mail tab.

3 Click the Compose Messages In This Format drop-down list and choose the format that you want to use for all your messages.

4 Click OK.

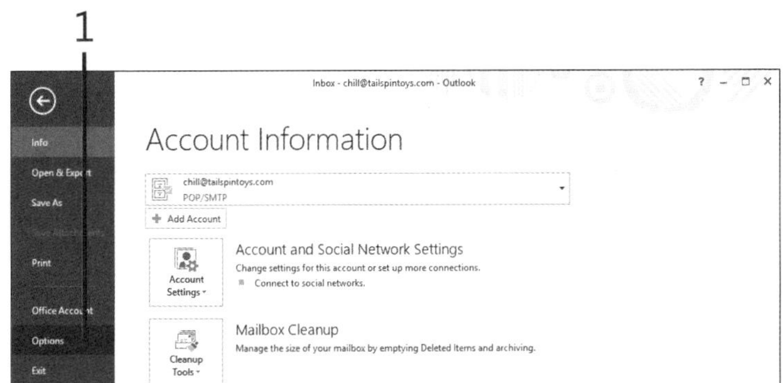

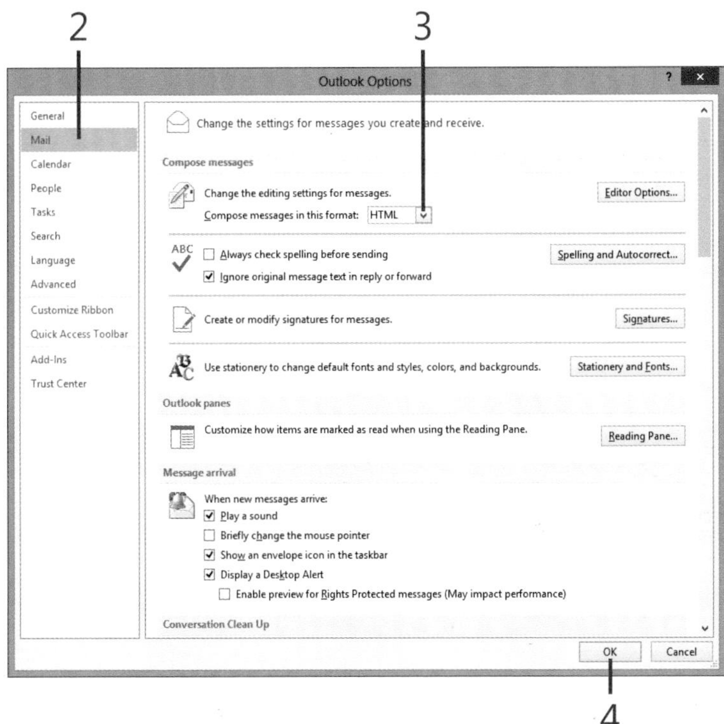

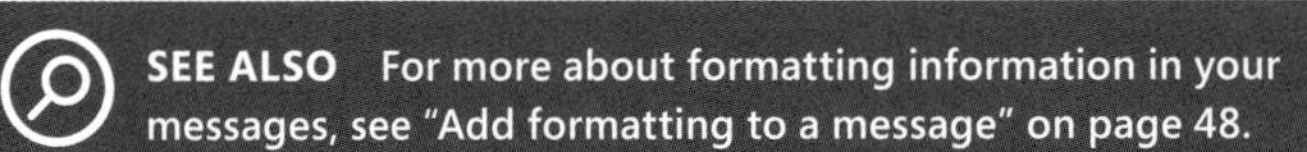

SEE ALSO For more about formatting information in your messages, see "Add formatting to a message" on page 48.

TIP With HTML formatting, your messages can include pictures that are located on the Internet. To embed a picture instead of creating a hyperlink to it, on the ribbon, click the Insert tab. Then, in the Illustrations group, click Picture. In the Insert Picture dialog box, click in the file name text box and type the picture's URL. Next, click the drop-down arrow beside the Insert button and choose Insert And Link. Outlook retrieves a copy of the image and embeds it in the message.

Setting Calendar options

You can change the way Calendar works in Outlook 2013. You can change the default Monday through Friday workweek to one that is specific to your schedule (perhaps you work Wednesday through Saturday). You also can set up holidays that aren't traditionally observed in your country or region.

Set the workweek

1 On the ribbon, click the File tab to display the Backstage view. Then, click the Options tab.

(continued on next page)

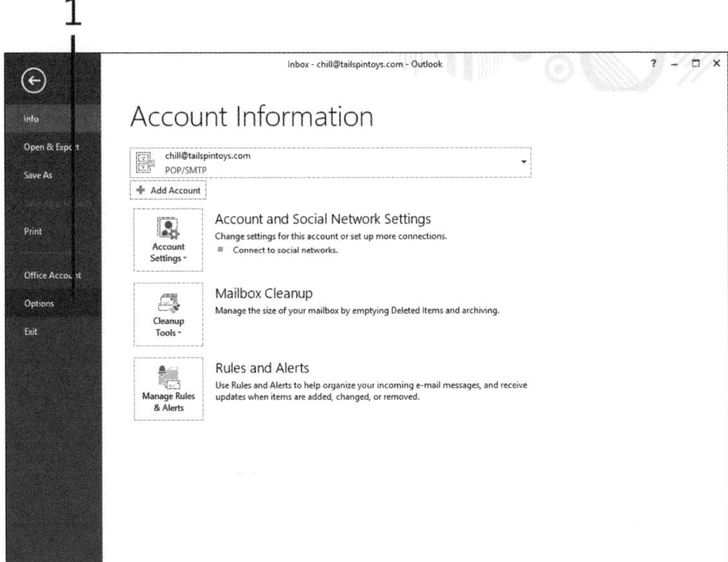

TIP You can specify which day of the week is the first day for you. To do so, in the Outlook Options dialog box, click the First Day Of Week drop-down list and then click a day .

TRY THIS Change your work hours to begin at 12:00 A.M. and end at 7:00 A.M. In the folder pane, click the Calendar icon and then, on the Home tab, click the Day button. Notice how the 12–7 range is shown in white to indicate your workday hours.

Set the workweek *(continued)*

2 In the Outlook Options dialog box, in the column on the left, click the Calendar tab.
3 Select the days of the week that you work.
4 Click the Start Time drop-down list and select the time your workday begins.
5 Do the same in the End Time list for the end of your workday.
6 Choose the start day for your workweek.
7 Click OK.

Add holidays

1 On the ribbon, click the File tab to display the Backstage view. Then, click the Options tab.

(continued on next page)

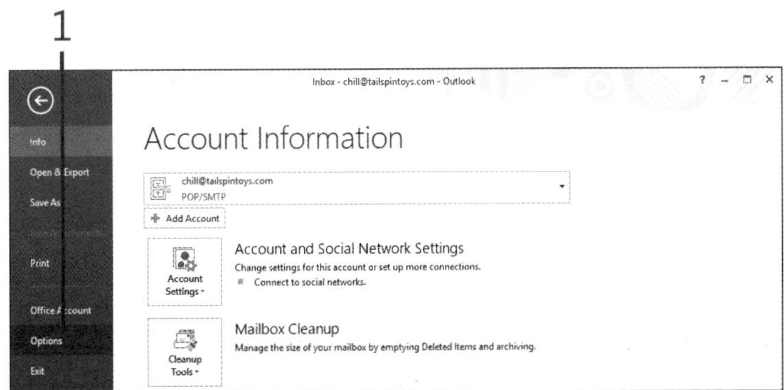

Add holidays *(continued)*

2 In the Outlook Options dialog box, in the column on the left, click the Calendar tab.

3 Click Add Holidays.

4 In the Add Holidays To Calendar dialog box, select the country or holiday set that includes the holidays that you want to add to your Calendar.

5 Click OK to save the settings and close the dialog box.

6 Click OK to close the Outlook Options dialog box.

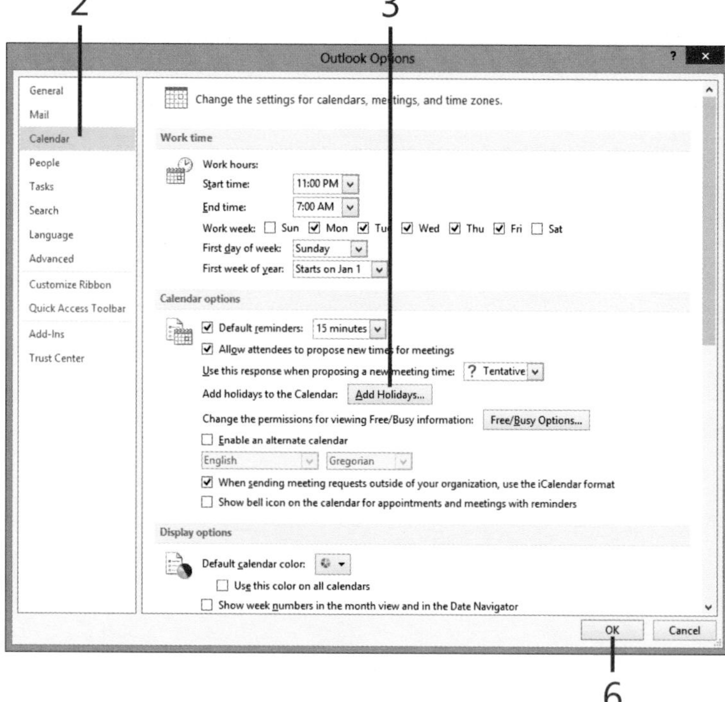

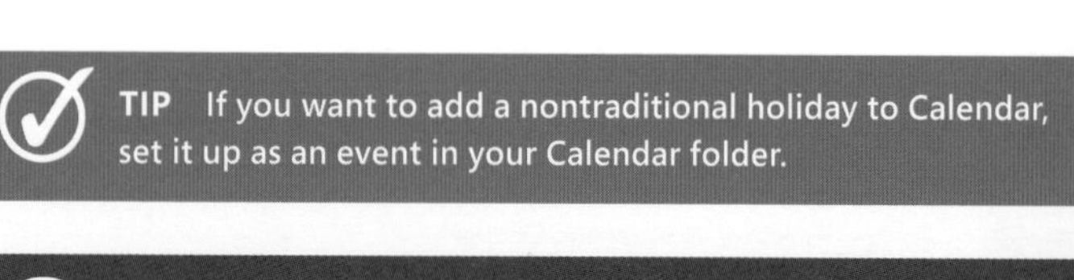

TIP If you want to add a nontraditional holiday to Calendar, set it up as an event in your Calendar folder.

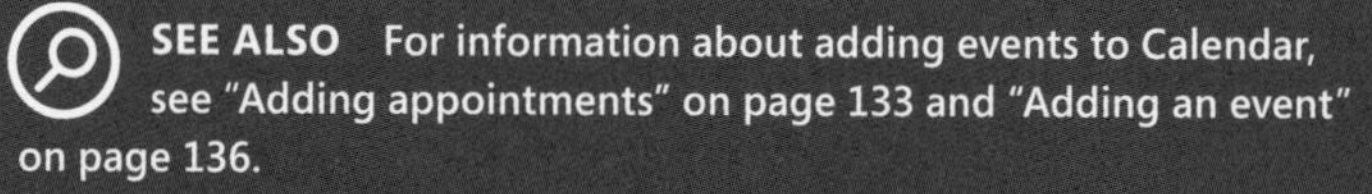

SEE ALSO For information about adding events to Calendar, see "Adding appointments" on page 133 and "Adding an event" on page 136.

Customizing the Folder pane

The Folder pane includes icons that you can click to quickly open an Outlook folder. You can customize it in several ways, such as by hiding it when you want more room to see items in Outlook or by adding or removing folders from it. You can also change the order in which the folders are displayed in the Folder pane.

Show or hide the Folder pane

1 In the upper-right corner of the Folder pane, click the Minimize The Folder Pane button.

(continued on next page)

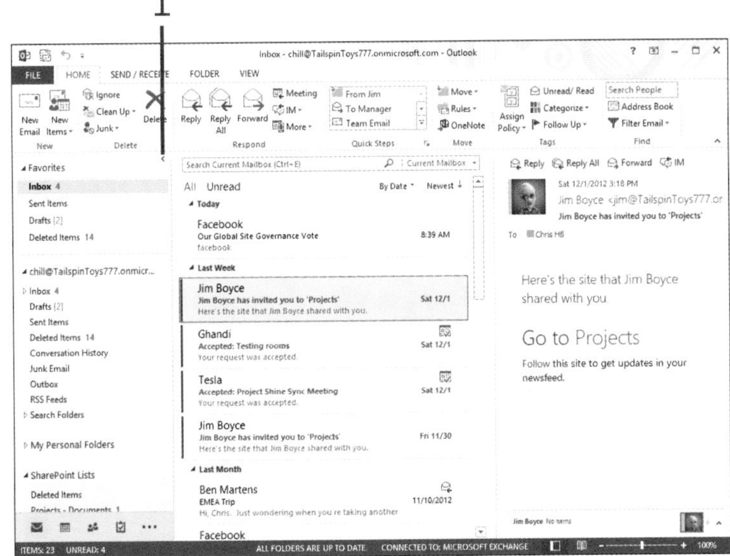

SEE ALSO To learn more about the Folder pane, see "Exploring Outlook folders" on page 23.

Show or hide the Folder pane *(continued)*

2 The Folder pane minimizes.

3 At the top of the minimized pane, click the Expand The Folder Pane button to expand the pane again.

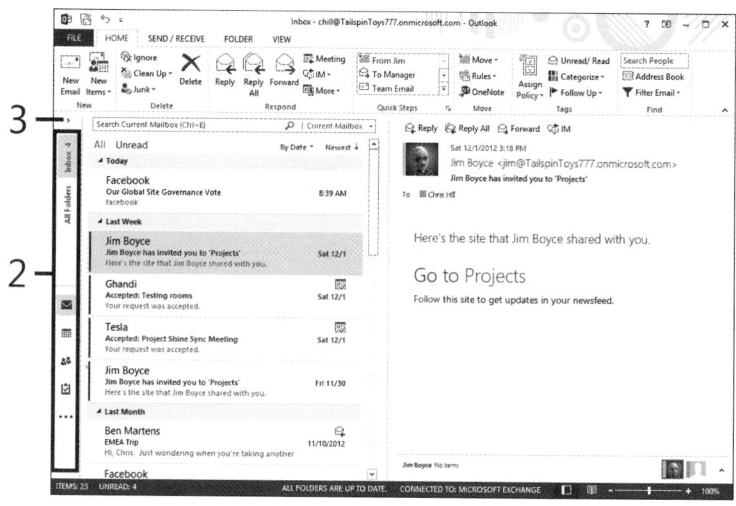

Add or remove Folder pane items

1 On the ribbon, click the View tab.

2 In the Layout group, click Folder Pane. On the menu that appears, click Options.

3 In the Navigation Options dialog box, select the Compact Navigation check box to use small icons instead of folder names.

4 Specify the number of folders to show in the Folder pane.

5 To change the display order of a folder, select the folder, and then click Move Up or Move Down, as needed.

6 Click OK.

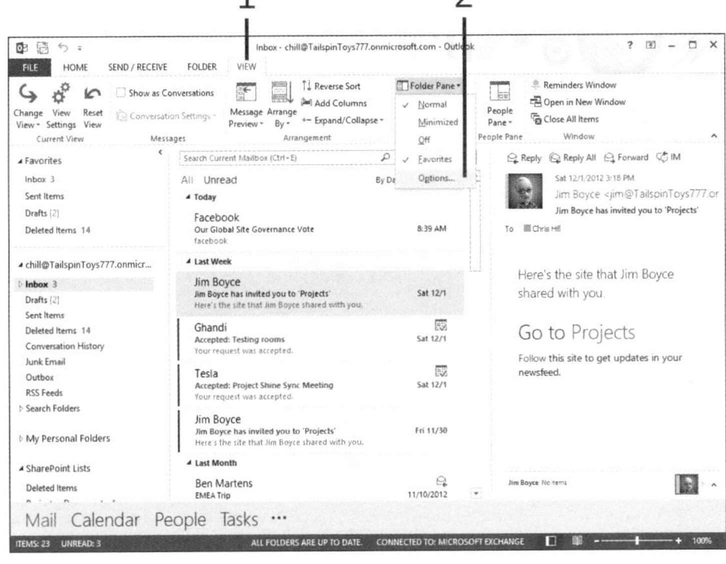

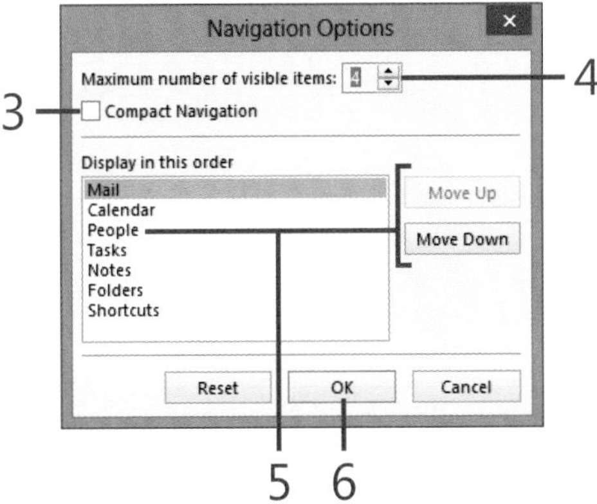

TIP You can hide the Folder pane by choosing Folder Pane from the View tab on the ribbon and then choosing Minimized.

TRY THIS Minimize the Folder pane by clicking the left-pointing arrow at the upper-right corner in the Folder pane.

Adding Outlook folders and SharePoint sites to the Shortcuts page

You can use the Shortcuts page in the Folder pane to add your own shortcuts and navigate quickly to those items from Outlook 2013. For example, if you have a certain combination of Mail, Calendar, Contact, and other Outlook folders, along with some SharePoint sites that you use regularly, you can add shortcuts to each on the Shortcuts page so that you can quickly and easily navigate to them.

Add a shortcut group to the Folder pane

1 In the Folder pane, click the Folder Options button.

2 On the menu that appears, click Shortcuts.

(continued on next page)

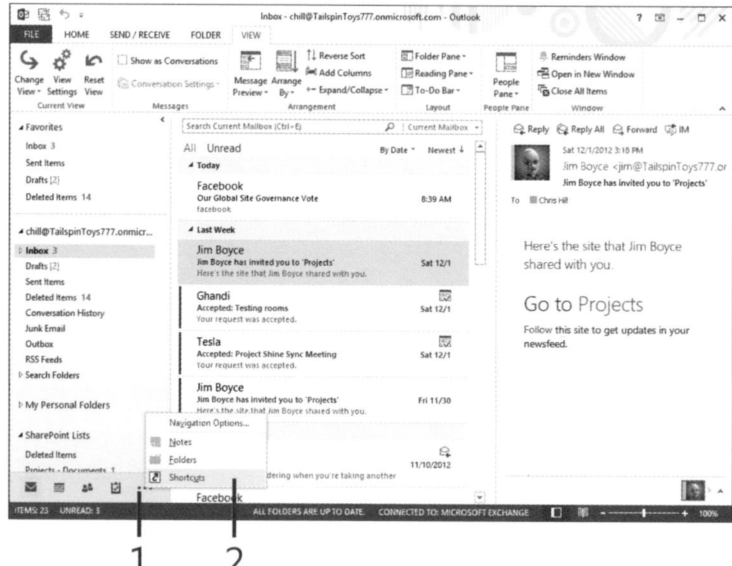

TRY THIS Add several shortcut groups to help you access Outlook items that you use often. For example, create a new contacts folder to store your personal contacts separately from your business contacts. Create a shortcut to that folder in the Shortcuts list. When you want to open that folder, just click its icon in the shortcut group. Add all of your most frequently used Outlook folders to the list.

Add a shortcut group to the Folder pane *(continued)*

3 Click a shortcut to view it in Outlook.

4 In the Folder pane, right-click Shortcuts and then, on the shortcut menu that appears, click New Shortcut Group.

5 Type a new name for the group and press Enter.

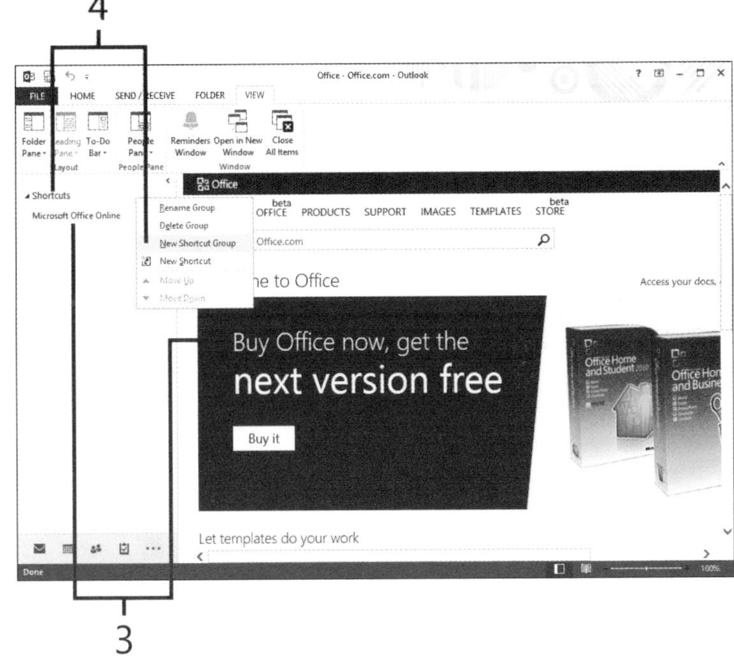

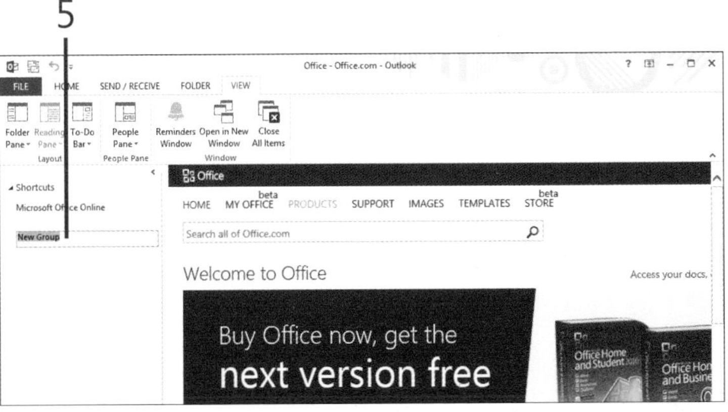

Add shortcuts to the Folder pane

1. On the Shortcuts page, right-click the target shortcut group and then, on the shortcuts menu that appears, click New Shortcut.
2. In the Add To Folder Pane dialog box, choose the Outlook folder for which you want to create a shortcut.
3. Click OK.
4. Note the new shortcut in the selected group.

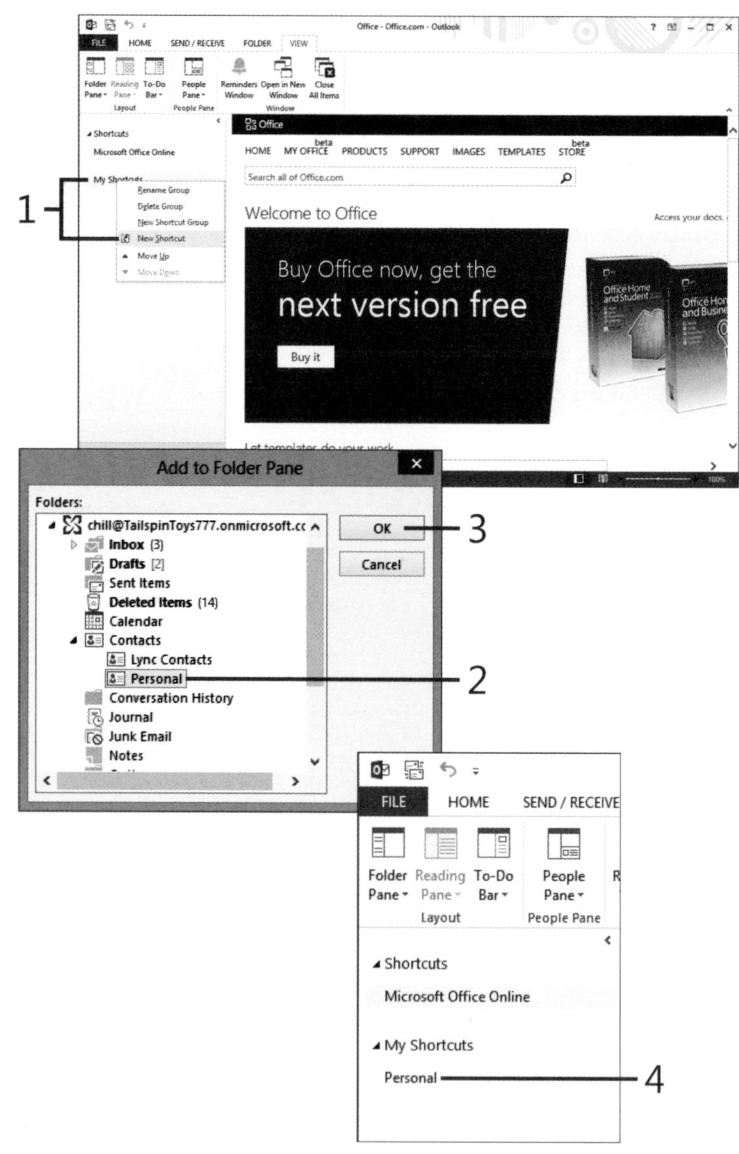

TIP To add shortcuts to your favorite websites and SharePoint sites in the Shortcuts list, just create a shortcut on the Windows desktop to the site and then drag the shortcut to the Shortcuts list in the Folder pane. You need to drop the shortcut icon exactly on the Shortcuts or on a group header for this to work correctly. These shortcuts open the website within Outlook.

TRY THIS You can add shortcuts for local file folders, network shares, and even documents and programs to the Outlook Shortcuts page in the Folder pane. Just drag the item to the Shortcuts group header (or other group header) to create the link to the item.

Customizing the Outlook ribbon

The ribbon is used throughout the Outlook 2013 interface to provide quick access to commonly used commands and features. Although the ribbon gives you quick access to these items in a very organized way, you also have the ability to change it to suit your needs. For example, you might want to add your own tab of favorite commands so that you don't have to switch back and forth between tabs. You can also turn tabs on or off altogether.

Turn tabs on or off

1 Right-click any tab on the ribbon and then, on the shortcut menu that appears, click Customize The Ribbon.

2 In the Outlook Options dialog box, scroll down, and select the Developer tab check box.

3 Click OK.

(continued on next page)

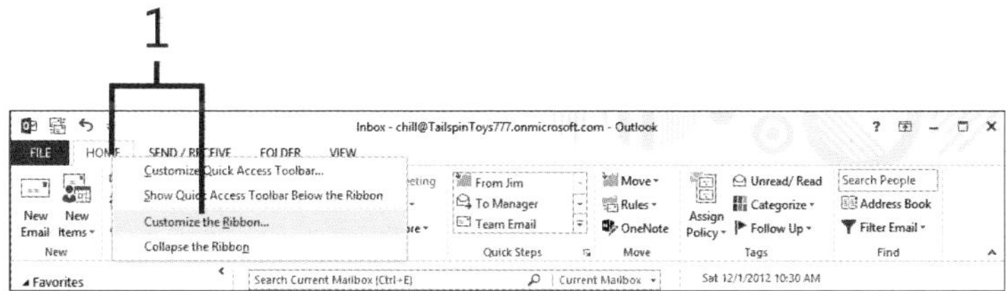

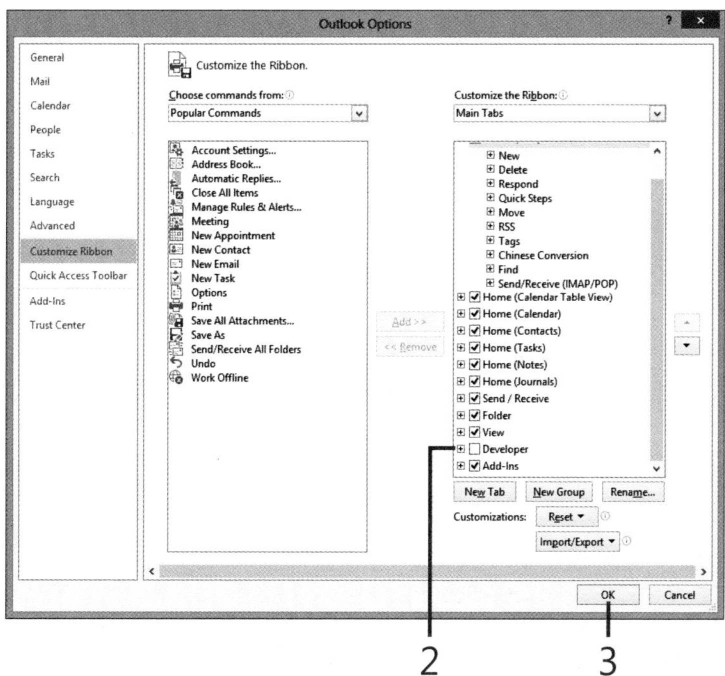

> **TIP** Use the Import/Export command on the Outlook Options dialog box to export your customizations so that you can easily restore them (or share them with others). If you want to restore the ribbon to its original, default state, in the Outlook Options dialog box, click the Reset button to clear all customizations.

Turn tabs on or off *(continued)*

4 The tab appears in the ribbon.

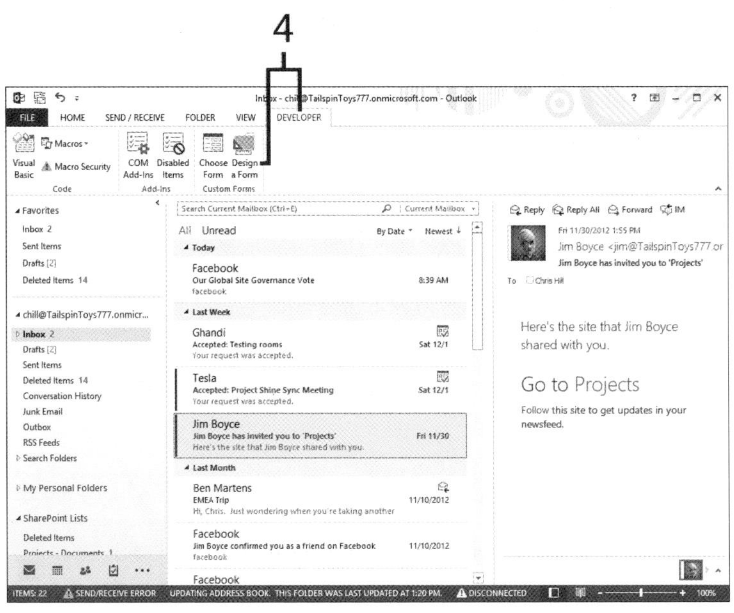

TRY THIS You can control the order in which the groups appear on a tab. To do so, select a group in the Outlook Options dialog box and then use the up and down arrows to the right of the group list to change the order in the list.

Add your own tab

1 Right-click any tab on the ribbon and then, on the shortcut menu that appears, click Customize The Ribbon.

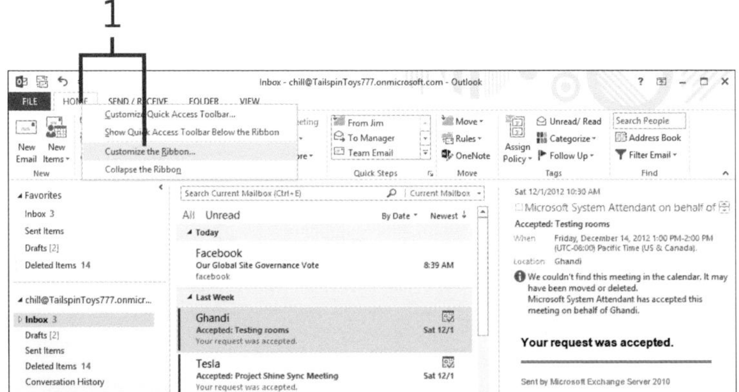

(continued on next page)

Add your own tab *(continued)*

2 In the Outlook Options dialog box, click New Tab.

3 In the list box on the right, click the newly created tab.

4 Click Rename.

5 In the Rename dialog box, type a new name.

6 Click OK.

7 Click New Group (created by default when you add the tab).

8 Click Rename.

9 Again, in the Rename dialog box that opens, type a name for the group.

10 Choose an icon for the group.

11 Click OK.

12 In the Choose Commands From list, choose a command group.

13 Choose a command.

14 Click the Add button to add the command to the selected group.

15 Add other commands and groups as you prefer and then click OK.

(continued on next page)

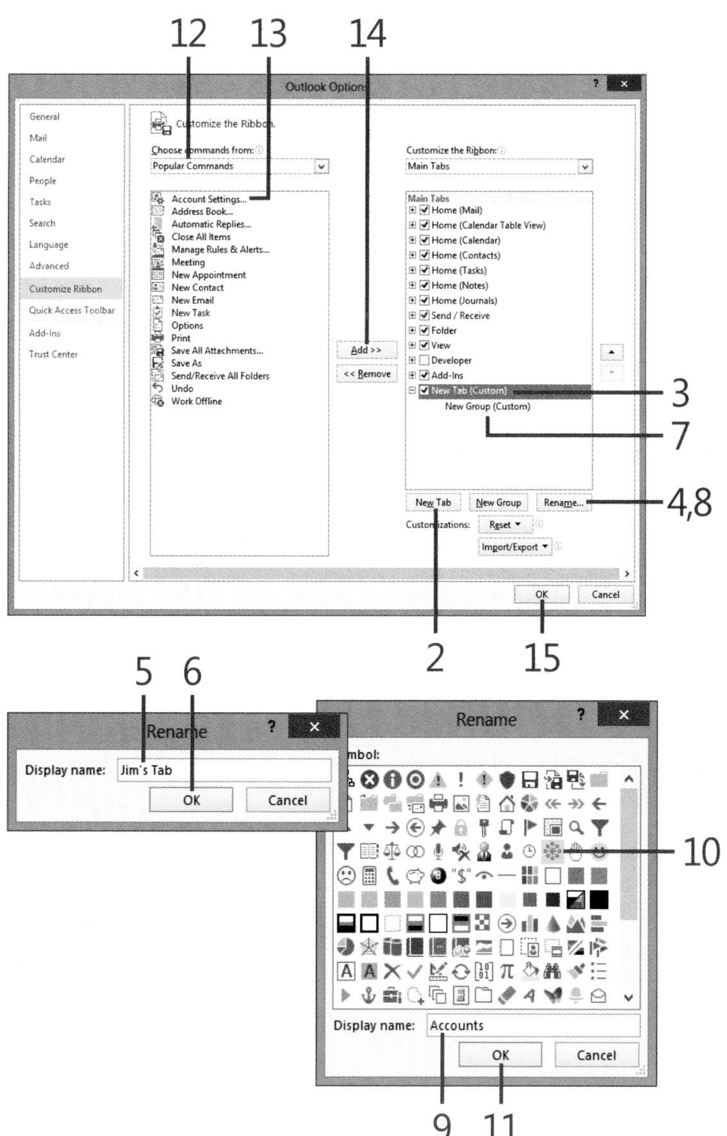

Add your own tab *(continued)*

16 The new items appear in your custom tab.

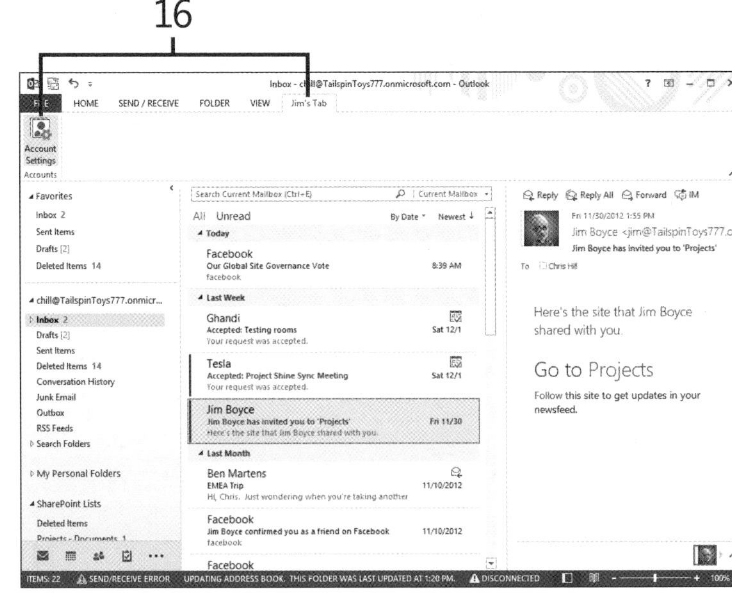

Customizing the Quick Access Toolbar

By default, the Quick Access Toolbar sits above the ribbon and provides quick access to frequently used commands and options. The Quick Access Toolbar takes up relatively little space, so it's unobtrusive. Although it already contains a handful of commands, you can add your own to suit your needs.

Add a command to the Quick Access Toolbar

1 On the right end of the Quick Access Toolbar, click the Customize button.

2 On the menu that appears, click More Commands.

(continued on next page)

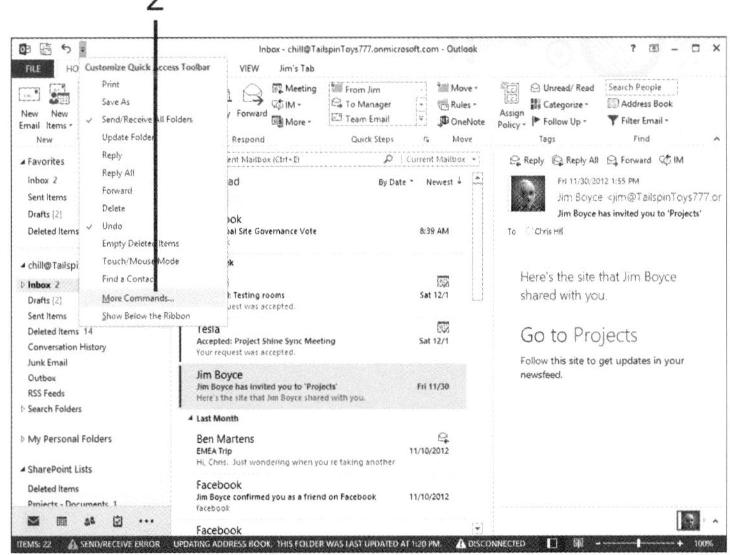

TIP The Quick Access Toolbar is a great place to add macros so that you can get to them quickly when you need them.

Add a command to the Quick Access Toolbar *(continued)*

3 In the Outlook Options dialog box, in the Choose Commands From list, choose a command group.

4 Choose the command you want to add.

5 Click Add.

6 Optionally, add any other commands and click OK.

7 The commands now appear on the Quick Access Toolbar.

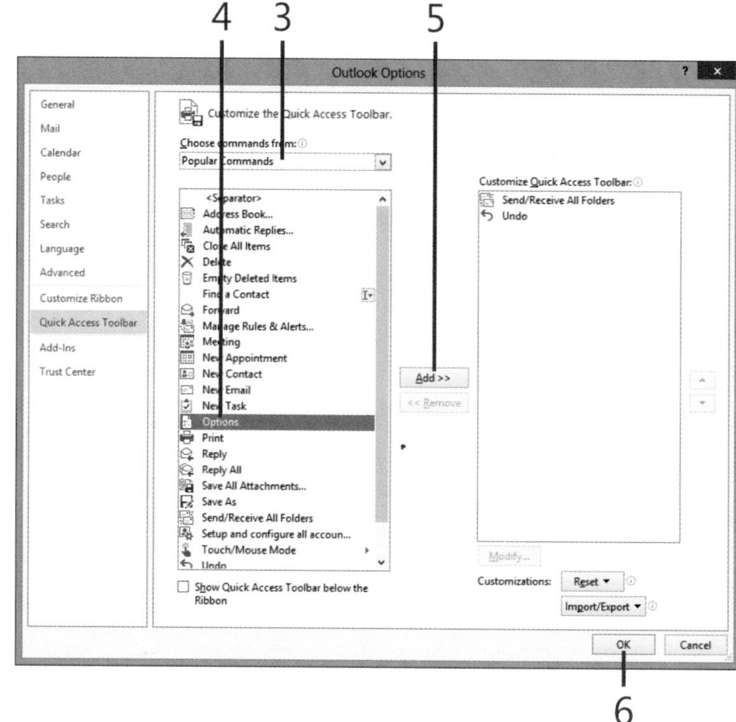

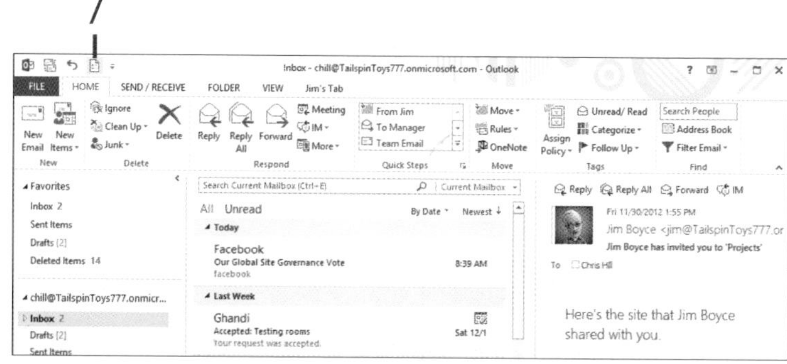

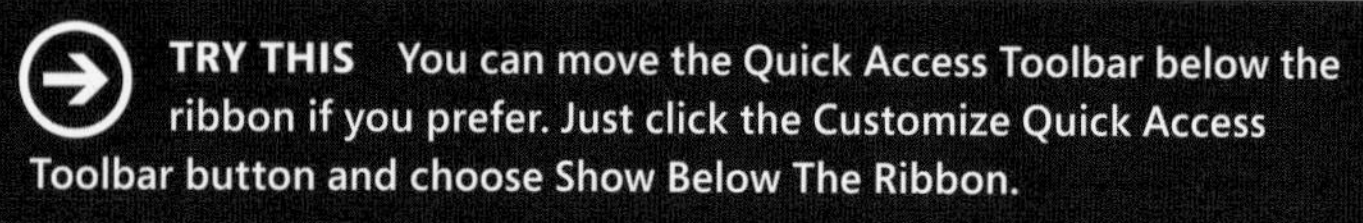
TRY THIS You can move the Quick Access Toolbar below the ribbon if you prefer. Just click the Customize Quick Access Toolbar button and choose Show Below The Ribbon.

Index

A

B

C

D

E

F

M

N

O

P

Q